CHURCH, STATE & THE ETHICAL IMAGINATION

A Phenomenological Study of Christian, Cultural and Constitutional Value Clashes In South Sudan

ZECHARIAH MANYOK BIAR

Copyright © 2022 Zechariah Manyok Biar

ISBN (Paperback): 9780645719147
ISBN (Hardcover): 9780645759051

No part of this publication may be reproduced, stored in a retrieval system, or transmitted, in any form, or by any means, electronic, mechanical, photocopying, recording or otherwise, without the prior permission of the publishers.

This book is sold subject to the conditions that it shall not, by way of trade or otherwise, be lent, re-sold, hired out or otherwise circulated without the publisher's prior consent in any form of binding or cover other than in which it is published and without a similar condition including the condition being imposed on the subsequent purchaser.

Cover design, typesetting and layout: Africa World Books
Unit 3, 57 Frobisher St, Osborne Park, WA 6017
P.O. Box 1106 Osborne Park, WA 6916

Catalogue records for this book are available from the National Library of Australia and Western Australia State Library

TABLE OF CONTENTS

DEDICATION	vii
ACKNOWLEDGMENTS	ix
INTRODUCTION	xiii
What this Book is About	xiii
Motivation Behind this Book	xv
Overview of the Book	xviii

CHAPTER ONE

BELIEFS AND LAWS	1
Background	1
Article 8 of the South Sudan Constitution	3
Islam	4
Other Scholarly Views	6
Schools of Thought, Tradition and Their Impacts	8
African Belief Systems	9
Central Value Systems	13

Social Imagination	14
Christian Ethics for Public Life	16
Separation of Church and State	20
The Role of Central Value Systems in Separation of Church and State	21
Crux of the Matter	23
The Contribution of this Study to Knowledge	25
General Approach	28

CHAPTER TWO
THE ORIGIN OF ARTICLE 8 IN SOUTH SUDAN'S CONSTITUTION — 32

Introduction	32
Obscurity of Article 8: Stipulation and Misinterpretation	34
Institution within Institution	37
Origin and Development of Islamism in Sudan	39
Mixing State and Religion	42
Islamic State and the Islamic Law	43
Oneness of Allah in the Sudanese State	45
Islamization and Introduction of Separation of Religion and State in Sudan	46
Perceived Marginalisation	49
Muslims and People of the Book	50
Resistance to Submission and Declaration of Violent Jihad	52
SPLM's Concept of the Problem of Sudan's Origin	54
Religion and Ethnicity	57
Politicised Religion and Repressions	58
Summing up the Project of Conserving Islam and its Marginalisation Policies	62

Imagined International Standards   63
Individual Conscience's Rights, Separation of State and
Religion and Sudan's Constitutions   64
International Standards and National Conditions   68
Article 8 of South Sudan's Constitution and its Tactical
Functions   72
Political Survival Strategy   75
Islamists and Manipulation of Religion and Politics in
Sudan   77
South Sudanese Politicians and their Survival Strategy   78
Political Survival Strategies and Central Value Systems   80
Preliminary Conclusion   85

CHAPTER THREE
CONCEPTS IN CENTRAL VALUE SYSTEMS   87
Introduction   87
Sketching Decision-Making Theories   88
Proponents of Modern Virtue Ethics and Ethical
Incoherence   91
Ethical Dilemmas in Ethical Decision-Making   94
Deontological Coherence in Decision-Making   96
Deontological Christian Ethics and Ethical
Decision-Making   98
The Primacy of Safety in Ethical Decision-Making   99
Values and Social Environments   101
Exploring the Theory of Basic Human Values   102
Ten Basic Human Values   103
Anxiety-Free Values   108
Anxiety-Avoidance Values   113

Turning the Circular Motivational Continuum Upside Down — 121
Central Value Systems and Decision-Making — 122
Values and Internal Motivations — 124
Central Value Systems and Different Worldview Traditions — 129
Central Value Systems and Worldview Traditions in South Sudan — 135
Preliminary Conclusion — 137

CHAPTER FOUR
CHRISTIAN AND GOVERNMENT VALUE CLASHES — 140

Introduction — 140
Security as the Common Good — 143
Religious and Constitutional Value Clashes — 144
Religious Values and Harmony — 147
Value Clashes in Secular and Liberal States — 149
Liberalism and Liberty of Individual's Conscience — 150
Mitigating Disagreements in Liberty of Conscience and Individual Choices — 152
Freedom of Choice and Doing-No-Harm Principle — 156
Central Value Systems and State Actors — 157
Value Clashes in Liberal and Non-Secular States — 160
Overviewing Interactions Between South Africa and South Sudan — 161
Constitutional Values Defining Ideological Status of South Africa — 162
Clashes of Religious and Governance Values in South Africa — 163
Central Value Systems and Value Clashes in South Africa — 167

Value Clashes in Non-Liberal and Secular States … 169
The Differences are in Liberal and Non-Liberal Aspects … 170
Nature of Value Clashes in Secular and Non-Liberal States … 171
Secularism and Harmony Value in Singapore … 172
Harmony Laws and Clashes of Religious and Governance Values in Singapore … 173
Value Clashes in South Sudan … 176
Nature and Ideology of State in the Sudanese and South Sudanese Constitutions … 177
Ideological Ambiguities in the State of South Sudan … 184
Power and Value Clashes in South Sudan … 188
Preliminary Conclusion … 191

CHAPTER FIVE
CHRISTIAN POLITICIANS AND ETHICAL POLICIES … 193
Introduction … 193
Cultural and Social Imaginations and Values … 195
Medieval Views on Church and State Relationships … 197
Premodern-Leaning Church Thinkers' Views on Church and State Relationships … 198
Modern-Leaning Church Thinkers' Views on Church and State Relationships … 203
Modern Views on Church and State Relationships … 205
Conflicting Views on Church and State Relationships … 206
Principles of State and Religion Separation and Central Value Systems … 212
Political Leaders and Value Cultivation in South Sudan … 213

South Sudanese' Love for Power and Self-Enhancement
Value 216
Power Value and Ethical Principles in South Sudan 219
Power and Public Harmony in South Sudan 223
Power Value and Past Experiences of South Sudanese 225
Religious Leaders and Value Cultivation in South Sudan 227
Guiding Principle in Religious Leaders' Power Value in
South Sudan 228
Peaceful Coexistence and Power Value 229
Dual Obligations in Caring for Oneself and Neighbours 230
Religious Leaders and Promotion of Harmony Among
Communities 232
Preliminary Conclusion 235

CHAPTER SIX
DIFFERENT MORAL CONVICTIONS AND
CONSENSUS IN SOUTH SUDAN 238
Introduction 238
Values and Different Levels in South Sudan 239
Common Values in African Traditions 240
Common Value-Clash Resolution Strategy in African
Communities 242
South Sudan's Constitution and Influence of Western
Constitutional Norms 243
Customary, Statutory Laws and Offenses in South Sudan 245
Prioritisation of Peaceful Coexistence 246
Moral Convictions and Traditional Consensus Building
in South Sudan 247
Value Differences and Peaceful Coexistence in South
Sudan 248

Imagination and Moral Beliefs	251
Elders and Conflict Resolutions	253
Consensus in Conflict Resolutions	254
Surrounding Environments and Moral Beliefs	256
Harmony Value and Justice	260
Conflicting Moral Convictions and Political Consensus Building in South Sudan	262
Conservation and Power Values	264
Political Tribalism in South Sudan	266
Principles of Harmony in Africa	269
Divergent Moral Convictions and Religious Consensus Building in South Sudan	270
Religious Leaders and Consensus-Building in South Sudan	271
Reconciling Divergent Enforcement of Values	277
Preliminary Conclusion	282

CHAPTER SEVEN
SOUTH SUDANESE CONTEXTUAL THEOLOGICAL ETHICS AND STATE-RELIGION SEPARATION 284

Introduction	284
Theology and Belief Systems	285
Contextual Theological Approach	290
Trinitarian God and Harmony	294
Nature Above Person	297
Person Above Nature	301
Unity and Beings	302
Different Understandings of the Trinitarian God	303
Unity in Diversity Versus Diversity in Unity	307
Foundational Approach in the Context of South Sudan	310

Eschatology and Harmony	312
Eschatology and the End of History	313
Hegel and South Sudanese	316
Hegel and Moltmann	318
Eschatological Orientation in South Sudan	319
Eschatology and Time	321
Theology of Harmony and Secular Responsibility	323
Religion and Secular Domains	324
Equal Treatment in Public Services	326
Political Power and Religious Roles in Secular Domains	328
Harmony as a Public Good	330
Preliminary Conclusion	332

CHAPTER EIGHT
CONCLUSIONS

	334
General Synopsis	334
Revisiting Research Questions	338

APPENDIX

Limitations and Future Studies	347

REFERENCES 351

INDEX 387

---- DEDICATION ----

I dedicate this dissertation to the Halbert and Harmon families that supported my graduate studies consistently during easy and difficult economic times in the United States of America.

Individuals that I should mention by name in these families include Dr. David Halbert, Dee Halbert, Bob Harmon and Belinda Harmon. Some of the other family members keep in touch with me. They consider me not just as a friend, but as one of their family members.

---- ACKNOWLEDGMENTS ----

Pursuing my doctoral studies would not have been successful without support from individuals and institutions acknowledged here. Some of these individuals and institutions supported me financially. Some gave me books and journal articles for free to enrich the concept I was developing. Others supported me with ideas, and others connected me to institutions for more ideas.

Bob and Belinda Harmon have consistently supported me financially and with ideas since my graduate studies at Abilene Christian University in Texas, USA where I pursued two master's Degrees. Belinda's father Dr. David Halbert and his wife Dee Halbert have always been with the Harmons' family in supporting my studies. They continually keep in touch with me and my family even when I am back to South Sudan. Ron Johns and the Church he shepherds are among the supporters of my academic journey. When I started the current PhD, my cousin Dr. Lual A. Deng was the first to pay the tuition for the first academic year at Stellenbosch. Dr. David and Dee Halbert together with Bob and

Belinda Harmon took over the payments of the remaining years of my studies. The Barnabas Fund subsidised the studies.

I cannot forget Dr. Michael Smith who encouraged me to pursue higher education. He followed through with his encouragement and supported me financially for my undergraduate studies. It was Dr. Smith who took me to USA to meet with my current sponsors.

On the academic side, I would not have finished within two years after my registration as a PhD student had it not been for the guidance from my supervisors: Prof. Dion A. Forster of Stellenbosch University and Dr. Christopher Sugden of the Oxford Centre for Religion and Public Life (OCRPL). Prof. Forster would go beyond normal supervision to buy books with his own money and give them to me for free to enrich the concept that I was developing. His expertise in systematic theology and ethics was likewise invaluable in shaping my theological thinking. Dr. Sugden is a thinker who can detect small philosophical inconsistencies in an argument. His comments made my work philosophically meaningful. He was also very helpful in shaping my academic language. Along this line, I thank Dr. Larry E. Fink, a professor of English at Hardin-Simmons University in Abilene, Texas (1988-2020), who edited the dissertation professionally and thoughtfully.

Dr. Patrick Sookhdeo whose work is quoted in various parts of this study is the thinker whose lectures inspired me to come up with central value systems concept. His style of teaching will remain in my memory for long time. Other people who helped me in my academic journey include Dr. Vinay Samuel, Dr. Joshva John, Dr. Andre Lombard and Dr. Ruth Samuel. My PhD colleague and the Director of Barnabas Fund, Hendrik Storm who, together with Dr. Patrick Sookhdeo, have been encouraging me to finish my studies as soon as I am able without worrying about payments of University fees. My mentor at the Oxford Centre for Religion and Public Life, Dr. Sara Afshari, has gone beyond her mentoring work to connect me to institutions that she believed would enrich my work.

I also thank my Church, the Episcopal Church of South Sudan, for different roles that its leaders and institutions played in ensuring that my studies go smoothly. First, I thank the Archbishop and Primate of the Episcopal Church of South Sudan, Dr. Justin Badi Arama for giving me time to study. Had it not been his permission, I would not have gotten time as the Diocesan Bishop to pursue PhD studies. Second, the administrators of Wanglei Diocese have done much by making sure that my family lacked nothing during my studies. Third, the administrators of Bishop Gwynne College and the Episcopal University have contributed to my research by providing me with an office and internet. Had it not been for them, it would have been difficult for me to access online journal articles.

---- INTRODUCTION ----

What This Book is About

In any society, it is common to hear older people complaining about how younger people are spoiled in their behaviours. Younger people, in turn, complain that older people stick to outdated values and principles. Researchers argue that such complaints result from fear of unknowns from both sides. Older people, for instance, fear new values that younger people are developing because such new values seem to threaten foundational norms of their society. Younger people on their part fear that older values could prevent them from exploring new ways of enjoying life. Each side flatters itself that its values are better than those of the opposite side. This relentless struggle seems to be motivated by an unceasing need of one generation to show its value superiority over the other. Often, this struggle is supported with power positions. When any group is in any kind of predominant power, for example, it tries to make sure that it effortlessly prevents the other side from advancing its values. This is true in conservative and liberal divides. It would appear that what one learns in his or her surroundings seems to have the upper hand in determining what one values. This could be why variations exist even among people of one generation. The same could explain confusions in implementing well-formulated legal provisions in legal documents.

South Sudan is no exception in the confusions related to implementing the provisions of its constitution. For this reason, I pursued a doctorate at Stellenbosch University in South Africa in collaboration with the Oxford Centre for Religion and Public Life in England. This doctoral study resulted in this book.

The book explores underlying reasons for the inconsistent implementation of Article 8 in the Constitution of the Republic of South Sudan which stipulates the separation of religion and state and the equal treatment of all religions. Yet, the state provides special treatment to Islam by giving it funds for building Islamic schools and for annual pilgrimages to Mecca. Other religions do not get the same treatment, as stipulated in the Constitution. The political leaders who provide this special treatment to Islam are Christians who fought against the former Sudanese government for two decades because they mixed Islamic religion with the state. I set out in this book to establish what could be behind how South Sudanese leaders make their decisions about religion and the state. I examine the roles that central value systems play in discrepancies in implementation. The notion of a central value system is a new concept formulated in this study. It is a conservation value composed of conformity, security and tradition.

No previous study has mentioned the concept of a central value system. The conservation value concept that engenders the central value system concept is taken from the theory of basic human values developed by Shalom Schwartz. This study considers as central value systems

Schwartz's (2012) conservation values that he places at the lower part of a circular motivational continuum. Schwartz believes that values are fixed in a motivational continuum that he arranges in a circular chart. The upper part of the circle always indicates liberal values and the lower part indicates conservative values. My study shows that values are so arranged that conservation values often stay in the centre of values.

It is likely that both conservatives and liberals employ conservation values of conformity, security and tradition to protect whatever values they cherish. For example, liberals may require conformity from their members to secure or protect the main values in their liberal tradition. Similarly, conservatives would employ central value systems to shield cherished conservative values. It is probable that the conservation value constitutes a central value system for any person or group of any persuasion or school of thought. It resists penetration from new values trying to change cherished values. In South Sudan, central value systems protect the values of power and harmony. Theology in the context of South Sudan would thus be a theology of harmony. Its base is the Trinitarian God, eschatological in orientation and secular in responsibility. The originality of this study is in demonstrating that conservation values form central values that direct how people react to values that they are uncomfortable with, regardless of whether they are conservatives or liberals.

Motivation Behind this Book

There appears to be deliberate inconsistency in the implementation of legal provisions. In South Sudan, for instance, laws are carefully written, but are infrequently implemented as transcribed (Kindersley, 2019). It is hard to understand why policymakers and implementers keep well-written laws on their office desks, while they carry out their daily activities in ways that seem to differ with provisions in these laws. One of these legal provisions is Article 8 of the Constitution of South Sudan. It stipulates the separation of religion and state. However, state authorities often facilitate Muslims' annual pilgrimages to Mecca. Muslim schools also occasionally benefit from state funds. Some Christians find it hard to understand why the President of South Sudan favoured Muslims in 2014 by offering them $200,000 for building mosques and Islamic schools and for pilgrimages to Mecca (Sudan Tribune, 2014, June 27). The same state authorities do not provide other religious groups with the same treatment in accordance with Article 8(2) of the South Sudan Constitution which demands equal treatment of all religions.

The inconsistency between written laws and their implementation does not seem to result from the inexperience of political leaders in South Sudan. Though South Sudan is a new country, the political leaders leading its state institutions are not inexperienced. Most were effective political leaders in united Sudan. Some were successful military commanders during the civil war between the Sudan government and the Sudan People's Liberation Movement and Army (SPLM/A). Their inconsistent implementation of legal provisions might be caused by something other than inexperience. Some form of reverse psychology may be at play in these potential inconsistencies. Having a particular constitutional provision and practicing the opposite could be understood as a form of reverse psychology, since South Sudanese political leaders appear to do what is opposite to what they actually desire. In other words, these leaders are trying to humanise former oppressors who are Muslims to make them behave in a different manner to their former ways of engaging with others in the united Sudan. However, this does not seem to be the case either, since South Sudanese politicians seem inconsistent in implementing Article 8 of South Sudan's Constitution.

All that contributes to confusion in any implementation of legal provisions is not clear at this point. It is this mismatch between well written laws and their implementation that I will explore. I hypothesise that central value systems might influence the incongruity between laws and their implementations. I first explore theories of decision-making such as teleology, deontology, and areteology among others. Nevertheless, these do not seem fully to explain reasons behind inconsistency in decision-making in relation to implementing laws. Shalom Schwartz's theory of basic values comes closest to explaining what influences decisions of policymakers and implementers. The shortcoming of the theory of basic values, however, is the postulation that values are fixed in the circular motivational continuum that I will explain later in chapter 3. Possibly, the upper part of the circle that Schwartz (2012) offers to explain liberalism can become the lower part that explains conservatism when it comes to value-related pressures on people's predispositions. It is likely that values are so organised that some form the central part of the circular motivational continuum. Values in the periphery of the circle are open to change. But values in the centre of the circle often resist change. They are conservation values which include tradition, conformity and security.

Given the above premises, I will not examine connotations and effects of religion and state separation in the Constitution of the Republic of South Sudan. Several scholars in different parts of the world have already examined meanings and implications of constitutional provisions on church and state separation. I will not analyse the impact that the separation of religion and state could have on either the state or religion in South Sudan. I will mainly scrutinise what could be behind likely confusions in the implementation of constitutional provisions on the separation of state and religion in the country. The emphasis will be on the role that central value systems play in the implementation-related decision-makings. If central value systems explain these confusions in the implementation, then I will explore implications for theological approaches in the context of South Sudan.

Overview of the Book

I explore potential roles that central value systems play in unpredictable decisions that relate to daily activities in state institutions. The same applies to religious institutions. The enquiry is guided by Article 8 of the Constitution of South Sudan which stipulates the separation of religion and state as well as equal treatment of all religions by the state. However, there seem to be inconsistencies in the daily implementation of this constitutional provision. My study examines reasons behind these irregularities in implementation. My hypothesis is that central value systems are what influence decisions, leading to irregularities in the implementation of legal provisions such as Article 8 of South Sudan's Constitution. Chapters two to eight explore this hypothesis.

Chapter two is about the origin of Article 8. No article in the constitutions of united Sudan before the year 2005 mentions separation of religion and state. Article 8 was first introduced in the Constitution of semiautonomous government of Southern Sudan after the signing of the Comprehensive Peace Agreement in Kenya in 2005. Chapter two explores possible reasons behind the introduction of Article 8. It explores existing literature to understand whether or not Southern Sudan's lawmakers added Article 8 in 2005 to prevent the then Muslim-dominated government of united Sudan from declaring the whole of Sudan as an Islamic state (Sudan Tribune, 2013 Feb 25). The other assumption that the chapter explores is whether Article 8 was introduced to meet international standards. Influence of other countries on South Sudan is also explored as one reason for the introduction of Article 8 in 2005.

Chapter three scrutinises theories of decision-making to understand how South Sudan leaders make decisions in implementing legal provisions. I begin by examining decision-making theories such as teleology, deontology, areteology and other decision-making approaches related to these theories. My intention is to understand whether South Sudan leaders make use of some of these theories in their decision-making. I then explore Shalom Schwartz's Theory of Basic Human Values to comprehend whether it is better than other theories of decision-making. I further examine the roles of central value systems in ethical decision-making in relation to social, religious and political matters in South Sudan. The scrutiny of central value systems looks at the probable influence these values have on ethical decision-making. This analysis may also help in answering how far central value systems could relate to other theories of decision-making. Examining central value systems, moreover, is crucial in demonstrating how people rank values in their thoughts and why the conservation values form central value systems. Conservation values vary from individual-to-individual for different reasons. However, what everyone appears to share is the significance of conservation itself. One group could regard some values as peripheral, while others regard them as central. Above all, the chapter discusses possible ways in which conservation values consciously and unconsciously affect ethical choices.

Chapter four examines value clashes between Christians and government. I explore different states that have provisions in their constitutions for the separation of church and state or religion and state: liberal and secular states, liberal and non-secular states and secular and non-liberal states. Do religious values and values of constitutional governance clash in these states? Understanding value clashes in these different types of states is crucial for this study. Are these clashes of the same nature or different? If they differ, what causes these differences? If the clashes are of the same kind in these different states, why? Exploring these different states in relation to separation of religion and state is important for understanding what type of system relates to South Sudan's constitutional provision for the separation of religion and state. Understanding how these states implement their legal provisions for religion and state separation will also help us comprehend why the implementation of Article 8 seems confused.

Chapter five explores additional theories of how value systems influence decisions on the acceptance or rejection of the separation of religion and state. The theories are grouped into those that relate to a belief in hierarchy of beings, the quest to achieve the ultimate good and the universality of norms. The chapter begins with how old experiences influence ideas in new settings, especially in religion and state relations. It first explores medieval views on church and state relationships in order to understand the roles that religious and political leaders played at the time to cultivate values. The second section explores the current understanding of church and state relationships and its associated value cultivation in the United States. The USA represents states that cherish secularism in public life and religious beliefs in private life. It is significant to grasp what kind of values religious and political leaders cultivate in secular and liberal settings. Since secularism is mostly promoted in opposition to private religious beliefs in modern and postmodern periods, are there people who still promote premodern and medieval views of the relationship between state and religion in the United States today? The last two sections explore values that political and religious leaders cultivate in South Sudan. The hierarchy of being in medieval philosophy and theology has implications for the exercise of power through a hierarchy. South Sudan leaders seem to have a very similar view. Therefore the chapter explores the medieval thought on church and state relationships in order to illuminate the current thinking on the topic in South Sudan.

Chapter six examines different moral convictions and consensus in South Sudan. It looks into how people or groups with conflicting values arrive at consensus in their efforts to live together in harmony despite their different moral convictions. I attempt to describe how differences in value orientations influence what individuals and groups of people accept or reject. In addition, I explore how South Sudanese arrive at consensus in their endeavours to live together in harmony despite their different moral convictions. The chapter explores traditional strategies of helping people with different moral convictions arrive at consensus in South Sudanese communities. It examines political and modern strategies of helping people resolve differences related to conflicting moral convictions. It then explores Christian ways of helping individuals and groups resolve different types of conflicts. Examples shed light on what South Sudanese do in relation to other strategies of value-motivated conflict resolutions.

Chapter seven is about theological approaches that South Sudanese employ to make sense of state and religion relationships. I endeavour to establish an approach that South Sudan theologians and religious leaders use or would use to develop their public theology. The other point that this chapter tries to grasp is types of values that guide public theology in South Sudan and to identify the foundation of its public theology. I contend that the theology dealing with religion and state relationships in South Sudan would be the theology of harmony which has its foundation in God. In other words, God is the starting point for the theology of harmony in South Sudan. The theology of harmony in South Sudan reflects the oneness of the Trinitarian God in its foundation, is eschatological in its orientation and secular in its responsibility. The chapter will explore each of these three elements.

Chapter eight is the general overview of the study. It mainly revisits the research problem and the research questions and how the analysis attempts to answer the research questions. The questions raised for future research are presented. The last part of the book discusses limitations of the study.

CHAPTER ONE

BELIEFS & LAWS

Background

South Sudan is a new country with old problems. The new and the old values seem to clash at many points. These clashes originate from its troubled past, from its relations with the now old Sudan, relations marred by religious and ethnic differences. Both the Arab-led government and the Islamic religion in Khartoum were hostile to Christians and African Traditional Religions (ATRs). It is important to mention here that when people talk of the Islamic regime in Khartoum, they refer to a regime that was controlled by Islamists such as Hassan Al-Turabi (Sidahmed, 2012). Sudanese Muslims associated with the radical Egyptian Muslim Brotherhood. This grouping are the ones who are often referred to as Islamists in Sudan (D'Anglo, 2010).

The hostility of Islamists against other religions in Sudan made the government a distant entity in the lives of South Sudanese. As a result, the traditional leaders and traditional values became strong in the South. When the civil war broke out in 1983 between the government in Khartoum and the SPLM/A in the South, radical changes took place in the lives of South Sudanese. Christianity rapidly grew because it was seen as a stronger alternative to the religion of the oppressors in the North. African Traditional Religions were seen as too weak to protect people in the face of danger. Many people left ATRs for Christianity between 1980 and 1990. Also, the SPLM/A replaced the government that was far away from the people with the SPLM/A's dictatorial bush rules. These bush rules interrupted the normal operations of traditional leaders but could not replace traditional leadership. The SPLM/A and the Christian religion were occupied with the liberation struggles. They neglected to cultivate the relevant values that suit Christians, and also values that would suit government norms. African traditional values in South Sudan remained intact in every community.

In the year 2005, the government in Khartoum and the SPLM/A signed the Comprehensive Peace Agreement (CPA) in Kenya, ending the twenty-one year long civil war and establishing the government of Southern Sudan (GoSS) in the South. The government of national unity (GoNU) remained headquartered in Khartoum. It was partly this liberation mind-set that led to the separation of religion and state in the Constitution to prevent the Muslim-led government from declaring Sudan an Islamic state (Sudan Tribune, 2013 Feb 25). Declaring Sudan an Islamic state was possible because Article 65 of the *Constitution of the Republic of the Sudan 1998* stipulates that 'Islamic law and the consensus of the nation, by referendum, Constitution and custom shall be the sources of legislation.' Article 1 of the same Constitution also mentions Islam as 'the religion of the majority of the population.'

When South Sudan seceded from Sudan in the year 2011, its leaders found it difficult to introduce the international norms required of South Sudan as a member of the international community. Yet, they struggled to adopt laws that met international standards. The separation of religion and state is one of the laws that was maintained in the new Constitution and is supported by the international community as meeting the international standards of protecting minority religions. There seems to be lack of clarity about the concept of separation of state and religion among politicians and religious leaders. This contributes to the confusion of having provisions of separation in the Constitution, on the one hand, and lacking the willingness to implement them as stipulated, on the other. In the year 2013, for example, the General Assembly of the Presbyterian Church of South Sudan invited its members who were leaders in the government to debate Article 8 in the *Transitional Constitution of the Republic of South Sudan 2011* (Sudan Tribune, 2013: Feb 25). The invited government officials included the then Vice President Dr. Riek Machar Teny. The Church leaders argued in favour of an Article 8 review for what they regarded as better alternatives.

Article 8 of the South Sudan Constitution

The government officials in the meeting agreed on the need to review Article 8 of South Sudan's Constitution. The Vice President called for dialogue between the government and the Church on the relevance of Article 8 to the situation of South Sudan. He said that the inclusion of Article 8 in the transitional Constitution was to ensure that no one should impose on the people any religion as the state religion (Sudan Tribune, 2013, Feb 25). Nonetheless, he argued that such concerns could be addressed without separating religion from the state. Yet, Article 6 in the 2005 Constitution of united Sudan does not talk about the separation of religion and state. It mainly talks about religious rights.

It is not yet clear what the leaders of the Presbyterian Church would like Article 8 to look like. Maybe they would like to choose a specific type of separation of state and religion in South Sudan's Constitution. Alternatively, they might be interested in full removal of Article 8 from the Constitution. The Christian government officials who attended the meeting at the Presbyterian Church are also ambiguous about what Article 8 would look like in the absence of the Islamic regime in Khartoum. It is unclear whether Article 8 is solely aimed at preventing the Islamic regime in Khartoum from declaring the whole of Sudan an Islamic state, or if it was put in the Constitution for the genuine equal treatment of all religions. Other denominations are silent on Article 8. However, their silence does not mean they clearly understand what Article 8 really means. Article 8(1) just mentions the separation of religion and state. It is ambiguous on the types of separation required. This ambiguity appears to give some government officials the impression that they can apply Article 8 as they wish. By using Article 8(1), for example, the government seems to keep Christianity away from government-related benefits.

Islam

The problem is not only in the ambiguous stipulation of state and religion separation in Article 8(1). What is more confusing is how government officials appear willingly to work contrary to Article 8(2), which stipulates that 'All religions shall be treated equally and religion or religious beliefs shall not be used for divisive purposes.' By choosing what is contrary to the equal treatment provision in Article 8(2) (Sudan Tribune, 2014, June 27), it seems government officials believe that it is right to fund minority religions such as Islam in South Sudan. It should be noted that Muslims have never opposed equal funding of other religious groups. There is still a good relationship among religious groups in South Sudan (Wilson, 2019).

Some government officials, including the President, do not appear to have any ill-intention towards any religious group even when they appear to favour some religious groups against others. Otherwise, they would not be supporting Islam since almost all top government leaders in South Sudan are Christians. This makes one wonder what the motivation behind these inconsistencies could be. Could it be that a cultural, and maybe religious, value of generosity is possibly rooted in Christian government leaders and unconsciously makes them violate the provision for equal treatment of all religions in Article 8(2)? Would another reason for government leaders funding minority religions such as Islam be political expediency that may aim at keeping politicians docile or to win political support from those supported? This need for Muslim political support might not be limited to the few Muslims within South Sudan. It could extend to Islamic countries which South Sudanese politicians could imagine would be ready to support them in ways that Christian nations are not prepared to.

It is, therefore, worth exploring what influences policy and decision-making, especially in relation to what is the ethical thing to do, among government officials in South Sudan when it comes to equal or lack of equal treatment of all religions as stipulated in Article 8(2) of the Constitution. I will explore what the most ethical thing to do would be for Christian leaders in South Sudan. Given the complexity of our political, historical, cultural and religious situation, I will try to comprehend what a Christian politician, or a political dispensation that includes a large number of Christians, should do in relation to Article 8.

Other Scholarly Views

My conversation partners in this study will include Graham Ward, Charles Taylor and Robin Lovin. A study like this, which explores issues in African context in comparison with similar situations in other continents, should balance views of scholars from different contexts. I have attempted to do so in all cases. However, my reason for the choice of primary conversation partners in this study is to focus on the role of the social, ethical and theological imagination in some, if not most, of the activities that people carry out in their daily lives. The predominance of academic literature in these fields comes from the persons I have engaged. Each chapter will also texture their perspectives with inputs from African scholars and other conversation partners from around the world. Chapters two and seven, for example, include African conversation partners like Abdel Salam Sidahmed, Mogobe Ramose, Robert Vosloo and Dion Forster. Chapters three, four and seven have Asian conversation partners such as Shalom Schwartz, Jaclyn Neo and S. N. Balagangadhara.

The concept of the ethical and theological imagination might not appear overtly in every chapter. However, it is present in subtle and important ways throughout the unfolding discussion. In particular, it is important in relation to the notion of a central value system. It explains how historical processes and surrounding environments that develop norms, influence an individual's ethical behaviours and decision-making, how they shape moral and theological concepts, and how these concepts (in turn) are shaped by lived realities. As Ward (2018: 6) puts it, 'the imagination is powerful and transformative, and textures every awareness of what is in us and outside us.' Ward (2018: 6) believes it is the imagination that 'relates us to the worlds we inhabit and fashion around us.' Taylor (2004), like Ward, is important as a conversation partner because he discusses how people imagine their lives in relation to their social surroundings. Such imagination plays a role in how people arrive at common practices that make up their social and political life.

Lovin's (2011) work helps us understand what makes people agree or disagree on ethical decision-making in supporting or rejecting a particular position, especially in relation to what is the right thing to do. Lovin is one of the best conversation partners for this study for two reasons: first, Lovin shows that the experiences and values that the ethicists mentioned in his work acquired in their surroundings, influenced their Christian stances and ethical positions. Secondly Lovin shows that Christian ethicists place their ethical choices within the framework of a Christian stance that starts with creation and ends with resurrection destiny. Christian persons in South Sudan, particularly Christian political figures, may find such a focus appealing in understanding, critiquing and shaping their social and political stances.

I intend to aggregate the views of Lovin with those from African ethicists. However, many African ethicists adopt a critical, and often combative, stance to Christianity. Such a critical perspective, while important, is unlikely to find purchase with South Sudanese Christian political leaders. But I aim to incorporate the perspectives, ideas and critiques of such philosophers in conversation with other well known, and generally accepted, Christian theologians and ethicists. This has a twofold aim: first, to engage the value systems that operate in our context; second, to re-evaluate critically these value systems from an African, Christian and ethical perspective. Indeed, such a task could not be undertaken without clear, and direct, engagement with African ethicists and philosophers. Their perspectives and contributions will be relevant to the question of how one's central value system relates to the cultural and social imaginations, and how these, in turn, influence policy choices in relation to what is the right thing to do, even contrary to constitutional provisions. This discussion will need to be carefully facilitated, since preliminary research shows that there are no adequate South Sudanese contributions in this field yet. In addition, more general contributions by African ethicists who explore questions of policy choices may not combine how one's deep rooted experiences and Christian stance influence ethical choices in public. Some African ethicists do participate in the debate on cultural, social and moral imaginations. Yet, even in these instances they often facilitate their own conversations between their historical, cultural and social perspectives and the contributions of leading scholars in this field, such as those identified previously (Graham Ward, Charles Taylor, etc.). I shall outline some of this preliminary research in the section that follows.

Schools of Thought, Tradition and Their Impacts

The importance of the separation of church and state has been debated for centuries, both in theory and in practice, but has not yet been resolved (Doshi, 2010; Sheeder, 2013; Lewis, 2014; Walsh, 2017; Deagon, 2017). It is likely that different schools of thought and traditions (DeGirolami, 2015) influence the belief in the importance of the separation of church and state, or lack of such separation. A new school of thought often tries to change beliefs and practices in the old school of thought and tradition (Garnett, 2013). Yet, old schools of thought and traditions do not end when new ones emerge (Copleston, 1993). They move in parallel, leading to parallel beliefs. The confusion in practice seems to happen when one tradition runs into another (Doshi, 2010). For example, the medieval thinkers favoured practices and ideas that conform to the principle of hierarchy, while most Renaissance and Enlightenment thinkers favoured ideas and practices that comply with individual rights and freedom. Today, some people strongly believe in hierarchy (Duffel, 2007) and others strongly believe in individual freedom (Garnett, 2013). Their understandings of the separation of church and state differ, resulting in likely confusion in the implementation of legal provisions.

As mentioned above, most studies done on the separation of church and state concentrate on two main arguments: 1) the need to achieve the ultimate good as the basis of church and state separation in line with the principle of hierarchy and 2) religious liberty as the basis of church and state separation in line with the principle of individual rights and freedom. Theories such as the Medieval Two Swords Theory and Two Kingdoms Doctrine fall under the 'need to achieve the highest good' arguments. Meanwhile, theories such as the Wall of Separation, Pluralistic Separationism, Institutional Separationism and Nonpreferentialism fall under arguments based on religious liberty. Most schools of thought and traditions seem to agree that practices are motivated by the need to do the good and avoid the evil that is the perversion of the good (Burroughs, 2013; Djupe & Calfano, 2013). Yet, they disagree on reasons behind doing the good. The medieval thinkers focused on social duties that achieve the good of society, while the Renaissance and Enlightenment thinkers focused on rights that ensure individual freedom. Schools of thought and traditions also differ on whether there is a universal or only a localised nature of the good (Copleston, 1993).

African Belief Systems

Some African belief systems can be likened to medieval belief systems, where doing good is part of one's duty in the community of which one is a member (Nkondo, 2007). In other words, some African belief systems put communal obligations and duties above individual rights (Sindima, 1990). This is because collective identity or communal belonging is what many African communities value most (Forster, 2010). Yet, different schools of thought may influence the central values of people differently in each country (Baird, 2016). South Africa is one African country in which the values of collectivism are shown to compete with values of individualism. This is evident in debates on the philosophy of *Ubuntu* (Ramose, 1999; Shutte, 2001; Metz, 2011). Some southern Africans understand *ubuntu* as humanity, while others understand it as humanness (Forster, 2010). Those who perceive the community as the foundation of individual identity would define *ubuntu* as humanness. Those who see *ubuntu* as the meeting point for individuals would define it as humanity. Humanity relates to individual rights (Metz, 2011) and humanness relates to a substance that makes individuals humans (Forster, 2010).

One's understanding of the nature of community, and its role in life, would influence his or her understanding of the nature of relationships among members of such a community. Scholars influenced by the values of individualism, for instance, would understand the community as an institution in which individuals enter into relationships (Shutte, 2001). Entering into relationships means that individuals come together under some sort of social contract to form a community (Hobbes, 1999). Consequently, this concept of community informs one's understanding of the nature of Trinitarian unity among individualists. Vosloo (2004), for example, believes that the nature of unity among the members of the Trinitarian God resembles the communion of persons in which a person participates in others (Vosloo, 2002). He talks of hospitality 'which celebrates otherness without forfeiting identity' (Vosloo, 2004: 78). This implies seeing the unity of God as a starting point in moving from hypostases to substance.

Other scholars in Africa understand the community as the foundation for individual identity (Forster, 2010; Ramose, 1999). This understanding 'rests on community as the primary ontological reality that gives rise to the nature of the beings' (Forster, 2010: 246). These African scholars seem to concur with other scholars around the world who believe that the manner in which a community (as the foundation for individual identity), relates to the unity of God in the Trinity, emphasises that the unity of God starts from substance and then is expressed in hypostases (Kariatlis, 2010; Zhyrkova, 2009). The substance is the base. It gives rise to diversity in unity, not unity in diversity (Raeder, 2017). To illustrate this point further, earlier Nicene Creeds describe Christ as consubstantial with the Father. Newer versions describe him as of one Being with the Father. This means that Jesus has the same substance with the Father (Zhyrkova, 2009). The Holy Spirit is described as having proceeded from the Father. Again, this means that three persons of the Trinity share the same substance or essence. It is from this substance that they come as individuals, not the other way around. Individuals emerge out of a community. We are not members of a community simply because we participate in it as individuals. We are individuals because we come out of one community. According to Forster (2010), this can be likened to the southern African philosophy of *Ubuntu*.

The above-mentioned different beliefs about the nature and role of a community show that what one learns in his or her surroundings has a major role to play in how such a person makes ethical decisions (Taylor, 2004). Even if people live in one country, it is likely that the manner in which they would make ethical decisions could be influenced by teachings that form their central value systems. Decision-making guided by central value systems may apply to political and theological arguments about communal norms and relationships. The ethical imagination would also differ according to different worldview traditions. Although imagination in relation to mental formation of images and concepts could imply the same thing psychologically to both individualists and collectivists. Some people may use their imaginations to relate the doctrine of Trinity to harmonious relationships in a top-down manner. Others would apply similar imaginative concepts the other way around, based on their different worldview traditions. It is probably along these lines that Vosloo (2004: 79) cautions theologians against using the symbol of the Trinity 'to serve as an ethical ideal or divine model for human society.'

Vosloo (2004: 79) argues that people who suppress symbols such as hospitality and the welcoming nature of God do 'an injustice to the rich biblical accounts'. Vosloo, however, is not suggesting that using the above-mentioned symbols is the only way that the doctrine of Trinity should be applied to ethical matters. His advice is mainly against using the Trinitarian model 'as something cast in stone' (Vosloo, 2004: 79). Vosloo cautions against the utilitarian use of models of the Trinity since he understands how underlying values influence different theologians when relating the doctrine of Trinity, and of course also to ethical matters, such as hospitality. Hospitality, for instance, would be a perfect example of the unity in Trinity for those who value unity in diversity, but not necessarily for those who value diversity in unity. Hospitality is doing the good or offering care to others. It implies care-motivated welcoming of other people who live outside one's family. Hospitality does not refer to doing good for one's family members in South Sudan, for example. In the South Sudanese context, doing good for one's family members is an obligation rather than an expression of hospitality. You are not welcomed into your own body. The family is like one's own body because it is the foundation of family members. This means South Sudanese would imaginatively use different symbols such as harmony for relating the Trinitarian life to political and religious ethical relationships.

Central Value Systems

Given the above discussions, the motivation behind this study is to understand what the most ethical thing would be for Christian leaders in South Sudan to do. In other words, I want to know what a Christian politician, or a political dispensation that includes a large number of Christians, should do in relation to Article 8. To do this, I will explore the roles in ethical decision-making of the cultural imagination (Ward, 2018), social imagination (Taylor, 2004) and Christian stance (Lovin, 2011), which relate to the idea of central value systems. The central value system is a concept, which researchers refer to as the inner value structure (Torres, Porto, Vargas, & Fischer, 2015; Schwartz, 1993). Value theorists define values generally as 'transsituational goals and principles that guide human behavior' (Manfredo, Bruskotter, Teel, Fulton, Schwartz, Arlinghaus, Oishi, Uskul, Redford, Kitayama, & Sullivan, 2016: 773). According to Schwartz (2017), ten values influence what an individual or group of people do. They are divided into four categories. The first is the openness to change. This includes values such as self-direction, stimulation and hedonism. The second is self-transcendence. This is composed of values such as universalism and benevolence. The third is self-enhancement. This includes achievement and power. The fourth is conservation. This category consists of values such as tradition, conformity and security. Deep-rooted values are difficult to penetrate because they 'serve as standards for evaluating whether actions, events, and people are desirable or undesirable' (Manfredo, et al., 2016: 773).

In most cases, the central conservation value system is difficult to penetrate, and the difficult-to-penetrate values define our traditional beliefs and loyalties. As Ward (2018: 183) observes, 'We are the inheritors of the way our minds have been shaped'. We do not directly experience some of the things that shape our minds. We acquire them unconsciously in our 'earliest development' (Ward, 2018: 183). We then add to these handed-down values 'our own experiences as they are filtered through our families, our friends, the things we have learned, the beliefs we hold and the sensibilities cultivated in the way we have been socialized' (Ward, 2018: 183). What imagination does in this process is to generate unconscious meaning from the repressed thoughts and perceptions to 'make sense of and even flourish in the surges of stimulation that comes to us internally and externally' (Ward, 2018: 184). Ward (2018: 184) argues that imagination is not chaotic but 'opportunistic as it gropes and ferrets out the most favourable and meaningful circumstances, and as it moves towards or away from some ideal attunement between inner propulsions and outer habitats.' Imagination sometimes would appear confusing because it 'may not perceive the way ahead or what it wants clearly; it may not even understand its own compulsions – but it is directed, not blind' (Ward, 2018: 184). As Forster (2019: na) concurs, 'What we believe, either knowingly or unknowingly, shapes our living, indeed our whole lives.'

Social Imagination

How people imagine their surroundings is crucial. It is what Taylor (2004) refers to as social imagination. Taylor (2004) differentiates premodern social imaginaries from the modern ones. He argues that premodern imaginaries were based on hierarchical order that differed in value and dignity rankings. Nobody would attempt to deviate from the hierarchical ranking of society or from roles that different actors would play within such a society. Any action that was done in compliance with the hierarchy in society was regarded as normal and right, even if the higher authority could not consult with the lower authority. The modern concept of order, however, is different from the premodern one. It does not give any status to hierarchical functional differentiation. Actions done in line with hierarchy in modern societies cannot in themselves be seen as defining the good (Taylor, 2004). Members of any modern society are expected to serve one another in a manner that anyone can rule and be ruled in turn as a rational being. Taylor (2004) argues that services in modern society aim at ensuring freedom and liberty of individuals rather than aiming at achieving the highest virtue or excellence. Generally, primary services in modern societies aim at ensuring security and prosperity for members of society. Taylor (2004) observes that reason in modern societies makes human beings believe that they have a duty to preserve not only themselves, but also all other human beings.

However, Taylor (2004) points out that a social imaginary is a complex thing. It sometimes defines how things usually work, but it also gives us an idea of how things ought to work. Mostly, social actors 'tap into the social imaginary of individuals and communities to shape their identity and form, or ill-form, persons, communities and societies' (Forster, 2019: na). Moreover, social imaginary of an individual does not just accept current practices without situating them within the historical understanding of how members of society got to where they are today and how they relate to others in their surroundings. This understanding of society's functioning is difficult to express explicitly in doctrines because of its unlimited nature (Taylor, 2004). In a social imaginary, people sometimes choose particular actions that they believe are normative. Yet, the imagined ethical practices in social imagination also differ. Some imagined moral actions are carried out in line with an established order or status quo, and others are done to change the established order in a revolutionary manner (Taylor, 2004).

CHURCH, STATE & THE ETHICAL IMAGINATION

Christian Ethics for Public Life

The ethical choices of the ethicists mentioned in Lovin's work deal with ethical issues in general. They are not only limited to questions about Christian isolated ethical living. They also include questions on how Christians should engage or not engage in public. For example, Lovin (2011) spells out different positions of four ethicists together with how they agree and disagree on what guides ethical decision-making. Some Christian ethicists believe that Christian ethics should be confined to living an ethical life within the community of faith. Others believe that Christians should advocate for the freedom of the oppressed. Yet, others think that Christian ethics should consider addressing issues within the dominant reality of social and political situations. Furthermore, some Christian ethicists argue that consensus should always define how Christians live with others. The leading advocates in these four different groups include Stanley Hauerwas, Katie Geneva Cannon, Reinhold Niebuhr and John Courtney Murray (Lovin, 2011).

Lovin (2011) points out that Hauerwas argues on Christian integrity that 'focuses on incarnation within the Christian stance.' Hauerwas (2010) sees values as integrated into narrative. He thinks what constitutes the moral self for a Christian is a narrative that stresses the importance of Christian habits (Hauerwas, 2016). In other words, believers would experience God 'as speaking to them authoritatively through scripture' (King, Abo-Zena, & Weber, 2017: 137). Moreover, Hauerwas (2010) believes that narrative rationalises moral reasons for particular behaviours, in particular traditions such as the community of faith. King, Abo-Zena, and Weber (2017: 128) also point out that other 'studies have noted the importance of faith communities, mentors, or religious educators' in spiritual development. Narrative, to Hauerwas, is crucial because it is not just used as an abstract communication that helps people know the world in which they live; it practically helps them change their behaviours and the world in which they live (Paul, 2013). Hauerwas (2015) further believes that actions are nothing more than enacted narratives. As Bafinamene (2017: 3) puts it, 'believers are called to learn, appropriate and absorb, practise and conform their lives to God's stories or the stories of Israel and Jesus.'

Hauerwas strongly believes in the distinctiveness of the church from the world. As Paul (2013: 16) reports, Hauerwas (1985: 5) believes that we as Christians 'must attend to the distinctiveness of our language, and to the distinctiveness of the community formed by that language, because it is true.' He argues that the church must not be diluted with the world's secularism by surrendering it to 'narratives that promise inner-worldly fulfilment' (Paul, 2013: 13). Hauerwas is mainly against cultural and political values that hinder the church's faithfulness to gospel narratives (Paul, 2013). He (as cited in Paul, 2013: 16) quotes Romans 12: 2 in which Apostle Paul warns Christians not to conform to the world, but instead 'be transformed by the renewal' of their minds. He goes further to think of 'the church as a political body, that is, as a community that not only preaches a political message, but actually embodies a politics' (Paul, 2013: 16). Lovin (2011: 51) observes that Hauerwas's Christian stance was influenced by 'the radical freedom from government and society that Mennonites and other radical Protestant groups sought during the Reformation.'

However, not every Christian ethicist agrees with Hauerwas. Some believe that Christian morality should be defined within the experiences of the oppressed people in society and in the community of faith. The womanist theologian Katie Geneva Cannon is a leading voice in this perspective. She believes that moral choices should be guided by the need to survive. In other words, the virtues of survival-guided Christian ethics are different from the cardinal virtues that include bravery-based courage. The courage of the oppressed is a sly courage. Alice Walker, who is a social activist, believes that 'This sly form of courage empowers a person to slip out of difficult situations by lubricating them with just the right amount of believable flattery and feigned humility' (Lovin, 2011: 60).

The focus on survival in the womanist theology of Cannon came from the long oppressive experiences that black women had within their black churches in the United States and the wider community, in which the Bible was used to justify the mistreatment of black people (Cannon, 2008). Cannon (2008: 131) argues that 'enslavers tried to indoctrinate Africans to believe that they were duty bound to serve Jesus Christ while they worked for their oppressors, performing their duties with great diligence and fidelity to God.' Because of these challenges, black people in general and black women in particular began to re-image Jesus Christ (Cannon, 2008). It is along this line of re-imaging Jesus Christ that Mouton (2011: 289) argues that the Church needs 'to reconstruct reality by courageously redefining and, where necessary, renaming (for our time emotionally laden) images such as *authority, power, obedience,* and *submission* as liberating practice for *all*, and as fundamental to a Reformed spirituality and view on humanity and creation.'

Even though other Christian ethicists agree with Cannon that Christians should work for the freedom of the oppressed, they believe Christian ethical efforts should include cautions against trying to do too much beyond their capacity. As Lovin (2011: 55) points out, Christian ethicists argue that 'the first task of Christian ethics is to match the requirements of the Christian stance to the realities of the present situation.' Christian realists such as Reinhold Niebuhr argue that American Protestants were disappointed in their inability to change events because 'They had put too little emphasis on sin, and they had estimated their own contribution to the work of redemption too highly' (Lovin, 2011:

56). Niebuhr (as cited in Lovin, 2011) argues that the Christian principle of ideal love that motivates serving others must be understood through the Bible's accounts of human nature. Human nature, to Niebuhr, is created in the image of God but has been separated from God's image by sin (Lovin, 2011). Therefore, it prioritises 'security and power in the self' over the genuine love for others in 'structures of politics, race, and nation that the Social Gospel had hoped to transform' (Lovin, 2011: 56). Niebuhr's realism originated from his experiences in Detroit in Michigan and in New York where he observed resistance to changes in economic equality by people with power (Lovin, 2011).

However, John Courtney Murray does not share Niebuhr's caution. He believes in the importance of consensus guided by reason (Lovin, 2011). According to Lovin (2011: 47), Murray argues that 'People in society use their reason to decide how they are going to live in order to create good lives for themselves.' In the process that leads to public consensus, Murray (as cited in Lovin, 2011) thinks that what matters is civil argument, not the sharing of faith or the settling of problems by force. Generally, consensus is a win-win public agreement in which people 'agree to continue reasoning together about what contributes to the common good and what kind of constitutional framework is required to sustain it.' Murray's Christian stance was influenced by his experience within the Catholic Church that was going through discrimination from the dominant Protestants who regarded it 'as foreign and undemocratic' (Lovin, 2011: 46). Murray's internal knowledge of the Catholic Church was different from what he heard the Protestants saying about Catholics. Yet, he knew there were some ethical areas where Catholics would differ from Protestants and the only way to promote harmony between these groups was consensus that aims at disadvantaging nobody.

Even though religious and social values differ among religious traditions as well as within each religious tradition today, the true conflict of values is between tradition and modernity. These differences are observed within each religious tradition such as the Anglican or Catholic. Starks and Robinson (2007: 18) argue that value differences that relate to traditional beliefs and modernity are 'more important than differences between Catholics, mainline Protestants, evangelical Protestants, Jews, and those with no religion, and more important than education or occupation.' For example, Protestant fundamentalists value traditional forms of obedience in their children more than non-fundamentalists do. Religious interest groups have been formed now in the United States to resist values that they see as conflicting with Christian values in the public domain. The conflict between modernist and traditional Christians is worsened by the fact that some modernists regard 'religious texts and teachings as human creations that should be considered in cultural context along with other moral precepts, and sees individuals as largely independent from God in determining their fates' (Starks & Robinson, 2007: 19).

Separation of Church and State

The above literature shows that different traditions and schools of thought influence individual and group values. Partly for this reason states with provision for the separation of church and state in their constitutions are more confused in day-to-day implementation of such laws today than states with no such provisions in their laws. The United States, for example, is known for valuing the separation of church and state, yet religion is mostly considered important in US elections and legislation (Garnett, 2007; Witte, 2003; Norris & Inglehart, 2004). In Sweden, the separation of church and state is accepted in some parts of the country, while it remains ambiguous in some areas (Sidenvall,

2012). Kenyans hold religious values important during elections, but politicians remind religious leaders of Kenya's secular status when elections are over (Riedl, 2012).

The idea of separating the church from state is sometimes violated by the church if state policies seem to threaten principles of holiness and the supremacy of God in line with premodern tradition. For example, religious groups are banned by law in the USA from engaging in political campaigns within religious institutions, but the Catholic Church violated this ban during 2008 general elections because it regarded some policies advanced by some candidates as ungodly (Flint-Hamilton, 2010). In addition, in line with premodern tradition's love for order, states today enact laws that they believe would maintain law and order (Kalkandjieva, 2011).

However, researchers and practitioners who are influenced by the Enlightenment tradition value laws that protect individual freedom. Along the line of the Enlightenment's promotion for individual rights, for example, protection against marginalisation is one of the main reasons that some scholars give today in support of the separation of church and state (Garnett, 2007; McCAuliff, 2010). In Africa, for instance, the support for the separation of religion and state depends on whether or not a religious group feels marginalised or favoured (Riedl, 2012). Those who feel marginalised would even make claims for the existence of separation of religion and state provision in a constitution where there is none (Mujuzi, 2011). Kenya is a good example.

The Role of Central Value Systems in Separation of Church and State

The existing literature, as shown above, seems to indicate the influence of the central value systems, which relate to cultural and social imaginations, in what individuals and groups of people support or reject. Yet, no study has been done to examine directly the role that central value systems (especially conservation values such as tradition, conformity and security) play in confusions prevalent in implementing legal provisions for the separation of religion and state in many countries. Some explored literature above focus on Christian involvement in public life. Nevertheless, this study explores the role that central value systems play in the confusion of religion and state separation in South Sudan. This can be done within the framework of a Christian stance, cultural imagination and social imagination (Lovin, 2011; Ward, 2018; Taylor, 2004). As Lovin (2011: 23) points out, the Christian stance is 'a set of convictions that work together to guide action by giving us an idea of the whole reality in which that action takes place and pointing out what it is within that reality that is most valuable and important.' It examines 'how all aspects of reality fit together' from the creation to the 'resurrection of Jesus Christ' (Lovin, 2011: 23).

Because of the above framework, theological reflections in this study will be done within the synergy between values that are influenced by Christian faith, and values that are influenced by cultural beliefs (Lovin, 2011). Other ways in which Christians develop their values to deal with moral problems will be explored in detail, guided by Christian theological contribution (which will be framed both in terms of the historical Christian traditions of the region, and also the hermeneutic choices that inform the chosen conversation partners in this study), cultural imagination and social imagination. As Ward (2018: 184) points out, the exploration of 'the imagination enables us to assess what is going on in a given cultural situation; what is going on beneath and yet through the symbolic.' Other perspectives that I will explore in detail include the concept of integrity that characterises the distinctiveness of Christian witness in moral decision-making, realism which matches Christian ethical actions with 'the realities of the present situation'

(Lovin, 2011: 55) and the liberation perspective which demands that Christian ethical decisions and actions be guided by the experiences of those who are oppressed in society. The purpose of exploring these different perspectives within the Christian stance, cultural imagination and social imagination framework is to understand what the most ethical thing would be for Christian leaders in South Sudan to do. Furthermore, I would like to know how differences in value orientations influence what individuals and groups of people accept or reject, and how consensus is used to let people of different moral convictions live together in harmony (Lovin, 2011).

Crux of the Matter

Article 8 of South Sudan's Constitution has brought into view the reality of clashes of values and inconsistencies in implementing legal provision in the country. Moreover, how contextual theological understandings of the constitutional separation of religion and state frames relationships between these two institutions is unclear. This study, therefore, poses the question: How would a contextual South Sudanese theology frame an ethical relationship between religion and the state?

Although the wording of Article 8 in the 2011 Constitution of independent South Sudan could point towards the respect for religious rights stipulated in Article 6 in the 2005 Constitution of united Sudan, the perceptions about the aim of Article 8 seem different. Some people appear to think that Article 8 was positioned in the Constitution in 2005 to prevent the Muslim-dominated government headquartered in Khartoum from declaring Sudan an Islamic state (Sudan Tribune, 2013 Feb 25). Others seem to think that Article 8 is in South Sudan's Constitution in order to meet the international norms of treating all religions equally.

It also appears that the modernist concept of equality is a marginalised value in South Sudan. South Sudanese are most likely to consider equality within the structure of hierarchy (McKinnon, 2000; Jaeckle & Georgakopoulos, 2010). Yet, the constitutional provision that aims at meeting the international standards must apply equality of religions in the modernist or postmodernist sense of the word. Equality in modernism and postmodernism is generally not situated within structural concept of hierarchy. This incongruence in the understanding of equality in South Sudan leads to various misapprehensions in the implementation of Article 8. State authorities, for example, hold the South Sudanese understanding of equality in relation to Article 8. Yet, the South Sudanese understanding of equality may fit better into a premodern conception of equality than it would into the modernists' or postmodernists' understanding of the concept. Religious leaders also rarely accept the modernists' and postmodernists' value of equality. They seem to side with so-called 'traditional values' that are grounded in the hope for a divine future. In other words, the churches (and their members) in this region adopt a particular eschatological worldview that is different from secular political focus which may have informed the drafting of Article 8 in South Sudan's Constitution (Paul, 2013).

Nevertheless, the lines of value clashes are not drawn between the church and the state. Some policy-makers and policy-implementers do not seem to agree with values contrary to their cultures, making the implementation of Article 8 differ from its clearly stated intention. South Sudanese rarely demarcate secular institutions from religious ones (Pendles, 2020). They operate in a complementarity fashion. The complementarity could be determined by friendship or necessity. Friendship would include unrestricted generosity towards each other. This unrestricted generosity might often be based on favouritism, not equal treatment. For example, the government helped 900 Muslims travel to Mecca in 2012 (Sudan Tribune, 2012 Oct 18). Muslims appreciated the assistance. Conversely, other religious groups not benefiting from the equal treatment of all religions stipulated in Article 8 of the Constitution were unhappy. Potential complaints by the Christians mentioned above indicate the unhappiness of disadvantaged religious groups.

The above value clashes need to be examined through the lenses of different value orientations. The emphasis will be on what the most ethical thing would be for Christian leaders in South Sudan to do. I will try to understand what a Christian politician, or a political dispensation that includes such a large number of Christians, should do in relation to Article 8(1). The study will examine the best possible relationships that should exist between religion and the state in South Sudan from the perspective of a South Sudanese theological context. In this process, the Christians' historical understanding of the state and its relations to the church will first be described. Then, how traditional values differ or concur with values that are stipulated in Article 8 will be analysed. This may be informed by traditional commitments and values but may also diverge from those values in some instances. It may draw upon, and aspire to, certain secular 'international' values, but also depart from them because of Christian theology, contextual history and current realities as well as cultural values.

The Contribution of this Study to Knowledge

As stated in the background of this study, the existing literature does not show the role that central value systems (especially conservation values that include tradition, conformity and security) play in inconsistencies prevalent in the implementation of constitutional provisions for separation of church and state in many countries. Researchers and practitioners dealing with the question of church-state relations focus much of their attention on either the freedom or lack of freedom that church and state separation promotes, or the question of Christians' involvement in public life. This study, unlike other studies dealing with church-state relations, analyses the role that central value systems play in confusion in the implementation of constitutional provisions for church and state separation. It asks how a contextual South Sudanese theology would describe the relationship between religion and state.

Therefore, the contribution of this study to knowledge is to start an academic discourse on how central value systems contribute to confusions in the implementation of the constitutional provisions for separation of religion and state in South Sudan, and probably in other countries. The conceptual model of this academic contribution is straightforward: CVS → CI where CVS = central value systems and CI = confusion in the implementation of constitutional provisions for religion and state separation. The straightforwardness of the framework is evident because the study will show how different traditions and schools of thought influence the central value systems of individuals and groups to the extent that such central values are hardly penetrated by operating legal provisions and dominant schools of thought.

The hypothesis of the study's contribution to knowledge is that since the central value systems would sometimes operate at the unconscious level of an individual, policy implementers would get confused between the importance of operating the national constitutional provisions and what they strongly believe in at the individual and special-group levels. How policy-implementers determine what the right thing to do is as Christians leaders could be influenced by conservation values that include tradition, conformity and security. A central value system may operate in a way that it guards against anything that threatens individuals' and groups' conservation. That is why implementation of Article 8 looks confusing.

This study mainly explores possible links between likely value clashes as well as conflicts in implementing the constitutional provisions in Article 8 of South Sudan's Constitution and its leaders' central value systems. That is, the study focuses on the role of central value systems in possible value clashes and inconsistencies in the implementation of Article 8 rather than on merely understanding the religion and state separation. Yet, special attention is given to how theology in the context of South Sudan can be framed to address ethical relationships between religion and state. The study postulates that an ethical relationship between state and religion in South Sudan would include no favouritism in the treatment of all religions. It also asserts that Article 8 calls for non-interference in the affairs of religion by state authorities or in state affairs by religious leaders. Religions, in this process, would often depend on their theologies' specifying principles to guide state and religion relationships. For this reason, the primary question of this study is: How would a contextual South Sudanese theology frame an ethical relationship between religion and state?

It is conceivable, nonetheless, that the above-mentioned primary research question will not lead to comprehensive analysis of potential reasons behind possible misperceptions in Article 8 implementation and decision-makings. In order to explore in detail possible roles that central value systems play in decision-making that result in likely inconsistencies in the implementation of Article 8 in the Constitution of South Sudan, other questions must focus attention on specific areas of analysis. Specific areas of enquiry include the origin of Article 8 and its probable implementation incompatibilities, and theories that may explain potential inconsistencies in implementation. The questions below focus on these specific areas of analysis. Put otherwise, these are secondary research questions to the above-mentioned primary research question. They focus on specific areas of analysis in that they ask:

What influences ethical decision-making of political and religious leaders in relation to social, religious and political matters in South Sudan?

What is the nature of the conflict between so-called 'Christian values' and the values of constitutional governance (as prescribed in Article 8) in South Sudan?

What are some of the roles that churches and government institutions play in cultivating values among South Sudanese?

How might different groups with different moral convictions arrive at consensus in South Sudan?

What would a South Sudanese theological ethics suggest is the 'best' approach to the separation of Church and State in South Sudan?

These secondary questions will form chapters that will systematically explore the hypothesis that central value systems often have direct and indirect influence on policymakers and the decision-making of policy-implementers. This step-by-step exploration of different questions may establish possible reasons behind confusions in the implementation of Article 8 in the Constitution of South Sudan. It may also establish the nature of a theology that would explain conditions established in the explored literature. Having mentioned these, I now set out the general approach that may help in exploring the above questions.

General Approach

The purpose of this study is to explore probable inconsistencies and value clashes in the implementation of constitutional provisions for the separation of religion and state in South Sudan. The study also looks into how different groups with different moral convictions arrive at consensus. The analysis focuses on where different values differ and where they converge (Migliore, 2004). The study employs a phenomenological approach, which is the study of appearances (Daniel, 2012).

This methodology fits the aims of the study well in the sense that the study explores what *appears* to be behind inconsistencies in the implementation of Article 8 in the Constitution of South Sudan.

Scholars often use two popular types of phenomenological approaches: Husserl's descriptive phenomenology (Giorgi, 2017), and Heidegger's hermeneutic phenomenology (van Manen, 2017). Both are mostly empirical in nature. Husserl's descriptive phenomenology aims 'to capture experience in its primordial origin or essence, without interpreting, explaining, or theorizing' (van Manen, 2017: 775). Heidegger's hermeneutic phenomenology differs from Husserl's descriptive phenomenology in that it focuses on the nature of being (Giorgi, 2007) and aims at interpretively describing what the phenomenon is (van Manen, 2017).

A hermeneutic phenomenology at first seemed to fit this study very well because it focuses on interpretive description of a phenomenon. However, since the study aims at exploring particular Christian and cultural value-orientations in relation to possible value clashes and discrepancies in Article 8 implementation, it mainly uses the phenomenology of religion to explore the phenomenon of value clashes. Schleiermacher initiated the discipline, 'phenomenology of religion.' He then inspired other phenomenologists of religion such as Otto, Kristensen, Van der Leeuw, Chantepie and Eliade (Cox, 2006).

The most influential phenomenologist among the phenomenologists of religion is Van der Leeuw. The analytical process in Van der Leeuw's phenomenology consists of five steps (Cox, 2006): The first is phenomena classification, the second is phenomena interpolation, the third is bracketing, the fourth is structural relationships clarification and the fifth is the storage through which manifestation emerges (Van der Leeuw, 1963). This study adopts Van der Leeuw's phenomenology as modified by Blum (2012).

Blum (2012) argues that the phenomenology of religion should be defined by interpretive function. It aims at disclosing 'meaning encapsulated and expressed in the religious discourse, text, or experience under analysis' (Blum, 2012: 1030). The interpreter, according to Blum (2012: 1030), should aim at understanding what 'a perspective is like', its implications on a religious subject's beliefs and behaviours, and 'how these particular attitudes inform and are informed by other, related attitudes, beliefs, and practices.' Blum (2010) would agree with Koopman (2010: 126) that theological analysis mainly addresses 'questions regarding the contents, rationality, and implications of Christian faith.'

In this interpretive process, Blum (2012) agrees with other phenomenologists of religion that *epoché* or suspension of judgment is crucial: it brackets 'committed participation in a faith community and analyzes the intentions or "meanings" of a religious community or tradition' (Blum, 2012: 1033). However, bracketing might not always be the case in interpretive processes since interpretation might unconsciously be guided by a researcher's central value systems. Blum (2012: 1034) believes that other disciplines such as 'Sociology, economics, and political science do indeed have much to tell us about religion.' Therefore, their connection to a phenomenon under study must be considered in interpretive processes. He also argues that religion is not autonomous from history. Therefore, its interpretive processes should consider historical issues that are important to the understanding of a phenomenon. This is also in line with the relationship method in Systematic Theology developed by Paul Tillich in which 'existential questions are formulated by an analysis of the human situation in a given period as seen in its philosophy, literature, art, science, and social institutions' (Migliore, 2004: 15).

This enquiry, as mentioned earlier, will be interactive. Mostly, the 'aim is to create genuine conversation' that associates 'rather than driving a wedge' between religious values guided by Christian faith and constitutional values guided by the international community's standards (Migliore, 2004: 15). I will first explore literature on issues to do with Christian and cultural values and how these values affect Article 8 implementation in South Sudan. I will then scrutinise theories and other concepts that try to explain theological reasons informing the need, or lack of need, for the separation of church and state. In associative approach, the analysis will mainly start with understanding concepts and theories on the separation of church and state, together with their underlying values and attitudes, through correct interpretation and 'how these particular attitudes inform and are informed by other, related attitudes, beliefs, and practices' (Blum, 2012: 1030).

---- CHAPTER TWO ----

THE ORIGIN OF ARTICLE 8 IN SOUTH SUDAN'S CONSTITUTION

Introduction

The Constitutions of united Sudan before 2005 make no mention of the separation of religion and state. The separation of religion and state was first introduced in the Constitution of the semiautonomous Southern Sudan in 2005 after the signing of the Comprehensive Peace Agreement (CPA) in Kenya. Arguably, Southern Sudan's lawmakers added Article 8 into the Constitution in 2005 to prevent the then Muslim-dominated government of united Sudan from declaring the whole of Sudan as an Islamic state (Sudan Tribune, 2013 Feb 25). Yet, one would still wonder about the true reasons behind the inclusion of

Article 8 in the Constitution. Could it be that Article 8 might have been introduced to meet international standards on the separation of religion and state as well as the need for equal treatment of all religions? Could the principle of the separation of church and state in the USA have influenced South Sudan's lawmakers at the time? South Sudanese might have adopted American values during their formal education in the USA. Some South Sudanese politicians, such as the founder of the Sudan People's Liberation Movement and Army (SPLM/A), Dr. John Garang de Mabior, pursued their academic and military studies in the USA (DeLaney, 2010). Garang's formal education in the USA would possibly lead to the assumption of a likely link between American constitutional values and Article 8 in the Constitution of South Sudan.

Despite the above likely conditions behind the origin of Article 8, it is not yet clear what the true intention of the lawmakers was for adding Article 8 to the Constitution. Politically, the principle on which Article 8 is based is not clear, whether it is mainly the separation of state and religion or the equal treatment of all religions or both. Moreover, it is unclear how these principles play out in real practice. No South Sudanese has done a study on Article 8 to demonstrate the reasons for its inclusion in the Constitution of Southern Sudan, given the fact that the constitutions of Sudan never had provisions for the separation of religion and state. The main conversation partner in this chapter will then be a Sudanese scholar named Abdel Salam Sidahamed. He explores the background of Islamists and how they have been trying to influence the government in the united Sudan in an attempt to turn it into an Islamic state. It is not implausible to argue that fear of Islamists, and their efforts to turn Sudan into an Islamic state, are behind Article 8.

This chapter will, therefore, explore the historical background of Article 8 to understand its historical development. The purpose of this historical exploration is mainly to understand what motivated South

Sudanese lawmakers to include Article 8 in the Constitution in 2005 and later in 2011. This is crucial because it may show what the constitutional and other legal experiences of South Sudanese were in united Sudan in relation to religion and state relationships. In addition, this chapter will examine how these constitutional and other legal experiences translated to political, religious and social relations between the North and the South of Sudan.

Obscurity of Article 8: Stipulation and Misinterpretation

Article 8 in the Constitution of the Republic of South Sudan is one of the articles that legal experts claim meet international standards such as 'the protection of human rights and, especially, freedom of conscience, belief and religion' (D'Angelo, 2010: 646). It seems the inclusion of Article 8 in the Constitution was to ensure the boundaries between state and religion were defined and demarcated. However, that definition is not clear in Article 8(1) which states very broadly: 'Religion and State shall be separate.' Specific principles for separation of religion and state are not clearly stated. Moreover, which institutions are intended to guide these not-well-stated principles of separation are not well stipulated. The lack of clearly stipulated principles sometimes leads to misinterpretations of legal provisions. What the court often does is to determine the meaning of the constitution's provision and whether or not it is being correctly applied. If not correctly applied, then the court determines what can or should be done to rectify the misapplication and by whom.

Different judges could interpret well-written provisions for separation of church and state differently, such as the United States of America's Establishment Clause. However, misinterpretations reduce when the legal provision is clearly stipulated. Many judges in the United

States agree that the Establishment Clause means that Congress should be neutral in religious matters (Esbeck, 2012). It is clear that 'Congress shall make no law respecting an establishment of religion, or prohibiting the free exercise thereof.' What judges sometimes disagree on in the United States is the nature of the neutrality of Congress. More importantly, the key question which the courts often struggle to decide, leading to occasional disagreement between judges at all levels, is what constitutes 'the free exercise of religion', particularly if it conflicts with other rights guaranteed by the constitution.

Moreover, it also seems Article 8(2) of South Sudan's Constitution was intended to ensure equality of all religions. However, the reality of this equality of all religions is not very clear in daily implementations of Article 8(2). Chapter one mentioned that the government had been facilitating pilgrimages by Muslims to Mecca in Saudi Arabia in addition to funding the building of Islamic schools within South Sudan. The government makes these provisions for Muslims when its top leaders are fully aware of Article 8(2) of the Constitution. This seeming intentional disregard for Article 8(2) implies that equality is not a straightforward concept. There could be hidden intentions attached to the idea of equality of all religions stipulated in Article 8(2). Alternatively, some unconscious values could be contributing to ambiguities in implementing Article 8(2).

This chapter tries to answer part of the primary research question on what ethical relationships between religion and state consist of. The purpose is to understand whether unethical conditions were prevalent in the Sudanese constitutions that never mentioned the separation of religion and state before the signing of CPA. It is also important to understand whether the absence of the separation of religion and state in united Sudan's constitutions contributed to the civil war that ended in 2005. The chapter will further explore whether theological reasons are involved in the inclusion of Article 8 in the Constitution of South Sudan. Further, the chapter will examine whether the reasons for the inclusion of Article 8 in the Constitution were exclusively political in nature or included reasons of theology and human rights. Christianity and Islam were two major religions in united Sudan. The chapter will explore Christian and Islamic theological issues that might be involved in the absence of constitutional separation of religion and state in Sudan's constitutions before 2005 and its inclusion in the Constitution of Southern Sudan in 2005. The chapter will also examine the relationships between Christianity and Islam in united Sudan and in independent South Sudan. Whether ethical issues are or are not involved in these relationships will be explored. Understanding historical issues involved in the inclusion of Article 8 in the Constitution of South Sudan before and after the independence of South Sudan is important. It will possibly open the way to more questions for better understanding likely confusions in the implementation of Article 8 in the present independent South Sudan.

Section two below will explore what the intention for adding Article 8 to South Sudan's Constitution was or could have been before South Sudan became independent and what it could be after its independence from the Republic of Sudan. It will focus mainly on whether or not the lawmakers intended to separate religious institutions from state institutions. The third section will examine whether Article 8 was a reaction to perceived marginalisation of South Sudanese by North Sudanese in united Sudan. The fourth section will deal with the claim that Article 8 was introduced in 2005 in order for the Constitution to meet international standards. The fifth section will discuss whether political survival was the motivator behind Article 8 in South Sudan's Constitution.

Institution within Institution

Intentions for moral actions are often very elusive, especially when they are closely connected with political and religious survival. O'Donovan (2003) argues that the relationship between politics and theology is full of suspicion. Politicians, who often like to force morality to serve their political order, corrupt religion or theology when they misuse it. According to O'Donovan (2003: 6), moral discourses and sentiments in politics 'are like bad coinage pumped into the currency, which can only lower its value and destroy it.' However, he also observes that the suspicion is not limited to the way that politicians or politics corrupt morality or theology, but also affect the way that theologians corrupt politics. This is because politicians believe that the intervention of divine authority in political order could not happen without overwhelming the structures put in place by political authority. In other words, revelation does seem 'to pose a threat to political freedom' (O'Donovan, 2003: 8).

Since theology and politics aim at different end goals, it is easy to see why one should manipulate the other. Moral intentions to establish and maintain any type of politically motivated relationships appear genuine sometimes on the surface when in reality they might be deceptive. This is even more complex when it involves a claim for political morality. O'Donovan (2003: 6) terms political morality as a forgery because it 'serves the convenience of political order.' A true morality would sometimes recommend actions that are not convenient for politics or political order. However, it is not that politics does not pay attention to genuine moral issues. It sometimes does. The problem is that politicians would mainly like morality to serve the purpose of political order. Political order, as O'Donovan (2003: 6) puts it, is 'a certain constellation of benefits and disbenefits of power which happens to suit one person rather than another.' Unlike political morality that serves the political order, religious morality aims mostly at directing actions in a way that complies with God's will. God's will would occasionally go against human will in politics and in social life. This is because 'there is a *true* order which endures no matter who finds it inconvenient' (O'Donovan, 2003: 6).

Yet, not every religion and government would see a problem in the relationship of state and religion. Islam and the state, for instance, would advance the interest of each other in a clearly strategized, though still elusive, manner. Strategically, Islam would even justify the religious policy of obtaining political power to advance the Islamic agenda in a country. Accommodation of different religious views and beliefs would be rare in such a country. Islam has a clear theological doctrine of divine unity known as *tawhid*. This divine unity leaves no room for fragmentation, whether political or social. As Sookhdeo (2014: 74) points out, '*tawhid* states that the universe is a unified, harmonious whole, in which Allah's rule is imposed on nature, knowledge and society.' The role of human beings under this doctrine of *tawhid* is to comply or conform. Muslim leaders under the guidance of *tawhid* expect people to reflect the oneness of God in their lives and work. This means that Muslim leaders would not give room to diversity under this doctrine of *tawhid*. The Quran and *sunna* also caution against the diversity of beliefs.

In contrast to Islam, many Christian theologians caution against mixing the state with religion in the name of the Lordship of Christ over all authorities and principalities of this world even though they believe in the Lordship of Christ over all creation. As O'Donovan (2003: 7) argues, 'we can think of a theological politician, who interprets the principles of political prudence in a way coherent with God's will, but we cannot think of a political theologian, who forges a theology to suit a statesman's advantage.' Even if we find such a theologian who makes theology support the advantage of a statesman, as is sometimes the case, then that theologian could hardly command a recognised theological authority. As discussed earlier, theologically motivated moral sentiments conflict with politically motivated moral sentiments. For this reason Christians in the West differ with the Aristotelian belief that ethics is 'a subdivision of politics' (O'Donovan, 2003: 6).

The doctrine of *tawhid* would hardly define coherent politics in the modern West. Western Christian missionaries, who educated most of South Sudanese politicians and theologians in mission schools before and after the independence of Sudan from the British colonial administration, were mixed in their beliefs on the separation of church and state. Mostly the missionaries from the United States of America firmly believed in the separation of church and state, and dominated mission fields after Sudan's independence from Britain. Therefore, most South Sudan Christians may have the Western, especially American, mind-set that regards politics as different from religion, in contrast to Sudanese Islamists who regard the two as one. It might partly be for this reason that the relationship between the Islamic religion and the government in Khartoum had been mysterious to South Sudanese politicians and theologians for decades.

Origin and Development of Islamism in Sudan

In the 1940s, the movement that later became Islamism in Sudan started in the universities and high schools. The Northern and Southern Sudanese paid less attention to the students' Islamist movement because the main mentor was the Muslim Brotherhood in Egypt, making it seem like a distant issue. The movement might have been ignored also because the British were still ruling Sudan, and might have seen those Islamist movements as those students' private religious affairs that could have little effect on national policies. In 1954, this limited students' Islamist movement developed into something much more. As Sidahmed (2012: 164) points out, 'a small number of Islamist groups came together and formed the Sudanese Muslim Brotherhood movement.' Yet, the influence of this Sudanese Muslim Brotherhood movement rarely extended outside the student body. Therefore, the Northern and Southern Sudanese still paid little attention to its threats. This student Islamist movement then took advantage of 'the October 1964 uprising that toppled the first military regime of General Ibrahim Abboud' (Sidahmed, 2012: 164). Politicians then took notice of what was developing, but still did not think it was of any major threat to Sudanese politics.

Real concerns about the Islamists and their political power started after the 1964 uprising. Some Southern Sudanese Christians and the Northern Sudanese moderate Muslims started to realise that what initially seemed to be the students' religious affairs would have a significant influence on politics in the country. The reality of the Islamists' political weight, for example, was seen when the first real Islamist political party known as Islamic Charter Front (ICF) was formed during the 1964 uprising. This party could not be underestimated because it was led by a prominent Islamist Hassan al-Turabi. Even though the ICF was still not a major political party at the time, its appeal to the Islamist agenda was felt in Sudanese politics. For example, ICF 'was the driving force behind the push to dissolve the Communist Party of Sudan in 1965 on charges of atheism' (Sidahmed, 2012: 164). The same ICF pushed the 'adoption of an Islamic constitution for the country onto the agenda of the mainstream, parties, the Umma Party and the Democratic Unionist Party (DUP)' (Sidahmed, 2012: 164-165).

The politicians' fear of Islamists increased in 1985 when President Nimeiri was toppled. The Islamists' role was effectual in Nimeiri's downfall even though they had been in what seemed to be political alliance before the fall of Nimeiri's regime. President Nimeiri had imprisoned some Islamist leaders just a few weeks before the public uprising and military takeover that toppled his government. The Islamists formed a new political organisation known as the National Islamic Front (NIF) after the fall of President Nimeiri's regime. The NIF became the third-largest party after Umma and DUP in Sudan after the collapse of Nimeiri's government when it won 51 parliamentary seats in the 1986 elections. When the Umma and DUP parties formed a coalition government and elected Sadiq al-Mahdi as the head of state of Sudan, the NIF became the official opposition party in parliament.

The political aim of the NIF was to expand its Islamist movement and capture the Muslim constituencies in the next elections or to force the regime of Sadiq al-Mahdi to share political power with the Islamists. To their expectations, the NIF managed to join the coalition government in 1988, though it left it again in 1989. Nevertheless, the NIF did not leave the government in 1989 out of choice. It was excluded from the government by the regime of Sadiq al-Mahdi. However, Sadiq al-Mahdi had to be toppled by the same Islamists in a military coup that brought President Omar al-Bashir to power in June 1989, ending parliamentary rule in Sudan. At this point, it became clear that the Islamists were ready to change Sudanese politics in their favour and that what they favoured was to use the government as the tool to advance Islamism in Sudan. As Sidahmed (2012: 166) puts it, 'Whether in government or opposition the NIF proved to be very influential in setting the political agenda and successful in mobilizing public opinion in support of its own agenda.'

Mixing State and Religion

The above developments show that there is no problem with mixing religion and state in Sudan. In reality, the Islamic religion and the government in Khartoum constitute an institution within an institution. For example, when the NIF took over political power on June 30, 1989, it formed a council of 300 unelected members that run the affairs of the Islamic Movement as a religious organisation as well as the affairs of the state. This membership of 300 Islamists, for example, 'became a reservoir from which ministers, top state officials, security officers and occupants of other essential positions were recruited' (Sidahmed, 2012: 168). Moreover, the Islamists did not restrict their activities to civilian politics; they also had a military wing known as the Popular Defence Forces (PDF) that provided the needed military support to the new Islamist regime of President Omar al-Bashir.

However, mixing the state together with the religion is not a practice for Sudanese Muslims alone. Right from its beginning as a religion, 'Islam created a fusion of politics and religion which were inextricably linked' (Sookhdeo, 2014: 32). Muslims generally believe that religious truth would sanctify political power. They also believe that political power confirms and sustains religion. Sookhdeo (2014: 29) observes that 'One aspect of Islam that makes it different from any other religion is the way in which it seeks to address the structures and institutions of society through political power.' Yet, the reality of this fused relationship between the Sudanese government and the Islamic religion in Sudan was implemented gradually for various reasons.

Islamic State and the Islamic Law

During the British colonial administration in Sudan, the Islamic law, known as sharia, was confined to Muslims as their personal law. This was mainly because 'under the impact of Western colonial rule, sharia was phased out in most Muslim countries' (Sookhdeo, 2014: 34). Mostly, the colonial administrations would only retain parts of Islamic law that dealt solely with family matters. Customary and English laws ruled non-Muslims that included Christians and followers of African Traditional Religions. Yet, Muslims tried to legitimise sharia by using the values of a good conscience, justice and equality (D'Angelo, 2010). They did this to ensure that they gradually introduced sharia law into the national laws without being opposed by the colonial administrators who initially accepted it as personal law, aiming at regulating relationships within Muslim communities. This is because Muslims are generally 'not satisfied with individuals' personal choices to embrace the religion; rather it sought political domination of the new territories and peoples and the total transformation of all their societal structures by imposing sharia and subjugating the non-Muslim population to Islamic rule' (Sookhdeo, 2014: 32).

After Sudan's independence from the British colonial administration, Muslims who had become the administrators of Sudan government decided to 'extend the nature of personal law and amplify its possible value as territorial law' (D'Angelo, 2010: 648). Muslim government leaders gradually extended Islamic law to marriage cases where one of the couple was a Muslim. Sharia law would bind the couple, regardless of whether one of them was a Christian. The other extension was 'the adoption of a civil code based on the principles of Islamic law, according to the Muslim model, or the acknowledgment of the sharia law as a general source of inspiration of the law' (D'Angelo, 2010: 648).

Sharia law was used in civil courts as early as 1971 in Sudan, but to a limited extent. As Kustenbauder (2012: 406) puts it, 'civil courts in Sudan were required to use sharia law as a source of their decisions, in the absence of other legislation.' However, at this point, non-Muslims were allowed to deviate from the principles of sharia law.

Radical changes from customary and English laws to sharia law started when Jaafar Nimeiri became President in 1969. President Nimeiri set up 'a committee for the revision of Sudanese legislation, headed by the influential figure of Hassan al-Turabi' (D'Angelo, 2010: 649) in 1977. One possible reason why President Nimeiri decided to form this committee was pressure from the Islamists. The Islamists opposed his policies because they considered them as liberal and, therefore, not compatible with the doctrine of *tawhid*. When he took over as President in 1969, for example, he pursued policies that were intended to unite his government with the Anya-Nya 1 Southern Sudan rebels. He also nationalised banks that could have been Muslim banks. The institutions in Nimeiri's regime were mainly lacking Islamic influence with which Islamists would be happy. Therefore, Islamists were not happy with Nimeiri's policies that they deemed leftist-leaning. For that reason, these 'Islamists joined the Umma and DUP to form the National Front opposition Coalition' (Sidahmed, 2012: 165).

President Nimeiri decided to reconcile with the National Front in 1977. This national reconciliation gave the Islamists the opportunity to organise as a powerful force that could not be ignored. In other words, they 'adopted a comprehensive strategy to transform the Islamist movement into a political force capable of assuming power in its own right' (Sidahmed, 2012: 165). In order to survive politically, President Nimeiri decided to form a strategic alliance with the Islamists, a decision that 'allowed the movement to expand its membership and strengthen its economic capabilities' (Sidahmed, 2012: 165). President Nimeiri's adoption of sharia law was partly intended to appease the Islamists, and it did.

The policy that resulted in introducing sharia law into the Sudanese laws also came as a possible result of a conference that the Muslim World League (MWL) held in 1975 to step up the Islamic mission to spread Islam around the world. President Nimeiri made it clear that the 'task of the committee was more specifically the adaptation of the current legislation to the dictates of Islamic law' (D'Angelo, 2010: 649). The work of this committee partly resulted in the rebellion of the Sudan People's Liberation Movement and Army in May 1983 in Bor. President Numeiri confirmed the rebels' fear by issuing some laws in September 1983 in which sharia law was 'explicitly recognized as the source of law for all the Sudanese' (D'Angelo, 2010: 649). For example, the September 1983 laws included 'the Basic Judgments Act requiring civil courts to apply sharia law, notwithstanding other legislative provisions' (Kustenbauder, 2012: 406). Kustenbauder (2012: 406) argues that the September 1983 laws 'effectively marked the Islamization of all laws in Sudan and their application to all citizens, regardless of religious, ethnic, or regional affiliation.'

Oneness of Allah in the Sudanese State

What the Islamists seem to regard as the most ethical thing to do in the government and in religious institutions in Sudan is to safeguard the divine unity or *tawhid*. The *tawhid* is also referred to as the 'oneness of Allah.' This oneness of Allah implies that 'there can be only one law for the world, which is Islamic law, sharia, and Muslims must impose it, by force if necessary' (Sookhdeo, 2014: 29). In order to safeguard the divine unity in all spheres of life, the Islamists in Sudan and in other countries make sure that non-Muslims stay away from any position that would influence them to make decisions that may go against the doctrine of *tawhid*.

Muslims are generally expected to conform to Islamic rules which are not only limited to religious institutions. They are also enforced in political institutions, because Islamists believe that 'Islam is both a religion and a way of life, and therefore is as relevant in the public domain as in the private sphere' (Sidahmed, 2012: 181). Mostly, conformity is seen as important in Islam because it is the best way to safeguard the divine unity. Because of this view, there is 'stress on the uniformity of Islamic views' (Sookhdeo, 2014: 34). Since there is oneness of Allah, for Muslims there must also be oneness of state. This unifying state is known in Islam as *umma*. As Sookhdeo (2014: 34) puts it, 'The *umma* is the religious, social and political embodiment of *tawhid* in human society.' This doctrine of *tawhid* might have contributed to the introduction of the separation of religion and state in Sudan by the SPLM/A.

Islamization and Introduction of Separation of Religion and State in Sudan

The first legal mention of the separation of religion and state came from the SPLM/A as an attempt to block the gradual Islamization of Sudan through government institutions. Article 24(c) of the Sudan People's Liberation Movement *Manifesto* of July 1983 stipulates that 'there shall be separation of state, and Mosque and church.' The same section (c) of Article 24 of the *Manifesto* talks of freedom of all religions. It reads, 'All religious faiths in the country shall have complete freedom to practice without hindrance or intimidation, provided that this freedom is not abused and used for political purposes.'

The leaders of the SPLM/A do not hide the reasons for introducing the separation of state and religion in the *Manifesto*. They argue in

Article 24(c) of the *Manifesto* against the way that 'the Sudanese ruling clique in both the North and the South' would continue to use religious fundamentalism and the nationality question as tools for deceiving and dividing 'the people in order to perpetuate their rule and exploitation.' This suggests the motivation behind introducing the separation of religion and state was to protect South Sudanese from being politically dominated and exploited by the religious fundamentalists ruling Sudan in Khartoum. In other words, the intention for the introduction of Article 24 in the *Manifesto* was more about political survival than the need to protect the right of minority religious groups.

The SPLM leaders wanted religion and state to be separate in Sudan so that non-Muslims like them could get the chance to rule and not be blocked on religious grounds from getting political positions. There was a common claim by Muslims that Christians should not rule Muslims. This belief is not limited to Sudanese Muslims. Sookhdeo (2014: 33) points out that Muslims 'feel that it would damage the honour of a Muslim if a Muslim had to submit to a non-Muslim, whether in marriage, employment or politics.' Their reasoning is that 'Just as Muslims submit to God, so, by logical extension, must non-Muslims submit to Muslims' (Sookhdeo, 2014: 33).

There is no doubt that the SPLM leaders who wrote the *Manifesto* in 1983 were fully aware of the Islamic traditional belief that makes Muslims feel ashamed when ruled by non-Muslims. For this reason, it would not be false to conclude that the SPLM leaders who introduced Article 24 in the *Manifesto* in 1983 were mostly worried about their political survival under the Islamic rule in Sudan. They were mainly afraid that Muslims could use religion to divide and turn the marginalised people against one another to make them engage in religiously motivated wars and keep them from thinking about having access to political power. The concern about the way that Sudanese politicians use religion to divide the marginalised areas under Islamic rule is implied in Article 7 of the *Manifesto* where it reads, 'These minority clique regimes have always used the questions of nationality and religion to isolate the struggle in the South from that of the underdeveloped areas in the North.'

South Sudanese, before the separation of South Sudan from Sudan, would complain that Sudanese politicians mostly used religion to turn African Muslims like the Darfuris in the North against African Christians in the South. Kustenbauder (2012: 405), for example, quotes a South Sudanese living in the United States as saying that 'Religion was used for a long time to divide Africans', even though these Africans later realised that 'they were being manipulated.' Most citizens in South Sudan believe African Muslims who were marginalised in the North would not realise their marginalisation since they perceived any opposition to the government in Khartoum as opposition to Islam. South Sudanese generally think that Muslim leaders manipulate Muslims in Sudan into believing that they are one nation or *umma,* excluding non-Muslims and, for this reason, should support one another against non-Muslims. Sookhdeo (2014: 33) would concur that Muslims in any part of the world mostly believe that 'they must support each other against non-Muslims, no matter how much they differ among themselves.'

However, the same politicians in Khartoum who used Islam as a uniting tool also used Arab identity as a divisive tool among Muslims. For example, they used Arab identity, as will be seen in the section below, to marginalise African Muslims in the North. This left little chance for Africans to rule the Arabs in Sudan even if these Africans were Muslims. It also means that if the separation of religion from the state was not put in the Constitution of Southern Sudan in 2005, then Christian politicians were going to be marginalised after the signing of the Comprehensive Peace Agreement (CPA) in 2005.

Overall, it was likely, as Sidahmed (2012: 179) puts it, that 'The Islamist regime sought to replace the secular state structure with an ideologically committed apparatus that could be trusted to pursue the movement's vision of change.' They seemingly wanted to consolidate the system in which political and religious institutions would be integrated. However, the only religious institution that should be mixed with the state, for them, should be Islam. And the leading members of this religion should be Arabs. This could be what made Christians and other religious groups in South Sudan and, perhaps non-Arab Muslims in the North, feel marginalised. Whether or not religiously and ethnically motivated marginalisation existed in Sudan as perceived by some people is not yet clear. The section below explores the perception that Muslims, especially the ruling elites in the North, marginalised Africans and Christians in the South and non-Arab Muslims in the North.

Perceived Marginalisation

The potential marginalisation of non-Muslim politicians on a religious basis before the signing of the CPA in 2005 started in 1940, as mentioned earlier. But the legal basis for the potential marginalisation of non-Muslim politicians was Article 1 of the 1998 Constitution of Sudan. This Article mentions that Islam is the religion of the majority, although it is recognised that Christianity and other traditional beliefs have a considerable religious following. Even though Article 21 of the 1998 Constitution stipulates that all the Sudanese citizens 'are equal in eligibility for public posts and offices not being discriminated on the basis of wealth' (D'Angelo, 2010: 652) and religion, there were still fears not addressed in Article 1.

The implication in Article 1 of the 1998 Constitution was that since Islam was clearly mentioned as the religion of the majority of the population, it would be easy for such a majority to dictate policies under the guidance of Islam that considers both the state and the religion as one. D'Angelo (2010: 651) points out that in Islam, 'the relationship between political power, institutions and citizens are quite marginal and irrelevant.' Considering this fact, policies guided by Islamic religion would make it difficult, if not impossible, for politicians from other faiths, such as Christianity, to rule Muslims.

South Sudan politicians and military leaders who rebelled against the government in Khartoum in 1983 believed then and still believe now after the secession of South Sudan from Sudan, that politicians in Khartoum marginalise South Sudanese (SPLM Manifesto, 1983; Garang, 2019). This belief is now not limited to politicians alone in the South. Other South Sudan citizens strongly believe it (Delaney, 2010). They credit Islamic religion and Arab identity as the motivators for marginalising African Christians in South Sudan and non-Arab Muslims in North Sudan (Kustenbauder, 2012). For example, Kustenbauder (2012: 403) paraphrases a South Sudanese living in the United States of America as saying that 'Sudan's political history since the colonial period has been characterized by the marginalization of non-Arabs.' The South Sudanese who uttered this statement, however, never stayed in the North of Sudan to witness the Arabs' attitudes towards the South. So his view is not likely to be taken seriously, as representing the experiences of the marginalised people in the South.

Muslims and People of the Book

Most of the South Sudanese who used to work in the then united Sudan are often more negative towards the Arab Muslims in the North than those South Sudanese who never got the opportunity to work or live in the North. This is because the Arab Muslims used to treat the Southern Sudanese working among them as lower class citizens. Southern Sudanese regarded this attitude as patronising. However, the Arab Muslims could patronise Southern Sudanese for no other reason than Islamic teaching and tradition. The status of people in Islam depends on one's religion. Muslims categorise citizens of any country into Muslims, people of the Book such as Christians and Jews, and other people who do not fall within the first two categories. The most important citizens for Islamists are free and mature male Muslims. They are the only ones 'seen as persons with full legal capacity, full citizens enjoying all rights and liberties offered by the Islamic state' (Sookhdeo, 2014: 93). However, some respects are accorded to non-Muslims. Muslims tolerate Christians and Jews whom they refer to as people of the Book, even though some Muslims sometimes despise them. The worse treatment is given to those who are not Muslims and not people of the Book. In other words, citizens 'who are neither Muslims nor People of the Book can, according to classical Islam, be killed' (Sookhdeo, 2014: 93).

South Sudanese in the 1950s up to late 1970s were mainly not Muslims and not people of the Book. A majority of South Sudanese became Christians in the 1980s and 1990s. This means that it was after the 1990s that most South Sudanese qualified as people of the Book. Because of this, the Islamists in Sudan who were familiar with the teaching and tradition of Islam would wonder why South Sudanese, who were mostly not Muslims and not people of the Book until the 1990s, could complain against the North for marginalisation instead of thanking Muslims in the North for sparing their lives. In other words, the Arab Muslims in the North thought the best thing they did for South Sudanese who were neither Muslims nor people of the Book was to ignore them and let them stay alive. Developing the South and giving political positions to Southern Sudan politicians would have translated to giving services and political powers to people who never deserved better treatment other than elimination from among living beings.

The Islamists expect no complaint from South Sudanese who are not people of the Book. They also believe that people of the Book should not complain against Muslims for anything. In Muslim-majority states such as Sudan, the people of the Book are supposed to be submissive to Muslims and Islamic rule. Instead of complaining against Muslims, people of the Book are expected to accept their low status and pay the *jizya* or poll tax so that they can receive *dhimma* (protection) from Muslims. Since people of the Book would be given *dhimma* in Muslim majority states, they are also referred to as *dhimmi*. *Dhimmi* do not have rights. They must comply with what the Muslims tell them. In Islamic history, as Sookhdeo (2014: 94) points out, '*Dhimmi* were excluded from public office and were not equal with Muslims before the law.'

Despite all the above, it is clear why non-Muslims such as people of the Book would complain against Muslims. They see the *dhimma* condition as 'the formal expression of legalised discrimination and oppression against Jewish and Christian minorities living under Islam' (Sookhdeo, 2014: 94). Yet, Muslims do not see *dhimma* as Christians and Jews mostly do. They often see it as true protection of the people of the Book who pay their *jizya*. In other words, it is normal for Muslims, especially Islamists, to see people of the Book seeking favours from Muslims in everything, including protection from other Muslims mistreating them.

Resistance to Submission and Declaration of Violent Jihad

Even though Islamists would see the submission of Christians to Muslims as normal, South Sudan Christians, together with the followers of African Traditional Religions, thought it was oppressive to require such submission from them on religious grounds. Nevertheless, the Muslims regarded such attitudes as rebellious. Because South Sudanese were perceived to be insubordinate and rebellious, the Islamists kept on making it difficult for the South to get services. This also applies to holding back South Sudan politicians from political positions.

When South Sudanese could no longer tolerate what they perceived as an ever-increasing marginalisation of non-Muslims, they decided to continue opposing the government in Khartoum. As a result, the Islamists under the leadership of Hassan al-Turabi declared violent *jihad* or holy war against South Sudan in the 1990s. They mobilised an army known as *mujahadeen* to fight in the South. When the government of Sudan declared *jihad* against the South of Sudan in 1992, the reason given was that Muslims were fighting the enemies of Islam in the South (Kustenbauder, 2012).

Islamic tradition has various reasons for the declaration of *jihad*. Violent *jihad* is sometimes declared against those who refuse to accept *dhimmi* status (Sookhdeo, 2014). Another reason is the perception that such a group is hindering the spread of Islam. South Sudanese, for Islamists, would fit conditions for the declaration of violent *jihad* against them. For example, a Muslim leader in Sudan is quoted to have said this: 'The failure of Islam in the Southern Sudan would be the failure of…the international Islamic cause. Islam has a holy mission in Africa, and Southern Sudan is the beginning of that mission' (Kustenbauder (2012: 407).

The anger of North Sudanese, especially the Islamists, against South Sudanese for lack of submission to Muslims was justified. It was likely that South Sudanese never regarded themselves as *dhimmi* in united Sudan. They believed they were equal to free mature male Muslims. Not only would Christians see themselves as equal to Muslims as people of the Book, but also the followers of African Traditional Religions (who could qualify for elimination under sharia law) could consider themselves equal to Muslims. For example, Chief Buth Diu, a believer in African Traditional Religion, is recorded in the minutes of Juba Conference of June 1947 as saying that 'there should be a law to prevent a Northerner calling a Southerner a slave.' In the same Conference, Chief Lapponya, who was also a believer in African Traditional Religion, made it clear that South Sudanese officials would like to be paid like the North Sudanese officials since both sides were equally important.

Concerning integrity, South Sudanese could even see themselves as better than North Sudanese. For example, Chief Leuith Ajak described the Arabs from Northern Sudan during the Juba Conference of 1947 as the crowd of hungry people who 'would invade the South and swamp them and cheat the people.' Nevertheless, South Sudanese thought their marginalisation would not have happened if the British had not favoured the Arab Muslims in the North. This is part of what the SPLM referred to as the problem of Sudan in the SPLM *Manifesto* of 1983.

SPLM's Concept of the Problem of Sudan's Origin

In the SPLM *Manifesto* of 1983, the SPLM leaders argue that the problem of Sudan developed because of the colonialists' policy that favoured the Northern Sudanese, especially the Arab Muslims, over against the black Southern Sudan Christians. Some scholars concur with the claim that the British empowered the Arabic-speaking Northern Sudanese at the expense of the citizens of other areas in Sudan. As Kustenbauder (2012: 398) points out, 'British officials recruited Arabic-speaking northerners, who became a bourgeois class of petty bureaucrats charged with running the colonial administration.' Yet, it is not clear whether this favouring was intentional or not. There are possibilities that favouring the Arabic-speaking Northerners might not have been intentional. This is because the British were not Muslims favouring Islam as the approved or official religion. The policy that ended up empowering Arabs and Muslims might have been put in place with different goals in mind.

What cannot be denied is that the British policies that resulted in the empowerment of the Northern part of the country led to imbalances in social and political status in Sudan. The social and political status of Northerners, especially the Arab Muslims, was raised above the social and political status of other areas of Sudan. Southern Sudan was the most neglected in comparison to other areas of Sudan for two reasons: being non-Muslims and non-Arabs. Other areas such as Darfur, Blue Nile, and Kassala among others, were marginalised only for being non-Arabs. The British did not seem to realise that Northerners were going to misuse the privileges they received from the colonial administration.

For the above reasons those who felt marginalised could blame the British for their policies of favouring the Northerners in Sudan. Yet, the policy for favouring the North was a necessity for Great Britain for economic reasons. As the SPLM leaders point out in Article 18 of the *Manifesto*, it was 'necessary to provide the North with general and technical education in order to produce the required native junior staff to assist the colonial administration in the extraction of surplus.' This policy of necessity, in turn, made it difficult for the colonial administrators to think about equity between Northern and Southern Sudanese when the British were about to leave Sudan.

When the British colonial administrators decided to leave Sudan to the Sudanese, they just 'handed over the reins of government to British-educated, Arab bureaucrats' (Kustenbauder, 2012: 405). At that time, the colonialists had limited choices as to whom to empower. Handing over of the country's administration to Sudanese Arab Muslims was necessary because there were very few educated Southern Sudanese public servants. These facts seem to confirm that the favouring of Arab Muslims in the North of Sudan was indirectly done. The policies that were favourable to the Arab Muslims were necessary to the British colonial administrators.

It is, however, plausible to argue that what was necessary for Northern Sudanese disadvantaged people from other parts of the country. For example, the Arab identity of the favoured Northerners in Sudan became important, and their Islamic religion later became the most important religion compared to Christianity and the African Traditional Religions which were neither directly or indirectly favoured. Arab identity and the Islamic religion gave access to power in Sudan after the independence of Sudan from Great Britain. This happened because the indirectly favoured, educated Arab Muslims in the North got all the powers they needed to make policies. And the Islamic beliefs and traditions supported with political powers promoted sharia above other laws or legislation. Sharia would then dictate national issues in favour of Islam as the religion and Muslims. In Islam, as Sookhdeo (2014: 99) puts it, 'sharia plays a large part in determining personal identity and social status according to religious criteria.'

Not only did sharia promote Muslim status in Sudan, but it also made government officials and policymakers believe that areas in the North were more important for development projects than areas in the South, Blue Nile, and Kassala, among others. Whether they understood it or not, the British who favoured the North out of necessity and imperialist conditions resulted in imbalanced policies being developed even before they left Sudan in 1956. This was mainly because the colonial administrators 'isolated peripheral areas of Sudan—especially the south—leaving them undeveloped and thus unprepared for political independence' (Kustenbauder, 2012: 398). Those on the periphery could not find any platform from which they could express their grievances. That was partly why some Muslims who could not be identified as Arabs were marginalised like non-Muslims.

Religion and Ethnicity

The non-Arab Muslims are sometimes treated like non-Muslims in the North. Kustenbauder (2012: 404) found in his research that 'even in Darfur, where all inhabitants are Muslim, the government still uses Islam as a tool of social and political control.' This political control could be one reason why the marginalised Muslims could only find a platform for expressing their grievances outside Sudan. Kustenbauder (2012: 403) paraphrases one North Sudanese Muslim living in the United States of America as blaming 'the Government of Sudan (GoS) for perpetuating an unrepresentative system of governance, failing to develop outlying regions while channelling resources directly to Khartoum, and using religion as a pressure mechanism to perpetuate an unjust and oppressive regime.' This person could not have boldly uttered these words in Sudan because of the negative consequences that such a statement could bring. He would have chosen to suffer in silence. The SPLM leaders probably misunderstood the silence of the marginalised people in Northern Sudan as complicity. For example, the SPLM leaders claim in Articles 6 and 7 of the *Manifesto* that professing Muslims in the marginalised Northern areas of Darfur, Kordofan and Kassala were 'the most deceived and neglected by the ruling minority clique regime in Khartoum.'

The marginalised people such as the South Sudanese were not the only ones who would complain in Sudan against the misuse of religion and ethnic identity. The Northern Sudan politicians could also complain against the misuse of Christian belief and African identity in South Sudan. And there could be some truth to their complaint. Some South Sudanese such as Deng (1995: 205), for example, observe that 'traditional identity and Christian Western influence have combined to consolidate and strengthen a modern southern identity of resistance against Islamization and Arabization.' As shown in the above section 'the Sudanese Islamist party, the National Islamic Front (NIF), came to power in 1989 with the explicit purpose of establishing a nationwide Islamic political order' (Kustenbauder, 2012: 401). But it could also be true in the South of Sudan that 'Christianity and Christianization became an identity of resistance' (Kustenbauder, 2012: 401).

Furthermore, it could be true that South Sudan provinces of Bahr el Ghazal, Upper Nile and Equatoria were marginalised like the Northern Sudan provinces mentioned above. South Sudan politicians sometimes claim that such ethnically motivated marginalisation was unjust and not morally acceptable. However, the claims could be more political than ethical. For example, Kustenbauder (2012: 403) quotes one Sudanese as saying that religion in Sudan 'has been heavily politicalized.' This could imply that the Arab identity was not a moral problem, but the way it was used in politics was. As Kustenbauder (2012: 399) argues, 'the language of politicized religion operates as part of a hegemonic narrative about the local conflict in Sudan.'

Politicised Religion and Repressions

Both the politicians in the North and in the South could have manipulated religion 'in order to mobilize popular support at home and win political allies abroad' (Kustenbauder, 2012: 400). For example, D'Angelo (2010: 649) points out that 'the introduction of the Sharia was not accompanied by a profound activity of Islamization of the civil society as well as the same government contexts that should have supported it.' It could be argued that President Nimeiri was more political than religious when he abolished, in the name of Islam, the 1972 Addis Ababa peace agreement that stopped the Anya-Nya 1 war. D'Angelo (2010: 649) observes that 'the politics of Numeiri did not have a large following in Islamic circles, as highlighted by the execution of Mahmud Mohammed Taha.' Taha was a Sudanese moderate Muslim who was executed for being a critic of Islamism in Sudan. He was accused of apostasy and sentenced to death in 1985 because he tried to 'reinterpret the Quran in a more liberal way and thus reform Islam' (Sookhdeo, 2014: 111). The Islamists believe they protect Islam by lawfully killing apostates. As Sookhdeo (2014: 124) points out, 'sharia decrees a death penalty for adult male apostates and for all infidels (pagans).'

For the above reasons, it is hard to deny that religion in Sudan 'has been used by the government to prevent people from organizing political opposition to Khartoum' (Kustenbauder, 2012: 401). Politicising religion mainly helped the Sudanese politicians in Khartoum to get financial and military support from the Arab and Muslim countries to fight the Sudanese rebels such as the Christian-dominated Sudan People's Liberation Movement and Army. Most Muslim countries regarded the military and financial assistance they had been giving to Sudan 'as their duty to help Khartoum defend and expand the boundaries of Islam' (Kustenbauder, 2012: 407). The Islamists in Sudan such as Hassan al-Turabi referred to the civil war in Sudan as a religious war mainly to get financial support from some Muslim-majority countries.

Moreover, calling the civil war between the South and the North a religious war in Sudan 'consolidated and activated political support for Khartoum among Muslims residing within Sudan' (Kustenbauder, 2012: 407). As Kustenbauder (2012: 407) points out, 'categorizing the conflict in terms of religious identity gave Muslims in Sudan a common enemy and an incentive to support Khartoum despite their grievances with the government.' One example of this religiously motivated internal military support to the Islamic regime was the *mujahideen* that Muslim leaders in Khartoum such as Hassan al-Turabi recruited to fight the Christian-dominated Sudan People's Liberation Army in South Sudan in the name of Islam.

The Islamists aimed at transforming the state in Sudan on Islamic grounds through what they called *al-mashru al-hadari* or the 'civilizational scheme' (Sidahmed, 2012: 179). The *al-mashru al-hadari* can also be referred to as the 'cultural authenticity scheme' (Sidahmed, 2012: 179). For this reason, the policies of the Islamist regime were 'geared towards consolidation of Islamist control of the state' (Sidahmed, 2012: 179). Because of this, the regime adopted a serious repression approach in dealing with anybody perceived as standing against the Islamic civilisational scheme policy. The regime advanced this policy of repression by creating state organs that could listen to the Islamists in the process of fulfilling the 'pursuit of repressive practices against opposition and the general terrorization of society at large' (Sidahmed, 2012: 180). Since the civilisational scheme policy was institutionalised in both politics and religion, the Islamists in Sudan made sure that political and constitutional state bodies were established in a manner by which the goal of Islamism could be achieved.

The above developments in the Sudanese system of government may have prompted the SPLM to include Article 8 into *The Interim Constitution of Southern Sudan, 2005* during the interim period of CPA implementation in the year 2005 even though *The Interim National Constitution of the Republic of the Sudan, 2005* never stipulated the separation of religion and state. Article 8(1) of *The Interim Constitution of Southern Sudan, 2005* stipulates: 'In Southern Sudan, religion and state shall be separate.' Like the motivation for the inclusion of Article 24 in the SPLM *Manifesto* in 1983, the SPLM leaders seemed to believe during the interim period of CPA implementations, that if Sudan was going to remain united, then what would help non-Muslims have access to political power was the separation of religion and state.

The fear of mixing religion and state in Sudan came from policies and laws that were already in place. By the time the CPA was signed by the government and the SPLM in 2005, for example, all the Sudanese, regardless of religious affiliation (Sidahmed, 2012) were required to make the mandatory payments of *zakat*, which is the Muslims' almsgiving in taxation. Article 10 of the 1998 Constitution of Sudan specifies *zakat* as 'a financial obligation collected by the State and its collection, expenditure and administration shall be in accordance with law.' The law referred to here could include sharia law that could not be applied to non-Muslims; the payment of *zakat* by all citizens who included non-Muslims was not mandatory in the 1980s.

Additional issues of concern were legal incoherence in protecting human rights in Sudan. For example, the 1998 Constitution of Sudan, Article 15, guarantees the liberation of 'women from injustices in all aspects of life.' Article 15 of the 1998 Constitution of Sudan also stipulates that the State should 'encourage women's role in the family and public life.' However, by 2005, directives were already in place in Khartoum which required women to dress in a particular way. This made the intention of the Constitution unclear and the writers in Khartoum suspicious to non-Muslim women. Not only were non-Muslims worried about the possible mistreatment of non-Muslim women in united Sudan, they were also worried about the possibilities of the state-aided Islamization of all aspects of life in the whole of Sudan. For example, the Islamization policies put in place before the signing of CPA in 2005 'included the extensive building of mosques and prayer places in all government buildings, educational institutions, and any other building used by the public' (Sidahmed, 2012: 182).

*Summing up the Project of Conserving
Islam and its Marginalisation Policies*

The literature explored in this section indicates possibilities that could explain the South Sudanese claim of marginalisation. It is likely that the Arab Muslims in Northern Sudan protected their Islamic religion and Arab traditional beliefs from non-Islamic and non-Arabic cultural influences. One way that Muslim leaders, especially the Islamists, guaranteed that their religion and tradition was protected from external influences was that the followers of Islam in Sudan should comply with Islamic teachings and Arab traditional beliefs. In the process of trying to ensure the conservation of their religious and traditional beliefs the Islamists put in place policies that would, at best, marginalise non-Muslims and non-Arabs in Sudan. These Islamization and Arabization efforts by the Islamists in Sudan and those who used to help them in the Arab and Islamic countries made it difficult for non-Muslims and non-Arabs to introduce any unifying policies that could accommodate the diversity in the country.

Therefore, the marginalised areas reacted negatively by staging resistance, including a military one, to what they regarded as the increasing marginalisation of non-Muslims and non-Arabs by the clique in Khartoum. The increasing Islamization of Sudan was mainly the strategy to block any policy that would threaten the Islamic traditions and beliefs. `The aim of resistance to the Islamist policies was to secure the interests of non-Muslims and non-Arabs in Sudan, and also, partly, to conserve non-Islamic and non-Arabic traditions and beliefs. Promoting Arab identity, however, was a lesser threat in comparison with imposing conformation to Islamic beliefs and traditions which was invoked to help the Islamists control non-Muslims.

These indications of increasing Islamization of the Sudan state could explain why Article 8(1) is ambiguously stated in *The Interim Constitution of Southern Sudan, 2005*. The ambiguity could possibly give non-Muslim politicians room to manipulate the Constitution in the same way that religion was manipulated by Muslim politicians to secure and keep political power. What seems to be a major concern for South Sudanese political leaders is their political marginalisation on religious grounds. Marginalisation in terms of development does not seem to count much even though it is part of the story.

However, some people argue that the intention behind the inclusion of Article 8 into *The Interim Constitution of Southern Sudan, 2005* and that of independent South Sudan in 2011 was to protect freedom of worship. Those who argue along these lines think the international experts who helped the South Sudan drafters of the respective Constitutions have played a part in the inclusion of Article 8 into these two Constitutions. Because South Sudanese felt marginalised on religious grounds in Sudan, it would also be possible to argue that they included Article 8 in their Constitution to help them avoid similar marginalisation again in the future. Article 8 is believed to be one of the articles in the Constitution that could fulfil this wish. Whether or not these hopes are justified is yet to be ascertained. The section below will, therefore, explore the assumption that Article 8 was included in South Sudan's Constitution so that it could meet the international standards regarding freedom of worship.

Imagined International Standards

Some people within and outside South Sudan imagine that Article 8 was included in the Constitution of South Sudan in order to meet the international standards guaranteeing the freedom of religion. Countries that are part of the international community are required by international law to guarantee the protection of 'the rights of individual conscience' (D'Angelo, 2010: 468). An enduring belief is that church and state are separated to 'protect the individual's liberty of conscience from the intrusions of either church or state, or both conspiring together' (Witte, 2003: 31-32). This protection of individual conscience is mainly about guaranteeing the rights of the individual to choose and follow any religion as directed by his or her conscience.

Some believe that the protection of individual conscience was Thomas Jefferson's main intention when he wrote his 'famous 1802 letter to the Danbury Baptist Association' (Witte, 2003: 32). In this letter, Jefferson 'tied the principle of separation of church and state directly to the principle of liberty of conscience' (Witte, 2003: 32). His main intention was to insist that the protection of individual conscience is plausible. Nothing in his 1802 letter shows that he was talking about the separation of religion and politics. Now, the United Nations seems to equate the freedom of religion with the idea of protecting individual conscience. For example, Article 19 of the Universal Declaration of Human Rights talks about 'the right to freedom of thought, conscience and religion.' This Article uses the word 'right' two times and 'freedom' three times, possibly to emphasise the importance of the protection of individual conscience in relation to religious beliefs. In other words, the international community sees freedom of religion as an issue of human rights

Individual Conscience's Rights, Separation of State and Religion and Sudan's Constitutions

The influence of the international community, especially regarding the belief in the importance of the right of the individual conscience in religious choices and practices, is evident in some minor cases in Sudan.

The 1998 Constitution of Sudan, for example, was approved by the Sudanese parliament in an attempt to reconcile the 'Islamic law with the postulates of Western constitutionalism and the ideology of human rights' (D'Angelo, 2010: 650). It 'adopted a rather moderate tone with regard to religion and state by being silent on the religion of the state' (Sidahmed, 2012: 175). In line with the international standards set for the protection of individual conscience, Article 24 of the 1998 Constitution of Sudan stipulates: 'Everyone has the right to freedom of conscience and religion and the right to manifest and disseminate his religion or belief in teaching, practice or observance.' This is exactly what Article 18 of the Universal Declaration of Human Rights states. In order to assure this protection of conscience, Article 24 of the 1998 Constitution of Sudan specifies what policy implementers should avoid: that the Sudanese citizens should not be coerced to believe in any religion that is contrary to the religion of their own choice.

Moreover, the 1998 Constitution of Sudan tries to meet international standards in freedom of opinion and expression. Article 19 of the Universal Declaration of Human Rights talks of 'the right to freedom of opinion and expression.' In addition, religious liberty is widely believed to have three elements: 1) religious expression; 2) individual conscience; and 3) religious organisations and practices (Esbeck, 1986). Article 25 of the 1998 Constitution tries to address freedom of opinion and expression. The first part of Article 25, for example, stipulates that 'Every citizen has the right to seek any knowledge or adopt any faith, in opinion or thought, without being coerced by the authorities.' Part two of Article 25 then attempts to address freedom of expression. The reason why the word 'attempts' is used here will become clear later in this chapter.

Furthermore, the 1998 Constitution of Sudan tries to recognise the rights of different groups and races, including religions, within the country. It attempts to comply with standards set in Article 2 of the Universal Declaration of Human Rights which stipulates that every individual deserves the entitlement to 'all rights and freedoms' regardless of 'race, colour, sex, language, religion, political or other opinion, national or social origin, property, birth or other status.' The 1998 Constitution tries to meet these international standards of the equality of citizens in regard to public life. It makes clear that 'Sudanese are equal in the rights and duties of public life without discrimination based on race, sex or religion.' It also seems to address the employment discrimination that could be based on a citizen's prior status. For example, Article 21 stipulates that 'All persons are equal in eligibility for public office and civil service positions without preference due to wealth.' These Articles show that the 1998 Constitution of Sudan tried to show the international community that political leadership in Sudan was ready to respect the rights of citizens in accordance with international standards.

What is unclear in the 1998 Constitution is the separation of religion and state. Article 18, for example, requires those who work in government offices as well as those holding other public positions to observe the Holy Quran in prayers in their public offices. The public officials are further required in Article 18 to observe the principles of religion in all that they do. As D'Angelo (2010: 651) observes, the 1998 Constitution of Sudan 'is nothing more than a further confirmation of a type of identification between religion and politics.' Religion is mainly used in Sudan as the legitimisation of politics, and the reverse is true. For example, sharia is the main source of constitutional legitimacy in the Sudanese state because it is set out 'as prevailing in absolute over the other forms of rulemaking as set out within the context of the same disposition' (D'Angelo, 2014: 652).

Yet, it seems to be common-sense that in the modern state politics and religion must be independent from each other. As D'Angelo (2010: 645) points out, 'It has been generally recognized that the independence of political power from religious power, within Western experience, marks the definitive transition to the modern State' even though this independence could 'not interrupt the relationship between law and religion.' This separation of religion and state implies the secularisation of the state. And this 'secularization represents a desired approach which should therefore be promoted and sustained with the perspective of a universal vision of the protection of human rights and, especially, freedom of conscience, belief and religion' (D'Angelo, 2010: 646). This could be why both *The Interim Constitution of Southern Sudan, 2005* and *The Transitional Constitution of the Republic of South Sudan, 2011* added the section stipulating the separation of religion and state in order to meet international standards. It is, however, important to note here that the Universal Declaration of Human Rights is silent on the separation of religion and state. Arguably, the United States of America introduced this constitutional requirement in USA for church and state separation.

If North Americans are the champions of separating church and state, then it is possible that the idea of including Article 8 in the Constitution of South Sudan could have come from North Americans. The assumption is plausible because most of the experts who helped the SPLM leaders during the CPA implementation were North Americans. Apart from this assumption there are other indications that the international community as a whole influenced the Constitution. One could argue that Article 8 was included in the Constitution to meet the international legal standards protection of individual liberty of conscience. For example, D'Angelo (2010: 646) points out that in Sudan, 'the international community decidedly push in the direction of the alignment to the standards relating to the upholding of constitutional rights.'

International Standards and National Conditions

What constitutes international standards in upholding constitutional rights is often debated, because laws are mostly guided by national conditions which include local traditions and beliefs that shape value and legal practices. As D'Angelo (2010: 646) argues, 'the forms, limits and legal consequences of the various systems of relationships between the State and religious groups are to be considered as dependant variables of the respective socio-cultural and political contexts.' The United Nations' conventions that are mainly aimed at protecting human rights define the common international standards in legal practices pertaining to human rights today. However, some countries, whose understanding of human rights differs from the Western understanding, find ways of redefining the United Nations Human Rights' conventions in a manner that suits their traditional beliefs. For example, Article 7 of the Universal Declaration of Human Rights stipulates equality before the law. And since this declaration was done in the United Nations, then it is supposed to define what member states of the United Nations should follow in their legal practices.

Despite the above, Muslim-majority states prioritise sharia over the Universal Declaration of Human Rights with regard to Muslim women and non-Muslims. For example, 'sharia says that when compensation is payable for an injury, a woman receives less than a man does for the same injury' (Sookhdeo, 2014: 47). A woman's testimony in court is also not treated with the same legal equality as that of a man. In Islamic tradition, it would look absurd to consider women and non-Muslims equal to free mature Muslim men. This is because 'it would seem an offence against Allah's plan for creation to raise them [women] up as equal to Muslim men' (Sookhdeo, 2014: 48).

In issues of religion, Article 18 of the Universal Declaration of

Human Rights 'guarantees freedom of conscience, including the freedom to change religion' (Sookhdeo, 2014: 47). Yet, sharia does not comply with this supposedly international legal standard. The standard in Islam is that non-Muslims can convert to Islam, but Muslims are restricted from leaving Islam and joining other religions. In these cases, what the West imagines as universal might not be imagined as universal in Muslim-majority states in Asia and in Africa. Given the differences between the West and other continents such as Asia and Africa, what the United Nations agreed upon as universal rights since 1948 'are not necessarily seen as such by large portions of the world's population' (Sookhdeo, 2014: 47).

When pressured as members of the United Nations to respect the Universal Declaration of Human Rights, Muslim-majority states can ratify what the United Nations have agreed upon but subordinate such a law to sharia. For example, the Organisation of Islamic Cooperation (OIC) adopted the Cairo Declaration on Human Rights in Islam on August 5, 1990 in a possible attempt to comply with the international standards on human rights. However, Article 24 of the same Declaration specifies that the Islamic sharia should trump rights and freedoms mentioned in the Declaration. Article 25 of the Cairo Declaration further stipulates that any explanation or clarification of rights and freedoms in the Declaration should be guided by sharia as the only source of reference. This means, as Sookhdeo (2014: 48) puts it, that the whole Cairo Declaration on Human Rights in Islam 'is nothing but the reaffirmation of sharia principles.'

These texts show that the inclusion of Article 8 in the Constitution of South Sudan to meet the international standards on religious freedom may be just an assumption. For the historical facts seen in the supposedly moderate 1998 Constitution of Sudan indicate that local values trump international values in Sudan. This influence of local values in national laws and policies might not be unique to Sudan. It could be true in South Sudan, too. It might generally be possible that central values and beliefs of lawmakers direct what they support or reject in legislation. This implies that values that one acquires from childhood may sometimes make that person unconsciously support or reject any legislation even when he or she were thinking of supporting legal practices that meet international standards. Taylor (2004) argues that practices and understanding go together: people cannot practice what they do not understand as important. Therefore, it is possible to argue that what one has been experiencing in his or her surroundings makes understanding new practices possible. That is, new practices would be easy to understand if they relate to practices with which one is familiar. If so, then in some countries, any legal requirement deemed necessary because it is meeting what the United Nations agreed upon as international legal standards could only be accepted fully when resembling, to some extent, local values that define local practices.

In the instances where lawmakers fail to guarantee in legislation the constitutional protection of their local central values, implementation of constitutional articles such as Article 8 of South Sudan's Constitution that the United Nations may accept as meeting the international standards could be difficult. Some articles could be included in some constitutions to legitimise such constitutions internationally, but that could remain merely a political survival strategy that has nothing to do with real practices. This is sometimes true within a country where opposition groups demand something and a ruling party includes it in legislation only gradually to mobilise the supporters of the opposition toward the opposite political direction. It is partly evident that what mattered to the ruling National Congress Party (NCP) in writing the Constitution of 1998 (in which some considerations for human rights and the rights of religions were included), was political survival. The NCP was facing internal pressure from Umma and DUP who were opposed 'to an Islamic transformation of the state and its policies' (Sidahmed, 2012: 175). For this reason, the Islamists in the NCP appeared moderate in approving the moderate 1998 Constitution because they were targeting constituencies of Umma and DUP to strengthen rather than weaken their central belief in Sudan's Islamization agenda.

Some articles in the 1998 Constitution guarantee the protection of the central values that the Islamists strongly hold. For example, Article 24 of the 1998 Constitution of Sudan seems to have been included to meet the international standards in recognising the importance of individual conscience in religious faith. However, the writers of the Constitution were aware that Article 1 of the same Constitution would always trump Article 24. In other words, the Constitution already secures Islam in Article 1 where it reads, 'Islam is the religion of most of the population' (D'Angelo, 2010: 651). Moreover, Article 18 assures that public officials are controlled through an official requirement to observe religious principles in their offices. This kind of official requirement for particular religious practices in government offices would fall short of the international standard of protection for individual conscience. As D'Angelo (2010: 659) says, the state institutions in Sudan tend 'to heavily interfere in the religious choices of individuals, favoring the conversion to Islam and forbidding, or rather discouraging, the abandoning of the Islamic faith.'

The genuine protection of individual conscience means that government officials avoid favouring a particular religion that the majority follows in order to overshadow religions in which minorities believe. However, this is what Article 1 of 1998 Constitution of Sudan implies in calling Islam the religion of the majority. Article 65 of the 1998 Constitution also shows that Islamic religion should always be used as the source of legislation. In cases where the Islamic law is not applied, then 'the learned opinion of scholars and thinkers' could be used to guide the national legislation. This learned opinion, as D'Angelo (2010: 652) clearly indicates, 'evidently refers to an internal and typical dynamic of the interpretation of Islamic law.' This also falls short of the international standard of protecting individual conscience.

Article 8 of South Sudan's Constitution and its Tactical Functions

Like articles in the 1998 Constitution of Sudan that were included for tactical reasons, Article 8 in South Sudan's Constitution seems to have been included for tactical reasons that have nothing to do with meeting the international standards. It is clear in Article 8(2) of *The Transitional Constitution of the Republic of South Sudan, 2011* that 'All religions shall be treated equally and religion or religious beliefs shall not be used for divisive purposes.' This seems to meet the international standard set in Article 18 of the Universal Declaration of Human Rights. However, contrary to treating all religions equally, South Sudan government has been supporting Islam since 2012, while not supporting other religious groups. The government of South Sudan sometimes officially gives funds to Muslims for building Islamic schools and other activities (Sudan Tribune, 2014, June 27). Muslims are also supported by government funds to go to Saudi Arabia for pilgrimage. On August 1, 2019, the South Sudan Broadcasting Corporation announced that about 220 Muslims were going to Saudi Arabia for pilgrimage. The Secretary-General for South Sudan's Islamic Council Abdallah Barach officially thanked the President of South Sudan for annually supporting Muslims for this pilgrimage.

The support given to Muslims in South Sudan is also visible in government positions. For example, President Salva Kiir appointed

Sheikh Al-Tahir Bior Lueth Ajak as the Presidential Advisor on Islamic Affairs on May 4, 2016 (Gurtong, 2016, May 5). When Al-Tahir died in 2017, President Salva Kiir appointed Sheik Juma Saeed Ali on September 6, 2017, as the Presidential Advisor on Islamic Affairs (Radio Tamazuj, 2017, Sep. 7). This conflicts with the fact that the Advisor in this position should only advise regarding Religious Affairs as introduced after the independence of South Sudan from Sudan in 2011. There is a Bureau for Religious Affairs in the Office of the President. The Director leading this Bureau and the Presidential Advisor are known to be responsible for general religious affairs, not for particular religions. The President followed this practice until 2016. For example, President Salva Kiir appointed Mark Lotende Lochapi the Presidential Advisor on Religious Affairs on October 19, 2011 (Gurtong, 2011, Oct. 20). The office of Presidential Advisor on Islamic Affairs, created in 2016, was the first of its kind since the independence of South Sudan from Sudan. In other words, there is no agreed-upon policy or law stipulating that a Presidential Advisor should be appointed for a particular religion. If that were the case, then there would have been an Advisor now on Christian Affairs.

Only after the secession of South Sudan from Sudan did the government in South Sudan led by the Sudan People's Liberation Movement (SPLM) officially side with Muslims. During the war, the Sudan government in Khartoum officially sided with Islam, and the SPLM in its liberated areas mostly sided with Christianity. Sudan's politicians in Khartoum were using fear tactics in saying that the SPLM/A was planning to change Islamic religion, Arab identity and Arab culture (Kustenbauder, 2012). They knew very well that Sudanese Arab Muslims could not accept any change to their religion and culture.

The SPLM/A politicians and military leaders countered the Sudanese religious propaganda by saying that the SPLM/A was the promoter of the freedom of religion. The intention behind this claimed that promotion of religious freedom was not only to meet the international standards regarding the protection of individual conscience. It was mostly to mobilise the marginalised areas, some of which were Muslim, against the government in Khartoum in a religiously neutral war of liberation. Kustenbauder (2012: 414) argues that Islam and Christianity are part of social imaginaries that 'provide meaning and allow local practitioners to develop transnational connections and generate support.' When it appeared later that liberating a unified country was difficult, the SPLM/A leaders decided to talk about the liberation of South Sudan, even though the leader Dr. John Garang de Mabior maintained the idea of liberating the whole Sudan. Probably, South Sudan's independence in 2011 showed that the SPLA was successful in mobilising different networks to support its case.

The shift from the war for the liberation of the whole Sudan to some focus on the liberation of South Sudan introduced what seemed to be favouring the Christian religion against Islam. Kustenbauder (2012) argues that Christianity symbolised potential political equality and self-determination for rebel leaders. In the 1990s, the SPLM began to use arguments tactically in favour of Christian religious freedom rather than the freedom of all religions. They were sure that their arguments for religious freedom would 'justify southern demands for political self-determination and independence' (Kustenbauder, 2012: 414). Kustenbauder (2012: 414) points out that the politics of identifying the South with Christianity began when 'an Islamist regime came to power in Sudan.' The leaders in the SPLM knew that not identifying with Christianity at that particular time would leave them with little support within South Sudan and in the mainly Christian countries. One example of the expected support came from the United States when the American evangelicals 'increased awareness among the

American public about the war and international political pressure on Khartoum to end it' (Kustenbauder, 2012: 415). Especially, 'the specter of Christian martyrdom and genocide grabbed the attention of US officials' (Kustenbauder, 2012: 416).

The SPLM/A leaders knew they were in a better position to appeal to Christians because most of them 'received their education in mission schools' (Kustenbauder, 2012: 414). But most importantly, the rhetoric about religious freedom became useful after the September 11, 2001 terrorist attacks in New York and Washington, D.C. The leader of the SPLM/A John Garang began 'to portray the SPLA as a bulwark against Islamic forces and ally his movement with America's "War on Terror"' (Kustenbauder, 2012: 416). Article 8 would have been put in the Constitution in order to avoid government-aided Islamization of Sudan that disadvantages Christian politicians. In other words, Article 8 serves to protect the politicians from the South from religious-aided government policies in the North. Therefore, Article 8 is a means for political survival. The next section will examine this assumption.

Political Survival Strategy

The impenetrability of Sudanese Islamic values by any laws seen as contrary to sharia could be the true motivator of Article 8 in South Sudan's Constitution. In other words, Article 8 was possibly put in *The Interim Constitution of Southern Sudan, 2005* as a survival tool for SPLM politicians. Article 24 of the SPLM *Manifesto*, which first introduced the separation of religion and state principle in South Sudan, demonstrates the SPLM's fear. The *Manifesto* mentions that the ruling clique in Sudan would continue to use religious fundamentalism 'as a tool to deceive and divide the people in order to perpetuate their rule and exploitation.' The SPLM writers of the *Manifesto* seem to have introduced the principle of the separation of religion and state to provide political protection to non-Muslim leaders in Sudan against sharia principles that prevent non-Muslims from ruling Muslims. This fear seems to have been worsened by the tricks that the Islamists played in the 1998 Constitution. This Constitution includes articles that seem to guarantee the rights of non-Muslims but cancels them out with articles that reaffirm the centrality of sharia law in any Sudan's legislations. Moreover, the Islamists in Khartoum refused to mention the separation of religion and state in *The Interim National Constitution of the Republic of the Sudan, 2005* although they agreed to mention religious rights in Article 6. These tricks further caused fear in South Sudan because the history of Sudan since its independence from the British colonial rule in 1956 shows that the Islamists in Khartoum do not respect any agreement that does not guarantee exclusive Islamic rule in Sudan (Sidahmed, 2012).

The SPLM decided to mention in an ambiguous manner the separation of religion and state in Article 8 of *The Interim Constitution of Southern Sudan, 2005* to possibly play tricks against the Islamists. This seems to be an attempt by the SPLM to prevent the Islamists in Khartoum from declaring the whole of Sudan an Islamic state. The assumption was that the Islamists might declare Sudan as an Islamic state before the referendum that would determine the status of Southern Sudan in 2011. Having said this, it is good to note that Article 8 was not removed from South Sudan's Constitution after the secession of South Sudan from Sudan in 2011. Maybe Article 8 remains in South Sudan's Constitution for a different reason. This is because Muslims are less than seven percent of the population in independent South Sudan today (U.S. State Department, 2018). This means the government of South Sudan cannot fear Muslims in independent South Sudan declaring South Sudan as an Islamic state today. The different reasons for the presence of Article 8 in the Constitution will be explored later. Now, the idea that Article 8 was included in *The Interim Constitution of Southern, 2005* to protect South Sudan Christian politicians from being prevented to rule by sharia law will be explored next.

Islamists and Manipulation of Religion and Politics in Sudan

South Sudan politicians are aware that Islamists know how to manipulate both politics and religion to serve each other. When Islamists see their chances of winning to be low, they accept any position that might not be favourable to them, knowing that they would change it later when they get the opportunity so to do.

Islamists follow stages to achieve their goal of Islamization. The first is to create an Islamic consciousness (Sookhdeo, 2014). This stage was completed in Sudan in the 1940s when students formed their Islamic associations in high schools and universities in Sudan under the rule of the colonial administrators. The second stage is to create Islamic institutions. This was completed in the 1970s and 1980s when the Islamists under Hassan al-Turabi formed Islamic political parties. The third stage is engagement with political and social structures. This stage forced the SPLM/A to rebel in the 1980s. The engagement of Islamists in political structures became a clear threat to South Sudanese politicians who were mainly Christians. The fourth stage is the use of *jihad* or holy war when other options cannot work for Islamists. This started in the 1990s when the Islamist regime in Khartoum declared *jihad* against the SPLM/A and the non-Muslims in South Sudan. The last stage of Islamization is the realisation of an Islamic society (Sookhdeo, 2014).

Even though the Islamists had successfully completed stages one to three in Sudan, the fourth stage was not successful. Their efforts motivated the Western World to rally behind the SPLM/A. As Kustenbauder

(2018: 414) observes, the SPLM/A's 'appeals to and through its diaspora, and rhetoric of martyrdom, oppression, and human rights were also important strategies that helped the SPLA connect its struggle to the wider world of geopolitics.' The terrorists' attack on the United States on September 11, 2001, increased the negative view of Islamists in many Western countries. The United States openly supported the SPLM/A after 9/11.

The Islamist regime in Khartoum realised that failure to sign a peace agreement with the SPLM/A would motivate the Bush administration in the United States to attack Sudan under the pretext of it being a safe haven for terrorists. When the pressure is high against them, the Islamists withdraw in a manner that seems to show they accept the new conditions. However, they reorganise and fight back when the opportunity avails itself (Sookhdeo, 2014). Since the Islamists managed to force President Nimeiri in the 1980s to nullify the 1972 Addis Ababa peace agreement between his government and Anya-Nya 1 Southern Sudan rebels, the Islamists thought that they would sign a peace agreement with the SPLM/A so that the American war on terror would not engulf Sudan. Their next strategy was to influence the Islamic leaders in Khartoum later to nullify the CPA that they signed with the SPLM/A in Kenya in 2005. The SPLM/A leaders were aware of this strategy. This could be why they put Article 8 in Southern Sudan's Constitution of 2005: to keep the Islamists away from government decision-making that could involve Southern Sudan.

South Sudanese Politicians and their Survival Strategy

The friendship between the SPLM leaders and Western countries such as the United States, which value the separation of religion and state, may explain why Article 8 is maintained in South Sudan's Constitution after South Sudan's independence from Sudan. Yet, this does not mean South Sudanese actually implement the separation of religion and state as stipulated. Article 8(2) stipulates that all religions must be treated equally. Now, South Sudan leaders, even though they are Christians, seem to favour Muslims over other religious groups. One would naturally wonder why South Sudan leaders are now supporting Muslims in a way that seems to strengthen future Islamism in South Sudan. The explanation for this irony is that South Sudan leaders are being consistent with their survival strategy. In united Sudan, Muslims were regarded as threat to South Sudanese leaders who could rarely have chances to rule Muslims. Now, the threat is Christians who question ways that South Sudan leaders rule. There are indications of South Sudan leaders' anger towards the Church. For example, Christian leaders told the U.S. State Department that 'the government shut down some Catholic radio programs in its efforts to censor media programs critical of the government' (U.S. State Department, 2017: 1). The Muslim leaders, however, do not condemn the government in South Sudan for anything. This makes them possible partners of the government.

The Muslims have different reasons for collaborating with the government even when some of the ways in which the government rules people in South Sudan may not be ethical. The primary reason is that there is no separation of religion and state in Islam (D'Angelo, 2010). Therefore, Muslims cannot consider themselves as outside constituencies holding the government accountable for what its leaders do. Another reason could be that since Muslims are the minority in South Sudan, they seem to have started from stage one of Islamization in which what matters is to make their presence known. It is possible that this is why Muslims do not criticise any bad leadership in South Sudan. Therefore, their silence means that South Sudan leaders see them as good partners.

It could be assumed that the government advisory position that treated 'Religious Affairs' was changed to 'Islamic Affairs' in 2016 in order to strengthen the partnership between Muslims and South Sudan leaders. This assumption could be true in the sense that the change of the position of the Presidential Advisor on Religious Affairs to Advisor on Islamic Affairs coincides with the level of criticism of government by Christian leaders and negative reactions of the government to these criticisms. For example, Church leaders issued a number of criticisms against violence that erupted on December 15, 2013 because of political disagreement within the SPLM (Wilson, 2019). The violence briefly ended in 2015 and then resumed in 2016 (Wilson, 2019). Church leaders continue to condemn violence after the second outbreak of violence in 2016. For instance, 'The South Sudan Council of Churches (SSCC) issued a statement in August [2017] condemning continued violence in the country and emphasized a return to the "path of dialogue"' (United States Department, 2017: 1). This condemnation was part of critical statements that the Church had been issuing since the start of civil war in South Sudan in 2013. The U.S. State Department report (2018: 1) notes that outspoken attitudes of Christian leaders 'toward what they stated were the forces driving the conflict made them targets, similar to humanitarian workers.'

Political Survival Strategies and Central Value Systems

Both South and North Sudanese are guided by their central value systems in dealing with religious and political issues. The central value systems consist of security, tradition and conformity. Anything that goes against these values would result in manipulation. As Kelly (2011: 167) puts it, in its attempts to respect the will of the people, 'the government of the day or other powerful elements of society often will try to gain the consent of the people through propaganda and manipulation.' These manipulations make implementation of some laws more confusing.

Above all, South Sudan politicians are being consistent in trying to secure their political interests in united Sudan and in an independent South Sudan. Nevertheless, what they do looks confusing to those who do not know what role central value systems play in influencing these leaders. The same thing is true of the Islamists in Khartoum. What is different is that what the Islamists value the most is the opposite of what South Sudan Christian politicians value. Central value systems are part of social imaginaries. Taylor (2004: 23) defines social imaginaries as 'the ways people imagine their social existence, how they fit together with others, how things go between them and their fellows, the expectations that are normally met, and the deeper normative notions and images that underlie these expectations.'

The social imagination of the Islamists and South Sudan politicians concurs with three aspects of social imaginaries that Taylor (2004) talks about. These three aspects of social imagination include the economy, the public sphere and popular sovereignty. First, economic interest was likely one of the factors that led to the SPLM/A rebellion against the government of Sudan in 1983. The SPLM *Manifesto* spells out this economic interest in Sudan clearly in Article 24(b). The writers say that the interests of both the Northern and Southern Sudanese bourgeoisfied bureaucratic elites were 'self-enrichment including the building of multi-storey buildings and amassment of other forms of wealth.' Concerning the public sphere aspect of social imagination, South Sudanese accept what Kelly (2011: 165) summarises as 'the expression of the informed public opinion of a whole society.' This claim is stipulated in Articles 24 and 25 of *The Transitional Constitution of the Republic of South Sudan, 2011*. However, *The Interim National Constitution of the Republic of the Sudan, 2005* has not mentioned anything about the freedom of expression regarding opinion even when Southern Sudan was still part of united Sudan.

Popular sovereignty, the third aspect of social imagination, is that to which Sudanese and South Sudanese appear mostly to incline. They seem to believe in the pre-modern 'notions of a chain of complementary hierarchies' (Kelly, 2011: 166). The idea of hierarchy is that God has ranked his creations in a purposive manner. The purpose of each creature's position does not conflict with the purposes of other creatures but complement them. As Kelly (2011: 166) points out, 'The hierarchies are complementary because both higher and lower have duties to one another and in an orderly society both fulfill those duties.' Pre-modern thinkers believe that God directs human beings through senses and reason to do things that would ensure their preservation. Deviation from the hierarchy of God's creation would result in disorder. For this reason, anything or any person that deviates from the order of things would be punished (Taylor, 2004).

Normative order is part of the hierarchical mindsets of pre-modern societies which order things in such a way that burdens be shared in a manner that one person overburdens no other person. For this reason peasants in Europe would protest burdens laid on them by property owners: church and state (Taylor, 2004). For the pre-modern societies, 'An orderly society works within the bounds given to the people in their founding' (Kelly, 2011: 166). Such a society expects nobody to deviate from society's established norms. In Sudan, for example, 'Public order and security frequently constitute the excuse for sudden and violent blitzes in places of worship, in particular non-Muslim' (D'Angelo, 2010: 659-660). In a supposedly orderly society the role of people, on the one hand, is to fulfil the established norms. The role of a leader on the other hand, 'is to occupy the appropriate place in the chain and/or to embody the ancient law of the people' (Kelly, 2011: 166).

Like the pre-modern societies, South Sudanese and Sudanese seem to believe in the importance of hierarchy and its complementarity role. They believe that God is above everything. Angels come next to God. Human beings are the third and the highest in the ranks of created beings as God's representatives on earth. Article 4 of *The Constitution of the Republic of Sudan, 1998* partly reads: 'God, the creator of all people, is supreme over the State and sovereignty is delegated to the people of Sudan by succession.' This means, in Sudan, as D'Angelo (2010: 651) argues, 'the State is nothing more than a vehicle for divine action, which is guided through the people.' In South Sudan's Constitution, 'Sovereignty is vested in the people and shall be exercised by the State through its democratic and representative institutions established by this Constitution and the law' (TCRSS, 2011, Article 2). However, the preamble of 2011 Constitution of South Sudan makes it clear that God is the one who gave 'the people of South Sudan the wisdom and courage to determine their destiny and future through a free, transparent, and peaceful referendum in accordance with the provisions of the Comprehensive Peace Agreement, 2005.' God is also recognised as the giver of wisdom in the preamble of *The Interim National Constitution of the Republic of the Sudan, 2005*.

These perspectives have implications for how Sudanese and South Sudanese understand the roles of the state, religion and leaders. Muslims seem to regard the state as the facilitator of religious activities. For example, Article 18 of the 1998 Constitution of Sudan does 'impose on public power and those in public office the respect of the fundamental religious inspiration (in) one's own actions and those of the State' (D'Angelo, 2010: 654). Although the belief in *Ecclesiocracy* (Church over State) by Catholics would differ from the belief in *Erastianism* (State over Church) by Anglicans, it generally seems in South Sudan that the church is assumed facilitate the state's activities and rule. This means that in Sudan, any leader seen as subordinating Islam to the state would be punished or sanctioned. And in South Sudan, any religion seen as not unconditionally conforming to anything that the state does would be dealt with severely. This could be why in 2017, 'the government shut down some Catholic radio programs in its efforts to censor media programs critical of the government' (U.S. State Department, 2017: 1).

It is likely that the wall protecting the conservation values of Sudanese and South Sudanese is hard to penetrate. Both groups seem to make sure that their established beliefs in power remain free of vulnerabilities. For example, pressures from the international community on Sudanese and South Sudanese leaders to enact laws that meet international standards can hardly penetrate their conservation values. Within both nations, conformity is the most desired value because it helps secure the established ways of doing things. It is partly in their attempts to ensure conformity in everything that the government of South Sudan appears confused in implementing Article 8 of *The Transitional Constitution of the Republic of South Sudan, 2011*, especially in treating all religions equally. Religious groups who do not seem to conform to whatever the government does in South Sudan are not seen as equal in importance to religious groups who agree with everything that the government does. And the leaders in both Sudan and South Sudan are seen as higher in rank than any other citizen in the State. State officials in South Sudan still believe in the sovereignty of God over the state and its rulers, but do not see religious institutions and religious leaders as part of the sovereignty of God. For this reason religious leaders' disapproval of any unethical action of the government is seen as mere undermining of political authority in the country.

Preliminary Conclusion

This chapter argues that the intention behind the inclusion of Article 8 in South Sudan's Constitution could be the political survival of political leaders in South Sudan. The need for political survival became the main policy focus for South Sudan politicians because the Sudanese government in Khartoum together with the Islamists were thought to have future plans to prevent any politician who was not Muslim from getting political power. Generally, Islamists who work within political institutions believe it is a dishonour to Islam for non-Muslims to rule Muslims (Sookhdeo, 2014). South Sudanese politicians regarded the perceived favouring of Muslim politicians over politicians from other religions as marginalisation. The same was true of the perceived favouring of Muslim over non-Muslim areas. As a result, South Sudanese and North Sudanese from the marginalised areas rebelled against the government in Khartoum under the umbrella of the SPLM/A. After the SPLM/A's rebellion, its politicians and military leaders introduced in the SPLM *Manifesto* in 1983 the principle of separation of religion and state to deal with the issue of political exclusion on religious grounds. The SPLM/A continued by putting Article 8 in the Southern Sudan Constitution of 2005 to deal with the same problem.

However, when South Sudan became independent from Sudan in 2011, Christianity, not Islam, became a potential threat to the unquestioned rule of South Sudan politicians. This was because Christian leaders continually condemned state activities that they regarded as unethical. Therefore, South Sudan leaders decided to team up with Muslims who constitute less than seven percent of the population in South Sudan. Government officials see Muslim leaders as trusted partners because Muslims do not condemn any unethical activity of the state in South Sudan, as Christians do. The fear of Islam shifted to fear of Christianity in political circles in South Sudan. This shift from the fear of Islam by South Sudanese politicians in united Sudan to the favouring of the same in an independent South Sudan makes the implementation of Article 8 appear confusing, when in fact the politicians are being consistent in their efforts to secure political power. Islam in united Sudan was a threat to South Sudanese politicians because it was intended to make it hard for non-Muslims to rule Muslims. Today, South Sudan politicians regard Christianity as a threat because it does not give them unquestioned freedom to rule as they wish. One could argue that the shift in what South Sudan politicians stand against clearly demonstrates the strong role of central value systems. The central value is the conservation value which consists of the three values of tradition, security and conformity. In this case, central value systems of Sudanese and South Sudanese prioritise security in order to safeguard political and religious interests understood in terms of traditional practices. The need to secure political and religious interests requires that citizens conform to religious and political requirements in all aspects of life. Chapter three will explore central value systems in detail.

---- CHAPTER THREE ----

CONCEPTS IN CENTRAL VALUE SYSTEMS

Introduction

The shift of positions by the politicians of the Sudan People's Liberation Movement (SPLM) raises a question. The question is: What influences ethical decision-making of political and religious leaders in relation to social, religious and political matters in South Sudan? To answer this question, this chapter will explore the role that central value systems play in decision-making by reviewing a wide range of related literature. South Sudanese scholars of various disciplines and policy researchers are yet to contribute to academic debate on the theories of decision-making. So the literature to be reviewed will mainly be international literature relevant to theories of decision-making that can be related, in reasonable ways, to the Sudanese context.

Scholars debated and are still debating different theories about what influences ethical decision-making. However, do these theories examine the roles of central value systems in the confusions that sometimes happen in implementing legal provisions? So I will first present some relevant theories of ethical decision-making to determine whether they can answer the above question. Section two will explore Shalom Schwartz's Theory of Basic Human Values to understand the roles that these values play in ethical decision-making. Finally I will examine the roles of central value systems in ethical decision-making in relation to social, religious and political matters in South Sudan. Examining the influence of central value systems on ethical decision-making will help answer the extent to which central value systems could relate to other theories of decision-making sketched in section one of this chapter.

Sketching Decision-Making Theories

Decisions of rational beings aim at some good or right (Baird, 2016; Hacker-Wright, 2010; Piazza & Sousa, 2014; Ronzoni, 2010: 455). However, the understanding of what is good or right may differ from person to person and from society to society. Ideological or belief orientations could explain why people differ in their understanding of the good or the right. Research shows that political conservatives differ from liberals in decision-making (Piazza & Sousa, 2014). For example, 'conservatives seem to react more strongly than liberals to violations of group loyalty, authority, and sexual/bodily purity—transgressions that arguably have more to do with the loosening of social bonds between individuals, or challenges to the status quo' (Piazza & Sousa, 2014: 334). Moreover, 'Political liberals and conservatives both place high weight on harm and fairness, whereas authority and purity are more strongly weighted by conservatives than liberals' (Holyoak & Powell, 206: 1185). Political and religious conservatism seem to overlap, as observed in the United States of America (Piazza & Sousa, 2014). This might be also true in South Sudan. Possibly, the difference between liberals and conservatives in any country or society within any country could be that 'conservatives have a greater psychological need to manage threats and uncertainty' (Piazza & Sousa, 2014: 334).

The difference between conservatism and liberalism in ethical orientation could explain what influences ethical decision-making. Another possible explanation could be that ethical positions that individuals hold may influence their decision-making. These differences in decisions could be explained by the ethical theory that an individual regards as important. For example, a tension often exists between deontology and teleology in decision-making, especially when a decision-maker is faced with conflicting ethical issues. Deontologists, on the one hand, put the right before the good in their decision-making. For example, 'appropriate prescriptions for conduct in a given situation can be derived from consideration of the rights of each agent' (Holyoak & Powell, 2016: 1186). Teleologists, on the other hand, put the good before the right.

The third position to resolve the tension between deontology and teleology is virtue ethics. Virtue ethics is also referred to as areteology from the Greek word *arête*, which means excellence or 'fulfillment of the purpose or function to which individuals are destined' (Pastura & Land, 2016: 244). In virtue ethics, the character of a decision-maker is what counts, not the duty or the end-goal of a decision (Piazza & Sousa, 2014; Hacker-Wright, 2010). Baird (2016: 181) shows how Aristotle understands a virtuous person: 'first of all, he must know what he is doing; secondly, he must choose to act the way he does, and he must choose it for its own sake; and in the third place, the act must spring from a firm and unchangeable character.' The excellence of one's character would make such a person make wise or prudent decisions in a given situation. Areteology is mainly concerned with the good of others rather than the good of an actor. Aristotelian virtue ethics aim at the median position in decision-making (Baird, 2016). Actions guided by virtue ethics are done 'at the right time, toward the right objects, toward the right people, for the right reason, and in the right manner' (Baird, 2016: 182). This understanding of virtuous action is the opposite of the virtuous action of the modern virtue ethics that does not seem to meet the principle of internal coherence. A virtue ethicist in modern understanding, for example, disconnects moral beliefs from moral attitudes by arguing that one can believe that what he or she is doing is wrong and still do it under the necessary conditions such as sacrificing one person to save five people.

Deontology claims coherence in the sense that 'the aim of the right is to delineate how and to what extent conduct ought to be justified to other agents—the *constraints on* action' (Ronzoni, 2010: 455). Holyoak and Powell (2016: 1182) argue that 'the framework of deontological coherence emphasizes how the concepts of rights and duties produce complex systems of moral rules and systematic relationships among those rules.' Any decision-maker influenced by deontology considers the constraints on actions to be undertaken. Deontologists pay attention to what should not be done, especially in relation to any action that violates the rights of others in an attempt to maximise the good. For example, deontologists 'argue that the right or wrongness of an act is inherent in its consistency with, or deviation from, a universal moral rule, or as a function of the act itself, irrespective of the act's overall consequences' (Piazza & Sousa, 2014: 335). Thus pure deontology hardly considers as ethical maximising good at the expense of the rights of individuals or groups of people.

Teleology also claims to be coherent by the good as defining 'what is valuable and worth pursuing—the *goals of* action' (Ronzoni, 2010: 455). A decision-maker influenced by teleology would pay attention to end-goals that an action aims at, possibly the end-goal that maximises the good. The maximisation of the good should be independent from consideration of the right thing to do. For example, teleologists are comfortable with the claim that happiness as the good 'has an independent status, intuitively distinguishable from all sorts of considerations about *how* happiness is achieved from a moral point of view, or about what is specifically *morally* valuable about happiness' (Ronzoni, 2010: 456).

Proponents of Modern Virtue Ethics and Ethical Incoherence

The proponents of modern virtue ethics find it difficult to judge their actions based on coherence. They argue that 'An action is right if and only if it is what a virtuous agent would characteristically do in the circumstances' (Zyl, 2011: 220). What guides decision-making in virtue ethics is what is common in all right actions. The logic behind this assertion is that 'the virtuous person chooses a certain action for reasons that are independent of the fact that this kind of action is what virtuous agents characteristically do in the circumstances' (Zyl, 2011: 221). This kind of assertion describes but does not explain the action taken by the agent. An action made by a qualified agent in virtue ethics is assessed as right on condition 'that the agent did what she ought to have done' (Zyl, 2011: 221). This logic of virtue ethics seems to fall short of being 'a complete normative theory' (Zyl, 2011: 221). As Zyl (2011: 221), who is a proponent of virtue ethics, acknowledges: 'it is its explanatory account of right action that ultimately distinguishes one normative theory from another.' The proponents of virtue ethics may not think that this objection needs attention. However, silence on an objection does not make it go away.

If these theories are effective in guiding decision-making, they may influence decision-making of people who are aware of them; the coherent ethical judgment of an action may or may not be realised from decisions of people who are not aware of the theories of decision-making. Research shows that 'an intuitive concept of rights and duties underlies laypeople's understanding of formal and informal social regulations' (Holyoak & Powell, 2016: 1183). It could be argued that the coherence of ethical action in the decision-making of laypeople would be accidental rather than deliberate. Possibly, South Sudan leaders are not aware of deontology, teleology or virtue ethics. What influences their decision-making might be deontological or teleological intuitions, an intuitive mix of the two, value-based reasons, virtue ethics or something completely different. Coherence in this case would be absent even though a decision may resemble one or more of the established ethical theories of decision-making.

Not only is it difficult for those who are not aware of deontological and teleological theories to differentiate them in decision-making; it is becoming difficult for those who are aware of these theories to differentiate them in real life decision-making even if they could use them well at theoretical levels. Some thinkers argue that there is now a confusion in the traditional understanding of the prioritisation of the right 'from that of deontology' because these 'two terms have come to be used interchangeably' (Ronzoni, 2010: 454). Some even assert 'that the most plausible version of utilitarianism—the teleological theory *par excellence* according to Rawls's taxonomy—is actually a form of deontology precisely *because*, on closer scrutiny, it is just as committed to the priority of the right as justice as fairness' (Ronzoni, 2010: 454).

Ronzoni (2010: 454) argues for a definite connection between the concept of the priority of the right and deontology because 'the function of the priority of the right is to single out a specific kind of deontological theory.' To him, the Rawlsian deontological idea of 'justice as fairness' correlates with the prioritisation of the right over the good. Rawls's version of deontology is pluralistic in its accounts of the good because it 'tries to remain as *neutral* as possible among different conceptions of the ultimate human good' (Ronzoni, 2010: 454). The 'justice as fairness' concept hardly accepts the idea that the consideration of the right in decision-making should include the consideration of the maximisation of the good. Yet, some deontologists believe that there is no need to distinguish the right from the good.

Those who think there is no need to distinguish the right from the good argue that the good may sometimes maximise the right and vice versa. For example, the maximisation of the good that would violate the rights of the people would 'have a negative impact on the evaluation of the goodness of states of affairs' (Ronzoni, 2010: 458). Some thinkers say that the combination of rights and good in distributive equality ensures comprehensive utility. These thinkers argue that the maximisation of the good does not mean that 'the good ought to be defined independently from the right, since concepts like distribution or equality are not goods that could be valued from a non-moral point of view—unlike, say, pleasure, utility, or happiness' (Ronzoni, 2010: 458). This means that there are constraints considered in the maximisation of the good. Happiness could even sometimes be associated with the right. For example, every act that maximises happiness could be described as right.

Yet, not every thinker would agree that right cannot be distinguished from the good on theoretical differences. Researchers show that Christians tend to be deontologists in their understanding of right and wrong (Hacker-Wright, 2010). They argue that 'the entire universe is under the direction of an omnipotent and benevolent deity whose moral code makes it a fact that actions will either be right, in the sense of being required or permitted by God, or wrong, in the sense of being punishable by God' (Hacker-Wright, 2010: 212). Muslims are similar to Christians in the way that they understand rightness and wrongness of an action. However, research shows that Muslims predominantly believe in fatalism (Aktas, Yilmaz, & Bahçekapili, 2017). This means that Muslims would not choose to interfere in what they believe 'fate has already in store for a person' (Aktas, Yilmaz, & Bahçekapili, 2017: 299).

Ethical Dilemmas in Ethical Decision-Making

These differences in theoretical perspectives feature mostly in ethical decision-making, especially when one is faced with ethical dilemmas. For example, participants were given moral dilemmas in which one person could be sacrificed to save the lives of five people. The findings show that those 'who judged the sacrifice of one person to be wrong chose the deontological principle as their justification in all four dilemmas' (Aktas, Yilmaz, & Bahçekapili, 2017: 300). Most of the participants who chose the sacrifice of one person to save five people justified their choice on the utilitarian principle. Other participants who sided, but slightly differed, with deontologists (against sacrificing one innocent person to save five people in danger of dying) used fatalism and virtue ethics as their justification.

Those who believe in fatalism think that when the fate falls on a person, you cannot change it. Take for example, a trolley moving in the direction of five workers on the railway which would kill them unless its direction is changed towards one worker who should be sacrificed to save the five. Muslims would argue that there is no need for the five to be saved from their fate by sacrificing one person for whom his or her fate has not come. Those who believe in fatalism like Muslims would argue that the death of these five people is 'determined by divine authority and is not under the purview of the participant' (Aktas, Yilmaz, & Bahçekapili, 2017: 299). The fatalists believe deciding to sacrifice one person to save the five would translate to standing in the way of divine authority's decision. The virtue ethicists, referred to sometimes as moral minimalists, would judge the killing of one person to save the five as wrong like the fatalists would do. However, such moral minimalists would differ from the fatalists and deontologists in the sense that they would choose to sacrifice one person to save five people even though such a decision could still be regarded as not required morally.

Some believe that rational decisions are guided by pluralistic goal-oriented accounts of epistemic knowledge in which a decision may be irrational in one account and fully rational in another. Kopec (2016) argues that what matters is the goal in which one believes. For example, those who aim at coherence in their decisions should follow coherentism, those who believe in the importance of evidence in decision-making should follow evidentialism and those who believe in accuracy should follow it. Kopec (2016: 3591) thinks pluralism in decision-making is important because beliefs 'are formed in messy localized processes where various previously formed epistemic preferences and beliefs guide our reasoning to eventually settle on further beliefs.' Yet, he acknowledges that there is still no 'well-articulated account of preference coherence, and one would need such an account before one could tell which epistemic preferences ought to be ruled out' (Kopec, 2016: 3593).

Deontological Coherence in Decision-Making

Moderate deontologists try to resolve the above complexities in the theory of deontological coherence. Deontological coherence asserts that moral rules are 'systematic products of interlocking conceptions of rights and duties' (Holyoak & Powell, 2016: 1182). For example, the authority that provides the legal grounds for human rights could 'include God, an implicit social contract among people, or a democratic government' (Holyoak & Powell, 2016: 1182). Even though theories would differ, they 'often support the same moral factor' (Holyoak & Powell, 2016: 1182). For example, 'Whether we trace our values to God, Thomas Hobbes, Thomas Paine, or what our mothers taught us, we can all agree that we should not harm a fellow citizen without cause' (Holyoak & Powell, 2016: 1182). The coherence in moderate deontology is partly realized in the fact that people from different value orientations mostly agree on the principle of doing no harm to anybody without a genuine cause. Immoral laws are sometimes enacted for selfish reasons. Alternatively, laws that meet moral conditions could sometimes be enforced in an immoral manner for selfish reasons. Yet, 'there certainly is overlap, and a legal system cannot deviate too far from the commonsense morality of its culture if it is to be respected and obeyed' (Holyoak & Powell, 2016: 1182).

The reason why decisions would sometimes appear confusing is that people would shift their moral reasoning. However, the attitudes and beliefs of a decision-maker would still maintain coherence. For example, 'in the course of reaching a decision, a reasoner will shift their interrelated attitudes and beliefs so that they cohere with the emerging decision' (Holyoak & Powell, 2016: 1186). This is because a decision-maker weighs moral conditions and chooses the higher condition over the lesser one. For instance, one would be aware that lying is bad. However, such a person would choose lying if telling the truth would lead to the death of an innocent person. Telling the truth about where an innocent person is hiding so that those who want to kill him or her without genuine cause would make the truth-teller guiltier than how he or she would feel after lying to save the innocent person. One would be proud to lie and save an innocent person, rather than to tell the truth and harm him or her. It is in this case that virtue ethics does not seem to achieve coherence.

It is clear that the claim 'that an action is morally right is to know that we cannot be blamed for doing it, although we might not also know whether it is wrong not to do it' (Hacker-Wright, 2010: 210). Particularly, an areteologist who believes that an action is necessary would be ready to explain how others may imitate such an act. As Hacker-Wright (2010: 210-211) points out, 'to say that an act is right is to recommend it.' To carry out a particular action on the basis of necessity and believing that it is morally wrong even though you are performing it, means that you are indirectly recommending it to anybody who would deem himself or herself virtuous for similar action in a similar situation. However, areteologists do not seem to think about necessary actions as guided by the question of right actions. Some areteologists, for example, believe that virtue ethics is reasonable when it is considered in its own right as an ethics not tied down to right actions (Hacker-Wright, 2010). Yet, such argument still does not seem to address the question of coherence very well if areteologists still believe that some actions can be taken on the basis of necessity with clear belief that what the virtuous person is doing is wrong but necessary under that condition.

In deontological coherence, even those who may not be seen by others as coherent in their actions believe that their reasoning is coherent. This is seen in chapter two where the attitudes and beliefs of South

Sudan leaders shift from regarding Islam in united Sudan as an obstacle to getting political power, to seeing Christianity as a threat to holding unquestioned political power in independent South Sudan. These leaders are coherent in their reasoning in protecting their unquestioned holding on to political power. In situations like this, 'local coherence can emerge during reasoning even if the person holds beliefs that are globally incoherent' (Holyoak & Powell, 2016: 1186). Both deontologists and teleologists 'have generally assumed that when a moral issue arises, people approach it with specific predetermined values—beliefs about their rights and duties, and/or about utilities (both their own and those of others) associated with possible outcomes' (Holyoak & Powell, 2016: 1186). This is what scholars refer to as bidirectional inferences (Holyoak & Powell, 2016).

Deontological Christian Ethics and Ethical Decision-Making

Closely related to moderate deontology is 'a deontological Christian ethics' (Vorster, 2009: 510). It focuses more on the conservation values along the line of the integrity of creation. Any decision guided by Christian deontology takes into consideration the protection of human life. In Christian deontology, Vorster (2009) mentions the image of God or *imago dei*, the Kingdom of God, and forgiveness as important factors that guide ethical decision-making in relation to religious, political and social matters. The understanding of human beings as created in the image of God helps people live in harmony, love and care for one another. Moreover, such an understanding makes institutions treat people with integrity, regardless of class, race or gender. The doctrine of *imago dei* 'teaches humankind that all people should be treated as bearers of a human dignity that is granted by God' (Vorster, 2009: 512). Under the Christian deontology, the decisions that political institutions make should be guided by the concept of the Kingdom of God. Vorster (2009: 513) argues that people should acknowledge God's rule and cooperate in 'the proclamation of this divine rule by acts of justice and promotion of peace.' The Kingdom of God 'enables humans to reconcile with God, with fellow human beings and erect new relations with the environment' (Vorster, 2009: 513). The proponents of Christian deontology believe that reconciliation among people can hardly be achieved without forgiveness. Vorster (2009: 514), for example, points out that 'Forgiveness leads to reconciliation and the reconciliation between people, amidst the brokenness caused by evil, manifests the new reality of the kingdom.'

The Primacy of Safety in Ethical Decision-Making

These different theories of decision-making seem to agree on the primacy of safety. The security value seems to cut across all the theories of decision-making. Yet, some contexts translate to valuing security more than others would (Schwartz & Sortheix, 2018). It is likely that what one learns from the environment would form the central value system of such a person (Taylor, 2004). The congruence of one's values with the prevailing values in one's society is important in what one considers crucial in life (Zilberfeld, 2010). Culture matters in how people form values. Even virtue ethics that puts saving lives of other people higher than one's own life is learned from one's culture.

Holyoak and Powell (2016: 1195) argue that differences in moral judgment 'may arise from the complex systems of moral beliefs and values those individuals hold, which can differ in many ways.' These beliefs form personal basic values. These basic person values influence decision-making in political, religious, and social matters (Piurko, Schwartz, & Davidov, 2011; Caprara et al., 2018). This is what explains the differences between right and left in Western political ideological thinking. For example, basic personal values can influence voting in democratic elections in Western countries such as the United States and Italy, among others (Piurko, Schwartz, & Davidov, 2011; Caprara et al., 2017). Moreover, values promoted in daily practices and how a particular society explains experiences in its surroundings shape cultural systems in such a society (Taylor, 2004).

The differences in value systems result from how these values develop. What often become values of a particular community are individual values put together for the common good of a society in which such individuals live (Manfredo et al., 2016). Values that develop as individual values become communal or societal in the sense that there is interrelatedness between individuals and groups. Individuals mainly adopt or feel comfortable with values of a group when they feel that such values resemble their own individual values (Sortheix & Lönnqvist, 2015; Ponizovskiy, Grigoryan, Kühnen, & Boehnk, 2019; Khaptsova & Schwartz, 2016). Moreover, individuals avoid values that seem contrary to values that groups to which they belong regard as the least desirable ones (Manstead, 2018). For example, individuals in Western countries such as the USA put a negative value on old age because the prevailing value in society is excitement, and excitement seems to reduce with old age (Tsai et al., 2018). Values 'inform people of their state in the world in reference to their complex personal and interpersonal goals' (Tamir et al., 2015: 68).

Now, when individual values become communal or societal values, societal values become the overall guarantors of the values. The societal values are overall guarantors of individual values because they transcend specific situations that normally define individual values (Smack et al., 2017). That is, 'Societal values cascade down through multiple levels of organizations, institutions, and individuals and are reinforced and modified through reciprocal processes that emerge upward' (Manfredo, 2017: 775). Moreover, shared values are guided by a society in terms of social sanction to contrary values (Schwartz & Sortheix, 2018). The perception of what is good for society potentially guides the integration of different values and political ideologies (Caprara et al., 2017). Anything that individuals living together regard as desirable probably aids their understanding of goals in life (Tamir et al., 2015). In addition, what individuals strongly believe in as desirable develops in their early upbringing.

Values and Social Environments

Values play a role in one's daily practices and decision-making. Decisions align often with how one has been socialized. As Ponizovskiy et al (2019: 2) point out, 'each individual has a different set of preferred values, informed by the multitude of influences he or she has been exposed to during socialization.' For example, research shows that religiosity determines what political ideology one would support (Caprara et al., 2018). Religiosity mostly relates to shared assumptions about important religious values in line with the will of God or gods. For this reason, it becomes difficult for any new concept or belief to change what an individual already believes in as important in life. This resistance to change is not limited to the individual level, it happens also at the societal level. This is because values play a role in a very complex manner in which they 'are integrated in verbal and nonverbal symbols, communication patterns, daily routines, material culture, social institutions, and the ways people structure and relate to their natural and social surroundings' (Manfredo, et al., 2017: 775). Religiosity is part of these integrated systems in daily practical routines. It determines political ideologies that one should support based on some shared assumptions. Like religion, 'ideology includes shared assumptions and beliefs about human nature and society and about ideals and priorities to be pursued' (Caprara et al., 2017: 390).

The sections below will discuss in detail the concept of basic human values. This aims at pointing out how people rank values in their thoughts and why the conservation values form the central value systems. They will attempt to shed more light on how values that one learns from his or her surroundings influence ethical decision-making in political, religious and social matters. The conservation values differ from individual-to-individual for different reasons. However, what everyone seems to share is the importance of conservation itself. Some people could regard some values as peripheral, while others regard them as central. The sections will explore why these differences exist. They will also discuss possible ways in which conservation values consciously and unconsciously affect ethical choices.

Exploring the Theory of Basic Human Values

Many scholars believe that the theory of basic human values explains the motivation behind human decisions and actions across cultures (Schwartz, 1992; Schwartz, 2012; Caprara et al., 2017; Piurko, Schwartz, & Davidov, 2011; Cieciuch, Schwartz, & Vecchione, 2013; Tamir et al., 2016). The theory is referred to as the theory of basic human values because it 'concerns the basic values that people in all cultures recognize' (Schwartz, 2012: 3). Values are beliefs that are connected to, affect, and mostly refer to desirable goals (Schwartz & Sortheix, 2018). Values mostly go beyond particular situations and actions because they set standards for evaluating people and their actions as well as events and policies. Moreover, values are hierarchical in their importance, and guide human attitudes and behaviours. Values have similar features. Only motivation goals differentiate one value from another. Understanding the roles of value systems is crucial because values are mostly 'used to characterize cultural groups, societies, and individuals, to trace change over time, and to explain the motivational bases of attitudes and behavior' (Schwartz, 2012: 3). This motivational role of values behind human attitudes and behaviours explains how people behave across cultures. It also explains motivations behind certain decisions and actions in religion and politics.

Shalom Schwartz developed the theory of basic human values in 1992. However, the early version which 'theorized that values form a circular motivational structure' (Cieciuch, Schwartz, & Vecchione, 2013: 2) was developed earlier than 1992 (Schwartz & Bilsky, 1987). The writings of Geert Hofstede on human values inspired Schwartz in the 1970s and 1980s. He built on Hofstede's ideas by doing his own research on pro-social as well as altruistic human behaviours. Educated in Columbia and Michigan Universities in the United States of America in social psychology, Schwartz taught at the University of Wisconsin-Madison before he moved to Israel and taught at Hebrew University of Jerusalem until he retired. Although retired now, Schwartz still contributes articles on the theory of basic human values to improve and promote it. Schwartz extends his expertise beyond his own theory that we will explore in this section. He is, for example, one of the contributors to social learning theory as well as social cognitive theory. This chapter will only explore his theory of basic Human values.

Ten Basic Human Values

The theory of basic human values arranges 'the value domain into ten motivationally distinct, basic human values' (Cieciuch, Schwartz, & Vecchione, 2013: 2). These ten values are organised in a circular manner in order to show how each one relates to or differs from the other. For example, 'openness to change' is placed on the upper right side of the circle, while its opposite, 'conservation value,' is placed at the lower left side of the circle. In the same way, 'self-transcendence value' is put on the upper left side of the circle, opposed to 'self-enhancement value,' that is put on the lower right side of the circular continuum. However, self-enhancement can relate to openness to change from the upper right side of the circle in terms of personal focus, and can relate to 'conservation value' opposite to it in the lower part of the circle in terms of self-protection. In the same manner, 'transcendence value' placed on the upper left side of the circle can relate to 'conservation value' placed at the lower left side of the circle in terms of social focus, and can relate to 'openness to change' next to it at the upper right side of the circle in terms of 'growth value.' Research findings show that 'all the value classes are located close to three combinations of the dimensional poles' (Magun, Rudnev, & Schmidt, 2016: 199).

To provide the understanding of how the theory explains human decisions and actions, Schwartz and other researchers developed instruments for testing human motivations (Schwartz, 2012). The instruments have proven reliable over time to test and provide explanations for basic human values underlying human decisions and actions. As Cieciuch and colleagues (2013: 2) point out, 'Research with these instruments has supported the theory in a wide variety of samples from more than 75 countries, demonstrating that the theory holds near-universally and is not instrument-dependent.' The theory is mostly near universal because it explains individual needs, social interactions and groups' survival needs (Schwartz & Sortheix, 2018).

Since values are crucial in explaining what individuals and groups of people hold important in their lives, researchers have explored how values relate and differ in different cultures and countries around the

Figure 1. Circular motivational continuum of 19 values in the refined value theory.
[*Source:* Cieciuch, Schwartz, Vecchione (2013: 3)]

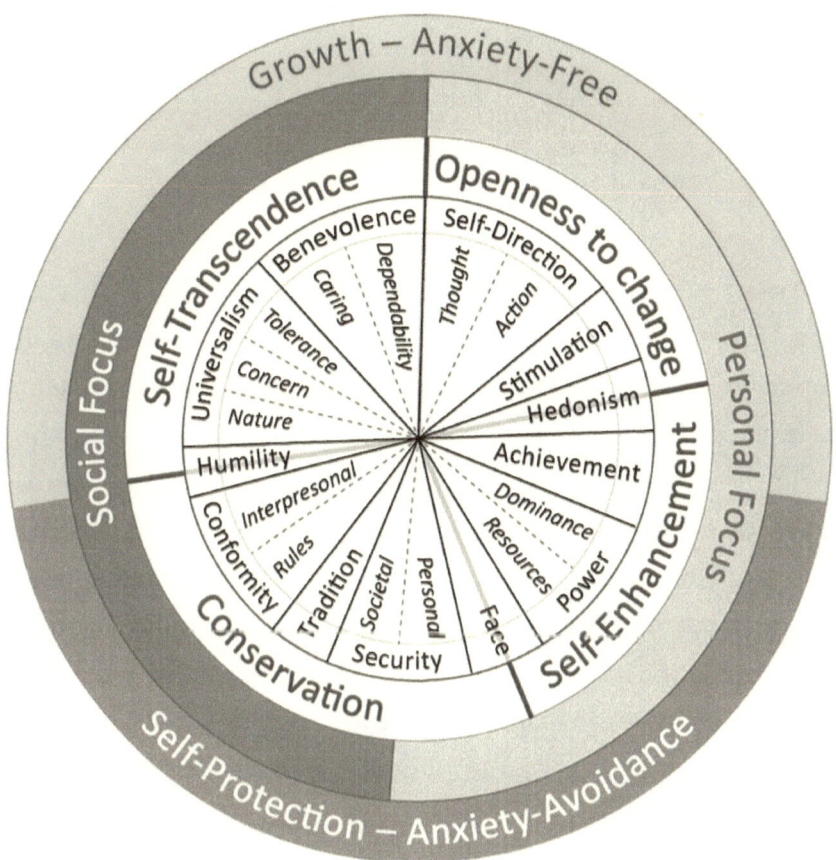

world. Schwartz (2012: 4) observes that what differentiates one value 'from another is the type of goal or motivation that it expresses.' Because of this, the theory of basic human values 'defines ten broad values according to the motivation that underlies each of them' (Schwartz, 2012: 4). The ten basic values are near universal because they explain similar behaviours in different cultures and countries, especially in relation to 'coordinated social interaction, and survival and welfare needs of groups' (Schwartz, 2012: 4). I will explore ten basic human values in two major categories: anxiety-free values and anxiety-avoidance values. The assumption behind these categories is that liberal values always fall under anxiety-free values and conservative values always fall under anxiety-avoidance values. Section three, however, will later show why this hypothesis might not be true.

Anxiety-Free Values

Anxiety-free values in the 'circular motivational continuum' (Cieciuch et al., 2013: 17) of the theory of basic human values are mostly on the top part of the circular structure. In circular motivational continuum, as mentioned above, values adjacent to each other 'share the same motivational emphases and are, therefore, compatible, while values that are further away from one another are less related or even conflicting' (Magun, Rudnev, & Schmidt, 2016: 190). This means that values under anxiety-free categories share the same traits even though they may slightly differ. There are two main categories under anxiety-free values: 'openness to change values' and 'self-transcendence values.' These are divided into subcategories that I will explain. These values mainly explain independence in thoughts and actions as well as feelings (Schwartz, 2012). Values that fall under anxiety-free are open to change. Yet, values that fall under openness to change differ from values that fall under self-transcendence. Values that fall under openness to change seek activities that promote self-direction and stimulation. Openness to change 'refers to a tendency to be curious, imaginative, intellectual, and open-minded versus conventional, cautious, and close-minded' (Cieciuch et al., 2013: 16). Values that fall under self-transcendence seek activities that promote caring for others (Schwartz, 2012). Other differences include the fact that openness to change has a personal focus and self-transcendence has a social focus (Schwartz, 2006; Magun et al., 2016).

I will first explore openness to change values that are composed of self-direction, stimulation and hedonism. Self-direction refers to 'independent thought and action--choosing, creating, exploring' (Schwartz, 2012: 5). Those who value self-direction yearn for autonomy in thoughts and actions. They like to be creative in their efforts to find new things in life. Their curiosity and independent-mindedness make them treasure freedom in choosing whatever goal they want to pursue in life, and they pursue it vigorously. Self-direction has a connection to 'stimulation value.' The goal of stimulation value includes 'excitement, novelty, and challenge in life' (Schwartz, 2012: 5). Those who value stimulation like to pursue activities that 'maintain an optimal, positive, rather than threatening, level of activation' (Schwartz, 2012: 5). They like a variety of exciting activities and lifestyles.

It is reasonable to argue that the need for an exciting lifestyle makes 'stimulation value' relate fairly well to 'hedonism value' under the category of 'anxiety-free values.' 'Hedonism value' refers to 'pleasure or sensuous gratification for oneself' (Schwartz, 2012: 5). Those who value hedonism pursue a lifestyle that capitalizes on enjoyment and self-indulgency. They mainly prefer emotions that increase pleasure in almost everything they do (Tamir, 2016). However, 'Hedonism shares elements of both openness to change and self-enhancement' (Schwartz, 2012: 8). Values under 'openness to change category' relate mostly to individualism rather than collectivism (Smack et al., 2017).

People who value openness to change are motivated by growth values and can be associated with the Growth class in basic human value categorisations (Schwartz, 2006; Magun, Rudnev, & Schmidt, 2016). Those who strongly value openness to change are committed to both openness to change and self-transcendence. However, some of them may combine the preference for openness to change and self-enhancement because they have larger leaning commitments to self-enhancement than they have to self-transcendence. Magun and colleagues (2016) found in their research that values related to openness to change are common in European countries with higher economic growth. In Europe, 'wealth is the most influential country-level trigger of the Growth values class formation' (Magun et al. 2016: 198).

These researchers mainly argue that 'indicators of country prosperity, health, and educational resources correlate positively with country probability of Growth values class and negatively or not significantly with all the others' (Magun et al., 2016: 198). Mostly, those who prefer Growth values such as openness to change are younger people, especially 'more educated females with parents of higher educational level, higher social status (employers versus non-employers), and non-migrant background' (Magun et al., 2016: 198). The same research shows that younger males mainly prefer strong 'personal focus values.' These differences were identified within each of the European countries in which Magun and colleagues (2016) did their research. The differences that the researchers identified were not differences among countries; they were class value differences within each country. However, the researchers admit that their findings could only be reflecting European economic structural realities that might be different in other social and economic settings.

It is likely true 'that growing up and living under such different social and economic contexts would have a considerable impact on people's thoughts, feelings and behaviours' (Manstead, 2018: 268). However, comparing attitudes within a group with the same economic status seems to show that what influences human beings is often more complicated than what the comparison of classes within one society seems to show. The findings that show the connection between socio-economic status and preference for growth values such as openness to change could be more of class-identification desirability attitudes than they are of fixed forms of basic human values. People with higher socio-economic status (SES) 'attached more importance to identities that are indicative of their SES position, but less importance on identities that are rooted in basic demographics or related to their sociocultural orientation (and vice versa)' (Manstead, 2018: 270). For example, research carried out by Manstead (2018) shows that one's status as working class has higher connection to empathy and willingness to help other people. However, this willingness to help other people does not stand the test under economic threats that these working-class people feel or perceive in relation to immigrants who have the same academic qualifications as they. Those who value openness to change in an environment where they feel secure appear hesitant to change when their comfort seems threatened by new changes. This also applies to the commitment to empathy and helping other people. Therefore, what influences people in decision-making in social classes could go 'beyond differences in financial circumstances' (Manstead, 2018: 268).

Sometimes wealthy people feel threatened by the influx of immigrants to countries in which these wealthy people own businesses. This economic threat does not appear to middle and upper classes immediately in the same way that it appears to lower-income working-class people. Working-class people are often keen on how their relations with others affect their social and economic life (Stephens et al., 2014). They are keen on the social context in which they live because it helps them develop resilience. They have 'a psychological orientation that is motivated by the need to deal with external constraints and threats' (Manstead, 2018: 273). However, the middle and upper classes pay less attention to external threats because they often feel, or perceive, they are in control of economic situations (Kraus et al., 2012). Wealthy people from middle and upper classes, for example, like immigrants to work for them as cheap labourers during high economic stability. However, they 'oppose immigration when economic instability was said to be high, rather than low' (Manstead, 2018: 276). People 'who grow up in middle- or upper-class environments are likely to have more material and psychological resources available to them, and as a result have stronger beliefs about the extent to which they can shape their own social outcomes' (Manstead, 2018: 273-274). They feel that immigrants would contribute to high economic instability. This means that there are degrees of anxiety in the face of economic threats in relation to immigrants. Working class, middle class, and upper-class people would all like to help immigrants when immigrants are not seen as potential or real economic threats, and would oppose them if they were seen as economic threats. This means that value relationships are more complicated than a simple straightforward 'openness to change value' seems to suggest.

Complexities in value relationships make some researchers believe that values are not universal, but cultural or situationally specific. People often behave in a manner that reflects their context. For example, religiosity would appear to value different things in different contexts. According to Ponizovskiy et al. (2019: 4), research 'found that in countries where the relationship between the state and the church was amicable, expected positive relations between religiosity and values of conformity and tradition were present.' Contrary to the above, 'in countries where church was in conflict with the state, religiosity correlated less strongly with conservation-type values, and more strongly with universalism' (Ponizovskiy et al., 2019: 4). Universalism in the theory of basic human values refers to 'understanding, appreciation, tolerance, and protection for the welfare of *all* people and for nature' (Schwartz, 2012: 7). It means that the church pays attention to the maintenance of a specific national tradition of religion in situations where a specific country is in a good relationship with the church and seeks universal religious solidarity in specific states where religious survival is under potential threat.

There seem to be some elements of specificity and universality in religious, political or social life. Schwartz (2012) explains how universalism connects and differs from specificity. In the concept of universalism, people derive their values from 'survival needs of individuals and groups' (Schwartz, 2012: 7). Schwartz (2012: 7) argues that 'people do not recognize these needs until they encounter others beyond the extended primary group and until they become aware of the scarcity of natural resources.' Universalism develops from specific contexts that provide universal convictions about how one should treat other human beings outside one's inner circle, and how they treat nature. Those who value universalism see the connectivity of all beings as important to their own survival and happiness. For them, the good life is not only realised in treating other human beings fairly, it also extends to treating nature fairly. This is because 'failure to protect the natural environment will lead to the destruction of the resources on which life depends' (Schwartz, 2012: 7). Those who value universalism combine the respect and protection of all human beings with the respect and protection of the nature that includes animals, birds, and fish, among others. Universalism makes people aware that the good life is inclusive and wider than one's inner circle. Along this line spirituality often falls within the value of universalism. As Schwartz (2012: 7) puts it, the 'goal of spiritual values is meaning, coherence, and inner harmony through transcending everyday reality.' We will later see how spirituality also fits into specificity. It was for the fact that spirituality would fit in different values that Schwartz (2012: 7) concluded that it 'did not demonstrate a consistent meaning across cultures.'

Universalism is a value located under the umbrella of self-transcendence values. For this reason it relates to the benevolence value that focuses on the welfare of others, transcending one's self-interest. The difference between universalism and benevolence is that benevolence focuses on 'preserving and enhancing the welfare of those with whom one is in frequent personal contact (the 'in-group')' (Schwartz, 2012: 7). It facilitates a smooth functioning of a group to which one relates. These groups include one's family and immediate community. Benevolence values often make people pay more attention to the welfare of people they know more than the welfare of outsiders. They give to their family members, friends but not strangers. Research, for example, shows that people of lower class help others more in private than they do in public (Manstead, 2012). Low-income people still help others, but they do not always see the need to help people outside their inner groups. Mostly, 'benevolence values provide an internalized motivational base for such behavior' (Schwartz, 2012: 7).

Piurko et al. (2011) argue that universalism and benevolence values have connection to the political left in ideological orientations. They believe that left political orientation motivates people to focus on the needs and welfare of every human being and the environment. Generally, the left and liberalism in political ideology 'emphasize the merits of the welfare state, express strong concern for social justice and tolerance of diverse groups (even those that might disturb the conventional social order), and emphasize pluralism and equality' (Caprara et al., 2017: 395). Piurko et al. (2011) also found that those who are liberals value equality of all people. Caprara et al. (2017) confirm the findings of the research done by Piurko et al. (2011) that there is a connection between liberalism and anxiety-free values. Overall, values that are under the anxiety-free category such as openness to change and self-transcendence, from which 'the higher order values' (Cieciuch et al., 2013: 8) such as universalism and benevolence come, have high connection to left or liberal political orientation. I will now explore values under anxiety-avoidance category to see how these values agree with or differ from the values under anxiety-free category that consists of openness to change and self-transcendence.

Anxiety-Avoidance Values

Anxiety-avoidance values are the opposite of anxiety-free values. They are placed at the lower section of Schwartz's 'circular motivational continuum' (Cieciuch et al., 2013: 2). Anxiety-avoidance values are divided into two main subcategories: self-enhancement values and conservation values. Self-enhancement values relate to self-transcendence values in terms of personal focus. Conservation values relate to openness to change values in terms of social focus. Minor components of the self-enhancement subcategory are achievement and power. Minor components of the conservation subcategory are conformity, tradition and security. The main aim of anxiety-avoidance values is to avoid anything that would make anyone feel uncomfortable or that is seen as a threat to one's life and ambitions. Anxiety-avoidance values mainly aim at keeping the status quo for security and traditional belief reasons (Schwartz, 2011). Security needs under the anxiety-avoidance value category could apply to both physical and emotional situations.

Conservation values focus more on security. Mostly, conservation values such as tradition, conformity and security 'emphasize order, self-restriction, preservation of the past, and resistance to change' (Schwartz, 2012: 8). It could be for these reasons that conservation values are more social-focused than personal-focused. On the contrary, self-enhancement values such as achievement and power focus on 'one's own interests and relative success and dominance over others' (Schwartz,

2012: 8). Yet, self-enhancement values still fall under the anxiety-avoidance value category in the sense that they emphasize the need to avoid or eliminate threats to one's ambitions.

As seen above, researchers in basic human values argue that values under the umbrella of anxiety-avoidance category are collectivistic or social-focused rather than individualistic or personal-focused (Smack et al., 2017). The 'individualistic versus collectivistic Orientations' (Smack et al., 2017: 2) are among the factors that explain what sometimes appears to be differences between Western countries with African and Asian countries in value orientations. What is interesting is that personal-focused values combine some values from the anxiety-free category such as self-direction, stimulation and hedonism with some values from the anxiety-avoidance category such as achievement and power. Social-focused values also combine other values from the anxiety-free category such as universalism and benevolence with other values from the anxiety-avoidance category such as tradition, conformity and security (Smack et al., 2017).

Values are generally connected with individuals' feelings or emotions. This is possibly because 'Acts of self-regulation are directed toward desired end states' (Tamir et al., 2016: 68). This end-states desire would focus on objective states of affairs such as peace for everybody all over the world. Alternatively, it could focus on phenomenological states of affairs such as the feeling of happiness. Values, especially the instrumental ones, 'inform people of their state in the world in reference to their complex personal and interpersonal goals' (Tamir et al., 2016: 68). To arrive at the desired end goals, emotions sometimes can be unpleasant. As Tamir and colleagues (2016: 68) point out, 'an unpleasant emotion may be desirable if it promotes goal pursuit, despite the fact that it involves displeasure, which itself is undesirable.' In this respect, contexts under which one learned his or her values are important in dictating the prioritisation of desired end goals or states of affairs that one pursues as well as emotional expressions accompanying choices of such desired goals. For example, emotions that express the need for anxiety-free values such as openness to change and self-transcendence could be different from emotions that express the need for anxiety-avoidance values such as self-enhancement and conservation. Moreover, emotions reflect engagement and disengagement in value expressions.

Engagement values are self-regulating in the sense that they promote intimate relationships, caregiving and protection of one another among the people. Because of the above reasons, people would often endorse values that are compatible with their emotional needs. Alternatively, they would adopt emotions that are compatible with their values. For example, those who endorse self-transcendence as their most important value desire emotions such as 'love, trust, empathy, and compassion' (Tamir et al., 2016: 69). Love, for example, promotes intimate relationships among people which could apply to in-group and out-group members. This is the same thing with emotions such as affection, trust, empathy and compassion. The experience of trust 'enables the maintenance of such bonds, when experienced as a source of security' (Tamir et al., 2016: 69). It 'facilitates the maintenance of satisfying relationships based on reciprocal concerns' (Tamir et al., 2016: 69). Compassion and empathy motivate people to take care of one another.

Opposite to emotions that promote engagement are those which prohibit engagement such as 'pride, anger, and contempt' (Tamir et al., 2016: 69). Emotions that keep people away from relating to others in a cordial manner are the disengagement values. Values under self-enhancement are disengagement values because they focus more on the need to have the power to dominate others rather than helping them. Those who fear being dominated because they have less power distance themselves from those who have dominant power. Those who have almost equal power do not engage very well either because they are often struggling to dominate one another. They are full of pride in their achievements. People who have dominant power are full of pride because 'Pride promotes self-esteem and propels further achievements' (Tamir et al., 2016: 69). Anger in those who love to dominate 'reflects the belief that one has the ability to control such offences and it serves to facilitate the restoration of power and dominance' (Tamir et al., 2016: 69). Emotions such as contempt, hatred and hostility serve the same purpose that pride and anger serve for actively restoring or maintaining power and dominance under some sorts of perceived or actual threats to such power.

Furthermore, some values are change-regulating rather than self-regulating. Emotions under these values can encourage either engagement or disengagement to 'desired stimuli' (Tamir et al., 2016: 69). For example, 'Emotions such as interest and curiosity motivate exploration and seeking of novel stimuli' (Tamir et al., 2016: 69). Some people desire openness to change because it helps them arrive at some new benefits or rewards that come with change. When people identify rewards that they would gain as the result of change, then 'emotions such as excitement and enthusiasm propel active engagement with them [new changes]' (Tamir et al., 2016: 69).

Opposite to values that give people emotional desire for change, conservation values give people emotions resistant to change. Particularly, 'emotions such as calmness and relief reflect the successful avoidance of potential threats and promote inaction' (Tamir et al., 2016: 69-70). Emotions such as relaxation and contentment play the same role that relief and calmness play under change-regulating values. Even though the findings from the research done by Tamir and colleagues (2016: 72) do not show strong connections between change-regulating values and emotions associated with them, they still concluded that to some extent, 'values can increase the desirability of value-consistent emotions.'

Anxiety-avoidance values are mainly disengagement values because they go better with emotions that keep the status quo than emotions that encourage engagement with new things. For example, the goal of achievement value under the self-enhancement category is 'personal success through demonstrating competence according to social standards' (Schwartz, 2012: 5). Letting go of social standards by which achievements are measured would mean that the person who is ambitious for the sake of social approval would not get the pleasure he or she wants from success. This would also apply to the value of power in changing situations where status does not matter to others. One who loves power for the sake of status would not like changes in how societies view status in relation to power, since that would lead to the meaninglessness of the social-esteem that makes power and dominance desirable.

Conservation values such as security, conformity and tradition are always likely to fall under the anxiety-avoidance category in relation to all values. Security leads to anxiety-avoidance because its goal includes 'safety, harmony, and stability of society, of relationships, and of self' (Schwartz, 2012: 6). For this reason, giving up security needs of individuals and communities to pave the way to new changes raises a host of anxieties. For this reason conformity is often needed alongside the security value in order to control 'actions, inclinations, and impulses likely to upset or harm others and violate social expectations or norms' (Schwartz, 2012: 6). Closer to conformity value is the tradition value. This is because the goal of the tradition value includes 'respect, commitment, and acceptance of the customs and ideas that one's culture or religion provides' (Schwartz, 2012: 6). The shared experiences that groups develop as their traditions, are often linked to their perceived or actual fates. These shared experiences 'symbolize the group's solidarity, express its unique worth, and contribute to its survival' (Schwartz, 2012: 6). It is for this reason that conformity and tradition work together to impose social expectations on each group's member. The imposed expectations, in turn, reduce insecurity in the general society and in individuals.

Research findings from studies based on Schwartz's theory of basic human values often show religiosity as connected to anxiety-avoidance values. This could possibly be because of the importance that many religions assign to traditional values and authority (Piurko, Schwartz, & Davidov, 2011). The association between religiosity and values that try to avoid anxiety is more common in traditional countries than in liberal countries. Research carried out by Caprara et al. (2018: 531) in sixteen countries in different parts of the world, for example, 'showed that individuals more committed to a religion attributed relatively high importance to the conservation values of security, tradition, conformity.' Tradition had a higher connection to religiosity. Israel was the highest with 60% connection.

The connection of religiosity to anxiety-avoidance values also corresponds to its connection to conservative ideologies. Research findings show that 'More religious individuals located themselves more to the right and conservative side of the political spectrum than less religious individuals' (Caprara et al., 2018: 531). Caprara et al. (2018: 533) argue that these connections are possible because religion gives people their worldview, especially in relation to how they cope with 'life and death' as well as 'the moral legitimacy to claim obedience for their rulers.' These connections were higher in countries 'where the majority religion had significantly influenced the moral education and socialization of children and the national identity of people' (Caprara et al., 2018: 534). More importantly, religions teach people values that lead to avoiding uncertainties in life. That is, religiosity goes well with conservation values.

Moreover, researches based on Schwartz's theory of basic human values associate political conservatism to anxiety-avoidance values. For example, some researchers found that people with right-wing political orientations or conservative ideologies prefer values under the conservation and self-enhancement categories (Piurko et al., 2011; Aspelund et al., 2013; Caprara et al., 2012). The connection between political conservatism and anxiety-avoidance values is found to be common in countries with major national religions (Piurko et al., 2011). This is because religions so institutionalised influence in such states that norms of these religions are a major part of citizens' lifestyles. However, the research shows no such strong association between political orientation and value priorities seen between value priorities and religiosity. For example, right-wing political orientation shows association with openness to change values in the Czech Republic (Piurko et al., 2011).

However, some countries fall between conservatism and liberalism in their value prioritisation: post-communist countries such as Slovenia, Hungary, Poland and Czech Republic (Piurko, Schwartz et al., 2011). Because of their swift transition from communism to capitalism, these countries possibly got confused in their value prioritisations. Caprara et al. (2017: 402) point out that the profound changes that took place after the collapse of communism 'resulted in confusion about the definition of left and right.' It is also possible that the orientations that citizens of these countries used to have under communism could sometimes have internal conflicts. Meaning and values under communism rarely cohere in ways that other value orientations could. For example, Sookhdeo (2019) explains that children in most of families under communism received one type of value orientation at home and another type of value orientation in public. Especially children whose parents were Christians used to receive Christian values at home and secular values in public. These values conflicted. Those different teachings resulted in cultural estrangement that makes individual values incongruent with societal values (Bernard et al., 2006). Currently, politicians of the political parties in post-communist countries such as Poland often reject the labels of right-wing and left-wing political orientations. Piurko et al. (2011) believe that post-communist countries still need enough time to develop basic human values that will make their value prioritisation consistent in terms of right-left political orientations. This is because values are very slow to change and change only when major changes force new shifts in values (Schwartz & Sortheix, 2018). Transition from communism to capitalism is a major change that could apply to relevant new values. Yet, letting go of the communist values may take time for citizens in post-communist countries that are now capitalist in ideology.

Although some countries fall between liberalism and conservatism in value prioritisation, researchers conclude that anxiety-avoidance values are mainly connected to conservatism or right-wing ideology (Piurko et al., 2011; Caprara et al., 2017). The connection is about avoidance of anxiety that results from new changes. Anxiety-avoidance values and conservatism also prefer to maintain the status quo. Conservatives do not like threats and uncertainties (Jost et al., 2003). Conservation values, further, influenced citizens when voting during democratic elections in many countries that Caprara et al. (2017) studied. Citizens who prefer tradition, conformity and security, as well as values such as power and achievement, vote for politicians who support these anxiety-avoidance values. Researchers believe that values that fall under the anxiety-avoidance category are unhealthy values (Bilsky & Schwartz, 1994). They argue that unhealthy values focus on transforming cognitive deficiency needs of individuals in ways that capitalise on self-protection or ego-protection from threats and deprivations (Schwartz & Sortheix,

2018). Security, conformity and power sometimes aim at extrinsic goals in the sense that they focus on pleasing other people as well as avoiding anything that would lead to social censure. Those who pursue anxiety-avoidance values would perceive other people as threatening, leading to unhealthy lives (Sagiv & Schwartz, 2000).

Turning the Circular Motivational Continuum Upside Down

Generally, the theory of basic human values ranks values in ways that make them appear fixed in a motivational circular continuum. The upper values of the circle, for example, determine liberalism, and values below the circle determine conservatism. In addition, values on the left side of the circle determine social focus and the ones on the right side of the circle determine personal focus. Some research findings show that growth value class or anxiety-free values have connection to countries with high gross national income (GNI) per capita (Magun et al., 2016). At the individual level, Magun et al. (2016) conclude that people who are highly educated and who belong to families with high level of education prefer growth class values or anxiety-free values. The opposite is that countries with low GNI per capita and individuals with lower level of education have connection to self-protection or anxiety-avoidance values. In terms of relationship between values and subjective well-being (SWB), research shows that the growth orientation or anxiety-free values promote subjective well-being (Schwartz & Sortheix, 2018). This is the same with personal focus values. On the opposite side, both the personal focus and the self-protective orientation or anxiety-avoidance values undermine subjective well-being (Schwartz & Sortheix, 2018).

The studies on basic human values often investigate relationships in Schwartz's motivational circular continuum. These relationships in the motivational circular continuum especially examine values that explain concerns for the welfare of others and those that explain concerns for personal interests (Schwartz & Sortheix, 2018). Recent studies particularly focus on how the ten basic human values relate to well-being (Joshanloo & Ghaedi, 2009; Haslam, Whelan, & Bastion, 2009; Karabati, & Cemalcilar, 2010; Bobowik et al., 2011; Sortheix & Lönnqvist, 2014; Sortheix & Schwartz, 2017). However, no one has done a study on whether there are values that could form the centre of the motivational circular continuum. Moreover, no study has looked into what could happen if the motivational circular continuum were turned upside down to make anxiety-free values take the place of anxiety-avoidance values. It is not yet clear how to explain circumstances under which conservatives sometimes behave like liberals and liberals behave like conservatives within countries in which liberalism and conservatism are not confusing. The countries in which conservatism or right-wing and liberalism or left-wing are not confusing include the United States of America and other countries that are not post-communist states. The section below will, therefore, go beyond value relationships in Schwartz's motivational circular continuum to examine whether some values form the central value systems and how such value systems influence decision-making on ethical issues in politics and religion.

Central Value Systems and Decision-Making

The central value systems concept is generally that there are values that form the centre of the circle. As Ponizovskiy and colleagues (2019: 9) argue, 'a value that is contextually salient, such as security at time of war, is likely to occupy a central place in the discourse.' However, the value at 'central place in the discourse' in such a time that Ponizovskiy et al (2019) refer to is not necessarily the central value system. Still, their idea about values that occupy the centre according to salient contexts is closer to the idea of central value systems. The circle referred to here, in relation to the concept of central value systems, is Schwartz's motivational circular continuum. The only difference is that Schwartz's motivational circular continuum does not have values that are placed in the centre of the circle to form central value systems. Schwartz's motivational circular continuum arranges values in a rounded relational manner in which values adjacent to one another relate. Conflicting values are far away from one another in the circle (Schwartz, 2012; Cieciuch et al., 2013; Schwartz & Sortheix, 2018). Central value systems, unlike the Schwartz's motivational circular continuum, arranges values in a way that values that are flexible are placed on the outer layers of the circle and values that are rigid are placed in the inner layers of the circle. The flexible values are anxiety-free ones such as openness to change and self-transcendence, and the rigid values are anxiety-avoidance ones such as self-enhancement and conservation. It is likely that new changes or new beliefs and schools of thought can easily penetrate flexible values, while rigid values are hard to penetrate by new changes or new schools of thought.

No research has explicitly mentioned the concept of central value systems in analyses of political decision making. It is now likely that even though the theory of basic human values explains the relationships of values in the motivational circular continuum, it implicitly explains the idea of central value systems and its role in resistance. For example, some researchers observe that some decisions are sometimes based on 'domain-specific core values, which let people make fast and frugal decisions that comport with abstract political beliefs' (Goren et al., 2016: 978). Core values guide fast decisions since people can unconsciously retrieve these core values from their central value systems (Vaisey & Lizardo, 2010). As Miles (2015: 681) points out, 'individuals carry around beliefs, predispositions, perceptual schemas, and other cognitively stored elements that influence how they act without requiring much (if any) conscious effort on their part.' This is possibly how central value systems influence decisions. It is these central value systems and their resistance roles, which are sometimes activated unconsciously, that I will now explore to understand how they relate to confusion in the implementation of legal provisions such as article 8 in the Constitution of South Sudan.

Values and Internal Motivations

Some values seemingly guide the internal motivation of individuals and society, especially in directing what people choose to follow or reject. For example, 'conformity and tradition values stress deference to and respect for external or socially constructed sources of authority such as culture or religion, whereas stimulation values prioritize excitement and novelty in one's private life' (Goren et al., 2016: 983). When it comes to 'cultural issues such as abortion and gay rights, beliefs about authority, conformity, tradition, tolerance, religion, and equality carry weight' (Goren et al., 2016: 978). And for 'foreign affairs, beliefs about warfare, ethnocentrism, patriotism, social intolerance, conformity, militant and cooperative internationalism, isolationism, and retributive justice shape opinion' (Goren et al., 2016: 978). Most importantly, Miles (2015) points out that some researchers have observed that different societies instil in their members some limited core values that give them common orientations around which they organise their thoughts as well as their actions. According to Miles (2015: 682), these instilled core 'values guide individuals in the conscious, rational selection of goals, provide a rubric by which strategies for obtaining those goals can be evaluated, and shape normative expectations in interaction situations.' This could

Figure 2: Central Value Systems
[*Source:* Developed by the Author]

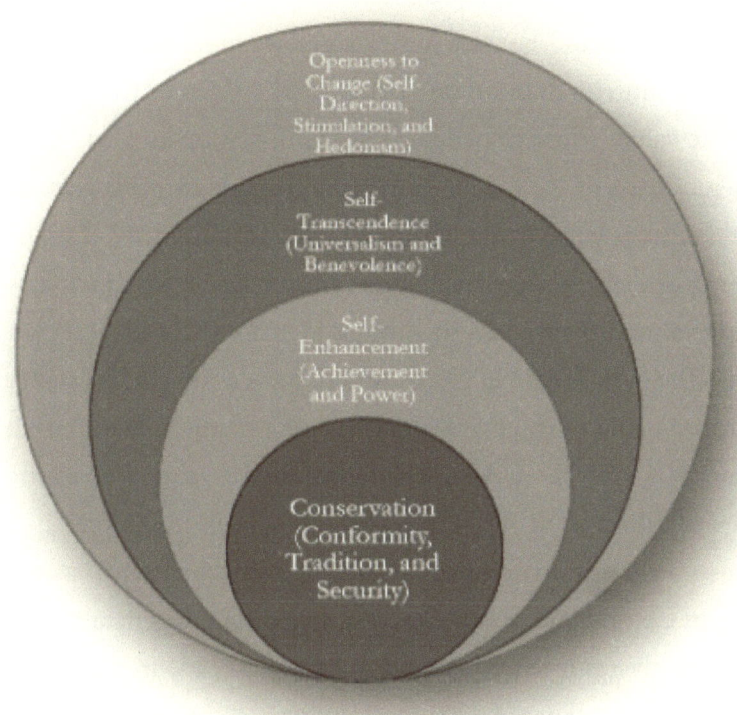

be why implementation of some legal provisions conflicting with central values of a particular society, or even particular individuals within a society, would look confusing.

It is likely that values that form the central system in any individual and in any society are values that people learn from their childhood. This is because 'value formation is inextricably tied to self-formation' (Miles, 2015: 683). As Ponizovskiy et al (2019: 9) point out, 'values are likely to affect attitudes and behavior stronger if the value or the attitude is salient in context.' Values that people learn from their childhoods possibly define specific 'needs of individuals as biological organisms, the need for coordinated social interaction, and the need for survival and well-being of social groups' (Ponizovskiy et al., 2019: 9). Specifically defined actions would serve these needs better than others in different countries. This could be why some values are more popular in some areas and countries than others. For example, Bayram (2015) argues that some values relate to people's self-identification as world citizens in different parts of the world. Those who strongly identify themselves as world citizens believe that what they value would work better in the wider world than in their local areas. This could be why people who strongly value universalism in Europe identify themselves as world citizens. The same is true in North America, even though 'resistance to conformity is the most critical predictor of a cosmopolitan self-view' (Bayram, 2015: 469). In Asia, self-transcendence values lead to strong self-identification of many people as world citizens. Achievement and hedonism values motivate people who identify themselves as world citizens in Central and South America. Even though generalised trust strongly motivates many Mainland Australians to identify themselves as world citizens, Bayram (2015) shows that stimulation values also lead to strong self-identification of people as world citizens in Australia. Security values motivate Africans to identify as world citizens.

Thus, those who consider themselves world citizens have different reasons for doing so. Some regard themselves as world citizens because they think about and care for people far away from them and provide humanitarian assistance (Brown & Held, 2010). Some regard themselves as world citizens because they believe they are open-minded and multicultural in worldview (Bayram, 2015). Moreover, some people who identify themselves as citizens of the world value autonomy in a manner that will let them live as free agents (Bohman, 2007). Mostly, 'World citizens are interested in personal success, wealth, and pleasure but they self-enhance without distressing others' (Bayram, 2015: 465). Research conducted by Bayram (2015: 470) shows that 'trust and urban residence positively relate to cosmopolitan attachment, while Left orientation and age relate negatively.' This could mean that inculcation of values in children in the past, when those who are old today were growing up, did not emphasise the importance of universalism that often leads to the idea of world citizenship as it does today. It could also be true that those who live in rural areas are still not exposed in their childhood to current universal value interests that often lead to valuing of world citizenship. Potentially it is through early exposure to universalism that 'those who are on the Right side of the political spectrum and are younger are more likely to be drawn to world citizenship' (Bayram, 2015: 470).

At the moderate level, many values are combined in people's self-identification as citizens of the world in many parts of the world. Nevertheless, some of these combined values could be more influential as predictors of world citizenship in some geographical areas such as North America, Europe, Africa, Australia or Asia. For the North Americans, for example, 'universalism, benevolence, achievement, hedonism, and stimulation each move world citizens' (Bayram, 2015: 470). Openness to change, universalism, stimulation, achievement and self-direction values motivate self-identification by some people as world citizens in Europe. For South and Central Americans, 'world citizens are primarily motivated by hedonism and achievement' (Bayram, 2015: 470). The combination of motivating values for people's identification as world citizens remain as generalised trust and stimulation values in Mainland Australia. For Asians, stimulation, universalism and hedonism values are the major combination of values that predict self-identification as world citizens. For Africans, 'values most conducive to cosmopolitan allegiance are benevolence and resistance to tradition' (Bayram, 2015: 470).

The above-mentioned differences in what people in different geographical areas value seem to indicate that different people regard different values as forming their central beliefs or central value systems. Moreover, different people who choose differently on core values would protect the value they treasure more than others would. If Africans, for example, regard security as their core value, then they would collaborate with those who guarantee their security around the world. On the opposite side, these Africans would negatively relate to those who cause insecurity among them. Africans would not be open to any change that moves in the direction of insecurity. This would imply that African countries could break partnership with countries that may appear a security threat. This could be why Ponizovskiy et al (2019: 9) argue: 'while values can be viewed as a reflection of the universal motivational continuum at the most abstract level, they can also be seen as relatively independent cognitive categories that are meaningfully linked to other mental representations.' Even though openness to change could always be part of the anxiety-free value category in Schwartz's motivational circular continuum, it would be the central value in Europe if it were forward-looking in introducing new values and getting rid of old values. The forward-looking 'openness to change value' becomes self-protective under the circumstances that openness to change is backward looking in restoring old values. This can apply to all other values where a threat to progress leads to self-protection. This idea will be elaborated later in this section.

Change can easily penetrate outer layers such as openness to change and self-transcendence values of the circle, but it is difficult to penetrate central layers such as self-enhancement and conservation. Values that are far apart in Schwartz's motivational circular continuum are openness to change and conservation (Cieciuch, Schwartz, & Vecchione, 2013). This means that openness to change values form the outer layer of the circle and conservation values form the centre of the circle. Some researchers point out that 'Multinomial logistic regression analysis using WVS [World Value Survey] data (2005–2008) shows that self-transcendence, self-enhancement (except power), and openness-to-change values lead to cosmopolitan allegiance, while conservation values hinder this attachment' (Bayram, 2015: 454). This means that self-enhancement of which power is part is closer to conservation in the circle, and self-transcendence is closer to openness to change in the outer layer of the circle. In the two layers that can be penetrated easily by new changes, one layer (openness to change) is personal focus. One layer (self-transcendence) is social focus. For the inner circles that cannot be penetrated easily by new changes or values, one layer (self-enhancement) is personal focus, while another one (conservation) is social focus.

Central Value Systems and Different Worldview Traditions

The concept of central value systems implies the important connection between values and different worldview traditions. Worldview traditions are mainly grouped in three distinct types: Premodern tradition, Modernist tradition and Postmodernist tradition (Baird, 2016). Premodern tradition was widespread until the Renaissance. Modernism began from the Renaissance and ended where German Idealism started. That is, the Modernist tradition started with the rejection of the Greek way of thinking in the Renaissance. The Postmodernist tradition started because of people's dissatisfaction with the Modernist way of thinking. These traditions are basically differentiated by distinct scientific models or paradigms around which they operate. Greek science, for example, emphasises explanation of issues in terms of forms and essences. That is, it focuses on clear explanation of patterns so that people can clearly understand them. Unlike the

Premodern tradition that focuses on forms and substances in relational explanations, the Modernist tradition operates on the basis of cause and effect. This scientific model is also known as mechanistic science (Baird, 2016). Mechanistic science tries to prove beyond doubt the reality or certainty of any object of study. It is in this focus on certainty from the starting point of doubt that Modernism differs from Postmodernism. The main approach of study in Postmodernism is phenomenology or the study of the appearance of things. Postmodernists never aim at proving the certainty or reality of an object. They aim at describing a phenomenon to let people see what such a phenomenon is. Postmodernists, for instance, describe a phenomenon until people are amazed at what such a phenomenon is. The scientific model of the Postmodernist tradition is organic: the idea that things are related to one another in an organic manner. This relationship of things in the Postmodernist tradition, however, differs from the relationship that premodern tradition emphasises.

Given all the above worldview traditions and their teachings, it is likely that what people do is guided by values and traditions they follow. It is likely that any new worldview tradition introduced at any time does not erase old worldview traditions, even though old worldview traditions would continue as weak belief systems. Those who hold onto older worldview traditions possibly live in perpetual struggles to protect old values in which they believe. In the same way, adherents to a new worldview tradition live under the pressure to make their new worldview tradition completely replace the old ones, leading to perpetual survival struggles. Considering these survival struggles, it is probable that what Schwartz has not thought about in the theory of basic human values is that anxiety-free values can sometimes become anxiety-avoidance values. Moreover, perhaps he never thought about the fact that some values could form the centre of the circular motivation

Figure 3: Value Changes in Relation to Traditions or Schools of Thought
[*Source:* Developed by the Author]

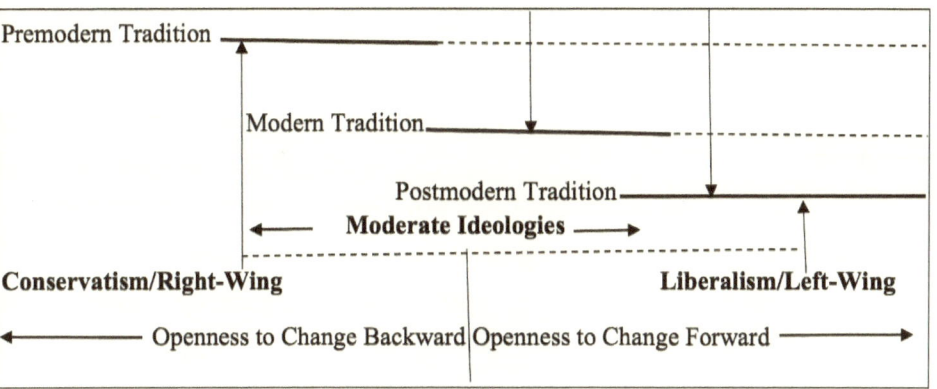

continuum in a self-protective manner. All values seem to use anxiety-avoidance as the tool for survival. When changes occur, for instance, any value system that appears threatened by new changes activates its self-protection mechanisms to protect its underlying beliefs from new changes. This means that what an individual or group of people value the most stays in the centre of value circle and so could resist the penetration from undesirable values. There seem to be times when liberal values take the centre part of the motivational circle and times when conservative values take the outer circle. For example, liberals support openness to change, when the change is forward looking, to values that support current Postmodernism, while conservatives do not support change because they are conserving values that they believe are being destroyed by postmodernism. If changes start going backward now to restore the modernist and premodern values, then conservatives can replace liberals in the anxiety-free circle, and liberals can take over the conservation values in the centre to protect the postmodernist values in which they strongly believe. This means that liberals can be in the anxiety-avoidance circle when they feel that their values are threatened by backward changes. As shown in the figure above, different worldview traditions influence people differently.

Fear seems to drive value struggles in any worldview tradition. Conservatives are often afraid to lose to liberals in elections because power is often used to advance ideologies guided by a particular worldview tradition. The reverse is true when liberals win elections and direct changes towards their valued worldview tradition. Conservation values become important to groups that are in a weak position. In this process, one's tradition means more. Tradition here means preserving anything that one strongly believes in. As Graburn (2001: 8) argues, 'Traditions are continually being created, not in some past time immemorial, but during modernity.' This means there is a liberal tradition in the same way that there is a conservative tradition. Liberals can use conservation values to protect their liberal traditions if conservatives are in power and are undoing changes made by liberals. Liberals do the same to conservative changes. Because of these continuous intentions to undo what the other has built, conservation values form the centre of any worldview tradition. Since worldview traditions keep coming up, any new worldview tradition often has the advantage of labelling old worldview traditions as outdated. This view sometimes influences research participants' choices in answering research questions. For this reason findings from basic human values seem to show fixed positions in the motivational circular continuum. Those who still strongly believe in old values would often be in a weaker position as shown by dotted lines in figure three above. While adherents to a current worldview tradition would be in a strong position as shown by the same figure. Yet, it is possible that dotted lines could become solid if people get dissatisfied with the current worldview tradition and turn toward values in an old worldview tradition. That is why adherents to both current and past worldview traditions use conservation values as means of protecting their values and worldviews. For the same reason those who are currently sitting in the anxiety-free part of the motivational circular continuum could move to anxiety-avoidance section when their worldview tradition is weakened.

Values in the world's major religions come from premodern tradition. Yet, some religions adopt new worldview traditions more than others do. Christianity, for example, has been changing to a smaller extent along with changing worldview traditions. William of Ockham who introduced modernism did it in the name of Christian religion. He never liked the fact that Greek philosophy was finding its way into Christian thinking. Martin Luther followed in the footsteps of Ockham, leading to the Reformation. Like many other thinkers in dominant worldview traditions, they rely upon their Christian faith in doing so. They use their Christian faith as part of the debate in their relevant worldview traditions. Some of them initiated these worldview traditions.

However, Islam has remained fixed in the premodern tradition. For example, it 'defines itself in terms of submission rather freedom, and of duties rather than rights' (Sookhdeo, 2014: 46). Like any adherent of premodern tradition, Muslims strongly believe in the oneness and the sovereignty of God. For this reason they believe that there must be one law in the world to safeguard the oneness and sovereignty of God. This demonstrates a belief in the hierarchy of beings. Because of this, 'All Muslims in the world are united into a supranational body by their submission to the one god Allah and to his revelation through Muhammad in the Quran and *sunna*' (Sookhdeo, 2014: 33). Anybody who tries to introduce any worldview that disagrees with the hierarchy of beings becomes an enemy to all radical Muslims who believe they are united in Muslim *umma* under God. In Islam, '*umma* is both the community of Allah and the community of Muhammad, the community that accepts Allah's unity (*tawhid*) and Muhammad's priesthood (*risala*) as part of its self-definition' (Sookhdeo, 2014: 33). Since hierarchy of beings would also apply within one class of beings, Muslims believe they are higher in the hierarchy than non-Muslims are. This could be why Islamists feel it is a dishonour for Muslims to submit to non-Muslims, such as Christians. In addition, Muslims would think that Islamic values would rank higher than values of non-Muslims. Which means, it is not acceptable to Muslims to replace Islamic values with values of non-Muslims. Unlike modernists and postmodernists who put individual needs above those of a community, Muslims believe 'The individual's needs and desires are to be subordinate to those of the *umma*' (Sookhdeo, 2014: 33). In relation to the current postmodernism, Islam looks backward to restore premodern values threatened by postmodernist values, making it a serious opponent to postmodernism.

Muslims are not the only ones who prefer premodern values to postmodern values; orthodox Christianity also values premodern values. The only difference between orthodox Christians and Muslims is how radical Muslims react to perceived threats to their values. Unlike radical Muslims, orthodox Christians mostly bemoan changes in values in silence. The orthodox Christians who still maintain premodern teachings make sure that they limit their interaction with the changing world. The orthodox Christians who limit their interaction with the changing world of religion and secularism are now referred to by scholars as 'land-locked Orthodoxy' (Herescu, 2019: 3). The orthodox believers who are engaged with the changing world are changing, even though they may not be aware of changes in their orthodoxy. Along this line Herescu (2019: 6) concludes: 'In the context of secularization, pluralism and multiple modernities, it is essential to rediscover the Church as a hospital, not a tribunal—especially in connection to sensitive and difficult issues that affect individuals and communities.' The changing orthodox Christians recommend rediscovery. But this is not possible with pure orthodox Christians who rely solely on premodern teachings of Christianity.

Central Value Systems and Worldview Traditions in South Sudan

South Sudan Christians do not fit into a one-worldview tradition in the same way Muslims do. Christian leaders in South Sudan hold mixed views based on where they got their academic education. This is the same with political leaders. They hold different worldviews, depending on where they received academic education. Government officials who mainly studied and worked in Sudan before South Sudan became independent in 2011 seem to hold the premodern worldview that they learned from Muslims. Some government officials and religious leaders who have less education hold the African traditional worldview that looks like the premodern worldview. These mixed worldviews among South Sudanese make it difficult to describe what values they strongly hold onto. Yet, given the closeness of many South Sudanese worldviews to premodern tradition, it is likely that their central values align with premodern values.

Different communities have different ways of transmitting their values to their members over time. As Herdin and Aschauer (2013: 2) point out, 'Cultural habits are deeply grounded in society, transmitted from generation to generation and clearly reflected in certain basic values of the citizens.' Moreover, these communities have different ways of protecting their respective values from external ones. For this reason communities differ in what they value. Two countries may differ because their citizens are shaped in different ways by cultural systems of the two countries (Piurko, Schwartz, & Davidov, 2011). For example, countries in the Western world today value individualism strongly and countries in Asia and those in Africa value communal life strongly. Each of these cultures is mostly resistant to the opposite values even when they practice them in their own terms.

Resistance to external values by any individual or society sometimes happens at the unconscious level. This happens in tribal communities as well as in social classes. Like tribes that condition people's behaviour, 'social class gives rise to culture-specific selves and patterns of thinking, feeling, and acting' (Manstead, 2018: 171). When any society introduces new values, these new values may occasionally appear to be succeeding. Nevertheless, successes of new values may not last for a long time because of the unconscious resistance that often comes from established values. For example, the 1998 Constitution of Sudan appeared to have recognised the importance of human rights, but the resistance to human rights by the Islamists influenced the writers to include parts of the same Constitution that could cancel out parts that do not support Islamic values. This is because these Islamic values, as shown in chapter two, 'are deeply entangled in a web of material culture, collective behaviors, traditions, and social institutions' (Manfredo, et al., 2017: 775). It is difficult for any member of any group or society to deviate from his or her group's values. Groups idealize their values in ways that maintain their internal coherence.

Cultures that are tight like those dominated by Islam are more resistant to change than are loose cultures. This is because values serve as principles on which people guide their behaviours (Schwartz, 2006). Mainly, tight cultures are the ones 'with strong norms and low tolerance for deviance' (Manfredo, 2016: 776). Elders in communities with tight cultures transmit the communally agreed-upon norms to younger generations who, in turn, transmit them to generations following them. Tight cultures communally rely on conservation values such as tradition, security and conformity. Conservation value, as mentioned earlier, is developed at an early age by children in any society. Children learn their cultures by imitation. When they grow up, they 'abide by and enforce norms associated with the cultural practices they learn, and their learning appears to be driven by the desire for acceptance within the group' (Manfredo, 2017: 776).

Conservation values often act as deterrents to any threat to people's survival. For example, researchers 'found an association between tightness and conditions of resource scarcity, disease, and environmental threats' (Manfredo, 2017: 776). In tight cultures such as Islamist cultures, 'Value priorities may change in the short term and then revert to their previous state' (Manfredo, 2017: 777). That is what conservation is all about. Conservation values are more resistant to external influences when observed by a group than when they are individually observed. They are difficult to penetrate in the sense that 'even in the event of severe threats to one's life and social stability, people will cling to the prevailing ideology, associated norms, and institutions as appropriate and desirable' (Manfredo, 2017: 776). Loose cultures, on the other hand, are easy to penetrate because they leave the security of values to individuals.

Preliminary Conclusion

This chapter began with the question on what influences ethical decision-making of political and religious leaders in relation to social, religious and political matters in South Sudan. The sketched theories of decision-making do not give a convincing answer to the question for many reasons. One is that South Sudan politicians are probably not aware enough of the theories of decision-making to use them in their decision-makings. The other reason is that these theories of decision-making are developed to suit particular worldview traditions.

And people tend to follow their own worldview traditions. The theory of basic human values is close to answering what influences ethical decision-making in South Sudan. But it cannot explain why South Sudan politicians shifted their position from aligning themselves with Christianity in the united Sudan to aligning themselves, seemingly, with Muslims in independent South Sudan.

The theory of central value systems tries to explain the shifting of positions based on the conservation values that act as self-protectors to any value system. It is possible that any worldview tradition would have values that can easily change and values that cannot easily change. Values that cannot easily change are learned from childhood. The conservation values such as tradition, conformity and security are activated to protect any threatened worldview tradition and associated values. For example, liberals activate liberal tradition when conservatives are in power and are restoring premodern and modern values with which postmodernists do not agree. They also use conformity to ensure that their members conform to liberal values and tradition. The tradition is then guarded with security values. The same thing happens when liberals are in power and are making changes to conservative values. In this process, those who find themselves threatened take refuge in the anxiety-avoidance section of Schwartz' motivational circular continuum, while those who are in power occupy the anxiety-free section. In the united Sudan, for example, Muslims were the majority and were always in top leadership positions. Since there is no separation between state and Islamic religion in Islamic countries such as Sudan, religious values were enforced by the state. This means Muslims were in the anxiety-free section of the motivational circular continuum. Since Islamic sharia blocks non-Muslims from ruling Muslims, government officials who were Muslims were free from anxiety. Christians and politicians who were Christians were always in the anxiety-avoidance section of the circular continuum, activating conservation values to protect Christian values. Politicians who were Christians joined with Christians in the anxiety-avoidance section of the circle in order to protect their rights to political power.

When South Sudan got its independence from Sudan in 2011, Christians became the majority, and politicians who were Christians found they had unchallenged opportunities to get top political positions. Christians then replaced Muslims in the anxiety-free section of the motivational circular continuum and Muslims moved to the anxiety-avoidance section to protect Islamic values from disappearing. Since the most important thing for politicians in South Sudan is either holding onto political power or getting into power, they realised in 2013 and 2016 that Christian leaders were often criticising bad leadership and Muslims leaders were always quiet. Criticism of bad leadership made politicians anxious who wanted to hold onto unquestioned power. Therefore, they moved to the anxiety-avoidance section of the motivational circular continuum where they found Muslims already sitting there. That is, possibly, how South Sudan political leaders and Muslims teamed up. This means that there is no fixed position on the motivational circular continuum. What seems to be fixed is central value systems. Yet, it always appears to change when different adherents to different worldview traditions activate it. The following chapter will explore the extent to which the role of central value systems influence ethical decision-making in political, religious and social matters.

CHAPTER FOUR

CHRISTIAN AND GOVERNMENT VALUE CLASHES

Introduction

What is the nature of the conflict between so-called 'Christian values' and the values of constitutional governance (as prescribed in Article 8) in South Sudan? To answer this question, this chapter will explore what Christian values have in common with values of constitutional governance and where they differ. This will be done mainly in relation to how Christian leaders and theologians agree or disagree with constitutional values that affirm or contradict Christian values. Christian values include doing good to all people (Galatians 6: 10), loving God and neighbour (Mark 12: 30-31), love for one's enemies (Luke

6: 27-28), and self-denial in which one regards others as better than oneself (Philippians 2: 3). The constitutional values in Article 8 of South Sudan's Constitution include the separation of powers and functions, liberty and equal treatment of all. The aim of exploring Christian and constitutional values is to gain a deeper understanding of what makes the implementation of Article 8 in South Sudan's Constitution appear confusing.

We have seen how South Sudan leaders sided with Christianity in united Sudan, especially during north-south civil war. Now, they seem to side with Islam in independent South Sudan, regardless of Article 8 provisions. How South Sudan leaders make their decisions about with whom to side and with whom not to side, and at what time, raises questions that have already been explored and others that are yet to be explored. To answer the question of what influences the decision-making of South Sudan leaders, chapter three showed that it could be central value systems. The central value is a conservation value that consists of three subsets of values that include tradition, conformity and security. It develops from a particular worldview tradition in which one grows up. People seem to protect values that they receive earlier in their upbringing more than values they receive later in life as grown-ups.

Islam seems to differ from Christianity in maintaining old worldview traditions. We have noted that Muslims seem to hold onto premodern worldviews when defining the relationship between religion and state. The idea of relationship in premodern tradition is hierarchical in nature (Baird, 2016). Thinkers in premodern tradition might not have been systematic enough in their enquiries, but still believed in the importance of hierarchy. These thinkers are known as Pre-Socratic thinkers who mostly believed in the orderliness of nature as a whole. They introduced Greek science. Greek science includes the idea of the hierarchy of beings in which God is above everything and the rest of creation is ranked from angels, who are next to God, down to stones, non-living things at the lowest level of the hierarchy. This hierarchy of beings provides unity under the highest Being who is God. Premodern tradition would regard the state as an institution situated within the hierarchy in which God is the overall head. No institution or being would define itself outside this hierarchy in premodern tradition, and Muslims seem to agree with this.

In Islam, the state or *umma* cannot function separately from the hierarchy in which God is the overall authority. This is shown by the doctrine of *tawhid* or the divine unity (Sookhdeo, 2014). The divine unity is formulated in a manner that it translates to the oneness of state or *umma* in Islam. Unlike Christianity of today, 'Islam provides governing principles about the conduct of public life, constitutionalism and international relations' (Ahmed & Gouda, 2015: 28). The doctrine of divine unity or one-ness of Allah requires that Muslims must conform to the teaching of Islam and the Islamic law. Any deviation from the *tawhidic* doctrine is seen as a threat to Islam as a whole and can be corrected by any means, including violent jihad or holy war. In this case, the clash between Islamic values and constitutional values happens when a constitution promotes values that go against values defined by the doctrine of *tawhid*.

Christian values, unlike Islamic values, seem to change with changing worldview traditions. Christians do not seem to understand that 'the solutions to the major problems of today can be found in the enduring principles of the past' (Epstein, 2018: 95). It might be plausible, however, to argue that not every Christian community is open to change for the sake of change. Yet, almost all Christian denominations accommodate some of the changes taking place in their surroundings. This is probably why the premodern doctrine of divine unity rarely defines Christians' behaviours today in the same way that it does Muslims' behaviours. Even if Christians had doctrines that might have resembled the Islamic *tawhidic* doctrine in the Early and Medieval Church, it might not be the case today in the postmodernist Church. However, Christians and Muslims seem to share the idea that religion and state should focus on 'public order and the common good' (McConnell, 2013: 772).

Security as the Common Good

Occasionally, states and religious groups disagree on the understanding of the common good and public order. Yet, what seems to unite them is the need for safety or security of human beings. Sometimes, some people would stretch this security need from guarding against physical harm to ensuring no emotional harm to individuals. Nevertheless, whether it is physical or emotional security, the agreement between religion and state is that security matters, while disagreeing in what security or guarding against harm consists. These disagreements often centre on activities that could mean different things to different people. There might be slight differences in how law and order is maintained in secular, liberal and non-liberal states. Clashes in governance and religious values seem to occur in matters perceived as threatening social or religious harmony or order. Mainly, the focus is on the rights accorded different individuals or groups and how such rights or responsibilities are hampered.

Constitutional provisions of separation of religion and state are likely motivated by the need to protect the life and interests of all people. It is also likely that religious values aim at directing believers to the will of God, which matters for the sake of salvation. The result or hope of salvation is to have eternal life. This, again, goes back to the idea of preventing harm to anybody. The difficulty in harmonizing the conception of security between religion and state is that changes give people different worldviews on safety and security and how they are guaranteed.

Religious and Constitutional Value Clashes

Sometimes, state authorities see some religious activities and values as a threat to national security and would try to control them. Religious leaders, on their part, see some activities of state as hampering religious activities and values. Religious leaders also differ from state leaders in the prioritisation of values. Religious groups in some states, for instance, may value collective rights, but state authorities may value individual rights over collective rights. These differences may result in perpetual disagreement since 'Weighing values such as privacy against ones like national security or free speech is difficult' (Manta, 2018: 117). Moreover, differences in worldviews exist even within one country. For example, the constitution of the United States of America seems naturally to support liberalism and secularism, but conservatives still exist in the USA who can interpret the same constitution differently from liberals.

Most US citizens value individualism (Epstein, 2018). However, some US citizens may still strongly value communitarianism (McIntrye, 1981). Sometimes, US citizens who value individual rights over collective rights would still 'disagree once they have crystallized the heart of the dispute, which is that the prior values they chose or were taught do not mesh with the other person's' (Manta, 2018: 118). Such disagreement happens possibly because the values in which one was raised at an early age take precedence over values learned later in life at home, in schools or at workplaces. Prioritisation of values by people with diverse underlying values would look arbitrary to those who are not aware of potential roles of central value systems in ethical decision-making.

Clashes between religious values and values of constitutional governance seem to occur when some values are perceived to cause or contribute to public disorder. As Neo (2017: 337) points out, 'since protection of religious freedom is an instrumental and not an intrinsic value, restrictions are viewed as legitimate when the exercise of certain religious beliefs and/or practices may undermine peaceful coexistence.' Any society has people who do not agree with the norms and values with which their community predominantly agrees. They strongly believe in the openness to change value and are often ready to explore new ways of life. These new ways of life often clash with the agreed upon old ways of doing things in such a society. This is because 'there are the religious believers who cannot or will not fit this new social order into their worldview and, therefore, assert rights against it' (Hamilton, 2018: 79).

Religious values are among values that are not easily changed. They change over time in ways that are difficult to realise. Religion generally 'is embedded in authoritative communities involving texts, stories, institutions, leaders, and tradition' (McConnell, 2013: 784). Constitutional values can quickly change when they have been amended. Nevertheless, nobody can amend holy books on which religious values are based.

Any group that wants quick changes in existing values would regard itself vulnerable when getting continuous resistance from majority groups who never like quick changes to existing values. When a group defines itself as vulnerable, and constitutional provisions protect vulnerable groups against discrimination, then values of constitutional governance that do not include provisions against discrimination could change to accommodate such a group (DeGirolami, 2017). However, religious values would hardly change even if some groups deem such values discriminatory. This could possibly lead to clashes between religious values and values of constitutional governance. Both those who desire quick changes in existing values and those who resist such changes would claim constitutional protection. As Epstein (2018: 100) notes, 'This point is of great importance because, under any general rule, all individuals have both rights against others and correlative duties to them.'

Those who like 'openness to change values' would often want to see religion confined to private life and private places. They argue, 'The vulnerable are at risk from some religious who insist that their liberty does not end with their own practices but rather expands to include the culture around them' (Hamilton, 2018: 80). These people mainly want to be given unrestricted freedom to explore freely whatever comes to their minds. That is what self-direction implies. This way of thinking is mostly part of postmodernism. For example, a postmodernist would argue that one is free to reconstruct the world according to his or her own culture or his or her specific experiences (Veerachary, 2018). Some thinkers refer to this understanding of meaning in the world as anti-realism. Philosophers such as Foucault are believed to promote anti-realism in postmodernism.

Some religious groups do not think their values only apply to private life in private places. They believe that what happens in public affects what happens in private and vice-versa. This means that religious liberty does not only imply being free in private, but in public life also. Such freedom could be very limited. Religious leaders would argue that religious liberty is beneficial to public order because it potentially 'reduces civil strife, buffers the power of the state, and encourages civic virtue' (Lund, 2017: 495).

Religious Values and Harmony

In situations where individuals or groups feel vulnerable because of resistance to what they believe in as part of religious practices, they become angry. This anger could result in religious disharmony in religiously diverse countries. This is why some countries value collective rights and religious harmony over individual rights. The need for religious harmony forces a state to formulate policies that promote such harmony. Values driven by the need for harmony require conformity in order to achieve uniformity. This is because 'Religious harmony as *uniformity* may go beyond ensuring a lack of open conflict and instead entail suppressing or discouraging any disagreement that may lead to conflict' (Neo, 2019: 971).

Religious harmony contributes to public order. Public order then promotes security in the sense that it reduces conflicts among people with different beliefs and values. Scholars such as Hussin (2018: 100) point out that religious harmony involves 'careful balancing between the requirements of the state for order, the demands of religious communities for freedom of practice, and the need for these practices not to overlap into the sensitivities of other religious communities.' In this situation, clashes between religious values and values of constitutional governance may occur in a situation where any of these values is perceived as an obstacle to the badly needed harmony among different groups.

The above differences show that different people hold that some values are more important than others in relation to separation of religion and state. This is possibly the result of changing values in Christian religion. In these continually changing worldview traditions, values influenced by premodern tradition might be different from values influenced by Modernist tradition. The same applies to values influenced by postmodernism. Postmodernism Postmodernism, in which everything seems to be relative seems to define policies in the twenty-first century.. German idealists started postmodernism by arguing that self-consciousness is the key to reality (Baird, 2016). This self-consciousness, however, was different from the relativism that is popular in postmodernism today. The similarities between German idealism and postmodernism are mainly on the importance of the self and the primacy of emotions. Self-consciousness leads to the recognition of the other which in turn leads to struggle for domination. The struggle for domination results in contradiction where those who dominate others are also dominated indirectly by people they think they are dominating (Baird, 2016).

Because of changes in Christian values, I have not yet clarified how Christian values clashed with values of constitutional governance in the past and how they clash today. So I will explore different states that have the separation of church and state provisions in their constitutions. These include liberal and secular states, liberal and non-secular states and secular and non-liberal states. The aim is to understand whether religious values and values of constitutional governance do clash in these states. Understanding value clashes in these different types of states is not only crucial; it will also be important to know whether these clashes are of the same nature or if they differ and if so, what causes these differences. If the clashes were the same in these different states, then it would also be important to know why. The importance of exploring these different states in relation to separation of religion and state is to understand what type of system relates to South Sudan's constitutional provision of the separation of religion and state. Understanding how these states implement their legal provisions for religion and state separation will also help us understand why the implementation of Article 8 in the Constitution of South Sudan seems confusing.

Value Clashes in Secular and Liberal States

How a constitutional provision on the separation of church and state or the separation of religion and state is framed often determines whether a system is secular or not. The formulation of laws in secular states ensures that nothing in the law shows that the framers of such a law are siding with one or more religion against other religions. A secular state is 'a state where political authority does not depend on religious legitimation or authority, and religious authority does not dominate political authority' (Neo, 2017: 336). Because of this, values that guide legal provisions in secular states are expected to be neutral. Secular states, for example, strictly maintain neutrality in matters to do with religious practices and values. The assumption is that there are state values that every citizen should follow regardless of their religious affiliation, sex, colour of skin, or social status, among others. In a secular state, no single religion can dominate the affairs of state, religious identity does not determine one's citizenship and individual right to worship is important though not a fundamental right.

Liberalism is slightly different from secularism. Liberal states, for example, prioritise the autonomy of an individual over that of a community. In a liberal state or states, 'the government's role is not to make theological judgments but to protect the right of the people to pursue their own understanding of the truth, within the limits of the common good' (McConnell, 2013: 781). Neither state nor religious groups should coerce an individual to make choices against his or her will in theological matters. This means that liberal states pay less attention to group rights. Regarding decisions on the common good, liberal states rarely prefer one view of the good over the other (Neo, 2017).

Liberalism and Liberty of Individual's Conscience

Some scholars argue that the concept of liberalism in the United States of America today was popularised by John Rawls (Chapman, 2013). Rawls (1971) popularised liberalism in his strong belief that the conscience of an individual is what counts and should be respected. This, to Rawls, is an important aspect of a liberal democracy. His argument is that since 'an individual has a duty to worship God with conviction, he has a right among men to do so according to conscience' (Muñoz, 2016: 370). Possibly, 'The central reason a liberal constitutional regime should protect liberty of conscience is to gain the assent of those who hold irreconcilable, yet reasonable, religious, moral, and philosophical commitments' (Chapman, 2013: 1472).

Yet, the current postmodernist idea of individual autonomy in relation to freedom of religion goes beyond Rawls' ideas. It is mostly a modification of the prior concept of the natural rights of the individual. For example, the framers of the Free Exercise Clause in the United States Constitution 'generally held that religious free exercise is a natural right that belongs to all individuals' (Muñoz, 2016: 369). To them, the natural rights of an individual to practice religious beliefs freely could exist in the absence of the state and its recognition of such rights.

When the United States of America was founded, the premodern worldview had not yet disappeared in many peoples' underlying values. It is possibly for this reason that the importance of God as a creator defined American founders' understanding of religious liberty. The framers of the US Constitution believed that religious liberty is outside of the state's regulatory power. For example, 'the framers held that whatever belongs exclusively to that right remains beyond the government's direct prohibition and regulation' (Muñoz, 2016: 371).

Mostly, liberal states recognize the sovereignty of an individual or of a state in matters connected to religious liberty.

Because of this perceived lack of state power in regulating religious matters, the US Constitution makes it clear that Congress shall make no laws prohibiting free exercise of religion. This restriction of Congress may extend to other state institutions such as the judiciary. If so, it is difficult to control even harmful practices of religion under the common principle of doing no harm to anybody. There are areas in which the state prohibits discrimination against anybody. However, the free exercise of religion would mean that what the state deems discriminatory might not be considered discriminatory by religious authorities, since holy books define what should and should not be done. This further implies that a state is prohibited from defining what is discriminatory in religion. The same restriction of the state from making laws that prohibit free exercise of religion may mean that religious groups or religious leaders could assume that what they believe matters in relation to national security. Such an assumption by religious leaders may lead to failures in guaranteeing national security as understood by the state.

Such failure would lead to clashes between the state and religious groups in such a state. To complicate matters, the naturally free religion is not only free as an institution in liberal states. It is also free as a collection of individuals who have natural rights to exercise their religious beliefs within religious institutions of their choice. These individuals are entitled to their natural freedom of conscience. Since these individuals have inalienable rights to their natural freedom of conscience, it means nobody, even religious leaders, could prohibit whatever these free individuals decide to follow as part of their religious beliefs and practices. Nevertheless, when decisions of these free individuals are harmful to others, deciding where the limit to their freedom of conscience is becomes complex. These complexities may explain many of the clashes between religious values and values of constitutional governance in liberal states. This section will, therefore, explore areas in which religious values and values of constitutional governance clash in secular and liberal states.

Mitigating Disagreements in
Liberty of Conscience and Individual Choices

The idea behind liberty of conscience is that an individual determines the answer to questions about the existence of God and how to follow religious practices in accordance with such an understanding of God's existence. In the process of choice, disagreements arise between individuals. To mitigate these disagreements, 'the principles of toleration and liberty of conscience must have an essential place in any constitutional democratic conception' (Chapman, 2013: 1473). However, mere toleration may not guarantee peaceful coexistence among individuals with different views about God's existence and religious practices based on such understandings. To secure meaningful coexistence among individuals, liberal states 'lay down the fundamental basis to be accepted by all citizens as fair and regulative of the rivalry between doctrines' (Chapman, 2013: 1473). However, this is not easy.

Any value system 'that bases itself on choice cannot help but rely itself on some assumptions, but it minimizes the number of these assumptions and holds the promise of creating a world in which individuals can coexist more easily than in alternative systems' (Manta, 2018: 118). The freedom of choice accorded to individuals is assumed to help them individually choose and follow what they believe to be good and reasonable. Yet, each person may possibly infringe the rights of others when deciding and following what he or she deems good.

Courts are important for adjudicating issues arising from competing rights and conceptions of the good among individuals in liberal and secular states. As Alexander (2019: 1071) points out, 'Courts have interpreted the Clause to mean that while the government can place no limits on one's religious beliefs, it can place some limits on the freedom to practice one's religion.' Free individuals in liberal states may avoid state regulatory powers on religious beliefs and practices, but it would be difficult for them to avoid state laws as interpreted by the courts. This is because a court 'permits limited restrictions on the freedom to exercise one's faith because religious freedom may affect others in society' (Alexander, 2019: 1072). However, in this process,

> ...*a court must first decide (a) whether an individual has a claim involving a sincere religious belief, and (b) whether the government action places a substantial burden on the person's ability to act on that belief. If these two elements are established, then the government must show (c) that it is acting in furtherance of a 'compelling state interest', and (d) that it has pursued that interest in the manner least restrictive, or least burdensome, to religion' (Alexander, 2019: 1072).*

Any court in liberal states such as the United States of America follows these steps in order to avoid arbitrary rulings on religious matters. Such arbitrariness would be highly likely in the absence of guidelines because the understanding of a 'compelling state interest' may differ from one judge to another. As McConnell (2013: 784) observes, 'much litigation involves religious ritual, ecclesiastical form, and tradition' that may be more complex than simply figuring out how they affect state interest.

In some court cases what seems simple may turn out to be complex. For example, Jack Phillips, a baker in Colorado in the USA refused to sell a wedding cake to a same-sex couple in 2012, arguing that 'he would not use his talents to convey a message of support for same-sex marriage at odds with his religious faith' (Alexander, 2019: 1096). This refusal angered the same-sex couple who sued Phillips. The Colorado Civil Rights Commission took on the case. Phillips was accused of violating the Colorado Anti-Discrimination Act (CADA). This Act prohibits anyone from discriminating against other people on the basis of their sexual orientations. The Colorado Civil Rights Commission investigated the case and found that Phillips had been refusing to sell wedding cakes to many same-sex couples based on his religious freedom claims. The Commission then tried the case and ruled that Phillips acted in a way that discriminated against people based on sexual orientation rather than just opposition to same-sex marriage. The Commission ordered Phillips to rewrite the policies and values of his bakery so that same-sex couples should not be refused services.

Phillips appealed against the orders of the Colorado Civil Rights Commission. However, the Colorado Court of Appeals upheld the decision of the Commission. Phillips appealed again to the Colorado Supreme Court. But the Colorado Supreme Court refused to look into the case. The case was then taken to the United States Supreme Court. The U.S. Supreme Court reversed the decision of the Colorado Civil Rights Commission in June 2018. The U.S. Supreme Court Justices argued that the Commission had not considered in a neutral and respectful manner 'Phillips's claim that his right to free exercise of religion entitled him to disregard the state's anti-discrimination law' (Alexander, 2019: 1097). Further evidence showing lack of state neutrality was that one of the members of the Colorado Civil Rights Commission threatened that Phillips would not be allowed to do business in Colorado if he continued to act based on his religious beliefs. Moreover, the U.S. Supreme Court Justices argued that the

Commission's lack of fairness towards Phillips was demonstrated by one of its members arguing that religion had been used in history to justify different kinds of discrimination.

Phillips' case is more complex than simple. It is complex because some people would argue that it generates more controversies than solutions. Alexander (2019: 1100), for instance, thinks the U.S. Supreme Court in its ruling 'did not address the larger question of whether the right to religious liberty must yield to an otherwise valid exercise of state power to ban discrimination in public accommodations based on sexual orientation' because it determined that the Commission was not impartial and fair to Phillips. Moreover, the U.S. Supreme Court 'did not determine whether the baker's religious freedom claim prevailed over the couple's antidiscrimination claim in denying the couple's request to purchase a wedding cake' (Alexander, 2019: 1097). The U.S. Supreme Court pointed out that a lack of state neutrality denied Philips of fair opportunity.

Liberal and secular states seem to have infinite opportunities for argument on questions about state neutrality on religious matters, non-discrimination and individual autonomy. Sometimes individuals would stretch this autonomy to try to control whatever other people say, even if what most of the people say would qualify as freedom of speech. They argue that they should be left alone in everything that they do. They seem to forget that 'the right to be let alone cannot mean that no one is entitled to comment on a wedding, even after a public announcement of the event' (Epstein, 2018: 105). The liberal and secular state, on the one hand, seems to provide legal principles governing its relationship with religion and on the other hand cancel them out. For example, provisions for the free exercise of religious exemptions exclude harmful practices. However, an individual's right to choose how to practice his or her religion would sometimes cancel out the Harm

Principle by making it difficult for judges to define what the harm is. As McConnell (2013: 804) points out, 'neither courts nor scholars have given serious analytical attention to what counts as "harm".'

Freedom of Choice and Doing-No-Harm Principle

There is no question about understanding obvious harmful acts such as torturing innocent people for being infidels or pagans. However, how one weighs practices that are harmful to other people's feelings is difficult. Sometimes, those who make more noise about what has been done to them might be considered more harmful than the actions or words of the people who offended them. Sometimes, what the majority says against the minority is considered more harmful, even if acts of the minority desecrate what the majority strongly believes is sacred. The underlying or central values seem to motivate people to make choices that they strongly believe in, though activities associated with such choices could be seen as harmful by people with different values. If the principle of engagement in issues to do with individual rights starts from unrestricted freedom of choice for individuals, then clashes of values become endless in the sense that no authority exists to define common ways of doing things.

A state might be the appropriate authority to define common ways of doing things because a state accepts some practices as normal and mandatory. The state would then require all its citizens to follow such practices. Nevertheless, whatever a state deems reasonable may not be reasonable to certain religious groups. For example, the United States government requires owners of health insurance companies to provide contraceptives that include abortifacient drugs to their clients (McConnell, 2013). Yet, some religious groups regard abortion as immoral, and would regard coercion to pay for such services as a violation of their consciences. Those denied contraceptives and abortion services would regard the act of religious people as harmful to them. But religious people who strongly consider abortion as immoral would deem being forced to do what they do not believe in as harmful, not just to their consciences but also to their salvation.

Some policymakers and policy implementers in secular and liberal states would argue that accommodation of religious practices should only be granted through legislation. Hamilton (2018), for example, argues that it is unfortunate that some people think that their freedom of religion would entitle them to cross the line of the doing-no-harm principle. This is 'because the Free Exercise Clause provides the clearest signal that the correct default position is that religious actors are accountable to the law and that accommodation should only occur legislatively after there is deliberate weighing of an accommodation and potential harm' (Hamilton, 2018: 94). The neutrality of the state, in this case, should apply in the sense that the enforcement of safety laws and regulations is done in an impartial and fair manner.

Central Value Systems and State Actors

State actors in secular and liberal states sometimes face the challenge of 'finding the right balance between the goals of protecting religious freedom and prohibiting discrimination' (Alexander, 2019: 1075). Occasionally, political leaders enact laws that do not balance protection of religious freedom and prohibition of discrimination. Moreover, some laws are enacted in a manner that gives license for discrimination. Above all, lawmakers in secular states are expected to enact laws without any favourite group in mind.

Yet, such neutrality could be undermined sometimes by central values of legislators in such secular and liberal states. For example, the

Trump Administration in the United States talked about the need to promote religious liberty globally. However, this seemed to be driven mostly by security values and the need for conformity more than by the neutral need for religious freedom. Spinelli (2019: September 23), for instance, argues that the Trump Administration liked to mention countries such as Nicaragua and Venezuela as suppressing religious liberty. However, the Administration rarely mentioned 'an ally which Pew rates as one of the worst suppressors of religious freedom: Saudi Arabia' (Spinelli, 2019: September 23).

In ten years of research by the Pew Research Center (2019), Nicaragua and Venezuela never appear among the twenty leading countries that suppress religious liberty, but Saudi Arabia does. For instance, Saudi Arabia is among the leading twenty countries that favour particular religions over others. It is among the leading ten countries with policies that are most restrictive of religious freedom and among the ten leading countries that most limit activities of religious groups and individuals.

Saudi Arabia has no provision in its Constitution for freedom of religion. In the kingdom, 'public practice of all non-Muslim religions is illegal in the country, including public worship, proselytization and display of religious symbols' (Pew Research Center, 2019: 18). Moreover, 'It is also illegal for Muslims to convert to another religion' in Saudi Arabia (Pew Research Center, 2019: 18). Even other Islamic sects such as Shia find it hard to operate freely in Saudi Arabia. In April 2019, for example, Saudi Arabia executed thirty-seven Shia Muslims, accusing them of being linked with terrorist organizations (Spinelli, 2019: September 23). In 2017, Saudi Arabia enacted a counter terrorism law which criminalizes people who would challenge, 'either directly or indirectly, the religion or justice of the King or Crown Prince' (Pew Research Center, 2019: 18). It would also be a criminal offense for anybody 'to cast doubt on the fundamentals of Islam' (Pew Research

Center, 2019: 18). The same offense would apply to anybody publishing anything that would contradict any provision in the Islamic law.

Despite all the above, the Trump Administration was willing to support Saudi Arabia against Iran to the point of trying to sell arms to the kingdom. The conflict between Iran and Saudi Arabia is not caused by mere political disagreements; it is religious. Yet, the Trump Administration accused Iran of religious liberty suppression more than it did Saudi Arabia. Vice President Mike Pence, for example, once criticised countries that criticised 'Iran for their persecution of religious minorities' (McArdle, 2019: September 23). The countries criticised by Vice President Pence never included Saudi Arabia. However, if freedom of religion in Iran and Saudi Arabia were compared, then Iran would rank better than Saudi Arabia because it allows other religions some limited freedom to operate in the country. There are, for example, about 500,000 to 1,000,000 Christians in Iran (World Watch Monitor, 2017: August 22) but almost no Christians in Saudi Arabia. Yet, the Trump Administration still overlooked the violation of religious liberty in Saudi Arabia and talks tough against the same in Iran, even when Iran is better than Saudi Arabia on the matter.

This likely contradiction in the promotion of religious liberty by the Trump Administration in the USA was possibly caused by a central value system. The values of security, conformity and tradition in central value systems seem to feature highly in whether or not the USA favours a country such as Iran or Saudi Arabia. Security and conformity values were probably the drivers of likely confusions in the Trump Administration's policies on religious liberty.

Economic and physical security seem to go hand in hand in the USA. President Trump, for example, believed that good relationships between the USA and Saudi Arabia would 'create hundreds of thousands of jobs, tremendous economic development, and much additional wealth for the United States' (Spinelli, 2019: September 23). Saudi Arabia seemed to represent economic security for the United States, but Iran seemed to pose a physical threat to the USA because its leaders do not conform to the United States' policies and norms. In relation to conformity, Saudi leaders listen to American leaders, but Iranian leaders do not respect any directives from them.

The literature explored above shows clearly that secular and liberal states focus more on the freedom of individuals and the neutrality of state in relation to religious beliefs and practices. However, the confusion in the promotion of religious liberty by the Trump Administration demonstrates the potential power of central value systems in decision-making.

Value Clashes in Liberal and Non-Secular States

Clashes of religious values with values of constitutional governance in liberal and non-secular states are different from such clashes in secular and liberal states. In these states, clashes of religious values and values of constitutional governance happen when rights of individuals are violated, and when state actors do not show neutrality in religious matters. Rights of individuals in liberal states are guaranteed in the sense that state and religious authorities do not coerce anyone to make particular choices in religious beliefs and practices. However, in liberal and non-secular states, rights of individuals are guaranteed, but religion is not separated from the state (Neo, 2017). Values of constitutional governance and religious values can overlap in non-secular states.

Individual autonomy remains the guiding principle in liberal and non-secular states such as South Africa. Because of this, a clash of religious values with values of constitutional governance results in coercion of individuals to make choices with which they are not comfortable. This section will, therefore, explore the nature of clashes in values in liberal and non-secular states. The comparison of value clashes in this section will mostly be between secular and liberal states with liberal and non-secular states. This will be done in order to understand how some aspects of these different value clashes relate to value clashes in South Sudan. The value clashes in South Sudan will mainly be explored in section five of this chapter.

Overviewing Interactions Between South Africa and South Sudan

South Africa is one example of a liberal and non-secular state. It is important partly because it interacted with South Sudan before and after South Sudan's independence. This interaction was often through a consortium of Christian organisations called Operation Lifeline Sudan (OLS) that was giving humanitarian support to people in the SPLM/A controlled areas during the North-South civil war. That interaction was not political, making it unlikely that issues of constitutional governance would feature in discussions between OLS officials, most of whom were from South Africa, and the SPLM/A leaders. Moreover, while OLS was operating in South Sudan, there was a very limited focus on constitutional governance within areas controlled by the SPLM/A since the SPLM/A was still a rebel movement. However, sometimes SPLM/A leaders would talk about their disapproval of mixing religion and state in Sudan. During those discussions issues of constitutional governance in South Africa might have come up.

Real political interaction between the two countries started after South Sudan became independent from Sudan. It came from political cooperation between the African National Congress (ANC) of South Africa and the SPLM of South Sudan and seems to have begun after Article 8 had already been included in South Sudan's Constitution. It would, therefore, be difficult to know whether the South African

Constitution inspired Article 8. Yet, one could still assume that South African constitutional aspects of governance might have directly or indirectly influenced the creation of South Sudan's constitution through these limited interactions.

The South African Constitution has no provision 'ensuring separation between state and religion' (Henrico, 2019: 5) and so could not have inspired Article 8(1) in South Sudan's Constitution. In this sense, South Sudan would constitutionally be like secular states and South Africa would not. Moreover, South Africa is legally liberal and South Sudan is not. Like liberal states, the South African Constitution of 1996 recognizes individual rights in religious matters. For example, 'section 15 is grounded on what the individual believes, irrespective of whether or not anyone else shares her belief' (Matthee, 2019: 120). Individual rights to religious freedom trump collective rights in South Africa as in many liberal states. In South Africa, 'the foundation for the collective right is the individual right to freedom of Religion' (Matthee, 2019: 117). Above all, 'religion is understood in an individualist sense' (Matthee, 2019: 124) in South Africa.

Constitutional Values Defining Ideological Status of South Africa

South Africa is not often neutral in religious matters in the way that secular and liberal states such as the USA are. Plaatjies van Huffel (2019: 137) believes South Africa 'upholds a form of the co-operative model' even though elements of separation of church and state would be missing. This is because 'the co-operative model is characterized by a constitutional separation between church and state coupled with mutual agreements between the state and various recognized religions' (Plaatjies van Huffel, 2019: 137). The South African Constitution has no provision on church and state separation. Some judges in South Africa seem to believe that the South African Constitution is strictly neutral on religious matters. However, Matthee (2019) argues that such constitutional understanding is flawed. South African lawmakers formulated the Constitution to make it clear that South Africa is not a secular state. For example, the word secular 'was deliberately not included in the 1996 Constitution of South Africa' (Plaatjies van Huffel, 2019: 139).

In real liberal and secular states such as the USA, state authorities and institutions do not get involved in sponsoring religious activities. They also try as much as they can to avoid religious influence in running state affairs. Real liberal and secular states are also strictly neutral in religious matters. However, in South Africa, 'allowance is made for the state to participate in and sponsor religions, but only on a basis of the equal treatment of religions' (Henrico, 2019: 4). In treating all religions equally, Article 8(2) in South Sudan's Constitution may resemble that of South Africa. Yet, the resemblance of these two constitutions on equal treatment of all religions might be a mere coincidence.

Clashes of Religious and Governance Values in South Africa

Clashes of religious values and values of constitutional governance in South Africa seem to relate mostly to the understanding of South Africa as a liberal and non-secular democracy. In liberal states such as South Africa, state actors do not regulate religious beliefs and practices since decisions on religious matters are left to individual conscience. For this reason, some religious people, such as Radley Henrico, openly opposed the proposal by the Commission for the Promotion and Protection of the Rights of Cultural, Religious and Linguistic Communities to regulate religious activities in South Africa. Henrico (2019: 12) argues that regulating religious practices would amount to 'violation of the constitutional guarantee to freedom of religion in the country.'

The main concern of the opponents of the bill was the violation of freedom of religion stipulated in the Constitution. However, the government wanted to minimize the danger posed by some religious practices. The Commission, for example, wanted to protect individuals from potential harm when it proposed a bill to regulate dangerous religious practices. As Forster (2019: 18) puts it, 'The reasons given by the state for wanting to regulate religion and religious leaders was for the safeguarding of the human rights of South African citizens.' For example, one self-styled prophet of doom 'sprayed an insecticide with the brand name Doom in the faces and on the bodies of congregants during church services for purported healing purposes' (Henrico, 2018: 8). Others include incidences in 2015 in South Africa where a church leader 'made congregants eat snakes, drink petroleum and remove their clothing as part of their religious worship' (Henrico, 2018: 8).

Religious groups and individuals believe that South African government authorities have the right to control dangerous religious practices. However, Henrico (2018: 16) argues that it would be 'more suitable that in instances where one seeks to limit religious freedom a court, as opposed to a regulatory body, should be the adjudicator.' Nothing justifies government's attempt to regulate religious practices. As Henrico (2018: 6) argues, 'Religion and the freedom to practice one's beliefs are matters left to the conscience and personal subjective belief of each person.'

Value clashes in South Africa are not limited to issues that seem to curtail individual religious freedom. The heart of value clashes seems to be the 'doing-no-harm principle.' Because of this principle the Commission attempts to regulate religious practices. There are things that religious leaders do not believe are harmful, but state authorities do. One example is whether or not corporal punishment is justified in schools. Some religious people believe that corporal punishment is justified for the greater good of a child, which state actors do not think right. The clash of state and religious values on corporal punishment was adjudicated by court in South Africa in *Christian Education SA v. Minister of Education, 2000 (4) SA 757 (CC)*. The court ruled against corporal punishment even if it is done on the basis of religious belief, arguing that limitation of this religious belief was justifiable (Matthee, 2019). The court gave the same ruling against harmful practices in the case of using dagga for religious purposes (Matthee, 2019).

Violation to equal treatment of all people is another area in which religious groups clash with state actors. For example, the 'South African Schools Act 1996' allows equitable free and voluntary religious observance for all religions in public schools. In 2003, the new national education policy 'meritoriously barred confessional, sectarian religion from public schools, but permitted the teaching of Religion Studies as an academic subject and allowed for religious observances, under the proviso that these were offered in a fair and equitable manner' (Plaatjies van Huffel, 2019: 145-146). Any violation of this law leads to clashes between religious groups and state actors. For example, diversity in dress code on religious grounds is accepted in public schools in South Africa. Some religious groups value some ways of dressing. They consider preventing them from doing so a violation of their religious freedom 'as stated in article 9 of the Constitution' (Plaatjies van Huffel, 2019: 147).

Yet, some public school authorities in South Africa would not consider banning headscarves 'as a violation of the freedom of religion of their learners' (Plaatjies van Huffel, 2019: 147). They base their disapproval of such dress on the legally approved dress code of a school. In this case, locally approved values of public schools seem to clash with both religious values and values of constitutional governance in Article 9 of the Constitution. However, locally approved laws in public schools would agree with the Constitution in the sense 'that in public schools a particular religious ethos must not exercise excessive control or authority over others' (Plaatjies van Huffel, 2019: 147). Yet, since South Africa is a liberal but non-secular democracy, issues may not be black and white in cases like these. Some people would argue that South Africa falls under a co-operative model. This 'model combines constitutional separation and mutual recognition' (Plaatjies van Huffel, 2019: 147).

Clashes between religious values and values of constitutional governance sometimes occur in issues to do with human rights. Palm (2019: 184) points out that some people believe that 'Christian values and God's sovereignty' would rank higher than human values that include human rights. Others argue differently. For example, Palm (2019: 186) argues, 'The historical lesson of the dangers of a systematic polarizing of rights and Christianity needs to be acknowledged as it has an ongoing legacy today.'

Value clashes in relation to human rights are likely based on individual perceptions. For example, religious people regard some practices as sinful, but state actors may not. State actors see decisions by religious leaders against individuals on those bases as human rights violations. Yet, the South African Constitution guarantees some rights for religious institutions. In the same way, the Constitution guarantees some rights for non-religious people or even for religious people with different understandings of biblical values and principles.

Some religious leaders hold that 'the Church believes in the Bible as the word of God and that it functions as the superior and ultimate instruction for personal life conduct and the collective life of faith, and that this finds expression in the church's statement of faith' (Van der Walt, 2019: 225). Others regard such a position as discriminatory and that it should change. Van der Walt (2019: 228), for example, argues that religious institutions should 'explore the values of human dignity and equality as proposed by the Constitution, considering how these link to values of radical hospitality, justice, and love, which are so central to the Christian gospel.'

Central Value Systems and Value Clashes in South Africa

People who strongly argue differently on the above-mentioned issues are mostly religious. However, their central value systems differ. In liberal and non-secular states like South Africa, some people may strongly believe in individual liberty and others may not. Some may even believe in secularism in a state that does not have legal provision for secularism. Seedat (2019: 201), for example, thinks South Africa is a secular state when she argues, 'Democratic secularism in South Africa has been guided by constitutional guarantees for freedom of religion.' It is likely her belief in values of secularism that makes her think the South African Constitution guarantees secularism when the reality is the opposite.

Postmodernist values such as self-direction seem to motivate others in opposing religious values in favour of what they believe are constitutional values. Yet, constitutional values could be open to different interpretation in Postmodernism. Postmodernism takes the consciousness of the self as crucial. Individuals define reality in Postmodernism, making it relative to consciousness of the self (Baird, 2016). Some scholars believe that Postmodernism was mainly influenced by movements of Continental Philosophy that used Structuralism and Existentialism alongside Phenomenology to understand reality (Veerachary, 2018). German idealism was part of this continental movement. However, true Postmodernism developed in the late twentieth century. Jean-Francois Lyotard, Jacques Derrida, Michel Foucault, Jean Baudrillard among others are some of the leading Postmodern philosophers. Their models of analysis include Post-Structuralism and Deconstructionism.

Postmodernists such as Derrida argue that a reader of any text can make a subjective meaning out of a text even if the author does not seem to mean what the reader understands as its meaning. This replaces the authority of an author in determining meanings with the authority of a reader, regardless of whether the reader's authority is misplaced. This way of looking at meaning in a text can also translate to looking at issues in one's environment. Continental movements including Postmodernism were mainly sceptical of analytical philosophy and most of its associated values.

Postmodernists mainly view themselves as non-absolutists. According to Vorster (2009: 508), 'Postmodernism posits that truth is relative and that moral codes can never be seen as fixed codes.' In Postmodernism, metanarrative that was popular in Modernism is regarded as less important.[1] Veerachary (2018: 35) points out that 'A metanarrative refers to a unifying story that seeks to explain how the world is in other words a metanarrative is a worldview.' Postmodernists generally put more emphasis on pluralism. They reject the notion that reason can explain the truth more than religion because religion and secularism are regarded as expressing faith positions that mean different things to different people. These faith positions might not necessarily agree on the definition of reality, but they are seen as equally valid (Vorster, 2009).

When one grows up in a particular worldview tradition, opposite traditions would stay in the periphery of such a person's value system. Many people who grow up in liberal tradition would see conservatism as backward. Those who grow up in a conservative environment would

---

1   Many scholars agree that Kuhn (1970) describes very well the reasons behind the emergence of Postmodernism. However, this study uses recent sources to sketch postmodernist thinking that has implications for the understanding of values today. Even though Postmodernism started in the first half of the 20th century, it was not popular until the second half of the century. Lyotard (1979) is believed to have popularized the term Postmodernism.

see liberalism as pointless. These differences, often seen within a country like South Africa, contribute to clashes between religious values and values of constitutional governance. This is because individuals with different worldviews are the ones who lead and are members of institutions. Judges who adjudicate clashes in countries like South Africa also have different worldview traditions that form their central values that may sometimes interfere with their interpretation of constitutional provisions and other laws. We now turn to how value clashes happen in non-liberal and secular states.

Value Clashes in Non-Liberal and Secular States

Separation of religion and state in secular and liberal states focuses more on liberty of an individual and the neutrality of state in the process of guaranteeing that liberty. A liberal and secular state regards its powers as limited in dealing with religious issues. This is probably because secular institutions cannot regulate the relationship of God and individual. Clashes between religious and state values in secular and liberal states happen when one oversteps its mandate and tries to force its values on the other. They only agree on values that they believe serve the common good. In liberal and non-secular states, the clashes of religious and governance values happen when regulators interfere with an individual's autonomy and liberty of conscience. We will focus on how non-liberal and secular states differ from secular and liberal states as well as from liberal and non-secular states in prioritising religious freedom and values. A non-liberal and secular state refers to a state that rarely promotes individual autonomy as part of religious freedom. Such a state might or might not be neutral in religious matters. It is neutral when it comes to favouring one religion over others but not so in rendering services to religious groups equally. For example, Article

152(1) of the Singapore Constitution gives the state the responsibility to take care of minority religions without favouritism.

Aspects of secularism are the same in liberal and secular states as well as in non-liberal and secular states. Neo (2017: 337) mentions four characteristics common to secular states:

> *First, the secular state must entail a rejection of permanent political dominance by any religion. Secondly, in such a secular state, citizenship should not be conditioned on a person's religious identity. Thirdly, such a secular state must recognize the availability of an individual right to religious freedom, even if such a right may not be prioritized as a fundamental right. Lastly, religious freedom must be protected as a function of the public good.*

The Differences are in Liberal and Non-Liberal Aspects

A non-liberal state, in comparison with liberal state, does not recognize individual autonomy as an important part of religious freedom (Neo, 2020) but protects the collective aspects of religions and their practices. The other likely difference from liberal states is that non-liberal states intervene in religious matters that they regard as threatening to safety and public good and also regulate relationships among different religious groups (Thio, 2010; Zaccheus, 2018)). A non-liberal state considers the promotion of public order as an important part of its mandate (Loh, 1998). Most such states are in Asia and Africa which seem to value harmony and social order over other norms (Okoye, Ezeanya, & Chukwuma, 2018; Kibret, 2015; Issifu, 2016; Neo, 2020; Hutchinson & Pendle, 2015). Laws focus on 'the importance of religious harmony as a legal, political, and constitutional norm in various Asian countries' (Neo, 2019: 968).

For simplicity, Singapore will be used to represent non-liberal and secular states just as the USA and South Africa represent states that constitutionally resemble each other in state and religion relationships. Reasons for choosing these countries are that court cases are available which demonstrate the clashes between religion and state values and literature is available which shows strengths and weaknesses of each system of constitutional governance. However, little has been written on the nature of secular and non-liberal states and so I am building on new work by Jaclyn Neo who is the only person who has differentiated secularism from non-liberalism in a way that is useful to my comparisons. I will use her limited work to interpret the situation in South Sudan. Neo is a professor of law at the National University of Singapore (NUS). She probably understands the nature of secular and non-liberal states in comparison with secular and liberal states better than other scholars partly because she did her academic studies at NUS in Singapore and at Yale University in the USA, giving her contextual understanding.

Nature of Value Clashes in Secular and Non-Liberal States

Exploring clashes of values in secular and non-liberal states will be important later in assessing where South Sudan belongs in its constitutional governance, especially in relation to the separation of religion and state. The nature of clashes of values in South Sudan are still murky at this point but may be clearer after exploring value clashes in Singapore. Even though there is no evidence of interaction between people in South Sudan and in Singapore, the two countries share a belief in collectivism more than in individualism.

Singapore is in Asia which resembles Africa in some value respects. Most Asian countries, like many African states, value collectivism over individualism. This makes it difficult for them to be liberal in the real sense of liberalism. South Africa is liberal in Africa because those who were mostly dominant in its constitution-making before 1994 were white South Africans who were mainly influenced by individual values in their former home states in Europe. Black South Africans were generally powerless in politics before 1994. They never had the privilege of making decisions on what should and should not be included in the constitution of South Africa. Otherwise, it would have been difficult to have liberalism in the South African Constitution today.

Secularism and Harmony Value in Singapore

Lawmakers in Singapore might have opted for secularism instead of liberalism because Singaporeans generally value public harmony, though secularism is not mentioned in the Constitution (Neo, 2017). Even though people in Singapore, like other people in Asia, naturally love harmony, 'religious harmony does not appear in the text of the Singapore Constitution, but is instead implied, presumably, as part of public order which is in the constitutional text' (Neo, 2019: 976). Yet, this love for harmony is shown by other laws in Singapore such as the Maintenance of Religious Harmony Act (MRHA). As Neo (2019: 967) points out, this harmony-motivated choice of secularism over liberalism in Singapore 'may be understandable because of skepticism that harmony is illiberal and entails the subordination of individual interests and rights to wider social, often statist, interests.' However, Singapore is not unique in its harmony-motivated choice of legal provisions.

The love for public harmony is mainly dominant in Asian and African values. But, it does not mean that other continents do not value harmony. The need for public harmony might exist as a minor or major value in other continents, though it might have different connotations and terminologies. In Europe, for example, the need for harmony is mentioned in Article 3(1) of the Irish Constitution. During the Enlightenment, harmony seems to have been one of major values in Europe, though referred to in different terms. As Neo (2019: 968) notes, 'one could possibly discern an idea akin to religious harmony in John Locke's writing when he speaks of tolerance and peace among religious groups.' What differs now among different states in different continents is the prioritisation of values. Public harmony could be an important value in many countries but might not be regarded as a priority value as in Singapore and some other secular and non-liberal states.

Harmony Laws and Clashes of
Religious and Governance Values in Singapore

Lawmakers in non-liberal states such as Singapore do not talk of religious neutrality. They are explicitly committed to managing religious pluralism for the sake of harmony. Since 'religious harmony points to the need to avoid inter-religious conflict' (Neo, 2019: 970), clashes between religious values with values of constitutional governance seem to relate to practices that promote disharmony among the people in Singapore. Religious leaders sometimes may not agree with how the state enforces its harmony-motivated laws which have aspects that might not be good for the advancement of religion (Grim & Finke, 2011; Rajah, 2012). One aspect is the restriction of freedom of speech even within the confines of religious institutions and places of worship (Zaccheus, 2018). Other countries such as the USA exempt places of worship from these restrictions because they consider them as sanctuaries.

Religious harmony laws may sometimes restrict what religious groups consider important to their religious practice. For example, religious harmony laws are used in Singapore 'to justify state prohibition of the headscarf—tudung or hijab—by students in public schools as well as in certain public sector jobs, such as in the police force or the military' (Neo, 2019: 976). This could go against religious rights that the same laws claim to guarantee. However, the reason behind these restrictions is that granting particularised religious rights to different religious groups by the state is sometimes counterproductive. For example, if one religious community aggressively asserts its rights such as wearing a headscarf or hijab, others may claim opposite rights that may lead to disharmony. For instance, 'if the Muslims were more assertive in seeking to be exempted from the current uniform rules, then the Christians may feel empowered to seek more space for religious proselytization, which tends to disproportionately anger the Muslim community' (Neo, 2019: 977). Since religious people are also citizens in the state, they should balance their religious values with values of good citizens. And it is likely that values for good citizenship trump values of good religiosity in Singapore.

Sometimes, religious groups that do not comply with state requirements are prosecuted. Jehovah Witnesses were once prosecuted for refusing compulsory military service in the country (Ong, 2019). The government differentiates religious beliefs from religious practices. In 1994, the High Court in Singapore affirmed these differentiations in the case of *Chan Hiang Leng Colin v. PP* (Lee, 2014). The idea behind the distinction between belief and practice is that the Constitution protects religious beliefs. However, practices that come from religious beliefs should comply with general legal requirements relating to social protection as well as public order. The need for public order trumps religious values.

Religious values also clashed with the values of constitutional governance in the case of *Faith Community Baptist Church v. Attorney-General*. The court ordered the Church to compensate the female employee it dismissed for having engaged in adulterous affairs (Goh,

2009). The Baptist Church argued against the court order, claiming that 'its employees and members were expected to adhere to certain moral standards' (Chuan, 2013, Aug. 20). This means that the termination of the woman's employment on the basis of adultery was justified under the laws of the Church. Unlike the Church, 'the employment tribunal did not consider adultery to be a sufficient cause for termination' (Neo, 2017: 365). The Ministry of Manpower also adhered to the employment laws of Singapore. It argued 'that employment law is a secular matter and that no religious considerations should be taken into account' (Neo, 2017: 365).

The literature shows that both religious groups and the state in Singapore agree on the importance of public harmony. There are now examples of court cases against requirements for public harmony which are mainly about the perceived or actual violation of religious people's freedom or rights to practice what they believe in. The court case explored above, *PP v. Ong Kian Cheong* was taken to court to deal with religious practices and speeches that would promote religious disharmony (Chen, 2014). Muslims argued that they were angered by a couple who referred to Islam as a false religion in the name of trying to turn people to Christ (Thio, 2010). The judges believed that such evangelism would result in hostility between Muslims and Christians.

The need for harmony is very important for secular and non-liberal states such as Singapore possibly because it falls within the Conservation value which comprises values such as conformity, security and tradition. The need for harmony or public order is the need for conforming to a particular way of doing things to avoid insecurity. Harmony also is good because it does not interfere with anybody's tradition. Individual autonomy in secular and non-liberal states might not be an attractive value because it can interfere with religious harmony and public order, leading to insecurity. Government neutrality in religous matters cannot guarantee public and religious harmony. This could be why a secular and non-liberal state is not neutral in religious matters in the same way that secular and liberal states such as the USA are. Having explored differences in relationships of state and religion in secular and liberal states, liberal and non-secular states and secular and non-liberal states, we now turn to see where South Sudan fits in its religion and state relationships as stipulated in Article 8 of the Constitution.

Value Clashes in South Sudan

South Sudan does not seem to fit into any value categories mentioned above. These value categories include secularism and liberalism. Some countries combine them in their constitutional designs and legal practices, some choose one over the other. These choices are not arbitrary. They seem to be guided by predominant values in a nation which define the nature of a state. The nature of state, in turn, defines how the state relates to religion. In some countries, 'A particular religion may be associated with national identity or with the foundational values of the community' (Ahmed, 2017: 4). In other countries, no one religion defines national identity. A clearly defined foundation of national values makes it easy for judges to adjudicate clashes between religious and constitutional values. In countries where such value definitions are not clear, the implementation of legal provisions on the separation of state and religion would often appear confusing, even to very sophisticated judges.

The issues that resulted in the inclusion of Article 8 in South Sudan's Constitution seem reactionary rather than carefully thought out in relation to national values. Historically, South Sudanese have seen their religious beliefs and cultures undervalued by the Arab Muslims in the North of Sudan. This is shown in speeches by leaders of SPLM/A during the north-south civil war. In 1986 John Garang made it clear that 'modern Sudan is a product of historical development before, during, and after the alternate colonial rule of the Turks, the British, and the Egyptians' (Khalid, 1990: 127). From the Turko-Egyptian occupation of North Sudan in 1820 to the SPLM/A rebellion against the government of Sudan in 1983, black Africans and their religions, including Christianity, have been seen as inferior to the Arab race and Islamic religion. For this reason, Garang complained against President Nimeiri in 1985 for dividing the country along ethnic and religious lines 'into Muslims and Christians, and into Arabs and Africans' (Khalid, 1990: 19). This division defined the Sudanese state and appears in different constitutions developed during the Arab rule in united Sudan.

Nature and Ideology of State in the Sudanese and South Sudanese Constitutions

The first constitution of Sudan differs in its definition of the nature of state because it was written by the British colonial administration in 1956 when Sudan became independent from the British colonial power. Article 2(1) of the 1956 Constitution of Sudan defines Sudan as 'a Sovereign Democratic republic.' Mo (2014) observes that the 1956 Constitution emphasises the sovereignty of Sudan simply because it was based on the self-determination agreement between the Sudanese and the British.

The definition of the nature of state by Sudanese themselves started in the Constitution of 1973, a year after the Addis Ababa peace agreement between the Anya Nya 1 Southern Sudan rebels and the Government of Sudan. Even though members of the regional government of Southern Sudan were involved in drafting and promulgating the constitution in 1973, they failed to recognize the danger of including ethnic group specifications in the Constitution. However, they were wise in excluding religion in the definition of the Sudanese state. Article 1, for example, included Arab and African nationalities in the nature of the Sudanese state. Yet, religion was not included in the definition, though mentioned in the section on religion.

The 1988 Constitution of Sudan clearly mentioned Islam as the religion of the majority in Article 1 in which 'Christianity and customary creeds' were mentioned to 'have considerable followers.' So the distinction between Arabs and Africans in Sudan in the 1973 Constitution has now in the 1998 Constitution included the divide between Islam and Christianity. Islam becomes the religion of the majority which has controversial implications on how the state relates to religion in Sudan.

The dissatisfaction with the definition of state in the 1973 and the 1998 Constitutions probably led to the definition of Sudan as a pluralist state in the 2005 Constitution. This was written as part of the operationalisation of the 2005 Comprehensive Peace Agreement (CPA). During the CPA negotiations, Sudan negotiators still wanted to stick to the religion-based definition of Sudan, and to define it as an Arab rather than an African country. SPLM negotiators wanted a Sudan defined by what John Garang referred to as *Sudanism* (Delaney, 2010) which, according to him, 'recognizes the ethnic, cultural, and religious diversity of Sudan' (Delaney, 2010: 3). Along the lines of Garang's *Sudanism*, Article 1(1) of the 2005 Constitution defines Sudan as 'a democratic, decentralized, multi-cultural, multi-lingual, multi-racial, multi-ethnic, and multi-religious country where such diversities co-exist.' The same Article 1 mentions justice, equality, freedom and human rights as important aspects of the nature of the Sudanese state. Religions and cultures are mentioned in Article 1(3) of the same Constitution as 'sources of strength, harmony and inspiration.'

It is naturally expected that the relations of religion and state would be defined by the nature of the state given in the Constitution. This expectation is partly true of Sudan because the nature of the state in the 1973 Constitution does not include religion. However, the relationship of state and religion in the same Constitution seems to be driven by the belief that Islam is believed to be the religion of the majority. In reality, the relationship between religion and state in Sudan is defined in line with Hassan al-Turabi's (1983) ideas on Islamic state, regardless of what the Constitution defines the nature of state to be. As Liu (2013: 38) points out, 'Turabi considered that in Islamic societies the only legitimate state system is early theocratic caliph regime; the best form of government in human society is Islamic representative republic.' Because it is theocratic, the Islamic state fits neither capitalism nor socialism (Liu, 2013). What matters is the sovereignty of Allah and the unifying nature of *umma*. Its ideological basis is *tawhid* under the *umma*. Therefore, an Islamic state cannot be secular (Liu, 2013). Turabi believes that 'Muslim cultural identity is religious loyalty beyond race, ethnicity, geography and language' (Liu, 2013: 39). However, Arab Muslims in Sudan, including Turabi himself, contradict this belief. They treat African Muslims in Nuba and Darfur as outsiders in Islam (Jok, 2012). The state acts as a tool for Allah in the teaching of Islamists like Turabi who argues that the Islamic state 'is only a social organization to safeguard the welfare and interests of religious people' (Liu, 2013: 39).

The Sudan People's Liberation Movement (SPLM) looks at the state differently. John Garang's *Sudanism* is based on 'the unity of all Sudanese of all races, genders, religions, and ethnicities' (Delaney, 2010: 9). Garang argues, as Delaney (2010: 10) puts it, 'that there are many different religions that are practiced in many different regions of Sudan, and that all of these religions should be accepted under the umbrella of the New Sudan, which represents all Sudanese peoples.' Garang believes that this unity in diversity should be implemented 'under a secular, democratic, socialist system that honors human rights' (Khalid, 1990: 23).

Some of Garang's statements about *Sudanism* resemble the definition of the state in the 1973 Constitution which includes terms such as unitary, democracy and socialism. Socialism was the state's political ideology when the 1973 Constitution was written. Garang and the SPLM he was leading, however, later disengaged from socialism, but maintained the idea of unity in diversity under a secular and democratic capitalist system of government.

Given the above differences between the North and the South in the definition of the nature of state, the understanding of religion and state relations differs. The Constitution of 1956 appears like a Western constitution in the stipulation of religious freedom. Article 7(1) states that 'All persons shall enjoy freedom of conscience and the right freely to profess their religion.' The only exception is when this right clashes with public order and morality.

The 1973 Constitution specifically defines religion and state relations. Article 16(a) stipulates: 'In the Democratic Republic of the Sudan Islam is the religion and the society shall be guided by Islam being the religion of the majority of its people and the State shall endeavor to express its values.' Article 16(b) also mentions Christianity as a religion that the state should encourage to express its values in Sudan.

There is no mention of other religions in the 1973 Constitution. The two religions mentioned, Islam and Christianity, are protected by the Constitution in a way that would disadvantage religions not mentioned. For example, Article 16(c) stipulates that 'Heavenly religions and the noble aspect of spiritual beliefs shall not be insulted or held in contempt.' This implies that any religious group criticising heavenly religions such as Islam and Christianity can be punished. Yet, the role of the state in the 1973 Constitution is to 'treat followers of religion and noble spiritual beliefs without discrimination as to the rights and freedoms guaranteed to them as citizens by this Constitution.' Politicians are also prevented by the Constitution from abusing religious beliefs for political ends. The 1973 Constitution seems to guarantee the non-discriminatory freedom of religions on one hand and prevent it on the other.

The 1998 Constitution which was written during the north-south civil war also sounds like a Western constitution despite the fact that the nature of state is clearly Islamic. Article 24 guarantees 'the right of freedom of conscience and religious creed' in a manner unusual in a country planning to be known as an Islamic state. It even prohibits coercion of anyone to adopt a religion that is not of his or her choice. Article 27 of the 1998 Constitution also guarantees different people's 'right to preserve their particular culture, language or religion, and rear children freely within the framework of their particularity, and the same shall not by coercion be effaced.' However, despite the freedom given to people's conscience in the choice of religion as well as in worship, Article 18 makes it compulsory for state officials to 'worship God.' Article 18 goes far in stipulating that these state officials 'shall maintain religious motivation and give due regard to such spirit in plans, laws, policies and official business in the political economic, social and cultural fields in order to prompt public life towards its objectives, and adjust them towards justice and uprightness to be directed towards the grace of God in The Hereafter.'

Mo (2014) observes a problem with this requirement in Article 18. To give regard to religious spirit in laws and policies seems difficult if religions were believed to be diverse in the country. It is difficult for both Christianity and Islam to influence laws and policies in an amicable manner because their value requirements may differ. For example, government officials required by law to worship God in their offices would do it according to what they believe in. For instance, Muslims would do it 'through the Quran, for others it is through the principles of religion' (Mo, 2014: 69). Moreover, this forceful requirement for government officials to pray in their offices would be 'problematic for many southerners who advocate secularism' (Mo, 2014: 69). The other problem is that Islamic law, Sharia, is mentioned in Article 1 of the same Constitution as the source of legislation. If religions are to influence laws and policies, then Sharia would guide this influence. This would be problematic to non-Muslims in the sense that 'Employment of non-Muslims will be conditional on his promotion and maintenance of the Islamisation program' (Mo, 2014: 69).

The above constitutional manipulations might have resulted in the removal of particular religions' names in the 2005 Constitution. Mo (2014: 69) believes that the removal of religion distinctions in the 2005 Constitution was possibly 'a measure to avoid controversy.' Article 6 and 38 talk mainly of religious rights, and the role of government in guaranteeing them. Unlike the rest of Sudan's constitutions, the 2005 Constitution 'is overwhelmingly concerned with all kinds of diversities in the country' (Mo, 2014: 69). Like the rest of Sudan's constitutions mentioned above, the 2005 Constitution does not mention the separation of religion and state. This reason for this is obvious: radical Muslims in Sudan such as Al-Turabi will not accept it. However, Mo (2014: 69) argues that 'It is obvious that the writers of this constitution had tried to separate religion and state, and as the country does not have a state religion, they have succeeded to a certain degree.' Yet, Mo (2014: 69-70) acknowledges that 'since Sharia still is the source of national legislation in the northern States, it is not possible to call Sudan a secular State.'

Having failed to convince North Sudanese leaders to include an article stipulating the separation of religion and state in the 2005 Constitution, South Sudan leaders included Article 8 in the Constitution of Southern Sudan to ensure a separation of religion and state in the South. Yet, the Article is ambiguous for some reasons, known and unknown. One known reason is that Sudanese politicians and religious leaders have been surviving through legal ambiguities. Even though the 1973 Constitution made sure that unity and democracy should be promoted, the same unity was negated by the importance given to Islamic religion. For example, 'stating that Islam is the religion of the majority could be an effort to legitimise an Islamic constitution.' Nimeiri thought that giving ambiguous powers to Islam would help him stay in power as long as he liked. Mo (2014: 60) captures it very well: 'In order to remain in power, President Numayri eventually allied himself with the traditional religious forces, which culminated with the implementation of the Sharia in 1983.'

Moreover, the 1998 Constitution is ambiguous or even contradictory in the sense that it gives all people freedom of conscience to worship God. Yet, public officials are required to worship God in their offices. The freedom of conscience to worship God was meant to let South Sudanese who had joined the so-called 'Peace from Within' in 1997 to convince those still fighting the government that there was constitutional freedom of worship in Sudan. Yet, the obvious reality remained. Mo (2014: 61) points out that when the 1998 Constitution places highest allegiance to God, 'it excludes non-Muslims and secularists within the country.' The 2005 Constitution was also ambiguous in avoiding a clear definition of state and religion relations. Article 1(3) just stipulates, 'religions and cultures are sources of strength, harmony and inspiration.' This was a calculated step to avoid controversies that would turn radical Muslims against Sudanese leaders who negotiated the CPA with an intention of sharing political power with the leaders of SPLM.

Power-motivated legal ambiguities are also evident in the relationship between the state and the African Traditional Religion (ATR) leaders in South Sudan. In united Sudan and now in independent South Sudan, 'various governments over the last century and a half have sought to sever spiritual and secular authority, to separate the political and divine worlds or, at the least, to assert government power over divine power' (Pendle, 2020: 44). However, this effort is not always successful because 'the actual secularization of authority proved hard to achieve' (Pendle, 2020: 44). Customary leaders such as chiefs 'often still relied on spiritual connections and remedial powers to maintain authority' (Pendle, 2020: 44).

Ideological Ambiguities in the State of South Sudan

The ambiguities arise when either state authorities or customary authorities shift their acceptance or rejection of the combination of government and divine powers. The shift occurs in relation to actual or perceived threat to holding on to power. Pendle (2020) gives examples of Nuer prophets who sometimes associate themselves with and sometimes distance themselves from the same government. The prophetess Nyachol is a good example of these power-motivated shifts. She uses customary laws to resolve disputes among her followers. She 'insists on compliance with the customary law including the rulings of the courts of the government-appointed customary chiefs' (Pendle, 2020: 47). But at the same time, Nyachol distances herself from the government. Mostly, 'she claims to offer a different type of power and political community than that of the government' (Pendle, 2020: 46). Nyachol even refuses to wear modern clothing because she associates them with the government. Those who visit her must leave their clothes far away from her hut (Pendle, 2020). Moreover, Nyachol does not allow anybody to take her photo. According to Pendle (2020: 47), 'Nyachol presents herself as the restorer and custodian of a Nuer-wide moral community that rebuilds a notion of a Nuer "customary" past that is backed by divine and not only government power.'

The issue is deeper than what Nyachol claims on the surface. Traditional leaders like Nyachol would often like to cooperate with government leaders who recognise their authority. They do not cooperate with government leaders who fail to recognise them. Government often asserted its authority over leaders of traditional religions. For example, in the 1930s during the British colonial rule, 'the government claimed the power to determine who was or was not an authentic "customary authority".' (Pendle, 2020: 48). Customary authorities who have been mixing divine and customary powers find it difficult to accept such government claims to exclusive powers and the associated definition of customary authority. The unrecognised spiritual leaders would often undermine the government's recognised customary authorities. This resistance would sometimes lead to flexibility in the government's definition of who should be considered an authentic customary leader.

When the government sometimes fails to have influence over local communities, it appoints ATR leaders as government chiefs to combine customary and spiritual powers. But when the government has the upper hand, then it side-lines these traditional leaders in the name of separating religious from secular powers. ATR leaders take advantage of such legal ambiguities in order to have greater power over their communities. In the 1920s, for example, the government decided to appoint a 'prophet' called Kolang Ket to be the paramount chief where the government had no control. But when Kolang died and his daughter Nyaruac became the 'prophetess', the government refused to appoint her as the paramount chief simply because she was a woman. This refusal by the government 'allowed Nyaruac to maintain a clear distinction between government and her own, divine authority' (Pendle, 2020: 52).

Because of this distinction, Nyaruac could not support the appointed paramount chief.

The distancing of Nyaruac from the paramount chief who succeeded her father made it difficult for him to control the people in the area. He kept complaining 'to Nyaruac and the government that he did not have the necessary authority to implement his chief's courts' rulings as people would run to Nyaruac's *luak* for justice or for sanctuary from the courts' justice' (Pendle, 2020: 52). (A *Luak* is a big grass-thatched roof building where cattle are kept. It sometimes functions like a conference hall because it is bigger than huts where people sleep.)

The powerless paramount chief later suggested that his position be given to Nyaruac's family male member since she could not be accepted as a woman to be the paramount chief. Nyaruac first refused the suggestion, arguing that it would be wrong to mix government's power with spiritual power (Pendle, 2020). When the powerless paramount chief insisted, Nyaruac allowed her brother Kuol to be the chief. Yet, she made it clear that since these two powers were mixed in her family, it would be impossible to separate them again later in an attempt to take chiefdom away from her family (Pendle, 2020).

The above examples make clear that legal ambiguity in Sudan and South Sudan has long been used as a tool for obtaining and maintaining political and spiritual powers. It could be for these reasons that the implementation of Article 8 in South Sudan's Constitution appears confusing. In Article 8 and other articles related to relationship between state and religions, it is not even clear whether South Sudan is liberal or not. If liberalism is about individual autonomy, then South Sudan is not a liberal state. Nor do any South Sudanese constitutions explicitly mention that the country is a secular state. The constitutions of united Sudan clearly state that Sudan is an Islamic state. But the constitution of South Sudan is not clear whether it is liberal or secular.

In the examples cited, value clashes adjudicated in court contribute to clarifying whether or not the country is secular or liberal. In South Sudan, no cases of value clashes have been adjudicated by courts. The only hint of what South Sudan is constitutionally might come from John Garang's speeches. John Garang talked of the need to have a democratic secular government in the New Sudan (Khalid, 1990). Yet, when both the Constitution of the national government and the Constitution of Southern Sudan government were written in 2005 before his death, they made no explicit mention of secularism. The separation of religion and state in Article 8 of the Constitution of the then Southern Sudan government never mentions whether South Sudan should be secular.

Yet, given John Garang's speeches on the need to introduce secularism in the Sudan and the day to day relationship of Christianity and the state in South Sudan today, one could argue that Garang intended South Sudan to be a secular and non-liberal state like Singapore. Like Singapore, South Sudan government regulates religious activities, especially newly registered Christian denominations. But it maintains some level of neutrality, though not at the level of neutrality in the USA. South Sudan government is not completely neutral in the secular manner seen in the USA because it occasionally funds Muslim activities.

Furthermore, South Sudan resembles Singapore when religious and political leaders team up to solve some political and religious internal disputes so that people live in harmony (Neo, 2019). Article 1(4) of the Transitional Constitution of South Sudan 2011 mentions peaceful coexistence of diverse groups as important. However, this love for public order and religious harmony is just an envisioned ideal rather than a guide for day to day practices. Public order and religious harmony rarely form part of central value systems in many South Sudan communities. There is little harmony even within tribes in South Sudan.

Power and Value Clashes in South Sudan

It is likely that the most important value in South Sudan is power. One evidence is that Garang complained about 'a practice of rule that keeps power in the hands of a few' in Sudan (Delaney, 2010: 8). Therefore, South Sudan might not really resemble Singapore in daily practices guided by a legally entrenched secularism.

South Sudan probably has a 'customary secularism' (Jok, 2012). This customary secularism was verbally promoted in the South during the north-south civil war as an alternative to 'Islamic nationalism' in the North (Jok, 2012). Gelvin (2005: 93) argues that new nationalisms are often 'defined by what they oppose.' Customary secularism was a perceived alternative to Islamic nationalism because the SPLM/A was trying to replace Islamic nationalism with John Garang's *Sudanism* of which customary secularism was a part. Since *Sudanism* was a tool of opposition, customary secularism is not well defined.

Islamic nationalism focuses on a constitution that derives its legislation from the Sharia law (Jok, 2012). Since South Sudanese wanted to change religiously-motivated laws, they decided not to mention any religion as the source of values. However, they also know that laws cannot come from a vacuum. There must be a value system from which legal principles are taken. For this reason South Sudan leaders chose customary laws and traditions as the basis for constitutional development and legislation. Yet, these leaders were not ready to disengage from religion. This could be why the Constitution of South Sudan is ambiguous. The separation of religion and state stipulated in Article 8 of South Sudan's Constitution seems to be a political power protection strategy rather than a belief system such as secularism and liberalism.

Islam in Sudan was used for divisive purposes in the sense that non-Muslims would find it difficult to occupy important political positions in the country under Sharia law. Radical Muslims seem to love a limited harmony within Islamic *Umma*. Other religions and their adherents have no place in an Islamic state which 'has a narrow utilitarian purpose' (Liu, 2013: 39) of taking care of the welfare of religious Muslim citizens of *Umma*. Unlike other Islamic *Umma*, the Islamic state in Sudan disregards non-Arab Muslims (Jok, 2012). Therefore, it was divisive in both religious and ethnic dimensions. It is partly to counter this Islamic divisive ideological belief that Article 8(2) states, 'All religions shall be treated equally and religion or religious beliefs shall not be used for divisive purposes.' Nothing in this provision shows South Sudan's commitment to secularism. However, if the government truly treated all religions equally and avoided using religious beliefs for divisive purposes, then South Sudan would fit into Singapore's pattern of secularism.

The customary laws that South Sudan leaders advocated as the foundation of their secularism are not exclusively secular. They mostly use values from the ATR. For example, murder is punishable by law in the customary courts whose decisions are often guided by religious principles in murder cases. It is religiously believed that a murder results in a curse that Dinka refer to as *tir* and Nuer calls it *nueer*. As Pendle (2020: 44) defines it, '*Nueer* is a potentially lethal pollution that arises after transgression of divinely sanctioned prohibitions, such as killing.' The curse from *nueer* can kill, not only the murderer but also his relatives. Thus, the main way of removing it is to pay blood compensations to relatives of a murdered person. The customary laws specify the number of cattle to be paid as blood compensation. This is often not necessarily a punishment for a murderer as in the legal system in the West. Almost all the members in the murderer's clan contribute cows to the blood compensation just to remove *tir* or *nueer* from their clan.

Some commanders from the Sudan People's Liberation Army

removed spiritual elements from murder laws in recent years, but this resulted in negative effects. These leaders argued that the *nueer* pollution or curse does not affect soldiers who kill people in government-authorised wars. This removal of the spiritual part of the murder laws emboldened others to kill without fear of any curse. For this reason some traditional leaders now call for the reinstatement of these spiritual values. They argue, as Pendle (2020,) puts it, that 'reinstating divine power behind the customary laws allows the customary laws to also be remedial.' Yet, it is clear that customary laws are not religious laws, though they are strengthened by religious values.

It is highly likely at this point that South Sudanese mostly value power. They do everything they can to preserve it. Clashes of religious values and values of constitutional governance are not yet clear in South Sudan. But the manipulation that took place during the different constitution-making processes in united Sudan was mainly motivated by the need to obtain and maintain political power. Islam has often been a religion preferred by those who wanted to hold onto political power in Sudan partly because 'Islam encourages intellectual conformity and an uncritical acceptance of authority' (Islam & Islam, 2017: 3). This differs from Christianity that is often perceived as critical of state authorities in matters to do with values. African Traditional Religious leaders are also like Christians in how they agree or disagree with state authorities on value-related issues. In South Sudan, clashes that sometimes happen between the state and the ATR leaders are motivated by the desire to have more power. Actual and perceived threats to one's power often lead to a redefinition of the religion-and-state relationship in South Sudan. It is likely that conservation values of security, conformity and tradition are used in South Sudan to protect one's underlying value for power.

Preliminary Conclusion

This chapter tried to answer the question of the nature of the conflict between so-called 'Christian values' and the values of constitutional governance (as prescribed in Article 8) in South Sudan. The chapter explored what Christian values have in common with values of constitutional governance, and where they differ. This was done by examining states that have provisions for the relationship between state and religion in their constitutions. These states are the USA, South Africa and Singapore. The aim was to understand whether religious values and values of constitutional governance clash in these states and how this relates to South Sudan.

In the literature that was explored, value clashes in different states happen when a constitutionally defined value system in the state and the values of religion do not match in practice. The clashes are mainly influenced by predominant underlying values in the nation even if values in the constitution are slightly different. For example, those who value secularism and liberalism resist values that seem to violate individual autonomy and lack of state neutrality on religious matters. Non-liberal states pay less attention to individual autonomy. But they resist any value that seems to go against communal values. What Christian values and values of constitutional governance have in common is the avoidance of any harm to human life.

South Sudan does not seem to have defined national values that guide daily activities in the country. The customary secularism for which South Sudan leaders have been advocating seems to resemble secularism in Singapore. Like Singapore, South Sudan is non-liberal. Yet, it is different from Singapore in value prioritisation. What is clear is that power value drives almost everything in South Sudan. What the Constitution stipulates is often disregarded when it seems to restrict one's powers. There is no evidence of this shift of value prioritisations in Singapore. Secularism in Singapore is guided by the love for public order and religious harmony.

The clashes between religious values and values of constitutional governance in Singapore happen when any institution does what would disturb public order or religious harmony. There is no individual autonomy, as in South Sudan, which justifies actions against public order or religious harmony in Singapore. Communal values trump individual values in both countries. However, what causes value clashes in South Sudan seems to be any act that is perceived to be a threat to one's hold onto power, be it political or religious. However, there is no evidence of court cases which show these clashes in South Sudan. Yet, some examples show that Islamic religion and ATR have been used to demonstrate these power-motivated value clashes in united Sudan and in independent South Sudan. This seems to explain why the implementation of Article 8 is sometimes confusing in South Sudan. We now turn to how ethical issues are imagined in relation to values explored.

CHAPTER FIVE

CHRISTIAN POLITICIANS AND ETHICAL POLICIES

Introduction

The love for power obviously poses a perpetual insecurity in united Sudan and in independent South Sudan. We have seen that Sudanese and South Sudanese value power for dominance, though they seem to focus less on achievements. In Schwartz's (2012) theory of basic human values, power value is a subset of self-enhancement value. The other subset is the achievement value. Schwartz (2012: 5) defines the goal of power as 'social status and prestige, control or dominance over people and resources.' Power is a threat sometimes when individuals and groups of people misuse it. In places where people misuse power, almost every person feels insecure.

In the two Sudans, power seems to be an attractive value that almost every citizen pursues (Jok, 2012). Yet, it probably stands on the shaky ground of violent competition to attain and maintain it. Since this one overarching value seems to stand on shaky ground, the cultivation of values that would form a firm national foundation in South Sudan is desirable. Therefore, the question is: What are some of the roles that religious and government institutions play in cultivating values among South Sudanese? It is likely that religious and government leaders are working to develop values that would lead to peaceful coexistence and pursuit of common benefits among different communities in South Sudan. Yet, it is unclear at this point what these leaders are doing practically to develop power values guided by ethical principles, be they religious or constitutional.

In South Sudan, the people have not yet understood their roles as independent bodies that have powers ranking above the powers of individual leaders. They are still manipulated in a divide-and-rule style prevalent in the former united Sudan. What South Sudanese knew and valued in united Sudan is what they know and value now in independent South Sudan. Past realities of united Sudan seem to define present ways of doing things in independent South Sudan. There seems to be no mechanism in place to control arbitrary decisions by the executive arm of government. Sovereignty of the people that Article 2 of South Sudan Constitution stipulates is not yet a reality. Political leaders probably regard popular sovereignty as an obstacle to obtaining and maintaining power. This makes the principle of equality of all religions stipulated in Article 8(2) of South Sudan's Constitution just an imaginary standard not yet necessary in practice.

Cultural and Social Imaginations and Values

This chapter will draw from the writings of Ward (2018) and Taylor (2004) in the process of answering the above question. Ward's (2018) idea of cultural imagination relates to how South Sudanese make sense of religious and government values. Cultural values in South Sudan mostly explain how things are done in state and religious institutions. Power is one of the attractive values in different communities in South Sudan. Ward (2018) argues that individuals are often immersed in practices and values that precede them in their communities. That is, 'We are the inheritors of the way our minds have been shaped' (Ward, 2018: 183). The imagination brings out underlying images and their associated meanings and uses them to make sense of new values and practices.

Like Ward's cultural imagination, Taylor's (2004) social imagination describes how past values and practices influence present values and practices. People use old values to interpret new ones. Social imagination is about how people perceive their existence in society, including how they fit together. When people get confused in new practices, they pull out old practices and values to explain present ones. Premodern and modern values, for example, could differ in some ways and have common features in others. These differences and commonalities manifest themselves when new ways of doing things are developed in disapproval of old ways. Yet, some aspects of older values remain in the unconscious and are often used to make sense of new ways of doing things.

Sometimes, people in different periods of time differ in their understanding of how the private relates to the public. For example, premodern societies believed that relationships between private and public practices aim at the good life, guided by high-ranking activities such as contemplation. The Catholics in the medieval age valued believers' dedication to celibacy as the ultimate form of Christian living. Unlike people in premodern and medieval periods, Reformers focused on the direct relationship of the individual to God, which makes private life more important than public life. These different understandings of private and public life have implications for how people in different periods of time understand popular sovereignty.

Transitions from one period to another are often both forward-looking and backward-looking in nature. Any transition from old norms and practices to new ones makes use of the old to explain the new. For example, the value of popular sovereignty in the United State Constitution is based on the ideals of natural law and traditions. The transition from natural law to the United States' modern constitution 'was made easier because what was understood as the traditional law gave an important place to elected assemblies and their consent to taxation' (Taylor, 2004: 110).

The ideas in Ward's (2018) and Taylor's (2004) writings will, therefore, be useful in understanding how South Sudanese use their old Sudanese values to cultivate religious and constitutional values in independent South Sudan. We will begin with how old experiences influence ideas in new settings, especially in religion and state relations. We will first explore medieval views on church and state relationships in order to understand the roles that religious and political leaders played at the time to cultivate values. Then we will examine the current understanding of church and state relationships and its associated value cultivation in the United States. The USA is chosen because it represents states that value secularism in public life and religious beliefs in private life. It will be important to see what kind of values that religious and political leaders cultivate in secular and liberal settings. Since secularism is mostly promoted in opposition to private religious beliefs in modern and postmodern periods, it would be important to understand whether there are people who still promote premodern and medieval views of the state and religion relationship in the United States today. The last two sections will then explore values that political and religious leaders cultivate in South Sudan. The hierarchy of being in medieval philosophy and theology has implications for the exercise of power through a hierarchy. South Sudan leaders seem to have a very similar view. Because of this, the chapter will mostly explore medieval thought on church and state relationships to illuminate the current thinking on the topic in South Sudan.

Medieval Views on Church and State Relationships

Premodern traditions seem to influence medieval thinkers in most cases. Medieval thinkers mainly focus on the importance of God in the hierarchy of beings. Since no species of God exists in this world to which people can compare God for an abstract understanding of His nature, premodern and medieval thinkers talk of God by the analogy of degrees and the analogy of proportionality (Baird, 2014). In terms of degrees, God is above all. In terms of proportionality, God is the perfect Being, the perfect Good and the perfect Truth. This section will examine whether medieval thinkers understand the relationship between church and state in terms of the hierarchy of beings in which God is the perfect Being, the perfect Good and the perfect Truth. This hierarchy-based analysis may enable us to know whether medieval thinkers rank either the church or state above the other or whether they put them side by side in importance. This will help understand what these two institutions governing human affairs understand their functions within the hierarchy of beings to be: that is, how they relate to God and one another, including implications for not adhering to such relationships.

Premodern-Leaning Church Thinkers' Views on Church and State Relationships

One church thinker who embodies premodern tradition is St. Augustine of Hippo, also known as Aurelius Augustinus Hipponensis in Latin (354-430). He was one of the great systematic thinkers of his time, and is still respected as a great thinker today (Baird, 2016). Augustine (2015) proposes what seems to be the separation of church and state mainly to deal with the sinfulness of human beings. To him, human beings are bad because of the original sin (Copleston, 1993; Harmless, 2010). To deal with this original sin in human daily life, Augustine (2015) argues that people should be governed by strong, capable government that enforces law and order since sinful people are incapable of doing what is good (Burroughs, 2013). He thinks human reason alone would rarely overcome sinful nature in that sinful nature takes advantage of any situation. Reason is inadequate in controlling opportunistic behaviours. Reason alone is also insufficient in enabling people to follow the ultimate good (Harmless, 2010). This is why the state is crucial in helping human beings achieve the ultimate good.

Yet, Augustine never advocates total church separation from state, although the state primarily promotes earthly good. He believes the City of God and the earthly city overlap in their existence here on earth (Feldman, 2009). That is, both cities overlap within each person. It is probably difficult, if not impossible, to divide one person into spiritual and secular lives (Buzzard, 1994). Augustine (2015) prefers Christian rule with true Christians to secular rule in that true Christian leaders could rule justly. He thinks true justice cannot be found in a pagan state (Copleston, 1993). True justice, according to Augustine, involves worshipping God as he requires, which can only be done by true Christians. Augustine (2015) thinks that Christianity is the one force that makes citizens truly good and peaceful. To him, Christian principles are not susceptible to desire for domination, and deceit presumably does not motivate true Christians.

However, Christian rule does not refer to the rule by the church. Augustine argues that the church could also be corrupt in its earthly form like an earthly government (Burroughs, 2013). Church leaders, to Augustine, are not necessarily already in the City of God. They are still on earth where they still participate in the sinful nature of human beings. The two cities that Augustine talks about are moral cities. The City of Jerusalem represents the love of God and the City of Babylon represents the love of self (Augustine, 2015). For example, a Christian whose principle is the love of self rather than the love of God belongs to the City of Babylon even if he or she is a church official. But a government official whose conduct is guided by the love of God morally and spiritually belongs to the City of Jerusalem (Harmless, 2010).

If a state only symbolises Babylon, the symbol of self-love, then Augustine would argue that a true Christian could not get involved in the running of its affairs or even be a citizen in such a state. But since both Jerusalem and Babylon are symbols of morality and lack of morality, Christians can be citizens of the City of Babylon as well as leading it. What matters to Augustine is the moral principle of those who run institutions in both the City of Jerusalem and the City of Babylon. That is why he stresses that a true Christian who lives by Christian principles should be a leader of a capable strong government (Augustine, 2015). Augustine stresses that Christian principles which promote Christian values are the ones that are perfect, not the need to promote the love of self.

On church-state relations, Augustine believes the role of Christians in the state is providing it with higher Christian principles of conduct (Burroughs, 2013). To him, Christians are mandated to act as the leaven in relation to a state (Augustine, 2015). This means that the church is higher than the state in status and roles because it represents the highest Good, which is the nature of God (Burroughs, 2013). Augustine's exaltation of the church over the state is motivated by his belief in the natural order or the hierarchy of beings which points to the supreme Good who is God (Harmless, 2010). The church, to Augustine, is the superior moral society that can influence the state and not the other way around. Yet, the state remains the enforcer of social order for moral ends (Harmless, 2010).

St. Thomas Aquinas (1225–1274), another great thinker among the Church Fathers, disagrees with Augustine's argument that the state exists as the result of original sin. He considers the state as existing in its own right 'to care for the common good' (Copleston, 1993: 414). Aquinas holds that the state would have been established even if there was no fall of human beings. He, however, agrees with Augustine that God is the ultimate Good (Naylor, 2017). That is why he bases his suggestions of what seems to be the separation of church and state on the nature of the good. Aquinas believes that other goods exist. However, he argues that these other goods must submit to the goodness of God (Naylor, 2017). To Aquinas, human beings aim at supernatural ends that include the ultimate Good.

For Aquinas, the law of God is the overall law because it is eternal. Other laws aim upward towards the Eternal Law of God. One would expect Aquinas to put other laws in the hierarchy of importance. For example, it would be easy for him to put the laws of government over religious laws and vice versa. However, Aquinas does not do this. Instead, he puts the Natural Law and the Divine Law side by side. These two laws have equal weight in the business of governing the affairs of human beings. The Divine Law, on the one hand, is the Law that is found in Scripture or in the Holy Bible. The Divine Law defines canon laws of churches. Natural Law, on the other hand, defines government legislation or human laws that constitutions and acts stipulate. Sometimes, no obviously clear divide exists between the Divine Law and the Natural Law in human laws and both aim upward towards perfection in the Eternal Law.

Moreover, Aquinas disagrees with Augustine's view of the church as the only perfect society through which the good life is realised (Copleston, 1993). He argues that the state, like the church, is a perfect society in relation to promoting the common good of the citizens (Aquinas, 1964). The common good that the state promotes includes peace within its borders and averting dangers, both internal and external, which prevent the good life among the people. However, Aquinas thinks the supernatural end that the church aims at is higher than the end at which the state aims. Therefore, the state must subordinate itself to the church in matters dealing with eternal life. It is along this line that Aquinas (1964) proposes roles that seem to indicate the separation of church and state.

Regarding church-state relations, Aquinas believes both serve one end-goal at which society aims, the promotion of the good life, 'and that the good life is a life according to virtue' (Copleston, 1993: 416). Yet, he does not consider the end-goal of society as the final end. The final end of virtuous life, according to Aquinas, is the enjoyment of God's presence in people's lives. And this is attained only by divine power and the divine rule. It is through this hierarchical process that Aquinas argues that 'under the new Covenant of Christ, kings must be subject to priests' (Copleston, 1993: 416).

Both Augustine and Aquinas are purely products of premodern tradition which views the highest Good as existing only in the nature of God. In premodern beliefs, all beings aim upward towards the highest Good or the One, which is God. Things that are low in hierarchical ranking, as Plotinus (1992) would put it, become beautiful and perfect when they participate in the highest form of the Good. This is why premodern thinkers do not talk of forms of evil. To them, no form of the bad exists. They argue that the bad is the privation of the ideal form of the Good (Baird, 2016). Anything that falls downward, like Satan who fell from his ranking as an angel, becomes imperfect because it loses its original form that connects it with the overall Good, which is God. Something that falls downward becomes ugly for not participating in the form of the Good. Plotinus points out that 'the beautiful body comes into being by sharing in a formative power, (*logos*) which comes from the divine forms' (Baird, 2016: 261). Those who do not aim upward to be like the Good destroy their good form or character. As Plotinus argues, 'greatness of soul is despising the things here and wisdom is an intellectual activity which turns away from things below and leads the soul to things above' (Baird, 2016: 263). In this sense, aiming upward means practicing anything good so that you become like the Good.

In premodern tradition, things are not separate particulars. They are unified entities under the universal highest Being. The form in which things participate to attain beauty 'approaches and composes that which is to come into being from many parts into a single ordered whole' (Baird, 2016: 261). God's thinking, for example, is universal in determining universally identical forms of his creations. Augustine and Aquinas regard the universals as archetypical exemplars or ideals in the mind of God (Baird, 2016). One form of one thing is universal for the whole class of that one thing in the mind of God. Justice, for example, even though it is an abstract ideal is universal in matters that relate to justice anywhere in the world even if people express it in different languages. In addition, moral concepts in premodern tradition are objective universal ideals. God is the efficient cause of all the existing universals.

Modern-Leaning Church Thinkers' Views on Church and State Relationships

Enlightenment tradition influenced some church thinkers. This tradition values individual freedom and rights over hierarchy and defines moral norms by universal reference. It rejected authority (through which hierarchy functions), tradition, and religion in favour of reason. For example, 'early modern philosophers such as Rene Descartes encouraged their readers to make a clean sweep of the past' (Baird, 2016: 371). Some of these philosophers argue that 'Previous thinkers had been deluded by errors in thinking or had relied too heavily on authority' (Baird, 2016: 371).

Luther is clear, as a modernist thinker that he is against all forms of hierarchy, including hierarchy in the church. He thinks all Christians are priests (Luther, 1991). To him, priests are only appointed for the sake of order in the church, not that they are spiritually higher than others. God, Luther (1991) argues, is the one who directly rules the church through the Holy Spirit. It is along this line that churches are autonomous to one another. The state and the church are also of equal rank because neither has power over the other. God, according to Luther (1991), rules the church and the state in different ways. Although God rules over both state and the church, Luther (1991) believes that what guides the state is mainly reason. Yet, outstanding members of society have rights to guide and provide for the church. The prince is one of these outstanding members when it comes to keeping peace and order and providing material support to the church (Luther, 1991). God, Luther (1991) argues, is hidden behind natural reason, which helps the prince to rule.

However, Luther cautions princes against interfering in spiritual matters of the church (Blayney, 1957). He advises Christians to obey a prince only in matters to do with the body and goods, but not in matters to do with faith (Luther, 1991). The prince has no authority in preventing the preaching of the Gospel. The prince also has no right to force anybody into a certain faith. Luther says that one must voluntarily obey God in matters of faith (Blayney, 1957). He believes in individual consent and rights. For this reason he thinks no human being has the authority to interfere in individual's relation to God. Yet, Luther (1991) seems to give room for the interference by one person in the affairs of another human since that is what the state does to maintain peace. This interference of state in the life of an individual is demonstrated by what he regards as two kinds of works. The first is the proper work of God, which is done in love and mercy. The second is the strange work of God which is done in strange love that uses punishment and threats as tools for enforcing compliance. It is the second work of God that state uses to maintain order, and the first is practiced by the church.

Calvin and Luther have slight differences in their theological views regarding church-state relations. Calvin in his argument on the separation of church and state differentiates the redemptive and providential works of God in the Two Kingdoms doctrine. The redemptive kingdom, to Calvin (1960), is the spiritual kingdom, while the civil or earthly kingdom entails the providential care of God.

Unlike Luther who does not believe in the hierarchy of beings, Calvin (1960) thinks the hierarchy of beings is important. He believes in the sovereignty of God above all other creatures which implies that other beings too are ordered in ranks of importance. Along this line Calvin (1960) ranks pastors and presbyters as the most senior clergy in the hierarchy in the church. This hierarchy of clergy serves effectively to advance the main work of the church, which, for Calvin (1960), is the education of the people in order to bring them to the invisible church which is the eternal kingdom.

In church-state relations, the work of state, for Calvin (1960), should be caring for both order and daily life of people. He wants magistrates to punish blasphemers and heretics in the church. Yet, he cautions magistrates against using the state's swords to punish those who express their private opinions. Calvin (1960) even urges civil authorities to act with mercy and moderation. To protect the church from state domination, Calvin (1960) advocates for the autonomy of the church from state jurisdiction. The law of God, to him, is the one that shall govern both the church and the state. Yet, he never encourages people to rebel against civil authority (Macleod, 2009). He favours passive disobedience to unjust civil authorities or rulers. Calvin only allows the revolution by the junior magistrates against the senior ones under the condition that the natural law is being contradicted (Macleod, 2009).

The modernists' rejection of premodern thoughts partly led to the crisis of rationality and knowledge. The Protestant Reformation was part of this period. Luther, however, minimally believed that reason would be necessary for salvation. He mostly believed in salvation by faith through the grace of God. However, the line of influence from schools of thoughts and traditions is not clearly drawn from tradition to tradition in different periods of time. As will be seen below, thinkers and policymakers living in the same period can vary in what they value. One example already mentioned is how Calvin differs from Luther. We now turn to modernist thought.

Modern Views on Church and State Relationships

Modern views on church and state relationships differ from premodern views in distinct ways. First, premodern views on church and state are mainly based on the importance of the hierarchy of beings and the role of God in this hierarchy. Second, they focus on the importance of collective duty for common good. Third, issues relate to one another under the overall authority of God. Contrary to these premodern views, modern views mainly focus on the rights of individuals rather than on collective duty for common good. Hierarchy of beings is not important. Some exceptions in modernism are the institutional separationists who still believe in the importance of hierarchy today, even though they reason like other modernists for church and state separation. Moreover, the idea of universality of issues is murky in modernist views. For these reasons, we will explore the modernist views of church and state relationships to see if premodern views have a certain influence on the modern views. The section will use USA as a comparative example.

Conflicting Views on Church and State Relationships

Individual rights rather than hierarchy of beings become the basis for church-state relations during and after the Enlightenment, as often shown by strict separationists (Esbeck, 1986). They demand the separation of church and state in the USA today to avoid discrimination against minority religions by majority religions and to avoid the possibility of religious values influencing state legislators (Hamburger, 2002). Strict separationists term this the 'wall of separation' between church and state (Gilpin, 2010). Values that they promote are mostly compatible with secularism and liberalism. For example, strict separationists would like the state to be nonreligious but at the same time not hostile to religion (Esbeck, 1986). They recommend that those who are religious should be secular in public life and religious in private practices of religion. That is, religious beliefs should be limited to religious institutions such as churches, homes and families.

The reason why strict separationists assign religious life to religious institutions, homes and families is that they believe that religion is a private matter for the individual believer. They argue that religious matters in public life disturb individual rights. It is for this reason that strict separationists demand that social and political issues be deliberated upon and approved only on a secular basis without any religious conviction openly attached to them. Even the educational support that Calvin wants the government to give to religious institutions is ruled out by strict separationists. For them, economic matters, military defence and the rule of law are secular issues, and thus fall under the responsibility of state.

Strict separationists reject the idea of the universality of ethical matters. To them, ethical issues which are related to politics and statecraft are relative to each state (Esbeck, 1986). That means individual's choice of values is not determined or judged right or wrong based on universal natural law. What directs strict separationists is the liberal theory of politics (Perkins, 2010). Churches and other religious institutions are deemed to have no institutional rights apart from the rights they have over their members (Perkins, 2010). Strict separationists believe that only individuals have legal rights, not institutions. Yet, they argue that the state should not coerce individual conscience informed by religious beliefs (Esbeck, 1986).

Pluralistic separationists agree with strict separationists on the importance of freedom (Horwitz, 2013). They argue that a state should be neutral in religious matters (Guirguis, 2014). To them, the state should not work for or against religious institutions since each is independent of the other. Pluralistic separationists are like the strict separationists in the sense that they believe in the secular and religious distinction (Terry, 2008). For them, the government can only play its neutral role well if it confines its focus to secular issues and protects minority rights (Danchin, 2008).

However, pluralistic separationists differ from strict separationists in that they believe that government policies might be influenced by religious values (McMahone, 2010; Cohen, 2015). They think the strict dichotomy between public-private realms is rarely practical since states are obliged to regulate personal morality in the private realm (Burroughs, 2013). In the same way, those who believe in the importance of a dichotomy between the faithful and the worldly in the church still argue that politics is dirty and must be corrected, using religious values. This means that the church should encourage 'its members to engage with the state in an attempt both to cultivate the goods of communion that it can foster and to limit the evils that it often legitimates and perpetrates' (Burroughs, 2013: 55).

Most importantly, the tolerance value that pluralistic separationists promote is closer to the universal belief that strict separationists reject. Yet, they agree with strict separationists that universal reference to ethical judgment in political matters is not necessary (Esbeck, 1986). To pluralistic separationists, the state is not bound by a particular theological belief or worldview in the same way that individuals are bound. Since the state, according to pluralistic separationists, cannot determine which religious worldview is correct, it should be neutral in religious matters (Walsh, 2017). For this reason, a state should avoid public theology or a national church so that there is no dominant religious worldview in public (Sheeder, 2013). To pluralistic separationists, the state is a human invention (Esbeck, 1986). God does not ordain it. This is why it should treat all citizens and their beliefs equally. Like strict separationists, pluralistic separationists believe that the state should protect individual conscience informed by religious values, unless such a conscience is a threat to public safety (Sheeder, 2013).

Institutional separationists differ from the secular belief held by both the strict and the pluralistic separationists. They argue that both the state and the church are subject to the will of God because he ordained them (Garnett, 2007). Institutional separationists believe that God is sovereign over all things (Esbeck, 1986). Nothing exists or operates outside the sovereignty of God. To them, the separation of church and state is just the separation of two institutions under one God to play different roles ordained by God (Burroughs, 2013). The roles, though different, serve society in the sense that the church gives the society, through the state, a religious moral agenda, and the state gives the church a platform for such a moral agenda (Garnett, 2007). This means that institutional separationists believe in the hierarchy of beings with each rational being having the right to perform its assigned roles. They, however, argue that no institution should be allowed to dominate another even when they are not independent of each other (Garnett, 2013).

The role of different institutions in the views of institutional separationists is to form people's characters from different directions. This comes from premodern tradition. In premodern tradition people are not born with a good character. It 'is formed by habit' (Baird, 2016: 178). Premodern thinkers such as Aristotle could argue that 'we become just by the practice of just actions, self-controlled by exercising self-control, and courageous by performing acts of courage' (Baird, 2016: 178). For this reason, good laws in any state are designed to inculcate good habits in such state's citizens. Good laws punish people when they deviate from the norms. The opposite is true when people follow correct norms. True virtue consists of both pain and pleasure. Premodern thinkers such as Aristotle believe that 'it is pleasure that makes us do base actions and pain that prevents us from doing noble actions' (Baird, 2016: 178). Bad laws do the opposite of the good because they allow citizens to learn bad habits. This is because 'the same causes and the same means that produce excellence or virtue can also destroy it' (Baird, 2016: 179). Premodern thinkers believe that inculcation of good character starts from childhood. They argue that 'men must be brought up from childhood to feel pleasure and pain at proper things' (Baird, 2016: 179). This is what they call 'correct education' (Baird, 2016: 179). And if this is the correct education, then it should apply to the development of good character anywhere.

Unlike strict and pluralistic separationists who reject the universality of values, institutional separationists opine that universal values are necessary for the state to maintain the values of human rights (Esbeck, 1986). Yet, they believe that states such as the United States of America are not bound to universal theocentric ideologies above the constitution. Institutional separationists maintain that individuals must differentiate the law from its source. Judeo-Christianity, to them, is the source of the law. This means that legitimacy of the state law lies in the source of law even if the source of law cannot directly be invoked in court rulings. It is the transcendent law, institutional separationists argue, that holds the state in check (Esbeck, 1986).

Institutional separationists argue that the state must protect religious speech and the religious press in the same way that it protects other speech and presses in public (Garnett, 2013). To them, religious values must be promoted in public in order to influence public policies (Lewis, 2014). For institutional separationists, the separation of church and state as institutions with distinct roles does not mean that the church must be silent in public (McMahone, 2010). An individual, institutional separationists argue, has the duty to use his or her religious values even in public realm to correct the bad and promote the good (Esbeck, 1986). However, they agree with pluralistic separationists that tolerance is crucial in public discourse. Institutional separationists also agree with pluralistic separationists on the importance of protecting the individual's conscience within the defined values held by such individual's institution (Garnett, 2013; Horwitz, 2013).

The other group that has views regarding the separation of church and state is the Nonpreferentialists. Nonpreferentialists agree with institutional and pluralistic separationists in the need for the state to be neutral when it comes to choosing among religious groups (Terry, 2008). Yet, they do not think the state should avoid giving support to church institutions, though the assistance must be on a nonpreferential basis (Lewis, 2014). Nonpreferentialists even argue that government aid to religious educational institutions is constitutional (Guirguis, 2014). They believe religious schools offer the benefit of education that has quality and personal values that government schools rarely offer (McMahone, 2010). Furthermore, religious schools offer a variety of choices to families and their children (Esbeck, 1986).

Nonpreferentialists share the Enlightenment values of freedom and individual rights. Nevertheless, they differ from the other church and state separationists in the sense that parochial school support enhances educational freedom (Guirguis, 2014). This educational freedom gives parents and students the freedom of choice in a variety of ways in comparison to monopoly educational systems.

Like the institutional separationists, nonpreferentialists believe in the universality of values. They argue that the government should be judged through transcendent universal ethical values that enhance human rights (Esbeck, 1986). It is this universal human rights value that prevents the government from discriminating against religious organisations and individuals based on their beliefs. Along the same line nonpreferentialists agree with institutional and pluralistic separationists that the state must protect religious speech and press in the same manner that it protects these freedoms in art, politics and philosophy. They also argue in favour of the protection of individual conscience, which is informed by religious values.

Principles of State and Religion Separation and Central Value Systems

Church leaders sometimes disregard the principle of religion and state separation if state policies seem to threaten principles of holiness and the supremacy of God. For example, religious groups are banned by law in the USA from engaging in political campaigns within religious institutions, but certain Catholic leaders violated this ban during the 2008 general elections because it regarded some policies advanced by some candidates as ungodly (Flint-Hamilton, 2010). In addition, in line with the love of premodern tradition for order, states today enact laws that they believe would maintain law and order (Kalkandjieva, 2011).

However, researchers and practitioners who are influenced by the Enlightenment tradition value laws that protect individual freedom. Along the line of the Enlightenment's promotion for individual rights, for example, protection against marginalisation is one of the main reasons that some scholars today support the separation of church and state (Garnett, 2007; MccAuliff, 2010). In Africa, for instance, the support for the separation of religion and state depends on whether a religious group feels marginalised or favoured (Riedl, 2012). Those who feel marginalised would advocate for the separation of church and state for their own survival. They would even make claims for the separation of religion and state in a constitution where there is no such provision (Mujuzi, 2011). Kenya is a good example. The roles that religious and political leaders play in South Sudan will be examined below to see whether they resemble roles played by religious and political leaders to cultivate values as discussed in the literature explored above.

Political Leaders and Value Cultivation in South Sudan

Political leaders seem to promote power values above other values in South Sudan. Almost every institution of government pays more attention to its ranking position among other institutions than services it is supposed to render. For example, organs of government are ranked vertically instead of the horizontal ranking common in other democratic countries. The Executive is the most powerful arm of South Sudan government (Jok, 2015), followed by the Legislature and then the Judiciary. This is, however, not what the Constitution stipulates. Article 51 of the Constitution arranges the organs of the national government from (a) the Legislature, (b) the Executive and (c) the Judiciary. Article 55 makes it clear that the Legislature oversees the Executive. Article 96 specifies the roles of the Executive. These roles do not include power over the Legislature or the Judiciary. However, since power value forms the central value of South Sudanese, politicians tend to disregard what the Constitution stipulates. Because the power value is central, leaders in South Sudan love to exercise unquestionable authority over both institutions and the individuals they lead. Yet, the Constitution is designed in a way that it 'does not provide ample checks and balances to ensure executive power is not abused' (Muita, Yitbarek, & Mnguni, 2018: 2). The President, for example, has powers to suspend the Legislature. He can also fire judges of the Supreme Court. These powers make it difficult for the President to be accountable to the Legislature. Most leaders in South Sudan seem to copy the idea of doing things without considering the views of the people they lead.

Decision-making is often power based in South Sudan. The Executive and the Legislature, for instance, often make decisions without consulting the people they serve even if such decisions negatively affect the lives of all citizens (Knopf, 2013). South Sudan politicians seem to have the 1920s understanding of leadership as 'the ability to impress the will of the leader on those led and induce obedience, respect, loyalty, and cooperation' (Ciulla, 2009: 306). Citizens, on their part, rarely complain against decisions that negatively affect their lives. Doing so would be tantamount to disobedience to leaders who make such decisions. Politicians who want to get into power and the ones who are holding onto power manipulate their communities to support them. This is because citizens are not aware of their power to question what their leaders do. A wider gap exists between educated elites in towns and those in rural areas. The elites in towns are engaged in a continuous power struggle and manipulating citizens in rural areas.

In South Sudan, citizens who are lower in public status depend on those who are above them in the hierarchy, who make sure that they hold power to employ others or connect them to employers with an intention to secure their loyalty. This scenario is not peculiar to South Sudanese. Taylor (2004) points out that in patriarchal societies, people have a strong sense of hierarchy which makes people depend on higher authority in many aspects of their lives. In patriarchal societies, people rarely question those who are above them in hierarchy. Sponsorship from these higher authorities is valued since one cannot access services without connections. In line with this patriarchal notion of social functioning, South Sudan leaders know that it is difficult for citizens depending on higher authorities to question actions of those who support them in any way, be it through financial or other privileges. Dependency on higher authorities in patriarchal societies starts from family heads and goes up to the president. South Sudan is a patriarchal society and the president holds unquestionable powers even to sack elected governors.

Services that elected leaders render to their electorates in South Sudan rarely show any accountability (Roach, 2016). This is partly because politicians in South Sudan never want to commit themselves to anything that would punish them or restrict them from exercising power as they desire (Jok, 2015). What seems to occupy politicians' daily activities in South Sudan is how to protect the political power they have which has nothing to do with making citizens happy. It has all to do with pleasing one's senior leader in one's institution. Political appointees would always want to please the President. Failure to show loyalty to top leaders results in being sacked (Rolandsen, 2016). However, most of the politicians removed from power positions by usual presidential decrees in South Sudan rarely remain silent. Some of them work tirelessly, including using military power, to regain their lost power positions (Wilson, 2019), whether or not the loss of a political power position is justified. Even those who lost elections in the year 2010 used violence to get power through the backdoor of elected government (de Waal, 2014).

Power struggles often lead to insecurity in South Sudan, both at national and state level, which could come in different forms. It could be incitement of the aggrieved politician's community against the community of the politician he or she is competing with. The goal of this community's incitement is that what such a politician is not happy about could be addressed. So-called grievances of politicians are addressed in South Sudan by giving the politicians political or military positions or ranks that would make them happy (Jok, 2015). This practice started during the North-South civil war and became normal after the signing of the CPA. When Paulino Matip Nhial's South Sudan Defence Force (SSDF) militias benefited from the 'big tent' policy in 2006, for example, it became a practice for many politicians and military officers to rebel against the government and get power positions that they might not deserve (Jok, 2015). The 'big tent' policy was the integration of about 50,000 SSDF soldiers into the national army.

The military ranks they gave themselves were left untouched during the integration. This signalled to others that they could get the same treatment whenever they rebel against the government and later re-join it. The insecurity resulting from this practice comes from attacks on military positions by armed youths or soldiers loyal to the aggrieved politician for the same aim of being heard and rewarded with power (de Waal, 2014). It was a power struggle that led to civil war in 2013 in South Sudan (Pinaud, 2014).

When power-motivated civil war breaks out and politicians engage in peace talks, power-sharing arrangements among the warring parties dominate the negotiations (IRRI, 2018). This was true during the Comprehensive Peace Agreement (CPA) negotiations in Kenya from 2002 to 2005 and in peace talks in which South Sudan's warring parties engaged from 2013 to 2018. Dissatisfaction with power-sharing arrangements often results in continuing the war, regardless of whether or not citizens are suffering (Roach, 2016). For example, when power-sharing arrangements did not work well in 2016, fighting renewed among the warring parties. '[P]eople who had been fully involved in the peace process increasingly came to the realisation that the settlement that was signed in their name was, in fact, unfavourable to them' (Jok, 2015: 10). Peace talks had to resume in Addis Ababa, Ethiopia and in Khartoum, Sudan to put power-sharing right. The Revitalised Agreement on the Resolution of the Conflict in the Republic of South Sudan (R-ARCSS) was initially signed in Khartoum and then in Addis Ababa in September 2018 after the warring parties agreed to have at least five vice presidents.

South Sudanese' Love for Power and Self-Enhancement Value

The power value in South Sudan is just one of the two minor values under Schwartz's (1992) Self-Enhancement value. Self-Enhancement value includes the minor value of achievement alongside power value. In South Sudan, there is often less focus on any achievements other than military and political achievements. For example, sections of peace talks that address developmental needs and other benefits for all citizens can easily be ignored during implementation of a peace agreement. The government would spend 70% of the national annual budget on salaries of the army and civil servants to secure their loyalty to political leaders (Jok, 2015). This is because lack of development and insufficient service delivery rarely form the core of what South Sudan leaders perceive as a national problem. The problem for South Sudan politicians is getting access to or maintaining power positions.

The SPLM Manifesto of 1983 mentions the love for power as one of the main factors that weakened Anya-Nya 1 rebels in the 1960s. Anya-Nya 1 officers could give themselves high military ranks even when the numbers and level of soldiers they led did not justify them. This self-promotion was often done contrary to set procedures for military promotion, leading to perpetual internal conflicts that the government in Khartoum could exploit to defeat the rebels. To remedy this problem John Garang of the SPLM/A decided to remain a colonel when he rebelled against the government in Khartoum and became the leader of SPLM/A in 1983. This meant nobody in the SPLA could be promoted above the rank of colonel.

However, Garang's idea could not end power ambitions in the SPLA. Military ranks closer to Garang's rank of colonel were still more desirable for almost every officer in the SPLA. It was clear that not only the rank of general was desirable. Since the rank of colonel was the highest, the rank of lieutenant colonel was called a commander. Almost every officer was aiming at the rank of a commander. Lower ranking officers in the SPLA often wanted to move one step higher. Even those closer to Garang in rank wanted to take his position, leading to many rebellions within the SPLM/A during the north-south civil war. This meant that the need to move to higher ranks did not go away although Garang maintained his Sudanese army rank of colonel. The problem for Anya-Nya 1 and the SPLA was not the rank level. It was power value. Therefore, it was mainly the overvaluing of power that needed to be addressed.

Addressing overvaluing of power does not mean doing away with the love for power. It is normal that power and control often dominate relationships between leaders and the people they govern. The difference mostly lies in the main goal of power. Some leaders disconnect power from ethics, and others keep the two together. Ethical leaders are often mindful of their moral obligations. Ciulla (2009: 302) points out moral obligations to 'justice, duty, competence, and the greatest good.' In South Sudan, the promotion of power value is not necessarily disconnected from claims of ethical principles such as justice and duty. The Bill of Rights in South Sudan's Constitution, for example, outlines moral responsibilities of government leaders towards citizens they lead. Article 9(1) of the Constitution shows that a covenant exists between the people of South Sudan and their government. This covenant means that political leaders should commit themselves to respect and promote 'human rights and fundamental freedoms enshrined in this Constitution; it is the cornerstone of social justice, equality and democracy.' One may think that there is a room for getting around these constitutional moral obligations. But the Constitution gives no space for the arbitrary exercise of power. Article 3(2) of South Sudan's Constitution clearly states that 'The authority of government at all levels shall derive from this Constitution and the law.'

Power Value and Ethical Principles in South Sudan

Despite unambiguity of the Constitution on how leaders should exercise power in South Sudan, politicians rarely talk about ethical principles in the day-to-day running of their affairs. If they mention anything that appears like an ethical principle, then it is vague because the connection of written laws to moral obligations in South Sudan's politics rarely exist. It is common for South Sudan leaders to say one thing and do the opposite which is a prevalent culture in Africa.. Africans know the difference between mere words and actions very well. Often, African leaders deliberately disregard rules in order to manipulate others for personal gain. As Garang (2019: 94) puts it, in African states 'the politics of the country runs according to the desires of leaders rather than a formalised ideological agenda and policy.'

Political leaders in countries like South Sudan seem to take power as a determiner of ethics. Ethics in South Sudan is what leaders say it is. In Nuer culture, for example, killing a person in any fighting is regarded as unethical because it pollutes the killer. Mostly, 'Various authority figures in South Sudan, including Nuer prophets, offer collective and individual healing against the consequences of this violence, partly as a way to build their own authority and ability to mobilize' (Pendle, 2020: 44). To neutralise this mobilisation power, Nuer political leaders justify killings that are ordered by government. Since Nuer religious leaders do not want to lose their powers to political leaders, sometimes ATR and political leaders get into a power struggle. For example, ATR leaders in Nuer resist claims of some political and military leaders that killing people in government-related wars never results in a curse on the killer. ATR leaders resist politicians' understanding of killing and its effects and maintain that killing pollutes the killer, regardless of who orders it.

The ethics of killing is not clear cut. So one could argue that both

Nuer politicians and religious leaders have a point. Political and military leaders could be justified in ordering soldiers to fight and kill other fighters if the war is a just war (Baird, 2016). Nuer ATR leaders, on the other hand, could justifiably maintain that a killer is cursed who kills people in an unjust war. This distinction can generate ethical standards for relationships between people and those in power. Ethics is about sincere and fair relationships between people. Nobody has the right to manipulate others for personal gain. Ethics bring into consideration aspects of right and wrong, regardless of the power position of any member in a group or society (Ciulla, 2009).

Yet, in South Sudan complaints of unfair treatment of citizens or problems of inequality often cover a hidden agenda of those who want to maintain or gain political power and then protect such power with financial resources (de Waal, 2014). For example, complaints during the CPA implementation were often 'about the need for the equitable distribution of peace dividends along ethnic or regional lines, however, in essence, they were about direct financial and power gains for the concerned individuals or groups of people' (Jok, 2015: 10). Even though claims for equal distribution of resources are often based on fairness in South Sudan, they still fall short of distributive justice principles in the sense that written laws rarely protect such equitable distribution. Law is supposed to define fairness and these clearly defined fairness laws should be binding on every citizen, regardless of their power positions. Put differently, ethical principles are not arbitrarily determined by those who want their self-interested wishes met. This is because nobody is free from legally defined ways of doing things.

The rule of law guides ethical or moral principles in politics. This is why new moral principles are often enacted into law. The enacted laws define how human beings within a territory should relate to one another. Violating enacted laws leads to punishment. Leaders' adherence to the rule of law demonstrates their ethical stance in the exercise of their powers. In most cases, misuse of political power comes from failing to adhere to the rule of law. Unethical acts which leaders in South Sudan sometimes seem to commit relate to power (Ruey, 2017). Those who hold onto power are likely regarded as unethical because they do not seem to care about others. The ones who want to get power are seen as unethical supposedly because all that they want is power. Mainly, political aspirants who have interest in political positions are labelled as people who want to get into or maintain power through the blood of innocent people. Sometimes, this accusation is true when one wants to get a political power position through military means. It is also true when incumbents want to maintain power by, with impunity, intimidating and causing their competitors to vanish.

Impunity in South Sudan seems to contribute to disregard for written laws and disregard for written laws encourages impunity. Pendle (2020), for example, describes how local government in South Sudan tries to separate the spiritual powers of ATR leaders from chieftaincy when a particular chief seems to undermine the authority of local government. But the same government leaders would encourage the combination of spiritual and customary powers in a particular chief who does not undermine state authority. For instance, local government leaders 'often sought out leaders with pre-existing authority to be chiefs on the condition that they accepted the government's overarching authority and instructions' (Pendle, 2020: 48). This manipulative implementation of laws seems to have its roots in South Sudanese cultures. Ward (2019: 180) points out that a person is 'an assembly of practices and performances and the interplay of multiple modes of memory.' This is where imagination plays a role by bringing to people's minds images of what they fear and love. Imagination, according to Ward (2018: 184), is 'opportunistic as it gropes and ferrets out the most favourable and meaningful circumstances, and as it moves towards or away from some ideal attunement between inner propulsions and outer habitats.' Sometimes a strange value that people fear may be the highest good in comparison with what they love in their culture. However, the fact that they are less familiar with such a new value makes them resist it, even if it is better. People rarely imagine the usefulness of what they are less familiar with in their socially and culturally constructed norms and values. Because of this interplay of different modes of memory in our underlying values, people tend to do what they are familiar with even if it is not what the written laws stipulate.

In many cultures in South Sudan, people rarely question what their leaders do. This gives leaders freedom to manipulate laws (Knopf, 2013). In united Sudan, 'Government officials claimed that the government power behind the law had transformed Nuer moral codes into Nuer law by providing sanctions' (Pendle, 2020: 48). However, religious sanctions seem to have existed against immoral behaviour before government sanctions were put in place, though these religious sanctions were less standardised (Johnson, 1986). Customary laws and ATR sanctions are less standardised because they are known by heart even by chiefs who adjudicate cases in customary courts. This makes people in South Sudan think of written laws as rules that leaders apply to any situation as they wish. This understanding of written laws is even evident in the South Sudan state where the Constitution has been amended several times since independence in 2011. Such amendments often relate to the power-sharing arrangements that the warring parties negotiated and agreed during peace talks such as in 2015 and 2019.

In South Sudan, the law seems to be beneath leaders instead of above them (Knopf, 2013). Because of this understanding of law, leaders seem free to twist laws in ways that suit their interests. This is one reason why Article 8 in South Sudan's Constitution seems to stipulate one thing, and leaders seem to do something different regarding equal treatment of religions. Religions that explicitly or implicitly demand accountability in South Sudan are suspected of having an interest in the potential downfall of political leaders even when they do not threaten the political power-structure in any way. All this manipulative implementation of laws in South Sudan comes from the culture that glorifies the use of power without accountability. Culture defines what people do. As Ward (2018: 183-184) points out, 'We are the inheritors of whatever was experienced in pasts we have never lived, but through which our species lived – particularly fears, anxieties and pleasures.'

Power and Public Harmony in South Sudan

The need to reduce fear sometimes motivates people to talk about the importance of public harmony. For example, public harmony and order seem to be what many people value in South Sudan. Yet, South Sudanese promote public harmony and order in relation to power or ambition to rule. Politicians seem to think that there must be harmony in order for a leader to rule without being disturbed. However, the law seems to stipulate harmony for the sake of peaceful coexistence among different communities. Article 2(3) makes it clear that South Sudan is 'a multi-ethnic, multi-cultural, multi-lingual, multi-religious and multi-racial entity where such diversities peacefully co-exist.' Despite this clear constitutional provision, political leaders in South Sudan rarely promote public harmony. They, for example, favour their relatives in employment (Atem, 2020: July 27). Segregated employment possibly serves to develop tribal supporters to whom politicians can run for political support when removed from power (Pinaud, 2014). Politicians make sure they secure trusted political supporters along tribal lines because politics in South Sudan is a poorly defined game of perpetual struggle.

Sometimes, people not related to politicians struggling for power know that these leaders lack integrity (Schomerus & Aalen, 2016). However, tribal supporters of politicians would not see such lack of integrity. Each side would blame the other for disturbing public harmony and order. Mostly, those in power think the ones who want to get into power do not care about public order and harmony among communities. Politicians who want to get into power seem to believe that the ones holding onto power care less about harmony among South Sudanese. Because of this, the notion of public harmony in South Sudan does not include civilities such as politeness. Hate speech is prevalent among South Sudanese (Clifford, 2017) who call one another names in public and expect public harmony in return. Because of this inconsistent understanding of harmony, public harmony in South Sudan seems attractive in theory rather than in practice.

Public harmony is attractive to South Sudanese in theory, but not in practice partly because what appeals to them is tribal pride (McGregor, 2014). Tribal pride seems to appeal strongly to them because many communities in South Sudan teach their children to be proud of their immediate clans and tribes in opposition to communities both near and far away (Yobwan, 2018). So communal or tribal pride rarely promotes social harmony because it does not glorify diversity in unity. Tribal pride is probably part of cultural imagination. As Ward (2018: 190) points out, cultural imagination 'is thick with dispositions, habits of mind and behavioural responses that have internalized the value systems that each of us lives.' Tribal pride is connected to power in that every tribe in South Sudan seems to believe it is more powerful than other tribes. This power-centred imagination is heightened when a member of a particular tribe is in a powerful position in the government. The favoured community believes they are honoured for having their son or daughter appointed to a higher position. This leads to rivalry among tribes in the sense that some communities would regard themselves excluded from government positions (Jok, 2011). Because of this rivalry and resentment among communities, there is often insecurity all over the country.

Power Value and Past Experiences of South Sudanese

How power is valued now is possibly linked to how it was valued in united Sudan. The same is true in various community traditions in South Sudan. They value hierarchical deference by younger ones to elders because power lies in hierarchy. Hierarchy was seen as the most important thing in Sudan, in the SPLM/A and local communities (Schomerus & Aalen, 2016). Different practices in different communities in South Sudan have some connection to power, often expressed in hierarchy. One of the practices was that chiefs always came from particular families and clans (Pendle, 2020). Another was that leaders could speak for others even when they had not consulted them. However, nobody would question leaders who would make decisions on behalf of others (Garang, 2019). This is because those who are higher in the hierarchy expect those who are lower always to remain silent, regardless of how much decisions made on their behalf affect their lives.

The SPLM/A was slightly different in that leaders often would get involved in power struggles (Nyaba, 1997). Those who were closer to top leaders would try as hard as they could to take power by force so that they could enjoy whatever top leaders like John Garang enjoyed. The Nasir Declaration of August 28, 1991, for example, 'was a political and military maneuver carefully calculated to snatch the leadership from Dr. John Garang' (Nyaba, 1997: 74). However, Garang was not free from overuse of power. He 'was the undisputed leader of SPLM/A, its chief ideologue, orator, decision-maker, negotiator and diplomat'

(Collins & Daly, 2016: 142). Garang was accused of having little tolerance for dissenting voices (Nyaba, 1997). The same was true of any other senior commander in the SPLA where junior officers who would dare question their seniors would be seen as enemies of the revolution (Nyaba, 1997). Because of this lack of freedom to question top leaders, followers of leaders struggling for power in the SPLA would fight one another without finding out exactly what they were fighting about. The senior commander was supposed to know it all. It was just a game of dominance. Other researchers observe that the focus on dominance makes each level in the hierarchy do little to complement the work of others (Taylor, 2004).

This literature confirms that politicians in South Sudan promote power value above other values. The need to preserve power seems to trump the need to preserve life in current South Sudan. It is partly for this reason that the power value has little relationship with achievement. Achievement value relates to power value under Schwartz's (1992) Self-Enhancement value. The understanding of achievement in South Sudan is to have more power, but not to use it for serving others to make their lives better. Yet, South Sudanese rarely blame a top leader like the President. A top leader is often seen as a pure person spoiled by people around him. This is to be expected in patriarchal societies in which people usually think that a leader has 'been betrayed by his local agents and officers, and that one needed to redress the situation in his name' (Taylor, 2004: 127). Now we turn our attention to how religious leaders cultivate values in South Sudan.

Religious Leaders and Value Cultivation in South Sudan

Religious leaders are no different from political leaders in South Sudan when it comes to overvaluing power. This is possibly because religious life is hardly disconnected from social and political life in the country. Different historical reasons contribute to this direct or indirect mixing of political and religious affairs. The same is true regarding the love for power. One possible reason is that the civil wars that resulted in the secession of South Sudan from Sudan in 2011 were mainly driven by religiously motivated love for power (Sidahmed, 2012). Islam was rarely disconnected from politics in Sudan (Jok, 2012). Because of this, Islamists believed they had legal, political and religious rights to rule in Sudan (D'Angelo, 2010). Christians found themselves marginalised politically and religiously when it came to power (Kustenbauder, 2012). The second possible reason that contributes to religious love for power is that before Christianity became a major religion in South Sudan traditional religions were not disconnected from community leadership (Pendle, 2020).

In both cases, spiritual leaders in Sudan and South Sudan would act on behalf of their communities with limited or no prior consultation. They would also support some politicians more than others on the basis of power solidarity. Any politician who would stand against spiritual leaders, especially Islamic ones, in Sudan risks losing such support (Sidahmed, 2012). This means that religious leaders have powers that political leaders rarely undermine in Sudan. To secure their unchallenged authority, Muslim leaders, and Christian ones to some extent, would side with politicians who promote religion in public (D'Angelo, 2010). Collaboration was the key to securing and maintaining power for both religious and political institutions. Given this background, religious leaders of leading religions such as Islam in united Sudan would hardly question bad leadership of political leaders as long as such leaders would not interfere with Islamic benefits and Islam's monopoly over other religions. True accountability would not have a space in this power collaboration between state and religious institutions in Sudan.

Guiding Principle in Religious Leaders' Power Value in South Sudan

The slight difference between religious leaders and politicians in South Sudan is that religious leaders rely on many past examples of religious servant leaders in holy books. Religious leaders in most cases easily make sense of new values and practices that have connections to old ones (Taylor, 2004). However, politicians in South Sudan seem to lack enough good examples of leaders with reliable records of servant leadership. It is in these reliable past examples that religions like Christianity seem to differ from others. Servant leaders in religion, especially Christianity in South Sudan, believe they work for something higher than authority in this world. Generally, Christianity aims at life beyond the life of this world. Mostly, the authority of God in Christianity has a connection to unconditional benevolence that goes beyond worldly flourishing (Baird, 2016). As Taylor (2004: 57) puts it, 'The paradox of Christianity, in relation to early religion, is that it seems to assert the unconditional benevolence of God toward humans (there is none of the ambivalence of early divinity in this respect), and yet it redefines our ends so as to take us beyond flourishing.' Christians believe in the renewal of the current disordered world (Taylor, 2004). This means that Christian leaders sometimes try to fix disordered governance systems as part of their focus on the new world of true flourishing.

Peaceful Coexistence and Power Value

Even though Christian leaders in South Sudan love power for the sake of it, they seem to promote values that are more than mere power value. For example, Christian leaders in South Sudan understand in principle that harmony among the people is something that God has ordained (Ashworth, 2013). Because of this, they do all they can in their power to promote peaceful co-existence among the people (Wilson, 2019). This understanding differs from that of South Sudan's politicians who seem to value harmony in connection to mere political stability to let them rule undisturbed. In their promotion of peace among the people, religious actors in South Sudan learn from history. For example, Catholic bishops issued this statement in 2014, a year after the civil war broke out in December 2013, in South Sudan: 'Our history is an open wound that desperately needs healing' (Catholic News, 2014). In this statement, the Catholic bishops seem to understand that history affects what people do or how they behave. Religious leaders also understand that Scriptures define what Christians do in their daily lives. This means that religious actors in South Sudan look backward to a people's history as well as to Holy Scriptures in order to deal with present and future social, religious and political problems. Since religious leaders often look backward first to age-old Scriptures in order to move forward, their new values often have connections to old ones. Harmony, for example, is one of the old values in Christianity that religious actors promote in South Sudan.

The old understanding of peaceful co-existence by Christians asserts that when they live in harmony with others, they obey a God-given duty to one another as God's creatures (Romans 12:16). It is this God-given obligation for one another that motivates Christians to care for one another, even for people they do not know. For example, 'religious actors and institutions across South Sudan have worked feverishly to preach peace, counsel war victims, and deliver services despite seemingly insurmountable odds' (Wilson, 2019: 4). This conception of Christian obligation is not new to South Sudanese. It is as old as Christianity.

Dual Obligations in Caring for Oneself and Neighbours

Christians do not merely think about their personal wellbeing. They also think about the wellbeing of people they do not even know. In early and medieval Christianity, this caring for oneself and others was understood as a dual obligation. Dualism was common in some Church Fathers' thoughts and theology. For them, issues often conflict within one person (Baird, 2016). It is not that dualism forms a dominant biblical theology in a way that agape or unconditional love does. It was mainly that existing schools of thought formed major parts of the worldview and traditions in which theologians grew up. Some of the Church Fathers were influenced by other religions and schools of thought that they were part of before they became Christians. Dualism was already part of their central value systems, a part that the new Christian way of thinking could hardly penetrate. Augustine is one of the Church Fathers influenced by earlier religions, in his case by Manicheian dualism, which believed in dual loves. To him, love for good and evil are often fused in one person (Baird, 2016). Augustine's teaching influenced other thinkers of his day and those who still admire his thoughts.

Christians today still believe in dual obligations, though it is mostly a revised Augustinianism. The difference between the medieval tradition and our time is that the concept of dual obligations at the time of Augustine was predominantly associated with duty, but now it is mostly connected to individual liberty, which is perceived to be the ultimate good today (Baird, 2016). What the dual obligations concept of the medieval tradition shares with the one of today is the motivation behind our actions towards others. As Taylor (2004: 117) puts it, 'what all these earlier conceptions have in common is that they suppose a duality of motivations in us: we can be tempted to serve our interest at the expense of others, and then we can also be moved—through fear of God, impersonal benevolence or whatever—to act for the general good.' Rousseau later argues that this dual obligation towards one another is somehow harmonised. He believes, as Taylor (2004: 117) points out, that 'the primitive instincts of self-love (*amour de soi*) and sympathy (*pitié*) fuse together in the rational and virtuous human being into a love of the common good, which in the political context is known as the general will.' When the self-love of a virtuous person is not 'distinct from love of others', there is harmony (Taylor, 2004: 117). Yet, the distinction in dual obligations remains in the sense that love for humanity still conflicts with love for self. Rousseau believes that this conflict comes from pride.

Not all religious leaders in South Sudan are aware of the concept of dual obligations. Muslim leaders probably have a different conception of love all together. However, Christian leaders and theologians are mostly aware of the two loves: the love for self and the love for others. This is what the Bible teaches, though love in the Bible prioritises others above oneself (1 Corinthians 13). The Bible harmonises dual obligations very well in that it discourages pride and envy that make the harmony of dual obligations tricky, though not difficult, in Rousseau's thought. It is probably along this line that Christian leaders in South Sudan mostly try to promote values that include love for one another and peaceful co-existence among citizens.

Religious Leaders and Promotion of Harmony Among Communities

The above examples partly indicate that religious leaders in South Sudan focus more on the promotion of harmony among the communities. Wilson (2019: 4) observes that religious actors in South Sudan 'are time and again cited by knowledgeable observers as the most important actors for peace in the country.' People mostly trust religious leaders in South Sudan. Wilson (2019) found that 82% of the citizens he interviewed reported that they confide in religious leaders whenever they face personal problems. This trust is not limited to solving personal problems. It extends to promotion of peace among communities. When Wilson (2019) asked interviewees questions about important actors and institutions for peace promotion in South Sudan, 83% mentioned religious actors and institutions as very important and 16% mentioned them as important. Only 1% mentioned religious actors and institutions as unimportant in peace promotion. The second most trusted group after religious leaders is elders. At least 10% of the respondents reported having trust in elders. One of the reasons why South Sudanese trust religious leaders is that they perceive them as God-fearing people who never promote violence. The legitimacy and influence that religious leaders and institutions have among South Sudanese make them important players in the cultivation of values.

Yet, religious leaders seem to be more effective at local level than at the national level in cultivating values such as harmony or peaceful co-existence in South Sudan. One of the reasons why religious leaders succeed in promoting peace at the local level is that they know how to make use of local values that encourage peaceful co-existence among communities (Ashworth & Ryan, 2013). People trust some religious leaders more than others because they work to promote peace and harmony among communities. One of the most trusted religious leaders is the former Archbishop of the Roman Catholic Diocese of Juba, Paulino Lokudu Loro. Wilson (2019: 11) quotes one interviewee as saying that Archbishop Lokudu 'talks about peace to his believers whenever he gets a chance. He always preaches a message of love, unity, and reconciliation.' Another is the Bishop Emeritus of Torit Diocese of the Catholic Church, Paride Taban. His record of peace promotion at local and national levels extends over decades of civil wars in Sudan and South Sudan (Ashworth & Ryan, 2013). Bishop Taban has mostly been effective in promoting peace and harmony at the grassroots levels. He has also been effective at the national level. Wilson (2019: 12) quotes one person describing Bishop Taban as 'a man who can change South Sudan because of his great ability in peace locally and at the national level. He is respected by many people including government officials.'

The former Archbishop and Primate for the Episcopal Church of South Sudan and Sudan, Daniel Deng Bul Yak is the third religious leader that people rank as one of the most popular religious leaders in peace promotion in South Sudan. Even though Archbishop Deng has been involved in the promotion of peace at the national level, he has been more effective at the local rather than national level. He is known for moving around from state to state with the torch of peace during his time in office. He is fearless in telling people the truth about the evil of war. Wilson (2019) quotes a nonreligious respondent as saying that Archbishop Daniel Deng does not fear to tell people when they are wrong or right.

Other church leaders mentioned as very important peace actors in Wilson's (2019) research include the Catholic Bishop of Yambio, Edward Hiiboro Kussala and the retired Bishop of the Episcopal Diocese of Rajaf, Enock Tombe. Both were effective at local level. Bishop Tombe mostly got involved in the peace negotiations in Addis Ababa from 2013 to 2018. As he was participating as an observer, he had little to do with changing the warring parties from war to peace. However, at local level Bishop Tombe has been promoting peace among communities such as Dinka, Nuer, and Murle among others. Bishop Hiiboro mainly promotes peace among communities in the areas of Yambio. One respondent in Yambio confirms this by saying, 'Hiiboro is very influential because he mediates between the community, rebels and government to bring peace in our community' (Wilson, 2019: 12).

Archbishops Deng and Lokudu had tried several times to convince national leaders to avoid war in favour of peace. But they could not succeed. They had been meeting with top political leaders in the country to promote peace and understanding among them. These meetings were often organised under the umbrella of South Sudan Council of Churches (SSCC). SSCC is known as one of the most important institutions for peace-building in South Sudan (Wilson, 2019). SSCC, for example, had to send facilitators to Addis Ababa in 2018, including this author, to resolve ten outstanding issues among the warring parties of South Sudan. This facilitation of peace by religious leaders was followed by the signing of the R-ARCSS in Khartoum, Sudan and later in Addis Ababa, Ethiopia in September of the same year 2018. The attempt by religious leaders to resolve the ten outstanding issues was not completely successful, though there were breakthroughs. It managed to introduce different ways of looking at things.

Christian leaders in Sudan and South Sudan have been consistent in their efforts to cultivate the culture of peace and harmony among the people. The Catholic Church has a clearly defined social teaching programme. This programme is known as the Catholic Social Teaching (CST). This social teaching puts into consideration issues to do with the common good and the dignity of human beings. More importantly, 'CST provides an image of peace as ultimately born of right relationships that resonates with the values and convictions of many others outside the Catholic community who also work for peace and justice' (Ashworth & Ryan, 2013: 53). Along this line Catholic bishops launched a program for pastor training in May 2011 with the theme 'One Nation from Every Tribe, Tongue and People' (Angle, 2011: 15) which can easily be internalised by pastors. Moreover, training like this can cultivate peace among Christians. It aims at transforming pastors' hearts and minds. When pastors are able to portray the value of peace and harmony among different churches, then Christians whom they shepherd may learn from them. This cultivation of harmony as a value among Christians may extend to people not Christians all over the country. As Ashworth and Ryan (2013: 53) point out, such a programme 'is a powerful reminder that the church's work of peace begins with the transformation of hearts and minds.'

Preliminary Conclusion

To identify the roles that religious and government institutions play in cultivating values among South Sudanese, the literature shows that political leaders in South Sudan promote the power value more than other values in their institutions. However, the power value that they promote rarely involves focus on achievement. In Schwartz's (1992) basic theory of human values, power value is a subset of Self-Enhancement value. Achievement is part of this category but is often missing in the exercise of power in South Sudan. Power seems to be exercised for its own sake without any focus on achievements for common good. Power and insecurity generate each other in South Sudan. For example, the love for mere power often results in insecurity which increases the use of power for self-defence. South Sudan leaders resemble what patriarchal societies do in the exercise of power (Taylor, 2004).

Patriarchal societies love power for both prestige and survival and

South Sudanese are no exception (de Waal, 2014). This overvaluing of power for prestige and survival is part of some cultures in South Sudan (Pendle, 2020). This means that cultural values define how South Sudanese behave in public. Mostly, cultural values influence what leaders do in the government regardless of written laws. In many cultures in South Sudan, hierarchy matters. This is where their cultures resemble medieval cultures. Medieval thinkers believed in the hierarchy of beings which has implications for how people exercise power.

In the literature, no evidence shows that religious leaders are different from politicians in the love for power, but many religious leaders in South Sudan do more to promote peaceful coexistence among different communities than political leaders. But religious leaders are not effective at all levels. They are more effective at local level than at the national level in promoting harmony among citizens within and outside religious institutions. At the national level, politicians seem to love power without much consideration for the common good or the welfare of all citizens. In other words, politicians in South Sudan exercise power in a self-centred manner. At the local level, however, chiefs understand their powers as tools for uniting the people they lead (Pendle, 2020).

It was clear in chapter four that Africans and Asians love harmony, though this harmony is often for the inner group. In this area South Sudan resembles Singapore in secular and non-liberal religion-state relationship. This means that religious leaders build on the love for harmony that communities already have. Ashworth and Ryan (2013: 54) seem to confirm this by observing that religious leaders succeed in cultivating peace in South Sudan because they make use of 'local values and practices.' Local values and practices probably diminish at the national level where the understanding of power as the ultimate value cancels out the love for harmony.

However, it is unclear at this point how differences in value orientations influence what individuals and groups of people accept or reject and why value orientations at the local level differ from those at the national level. We might assume that what people value locally would be the same thing that they would value at the national level. But that does not seem to be the case. It is also not clear in the literature how people arrive at consensus in their attempts to live together in harmony at the local level despite their different moral convictions. Chapter 6 will, therefore, explore these differences in value orientations as well as consensus-making.

CHAPTER SIX

DIFFERENT MORAL CONVICTIONS AND CONSENSUS IN SOUTH SUDAN

Introduction

We have argued so far that political leaders in South Sudan overvalue power. They seem to use it heavily without consulting their constituencies (Kopf, 2013; Jok, 2015; Muita, Yitbarek, & Mnguni, 2018). This power value, however, seems to lack the achievement value that goes with it in Schwartz's (2012) Self-Enhancement category of values. The implication of valuing power heavily without valuing achievement at the same level is that such power would neglect to render services to the people who are being led. Lack of services would then force the less privileged to resist those who are in power as shown earlier. And resistance to those who are in power results in wars that undermine peaceful coexistence among communities.

However, politicians are not alone in overvaluing power in South Sudan. Religious leaders also seem to overvalue power. The difference between the two is that religious leaders make use of local values to promote peaceful coexistence among communities (Ashworth & Ryan, 2016). But political leaders seem to capitalise on ethnic divisions in order to obtain or maintain power. They may intentionally disrupt local values that encourage peaceful coexistence among communities because peaceful coexistence among people would limit their support base.

Values and Different Levels in South Sudan

The understanding of values and their functions at the community level seem to be disconnected from values at the national level. It is highly likely that political and military leaders think that what qualifies as a taboo at the local level hardly qualifies as the same at the national level (Pendle, 2020). This indicates that different institutions and the people leading them differ in their promotion of values. Given this lack of harmony between the understanding of local and the national values, it is possible that fragmented moral convictions about the common good exist among customary, political and religious institutions. These worldview incompatibilities make it difficult for different institutions to agree on common values for the advancement of the common good within the country, and often lead to conflict.

Conflict results from the incompatibility of values and goals. As Lamle and Aigbovbioisa (2019: 194) summarise, people sometimes 'pursue incompatible goals, interests, status, values, beliefs, resources or positions that ultimately lead to mutual disagreements or conflicts.'

South Sudanese currently seem to have fragmented worldviews in relation to the common good because they are scattered in many countries around the world. Those who resettled in Western countries at a young age know little about traditional values in South Sudan. The ones who went to these countries as adults know much about their traditional values. Because of this variation in experience, some South Sudanese now value Western ways of resolving disagreements and conflicts that result from mismatched values. But others still value African ways of resolving value-motivated conflicts. Members of these two different groups in the diaspora are now well-educated and financially better off than those in rural areas in South Sudan. Because of these two advantages, those in the diaspora have influence on communities in South Sudan. They claim to be modern in their thinking and have the financial strength to care for others. Their influence potentially contributes to fragmented worldviews in relation to values and the common good which then raise a question: How might different groups with different moral convictions arrive at consensus in South Sudan?

Common Values in African Traditions

Local values may differ from community to community. Yet, some values are common in many African traditions. In Africa, 'traditional values are relationships, selflessness, hospitality and a spirit of inclusiveness' (Johnson, 2016: 27). These values may fall under Schwartz's (2012) major value category of Self-Transcendence, although Self-Transcendence consists of only two minor values: universalism and benevolence. South Sudanese share the above-mentioned common values. But, local values in South Sudan are religious in nature (The same may be true in other African countries.). They are religious in the African Traditional Religions' sense. In relation to religious beliefs,

Africans consider values as taboos. They are not just practices or ways of life that communities love to follow. Since values are taboos in Africa, members of any society are expected to adhere to common values since failure to do so would bring a curse onto the whole community (Okoye, Ezeanya, & Chukwuma, 2018).

South Sudan is no different from many African countries. As Johnson (2016: 27) points out, 'there exists a commonality of core traditional values and world views among the diverse people of Africa, which makes it easier for them to understand their perception on the concept of peace.' Yet, a tension often exists between public morality and the law. Public morality here refers to how a particular society conducts its daily affairs in relation to pursuit of the common good and shared values. Public morality in Africa prioritises social order above individual competing interests. Africans give more weight 'to maintaining social order than meeting individual interests' (Kibret, 2015: 1). In most cases, they believe that each member should promote what is good for the community as a whole. Africans understand ethics as 'what a person does in accordance with the established norms of the society, which eventually contributes to the welfare of the whole community' (Okoye, Ezeanya, & Chukwuma, 2018: 11).

An overarching need for conformity guides what individuals do in African communities. A community consists of individuals who have different moral convictions in relation to how they are raised in their families. Yet, these individuals live in a community in which they are expected to conform to norms that they receive from their ancestors. Mostly, 'every member of the community is expected to act in ways that will enhance the good of the entire society' (Okoye, Ezeanya, & Chukwuma, 2018: 10). To maintain consistency on how community members behave, community elders acts as custodians of community values. They keep a close eye on what an individual does in public in order to make sure that each member of a community conforms to norms that their ancestors have passed down to them through generations. Public morality mainly relates to how a society regulates behaviours of its members who are individuals living in a community.

In Africa, 'the society is a series of interrelationships in which each one contributes to the welfare and the stability of the community, and avoids anything that is disruptive or harmful to the community's life' (Okoye, Ezeanya, & Chukwuma, 2018: 10). The way that elders police their people in African communities differ from how police do their policing in the Western world. Statutory laws guide the police in the West, while customary laws guide elders in African societies. Statutory laws, which are a body of rules usually adopted from social norms, are mostly written down in Western countries. This means that laws are formal in Western states. However, they are largely common or informal in many African countries. Legal norms of customary laws seem flexible when compared with legal norms of statutory laws (Lamle & Aigbovbioisa, 2019).

Common Value-Clash Resolution Strategy in African Communities

When values clash in African communities, the resolution is guided by the need to restore harmonious relationships among the conflicting parties (Issifu, 2016). Conflict resolutions in Africa 'focus on the principles of empathy, sharing and cooperation in dealing with common problems which underline the essence of humanity' (Kibret, 2015: 12). However, the same value-clashes are resolved differently under statutory laws (Alexander, 2019). Resolutions of value-motivated conflicts are consensus-based in Africa, but are not under Western statutory laws. It is likely that the difficulties that South Sudanese face today in resolving value-motivated conflicts come from legal systems that differ from customary laws that the country prides itself in championing (Jok,

2012). Other modern African states seem to face the same problem. This is because whenever African states get their independence from different colonial rules, they usually borrow Western statutory laws because colonial administrations are mainly Western.

South Sudan resembles other African states in their seemingly unintentional adoption of Western constitutional values. One would expect that since South Sudan seceded from Sudan in the year 2011, its laws would closely relate to Sudanese laws. Yet, this is far from the reality that South Sudan laws predominantly relate to Western statutory laws. South Sudan has always related to the West more than to the Arab world. It is partly for this reason that South Sudab's Constitution resembles Western constitutions. This indicates that South Sudan does not get its legal norms from the Arab-leaning Sudan.

South Sudan's Constitution and Influence of Western Constitutional Norms

If South Sudan had borrowed its Constitution from united Sudan's Constitution, legal norms of such a constitution would still resemble the Western norms rather than the Islamic ones because Sudan's legal system is not entirely Islamic. The British colonial administrators wrote Sudan's first Constitution of before its independence in 1956. The Bill of Rights of the 1956 Constitution adopts Western legal norms. For example, Article 7(1) of the 1956 Constitution stipulates that 'All persons shall enjoy freedom of conscience and the right freely to profess their religion, subject only to such conditions relating to morality, public order, or health as may be imposed by law.' Freedom of persons, or individuals, is the guiding principle in this Article. Other Constitutions of Sudan follow the same line of this Article, though they eliminate the idea of individual rights in favour of collective rights.

Today, many people may think of Sudan as an Islamic state simply because provisions sympathetic to Islamic laws have been added to Sudan's 1973 and 1998 Constitutions. Yet, that does not destroy Western constitutional norms that were put into the 1956 Constitution. What is important is that all constitutions of Sudan mention morality and public order as exceptions to religious freedom. For example, Article 47 of the 1973 Constitution guarantees the freedom of religion 'without infringement of public order or morals.' The 1998 Constitution stipulates the same freedom of religion 'without prejudice to the right of choice of religion, injury to the feelings of others, or to public order.' Article 38 of the 2005 Constitution guarantees the same rights of religion, 'subject to requirements of law and public order.' The 1998 Constitution is particular in guaranteeing the Islamic value of not injuring people's feelings.

Unlike Sudan that flavours its Constitution with Islamic values, laws of independent South Sudan were entirely copied from Western laws with the aid of legal consultants from the West. One example of copied constitutional principles is the provision for separation of religion and state in the 2011 Constitution. Yet, South Sudan professes to be a customary secular state (Jok, 2012). In customary laws, there is no idea of state-religion separation. A chief sometimes performs both religious spiritual responsibilities and customary court duties (Pendle, 2020). In most cases, the tension between customary and Western legal values leads to confusion in the implementation of such constitutional provisions because traditional norms potentially form central values of many people. The confusion results from the clash of familiar and unfamiliar values that define these legal provisions.

Laws that are borrowed from Western traditions, on the one hand, differ from African ways of doing things in that these laws focus mainly on preventing harm to individuals and their property. African public morality, on the other hand, focuses on limiting individuals from doing harm to the community in which they live. It is common in African societies to consider anybody who acts against the interest of the community as having gone against the common good of the whole community. In Africa, an individual's duty is to protect the common good of all in the community. Preventing an individual from causing harm to a community where they live goes against the notion of individual rights that the Western laws mainly protect. How South Sudan manages this tension between the public and an individual is not yet clear nor whether South Sudan prioritises duty over rights in its public morality or not.

Customary, Statutory Laws and Offenses in South Sudan

Ethical issues that customary courts deal with in South Sudan relate to sexual matters, family disputes, murder, and stealing, among others. Offences relating to these issues are common in different communities (Kibret, 2015). Nevertheless, legal norms behind some of these offences differ between customary and statutory laws, such as the Penal Code and Criminal Procedure. For example, criminal courts normally treat impregnation as a non-criminal act. This is because adult males and females have legal rights in statutory laws to consent to engaging in love affairs with any non-relative of the opposite sex of their choice. However, traditional norms are against love affairs and pregnancies outside marriage. Also, defilement is not seen as a problem in traditional norms in many communities. In customary laws and traditions in most South Sudanese societies, puberty indicates readiness for engaging in marriage-related love affairs. Yet, defilement is a problem in Western-borrowed criminal laws of South Sudan. What determines readiness for engaging in love affairs in Western legal norms is the age that gives a person the ability to make informed decisions. This means that criminal courts would adjudicate offences differently from customary courts. The implication of all these differences is that neither customary nor criminal laws define public morality satisfactorily to accommodate all values in the country. Because of this, moral convictions regarding values and their violation would normally differ based on an individual's familiarity with certain values.

Prioritisation of Peaceful Coexistence

It is likely that in cases where tensions between Western and traditional norms exist, South Sudanese would prioritise any action that could promote peaceful coexistence among communities and individuals. The same applies to clashes of various traditional norms. South Sudan seems to resemble other African countries in traditional ways of doing things. In other parts of Africa, resolutions to any conflict prioritise harmonious relationships among conflicting individuals or groups. As Okoye, et al. (2018: 2) point out, 'Traditional African world cherishes harmony which means living in accord with the various spheres or levels of reality.' Sometimes, elders who often act as mediators invoke spiritual powers to help people involved in conflict comply with decisions made to reconcile them (Kibret, 2015). For this reason individual moral convictions matter less in South Sudan's traditional societies. One person may have a different moral conviction than most. However, few, if any, would dare go against spiritual sanctions. Partly due to this traditional belief, Christian and other religious leaders seem effective in solving disputes at local level. At community level, people fear spiritual sanctions because they lead to both individual and collective curses. This traditional belief in the danger of curses means that South Sudanese may see state laws as irrelevant, but would not regard spiritual sanctions with disrespect.

Given the above pairings of problems and solutions, I will describe how differences in value orientations influence what individuals and groups of people accept or reject. In addition, I will explore how South Sudanese arrive at consensus in their attempts to live together in harmony despite their different moral convictions. I will then explore traditional strategies of helping people with different moral convictions arrive at consensus in South Sudanese communities. The third section will examine political and modern strategies of helping people resolve differences related to conflicting moral convictions. The fourth section will explore Christian ways of helping individuals and groups resolve different types of conflicts. In each section, examples will be used to shed light on what South Sudanese do in relation to other strategies of value-motivated conflict resolutions.

Moral Convictions and Traditional Consensus Building in South Sudan

It is one thing to have strong moral convictions as individuals or groups. It is another to convince others to have the same convictions. For example, most traditional communities in South Sudan value human life highly. They believe that taking human life under whatever circumstance results in the pollution of the killer's whole community (Pendle, 2020). Others do not have the same conviction. Government officials and those who stay in haven areas may have slightly different moral convictions in relation to killing in state-ordered wars. It is easy for people who have a high regard for human life to avoid taking such a life, but difficult for them to convince those who do not value human life highly to have the same moral conviction. The same applies to other moral principles.

Value Differences and Peaceful Coexistence in South Sudan

In South Sudan, activities and behaviours that many people regard as immoral include disrespect for elders, stealing, adultery, rape, killing, abduction of children, and sex before marriage, among others (Kibret, 2015). Positive values that counter these negative behaviours matter for maintaining peace among communities and have roots in many Africans' central value systems. For example, respect for elders in many African societies is 'a virtue well entrenched in the customs, traditions and taboos' (Muigua, 2017: 6). Those who engage in such negative activities are seen as rebels in their communities and can be treated like criminals.

In almost every community, elders teach children and young adults how to avoid these immoral activities and behaviours. Africans respect elders partly for their teaching role and regard them as knowledgeable about the values and traditions of their societies (Johnson, 2016). Yet, some people continue have behavioural problems that elders often caution them against (Kibret, 2015). Individuals' passions may sometimes be stronger than their reasoning when engaging in such activities. It could be also that the upbringing of children may differ from family to family and community to community in relation to such problems. It could be that individuals would naturally develop their own ways of looking at things even if they know that what they do is contrary to common ways of doing things in their communities. Some may not see a vice in the same way that others would see it. This perhaps accounts for different moral convictions within a society.

Different moral convictions make people feel hostile to those who differ from them. That sometimes leads to conflict which 'is a struggle over values and claims to scarce status, power and resources in which the aims of the opponents are to neutralise, injure or eliminate the rivals'

(Okoye, Ezeanya, & Chukwuma, 2018: 2). Conflict would result from groups' value differences or an individual's rebellion against common values in a community. This is because people would feel disgusted to see or experience anything that goes against their normative ways of looking at issues. When those who rebel against community's norms have power, they are sometimes tempted to force those holding onto traditional values to give them up for new ones (Biar, 2014). Lobbyists do this in countries like the United States of America when a president who shares their moral convictions is in power. Yet, the use of force rarely penetrates the central values of many people because force does not change people's values overnight.

People who believe that protecting traditional values is right would fight back against changes, regardless of their weak power positions. For example, South Sudanese who were either Christians or followers of African Traditional Religions were weak in comparison to Muslims in united Sudan (D'Agoot, 2019). However, for decades they refused to accept Muslims' values. Attempts of Arab Muslims to force non-Muslim South Sudanese into Islamic values embodied in sharia laws resulted in civil wars until South Sudan seceded in 2011 (D'Angelo, 2010; Sidahmed, 2012; Kustenbauder, 2012).

Yet, different communities have different ways of solving moral issues over which they disagree. They rarely break up on the basis of value differences as did Sudan and South Sudan. More often, African societies and states break up at both micro and macro levels for administrative reasons rather than value differences. In most cases, Africans compromise for the sake of relationships when they disagree on moral issues.

Arab Muslims in Sudan seem to have a different way of looking at things. They probably believe in the winner-takes-all principle that rarely considers compromise as a win-win outcome. Arab Muslims rarely aim at mending relationships between them and those who have different moral convictions or values from them. The winner-takes-all mindset rarely focuses on harmonious relationships among groups with diverse values and worldviews. It becomes difficult for Muslim-dominated states such as Sudan to solve moral differences because they are not flexible during discussions about them. Muslims, especially Islamists, believe that their values are superior to those of non-Muslims (Sookhdeo, 2014). The same could be true for any community in Africa in which people have the mindset of the winner-takes-all.

Africans generally value flexibility in conflict resolution since they aim to restore harmonious relationships among communities which implies that rigidity is not productive. Any participant in the talks is believed to have some wisdom that would help the conflicting parties reconcile (Kibret, 2015). In this process, nobody has a monopoly of knowledge, and no values are assumed to be superior. Some humility is required from participants, even if those involved in the conflict are bitter for the wrong done or perceived harm inflicted on each side. This humility that often discourages extreme positions gives mediators enough room to deal with the conflict comprehensively. Put differently, African conflict resolutions focus on 'simplicity, participatory, adaptable flexibility, complete relevance, and comprehensiveness' (Kibret, 2015: 2). Since they mainly value restorative justice in conflict resolutions, a community that does not value win-win solutions in Africa may lack mechanisms for value-related conflict resolutions. If no mechanism exists for resolving moral disagreements, there would be no end to conflicts between any two conflicting parties.

The sixty-four tribes in South Sudan are grouped into four related ethnic groups. They include Nilotics, Nilo-Hamites, Bantus and the Sudanic groups (Wassara, 2007). These groups have common ways of solving value-related disputes or other conflicts. They all aim at restoring harmonious relationships between conflicting parties, so the solution to any disagreement is often based on a win-win model which avoids escalation of a problem. An escalated problem often ends up in civil courts. However, in many African communities, 'people tend to associate courts with the danger of creating a permanent rift in social relations, which in turn risks the wrath of the ancestors, spirits, and divinity, or the potential use of harmful magic by an enemy' (Agwella, 2020: 149). A conflict solution that elders provide is preferable in Africa for harmonious living.

Imagination and Moral Beliefs

Sometimes, value-related conflicts are imaginable in traditional South Sudanese communities. For example, Bantus in Western Equatoria believe that evil people with mysterious powers cause bad fortune to good people. Imagination uses images which might not necessarily exist. As Cronin (2010: 72) points out 'It is the function of imagination to receive images and to produce images of things that do not necessarily exist.' They might just mirror existing realities because imagination is based on what people believe to exist or have existed, without having physical access to it. This is why it is difficult to imagine any object that a mind cannot conceive of. Bantus in Western Equatoria in South Sudan, who still believe that some people have mysterious powers that harm others, use the power of imagination to assign immorality to invisible actions.

Africans do not overlook imagination-based moral beliefs because they may lead to conflict. Wassara (2007: 10), for example, points out that 'relationships deteriorate in the society and tension builds due to imaginary causes of conflict associated with magic and sorcery.' These ethical imaginations come from the fact that Africans do not separate religious life from secular life. They take life with its daily events holistically. Politics, religion and social life interact. 'Traditional approaches cannot be classified into political and juridical, rather they are holistic, comprising also social, economic, cultural and religious-spiritual dimensions' (Agwella, 2020: 146).

To South Sudanese, as in other African societies, conflict has spiritual dimensions (Agwella, 2020). Mediators who reconcile those who disagree on matters that involve spirituality perform spiritual activities during the reconciliation stages. In this process elders and chiefs of customary courts interact with spiritual leaders in the African Traditional Religions in South Sudan (Wassara, 2007). Other African communities resemble South Sudan communities in this process, among whom for example, 'Conflicts that have spiritual dimensions involving incantations, curses, witchcraft and oath-taking, among others, are brought before the traditional and spiritual leaders including the chief priests of deities, herbalists and diviners' (Johnson, 2016: 31). When a disagreement in South Sudan] results in bloodshed, people believe that gods would be angry not only with the murderer but with his whole community (Pendle, 2020). Spirits of such community's ancestors can also be angry with the living members.

Traditional societies in South Sudan also never look at events as isolated issues. They see them holistically as having connections to past, present and even future. Therefore, negative impacts of conflicts can have connections to the past in that the good name of one's family could be spoiled by today's wrongdoing. This is why 'Individuals in the communities are socialized to eschew behavioral dispositions that might bring disrepute to their fellow members' (Johnson, 2016: 30). Negative impacts of one's actions may potentially have connections to the present time in that community members could be harmed by one person's immoral behaviour. Negative impacts of one's actions could also have connections to the future in that unborn children would inherit a bad name from their parents.

Mending broken relationships between communities in conflict often includes repairing relationships among the living, gods, ancestors and spirits (Agwella, 2020). In reconciling conflicting groups or individuals, many Africans would sacrifice an animal 'and its blood is sprinkled on the shrine of the gods of truth and reconciler' (Lamle & Aigbovbioisa, 2019: 201). Some communities would even mix a little blood of their members with the meat of the sacrificed animal and cook it together to eat as a symbol of reconciliation or covenant (Johnson, 2016). This blood covenant is a major sacrifice for those who do it because it stops a conflict between communities. It also stops intermarriage between them. Because of these different relationships Africans perform ritual ceremonies in the process of reconciling conflicting parties. As Agwella (2020: 147) puts it, 'Ritual ceremonies bring together the people, the past, the present and the future, the ancestors and the gods for the sealing of the conflict resolution.'

Elders and Conflict Resolutions

Conflict resolution in Africa is done by people of integrity. Elders who lead efforts to reconcile communities in conflict are old people who are widely respected in such communities (Muigua, 2017). These leaders with integrity appeal to moral norms of conflicting communities while aware that nobody would question their own morality during the process. In traditional communities, respected elders lead by example. They are also knowledgeable about the history of their community as well as its values and norms. During discussions, such elders would share examples of how a similar dispute was solved in the past (Agwella, 2020) to demonstrate the possibilities for overcoming disagreements in similar situations for the common good of societies.

Resolutions of African conflicts start with exploring the root cause of a problem which requires the wider knowledge of elders. More than just what triggers a problem at hand is involved. Problems embody historical realities between the conflicting parties or individuals. So elders focus on knowing the root causes of conflict is to address them so that meaningful reconciliation can be restored (Johnson, 2016). Understanding historical facts helps parties appreciate how their relatives or communities related to one another in the past. If the relationship was cordial, their duty is continue such a cordial relationship. If there was historical conflict between the parties, elders will design ways of stopping such historical animosities. To get to the root cause of a problem, elders leading discussions and any other participant in the meeting ask questions that dig deep into the origin of the conflict. After clear understanding of the root parties in conflict can arrive at consensus in their problem solving.

Consensus in Conflict Resolutions

Consensus in Africa is important in any resolution of disagreements because it gives the parties in conflict the sense of ownership of the decision made to resolve it (Muigua, 2019). Consensus is often based on a win-win strategy in which no party feels like a loser. Elders in of conflict resolution make it clear to parties in conflict that after understanding the root causes of the dispute they would like to see a harmonious relationship among their people. Therefore any side in a dispute must give up something little in all that they value for the greater good of all. The Harambe Women's Forum (HWF) in South Africa, for example, decided to give up their bitterness against the Whites who mistreated them during the apartheid era in order 'to find a lasting security during the post-apartheid regime and created a better future for children as it fought against poverty' (Issifu, 2016: 149). The importance of lasting security is that it could bring harmony among parties in conflict so that current and future generations may flourish.

One might assume that applying traditional African consensus method to resolving value-based disagreements would be difficult. Yet, the love for harmonious relationships trumps any other value in resolving value-based conflicts in Africa. Africans resolve disagreements or conflicts based on harmonious relationships. For example, a disagreement between the government and Nuer prophets on the morality of killing exists today in South Sudan. Nuer and other Nilotic communities believe that killing a person under any circumstance pollutes the killer's whole community (Pendle, 2020). The government contests this unconditional pollution claim by differentiating killing in a state-ordered war and killing in a tribal conflict. According to the government, it is only in a tribal conflict that killing pollutes the killer.

To resolve the above-mentioned value-based disagreement, traditional leaders agree with politicians' differentiation of the two types of killing. However, ATR spiritual leaders still perform cleansing ceremonies to purify killers, regardless of who ordered the war in which such killers have slain their victims. The cleansing ceremonies that Nuer prophets perform to purify killers form a potential compromise between the state and ATR leaders. As Pendle (2020: 44) points out, healings that Nuer prophets perform 'do not only meet people's need for "health", but also resonate with beliefs that the political and the divine, even in matters of war and government, are intimately linked.' Moreover, a Nuer prophetess called Nyachol who has formed a moral community in her area would sometimes act 'as an informal appeals judge on the margins of an otherwise dysfunctional government court system' (Hutchinson & Pendle, 2015: 424). Chiefs would refer cases of killing to her so that she could reconcile a killer's family with a victim's family. The way Nyachol reconciles the two families or communities is to order for blood compensation for the slain person and then ritually purifies the killer from the pollution of killing before readmitting him into the moral community of youth that she has formed.

Surrounding Environments and Moral Beliefs

Nyachol is a peacebuilder, but in a limited sense. She promotes harmony within the Nuer community only. To her, it is immoral for one Nuer person to kill another Nuer. However, Nyachol does not hesitate to order attacks on other communities neighbouring Nuer (Pendle, 2020). The government once ordered Nyachol's arrest because she incited violence against neighbouring tribes. But her armed youth protected her from government arrest (Hutchinson & Pendle, 2015). Although she does not see any problem with inciting violence against neighbouring tribes, she still maintains her moral belief that killing within Nuer would pollute a killer, regardless of who ordered it. Because of this belief, Nyachol disagrees with government's officials on the claim that a state-ordered war does not pollute the killers. She purifies anybody who has killed before readmitting such a person into the moral community she has formed within her local area of Nuer community. However, the killers she purifies are 'all Nuer who have killed fellow Nuer and on the formal resolution of local blood feuds before she admits the perpetrators of such violence into her moral community' (Hutchinson & Pendle, 2015: 416). This all shows that Nyachol's moral community rarely extends to other communities since she orders revenge attacks on others.

The surrounding environment and the time in which Nyachol grew up may have influenced her moral beliefs. She grew up in the 1980s during the civil war in Sudan which encouraged violent ways of solving problems. For example, political and military leaders in both government and SPLA controlled areas glorified violence in dealing with one's enemies (Hutchinson, 2001). The enemies were often those who disagreed with top leaders. Disagreements among leaders in the SPLM/A controlled areas often related to a power struggle. Such internal power struggles set communities against one another inside South Sudan (Brosché, 2014). The rivalry caused by power struggles among leaders is worse between Dinka and Nuer because they are the majority tribes (Elhag, 2008) from which most of the leaders who engage in power struggles come.

All the above practices make the government care less about providing protection to any community. Therefore, 'Nyachol has responded to the government's abandonment of the local population to increased vulnerability to conflict by encouraging her followers to arm themselves and by sanctifying their protective stance through ritual' (Hutchinson & Pendle, 2015: 416). Whenever, a particular Dinka community would attack a Nuer village or cattle camp, Nyachol would order revenge attacks on Dinka villages and cattle camps. She saw no problem with her violent actions because she grew up in an environment that glorifies violence among communities. However, her local moral orientations make her believe that killing of one's community member pollutes the killer.

Nyachol rarely travels outside her home village. She does not even wear clothes, let alone use a car to travel. She once argued when one of the state government's ministers invited her to visit the state headquarters of Bentiu 'that she was unable to travel to Bentiu using a car because cars were part of the "modernity" she rejected' (Hutchinson & Pendle, 2015: 426). This limited exposure to other communities possibly contributes to Nyachol's moral worldview. Robinson (2016) observes that when people stay in their local areas with less exposure to other communities, they hardly trust other people. Also, any perceived or real political competition makes leaders play ethnic cards that result in ethnic hatred and prejudices. These factors combine to make Nyachol think that killing people from outside her community is not as morally bad as killing people within the same community.

When Nyachol is compared with another Nuer prophet, Gatdeang Dit, who grew up in the 1960s in Nuer areas, we see a major difference. Gardeang 'rejects all forms of violent aggression and fosters relations of peace and intermarriage with Dinka neighbors' (Hutchinson & Pendle, 2015: 415). He believes that intermarriage brings people of different communities together in a chain of extended family relationships which prevent communities and tribes from attacking one another. Leading by example, 'Gatdeang himself has married 30 Dinka wives, and many of his sons have followed suit' (Hutchinson & Pendle, 2015: 422). The Dinka responded to Gatdeang's example and married most of his daughters.

Gatdeang does not encourage anybody from his community to attack another community. He only believes in self-defence. He tells his people that the god he serves would not tolerate anybody who could fire a first shot against another person (Hutchinson & Pendle, 2015). He says that wounded or the captured people should not be killed during self-defence against external attackers. He lives by example, employing non-violent solutions to problems. In 2008, youth from Dinka in Warrap raided Gatdeang's cattle camp, looting more than 2,000 head of cattle. The Bul Nuer youth, the community of Gatdeang, considered the attack on his cattle camp intolerable. They wanted to raid Dinka communities in Warrap in revenge for what they had done. However, 'Gatdeang adamantly refused to condone their plans' (Hutchinson & Pendle, 2015: 425). He argued that one day, the attackers would bring the cattle back. As Hutchinson and Pendle (2015: 425) point out, , 'Gatdeang was alluding to the fact that he, personally, had received many gifts of cattle from visiting Dinka dignitaries, government leaders, and other supplicants from neighboring Warrap State over the years.'

When President Salva Kiir Mayardit learned about what had happened to Gatdeang and how he responded, he personally visited the prophet in his village. Instead of showing any anger, Gatdeang told the President that he was not angry against those who stole his cattle (Hutchinson & Pendle, 2015). He only pleaded with the President that the remaining calves of the looted cows be taken to their mothers in Warrap so that they would not starve to death. He never requested the return of his stolen cattle and refused the government's offer to do so because he understood that such operations often lead to violence and the death of innocent people. The President responded to Gatdeang's peaceful attitudes by providing the whole of his village with military and police protection from any possible external aggression in the near future. Although the military was later withdrawn from Gatdeang's village, more than ten police remained as his personal guards.

Gatdeang who grew up in the 1950s and 1960s was likely influenced by the Nuer values of the time. In Nuer and Dinka traditions, it was a taboo for anybody to kill vulnerable people such as children, women and older men during any fighting. (Mackenzie & Buchanan-Smith, 2004). One would also guard against killing a relative even if such a person belongs to the attacking community. Generally, however, killing a person considered evil in the Nuer community would still happen frequently among initiated men. As Nylapo (2017: 6) points out, 'any killing disturbs the social equilibrium by disrupting the "balance of blood" between the groups, which must now be redressed as part of the interplay of the rights they have against each other.' Gatdeang likely possesses these traditional values against killing. Having relatives in different clans and subtribes in Dinka and Nuer were signs of security. One could travel around easily without any fear of being harmed by strangers. This sense of security contributed to harmony among communities.

Harmony Value and Justice

The love for harmony in Africa could sometimes violate individual's rights to pursue justice the way he or she wants. Justice in Africa is often restorative. Africans value restorative justice because it avoids litigations that often result in retributive settlement of cases (Mutisi, 2011). Restorative justice mostly focuses on reconciliation of the victim and the perpetrator. There is often no real loser on any side of conflict. Africans see justice 'as the equality of opportunity and also points to the equality of all human beings' (Okoye, Ezeanya, & Chukwuma, 2018: 11). As Kibret (2015: 2) notes, 'Reconciliation comes as an end product of adjudication in which after the disputants have been persuaded to end the dispute and give concessions restoration of peace and harmony takes shape anchored on the principle of give a little and get a little.' Those who pursue punitive justice in Africa do not achieve such a goal since it is believed to disturb harmony among communities. But giving up what an individual believes to be a just way of settling his or her problems in favour of what a community wants may amount to coercing individuals to conform to community goods against the their will (Sabala, 2019).

Yet, Mason (2014) does not see justice and harmony as incompatible. He argues that only different worldviews make justice and harmony appear incompatible. For example, those who value harmony, like the Chinese, differ with those in the West who value justice because of how they understand the right and the good. The West and other regions in the world put the good and the right in opposition to each other. The West identifies the right with justice, and the Chinese identify the good with harmony. Mason (2014) argues that justice and harmony are complementary to each other. Mostly, 'there is a constant striving to do better, to use our understanding of the good to improve our pursuit of the right and to use right actions to further the good life' (Mason, 2014: 216).

Mason (2014) thinks that putting the right and the good together leads to restorative justice, and restorative justice leads to harmony among different groups. In issues to do with value differences or any other dispute, one may have to give up something in order to resolve such conflict. That is a win-win solution that many Africans value. To them, harmony matters more than punitive justice because it balances issues in conflict resolution. For example, 'We may lose a high level of harmony to ensure that an individual is not unfairly burdened, or we may put extra burdens on someone to bring about a greater harmony' (Mason, 2014: 216). This, to Mason, overcomes the polarity of the two. Mason (2014) believes that the combination of justice and harmony leads to practical wisdom.

Africans are similar to the Chinese in their efforts to combine the right and the good during any conflict resolution. Resolution of conflict focuses on restoration of relationships because it guarantees a greater good for all members of conflicting families or communities. Yet, justice is done to victims through compensation which restores damage without affecting relationships. Africans do not see value differences or different moral convictions as difficult to resolve. They believe that each person may maintain what values he or she treasures, but such differences cannot disturb harmony among the people. Even common values are maintained by persuasion, not by force. They are guaranteed through continuous persuasion of those who deviate from them. Words spoken to persuade people who deviate from common values effect harmonious relationships. But deviating from common values disturbs harmonious relationships among members of a community.

Traditional communities in South Sudan are truly Africans in how they resolve value differences among groups and individuals. They prioritise harmony over disagreement or any difference in moral convictions to arrive at consensus. Yet, they guarantee restorative justice in issues to do with justice. We now turn to how politicians resolve value differences in South Sudan.

Conflicting Moral Convictions and
Political Consensus Building in South Sudan

In conflict resolution, South Sudanese seem too flexible in both their local communities and at the national level. There is little evidence that politicians and civil servants disagree with the prioritisation of harmony in conflict resolution in their local communities. The same is true for leaders in the army and other organised forces. For example, SPLM/A leaders agreed with harmony-focused traditional conflict resolutions in 1999 at Wunlit to unite their warring factions (Ashworth & Ryan, 2013). This means that political and military leaders seem to understand that South Sudanese, like other traditional Africans, care more about relationships than an individual's or a group's feelings regarding different moral convictions. They also seem to understand the importance of consensus that often focuses on win-win solutions to disagreements. Yet, it seems difficult for politicians in South Sudan to prioritise harmony in conflicts that relate to politics. Political consensus that aims at long term stability all over the country is missing at the national level. According to Awolich (2015: 3), 'political consensus may be defined as a state of the nation when all the political forces are in complete agreement on foundational issues that affect its stability.' Possibly, South Sudanese focus on power value rather than on harmony at the national level, but focus on conservation values at local levels. This is why the implementation of constitutional and other legal provisions appears confusing.

South Sudanese love power without the achievement value (Jok, 2012; Knopf, 2013; Wilson, 2019; de Waal, 2014; Pinaud, 2014). Compromises that politicians make in peace talks support this conclusion because they often focus on power sharing arrangements rather than restoration of harmonious relationships or stability. This focus on power sharing during peace talks started with the 2005 Comprehensive Peace Agreement between the Sudan government and the SPLM. The same power sharing compromise was repeated in the Agreement for the Resolution of Conflict in South Sudan signed in 2015 and the 2018 Revitalised Agreement for the Resolution of Conflict in South Sudan. Particularly, the R-ARCSS compromise was done after the introduction of five vice presidents, each for a party involved in the peace talks.

Disagreements that resulted in civil war in 2013 in South Sudan were mainly about principles of voting in party primaries within the SPLM party. However, the agreements that different parties arrived at in Addis Ababa and Khartoum in 2015 and 2018 turned out to be based on power sharing. This shows that the aim was on how to maintain or get into power. It had little to do with the universal norms of democracy. Norms of democracy focus on the right of majority to choose their leaders who serve them. Democratic norms are not about getting power for the sake of it. Mere power value often prioritises domination over citizens (Schwartz, 1994). Leaders who dominate rather than serve their people also control resources. This is because successful control of citizens by a leader necessitates that such a leader be financially strong to maintain unchallenged power. Above all, leaders who value mere power treasure prestige in social status (Schwartz, 2012) which may sometimes have little to do with achievements in service delivery since doing so would raise the social status of others.

Conservation and Power Values

Conservation values differ from power values in that they are mostly used to protect one's underlying values. Those who value power use security value to protect it. Conservation values protect values generally by ensuring that no action disturbs any value that one holds as a very important part of his or her belief system. For example, 'People for whom independence is an important value become aroused if their independence is threatened, despair when they are helpless to protect it, and are happy when they can enjoy it' (Schwartz, 2012: 3). South Sudanese apply conservation values in their day-to-today interactions at local levels more than they do at the national level. Conservation values that include tradition, conformity and security focus on social order and stability. This is why any member of any community should respect and maintain customs provided by his or her tradition (Schwartz, 1994). It is also for social order that one should avoid actions that could harm others. Harmony and safety are very important in conservation value.

At local levels in South Sudan moral convictions relate to conservation values because local communities put harmonious relationships above other values. Some conservation values such as security emphasise 'safety, harmony, and stability of society, of relationships, and of self' (Schwartz, 2012: 6). Because of this, South Sudanese prioritise harmony in resolving conflicts caused by different moral convictions at local levels. However, they prioritise power in resolving issues at the national level possibly because power focuses on 'control or dominance over people and resources' (Schwartz, 2012: 5). Resources are very limited at community levels in South Sudan today because we still heavily rely on oil, making it less attractive to exercise power at local levels for dominance and prestige. This leaves local levels with traditional love for harmonious relationships that are important for survival.

The differentiation of the local from the national started right from the British policies that restricted southern Sudanese from having access to the north of Sudan during the colonial rule. The policy known as the Closed Districts Ordinances might have been put in place for reasons known only to the British. It led to divide-and-rule politics later adopted by the Muslim fundamentalists who ruled Sudan from its independence in 1956 until South Sudan's secession in 2011. Kon (2015: 3) argues that 'the colonial policies of divide and rule have constructed a sense of regionalized socio-political identity which in many aspect delayed conducive environment for a peaceful co-existence and socio-cultural and economic development, and most importantly contributed in cycles of regional political tensions in the politics of representation nationally.' This gave South Sudanese a different way of understanding the national government in Khartoum. They seem to think that there is no moral connection between what they do in the national government and what they do in their local communities since the national government belongs to nobody. To them, the national government is where people get political power that would give them the chance to become powerful and rich. The local community is a place where relationships are built and maintained for generations. Because of this potential misunderstanding of government, anybody who misbehaves at the national level would still be a hero at the local level where he or she builds relationships with local supporters, using national resources to buy their loyalty.

Political Tribalism in South Sudan

Since the national level is where people exercise absolute power for the sake of pride and prestige, relationships are often guided by private interests. Those who do not want to support a leader's interests are regarded as enemies with whom one has nothing to do. Instead of discouraging disharmony among communities, South Sudan leaders seem to encourage people from their tribes always to work against their political rivals (Kon, 2015). This is what Rolandsen and Kindersley (2017: 3) term as 'political tribalism.' To them, 'This political tribalism has been mobilised by colonial and post-colonial governments, and by the independent government today, as a useful tool in seeking constituencies of support' (Rolandsen & Kindersley, 2017: 3). Because of this, violence is often part of political disagreements. For this reason leaders of SPLA tried to change people's moral convictions against killing other humans in Nuer by saying that killing in government war never pollutes the killers. That is, government enemies should be eliminated without any fear of killing pollution or curse. Yet, people at local levels still consider the curse related to killing 'to be so pervading in society that it has itself become the cause of government wars' (Pendle, 2020: 47).

South Sudanese politicians mostly engage in identity politics rather than promoting true consensus-based politics. At the level of politics, 'some in the SPLA/M claim to be more "SPLA/M Proper" than others because they claimed not to have rebelled against it and to have sacrificed more for the cause of freedom than others and as such feel entitled to government privilege' (Kon, 2015: 4). They seem to have learned this identity politics from Sudan. Politicians in Khartoum ruled Sudan for decades on the basis of Arabs against Africans and Muslims against Christians (Sidahmed, 2012). To make matters worse, 'religious sectarianism created frictions not only between Muslims and Christians but also between Muslims who claim to be more Islamic than others in Sudan' (Kon, 2015: 3-4). Fundamentalist Muslims in Sudan could not imagine arriving at consensus with non-Muslims and moderate Muslims who could not follow the fundamentalists' version of Islam. Compromise for the sake of harmonious relationships is not the culture of fundamentalist Muslims in Sudan.

Since Islamic religious values were considered government values too (D'Angelo, 2010), it was difficult among politicians in Sudan to compromise their moral positions for the sake of harmonious relationships. Sudanese politicians would never compromise what Arabs and Muslims, especially the fundamentalists, believe in for the sake of the common good among ethnic groups in the country. They believe that their Muslim and Arab values are better than values of other religions and races. (Sidahmed, 2013; Jok, 2012). Their 'policies were rather placed on social engineering and reconstruction of peoples' cultures and communities, through introduction of Arabic and Islam culture and religion to build (what was thought at the time by Northern Sudanese) a more homogeneous identity and society' (Kon, 2015: 3). South Sudan politicians seem to have adopted this way of doing things in their problem resolution at the national level, but not at local levels. Working at the local level seems to represent the African way of solving disagreements, while Arab Muslims seem to deal with moral disagreements on the national level.

South Sudan politicians seemed to believe that it was immoral for some people to support the Arab Muslims during the north-south civil war in government-controlled areas. This is because Arab Muslims were mistreating Africans and Christians in those areas. Politicians also seem to think that those who disagreed with John Garang during the war and rebelled against the SPLM/A have no moral grounds to lead. In most cases, those who consider themselves sole liberators of South Sudan consider some tribes as traitors because most of the leaders coming from these tribes rebelled against the SPLM/A during the liberation war. Other tribes are considered cowards because only a few of their members participated in the liberation war. These views imply that those who liberated others have rights to special privileges. Rolandsen and Kindersley (2017: 10) point out that President Kiir 'has repeatedly made the ahistorical claim that Dinka people made disproportionate sacrifices in the SPLA wars, and thus are implicitly entitled to a disproportionate share of government and military positions.'

There are some truths in the above-mentioned views. Many people would agree that it is immoral for anybody to rebel against a system, on the basis of internal political disagreements, turn the issue tribal and kill innocent people simply because they belong to the tribe of a leader with whom he or she has disagreed. In 1991 and 2013, internal political disagreements within the SPLM that ended up in the rebellion of Riek Machar and other SPLM leaders led to innocent civilians being killed on a tribal basis on both sides of the warring factions (Johnson, 2014). One would also agree with those who morally argue against rewarding military and political leaders who break away from the government and re-join it with enhanced rank. Yet, labelling whole communities as immoral for mistakes or atrocities that a few of their members commit is not ethical either. These generalisations are common in South Sudan even when those who feel that they stand on moral grounds in relation to the liberation of the country would hardly stand close scrutiny on values that they accuse others of failing to uphold.

South Sudan politicians who feel that it is not right for leaders who rebel against the system to use their tribes against other tribes often fall into the same temptation of using their tribes against others in the name of protecting the system. This seems to encourage identity conflict which leaders sometimes encourage under the disguise of law and order. The irony is that the practice often results in a lack of law and order. Kon (2015: 1) points out that 'Since its independence, the South Sudan embraced ethnic rule, supported by the military, thereby weakening the establishment of the rule of law and order, as well as peace and security.' Identity conflict results in a lack of law and order because it goes against the traditional principles of harmony among communities.

Principles of Harmony in Africa

The principle of harmony in Africa is to live in peace and let others live in peace as well. There are no hard-line positions in this principle. Elders of any community often condemn hardliners in conflict resolutions since their behaviour disturbs harmony in a community. Africans generally believe that they need one another within each community in order to live a better life. It seems normal that Africans struggle together 'to overcome their difficulties and share their joy' (Okoye, Ezeanya, & Chukwuma, 2018: 8). When they disagree on mismatched goals and values, they compromise for the sake of cordial relationships among community members. More importantly, Africans seemingly tolerate diverse views for the sake of harmonious relationships. It is not that their views and values are homogeneous. African values are as diverse as the tribes on the continent. Tolerance of diverse views 'is built on the principles of solidarity and complementarity' (Okoye, Ezeanya, & Chukwuma, 2018: 8). For traditional communities, complementarity is hierarchical, in which 'people at different levels made their own essential contribution to each other's well-being, inferiors providing service, while superiors provided rule and protection' (Taylor, 2004: 144).

The literature seems to show that South Sudanese politicians hold hard-line positions at the national level on what they believe to be a moral practice, against what they believe to be an immoral one. This is why they keep on blaming those who rebelled against the SPLM in the past. However, there is no evidence that the same leaders hold hard-line positions when disagreeing at their local community levels. They seem to believe in the importance of flexibility for harmonious relationships at local, but not at national, level. The compromise that South Sudan politicians often arrive at in their peace talks is a power sharing arrangement. It appears that what these politicians learned from Sudan has influenced them politically, but not traditionally. Like South Sudanese, Sudanese politicians hold hard-line positions at the national level on moral issues. But they value relationships at their community levels as Muslims. We will, therefore, explore how religious leaders in South Sudan build consensus when they have divergent moral convictions among religious institutions.

Divergent Moral Convictions and Religious Consensus Building in South Sudan

Political leaders behave differently when solving conflicting moral convictions at national and local levels. They hold hard-line positions in negotiating differences at the national level. For example, it took more than twenty years of different kinds of negotiations between the Sudan government and the SPLM/A since 1983 to sign the 2005 CPA. Even the civil war in South Sudan that was caused by a power struggle within the SPLM in 2013 took more than four years of negotiations before the signing of the R-ARCSS in Khartoum, Sudan and Addis Ababa, Ethiopia in 2018. However, the same politicians value flexibility for the sake of harmonious relationships among people at local levels. People to people traditional peace making among the Dinka and Nuer in Wunlit is one example (Pendle, 2020).

Religious leaders seem to differ from politicians in dealing with value and other differences among individuals and groups. They seem to borrow from different traditions in dealing with divergent moral convictions that cause conflicts among believers. This practice of deriving values for conflict resolution from religious and other traditions and from Holy Books is true of monotheistic religions such as Judaism, Christianity and Islam in many places around the world. As Schiffman (2016: 10) points out, 'Each one of the three monotheistic faiths includes in its foundation text and later traditions concepts of peace and reconciliation.' For example, Christian leaders borrow from Church traditions, the Bible and African traditions in their various communities when resolving value-related conflicts among the people. The same borrowing applies to resolving political conflicts that Church leaders usually engage in to unite conflicting political groups. We will explore how religious leaders have been building consensus among conflicting individuals and groups during and after successive civil wars in Sudan and South Sudan. The analysis will also consider how religious groups resolve their value differences in the country.

Religious Leaders and Consensus-Building in South Sudan

One could argue that religious leaders must first know how to arrive at consensus when they disagree among themselves before they can go out from their groups and help others resolve their differences on consensus principles (Schiffman, 2016). This expectation would be high when it comes to religions in that their adherents believe in One God and have similar Holy Books. However, monotheistic religions such as Judaism, Christianity and Islam are not uniform in their traditions. Different religious leaders and scholars often interpret values in relation to their respective religious traditions. Moreover, understanding of the will of God differs among them. Some argue that the will of God is for all people to respect the sanctity of life since people are created in the image of God. Others say that the will of God is for people to love one another unconditionally. Another group argues that the will of God is that 'a person must stand up for the right under all circumstances, for justice may not be distorted by considerations of those who hate him, who is rich and powerful or poor and unable to protect himself, even if the judgment may likely affect oneself, one's parents or one's relatives' (Schiffman, 2016: 13). These different understandings of the will of God often lead to disagreements on moral principles and values within each of the monotheistic religions.

Religious values seem to be combined in the love for God and for neighbour. For example, both Judaism and Christianity teach that one should love one's self and one's neighbour (Leviticus 19:18; Matthew 22:34-40). The same is true of Islam. Islam puts the value for love of self and the neighbour this way: 'None of you [truly] believes until he loves for his brother what he loves for himself' (An-Nawawi's 40 Hadith No. 13). It is because of love that religious teachings encourage the Golden Rule of doing to others as you would like them to do to you. Values that specify how one relates to God and neighbours are almost the same among the two monotheistic religions of Christianity and Islam, though slightly different. In Matthew 7: 12, Jesus says: 'So in everything, do to others what you would have them do to you, for this sums up the Law and the Prophets.'[2] Prophet Muhammad puts the Golden Rule in almost the same way to that of Jesus: 'To do unto all men as you would wish to have done unto you, and to reject for others what you would reject for yourself' (The Sayings of Muhammad,

---

2 The translation of Matthew 7: 12 cited here is from the New International Version (NIV).

1954: No. 138).³

Values in many religions consist of 'justice, mercy, compassion, love, and includes virtues of beneficence, charity, truthfulness, trustworthiness, courtesy, self- sacrifice, the defence of others and piety' (Genyi, 2016: 105). However, religions do not rank values equally. Some religions rank love above other values, others rank justice above love, compassion and mercy. How a religion ranks values has implications for how adherents of that religion relate to groups outside their own. The same is true about consensus-building.

Christianity ranks love above justice, mercy and compassion. Jesus and Paul make this priority of love over other values clear in their teachings. For example, in Matthew 22:34-40, a man who is said to be expert in the law required to know from Jesus what the greatest commandment in the law could be. Jesus answered that love of God and neighbour is the greatest commandment. Like Jesus, Paul in 1 Corinthian 13:13 makes it clear that among 'faith, hope, and love', the greatest of the three is love. Because of this prioritisation of love, Christians believe that they can live in peace with one another as brothers and sisters in the world. Mainly, 'Christianity began as a peaceful religion seeking to establish the kingdom of God here on earth, that is, to create a world in which love, peace and reconciliation would be the dominant values' (Schiffman, 2016: 8). Later, surrounding environments corrupted the message of love among Christians. At times Christians used violence under the disguise of love to bring unbelievers to Christ so that they could have salvation.

Dissatisfaction with religious violence led to different schools of

---

3   The above quotation is taken from Allama Sir Abdullah Al-Mamun Al-Suhrawardy, *The Sayings of Muhammad* (London: John Murray Publishers):   72. https://themuslimtimesdotinfodotcom.files.wordpress.com/2013/11/sayings-of-muhammedsaw.pdf

thought that rearranged values. For instance, the Enlightenment introduced justice as the most important value that humans should pursue (Baird, 2016). As Gholson (2016: 41) puts it, 'The philosophical ethics of the Enlightenment were in many ways a response to the collapse of the Christian world into holy wars and violence.' Enlightenment thinkers might have thought that justice was the right value to bring order and fairness to the world that had gone wild with violence. Yet, prioritising justice over other values such as love came with its own challenges. For example, people would sometimes pursue justice in the form of legalised revenge against anybody who offended them. This likely deficiency of justice elevates love as a priority value for some people in Christianity.

People who maintain love in their central value systems as a priority mostly rely on the Holy Bible, be they Jewish or Christian. This is because in biblical teaching, 'one is taught to care for one's enemies through charitable acts of prayer and to refrain from revenge' (Genyi, 2016: 109). Others rely on traditions in which they grew up, especially if such traditions hold love as a very important value. In Jewish and Christian teachings one does not only love neighbours, he or she also loves strangers. This is because human beings are created in the image of God. Moreover, God does not see any racial difference among humans. He sees all humans as children of Adam. This is clear in Jewish scriptures and tradition. According to Schiffman (2016: 10), 'Rabbinic tradition teaches that God initially created one human being in order to emphasize the sanctity of every human life and to show that all human beings are related since they share a common ancestor.' Jesus, however, acknowledges the reality of differences in human beings. Not that human beings come from different ancestors other than Adam. But children of Adam have filled the earth in a way that they regard one another as strangers. Despite this reality, Jesus teaches that one should not only love those who love him or her, or only neighbours. He or she must love strangers, too. This is specifically clear in Jesus' teaching in Matthew 5:43-48. True love in Christianity is universal in the real sense of the word. As Genyi (2016: 109) points out, 'Christian teaching portrays love of neighbor irrespective of religion or tribe or race or any other form of identity.'

Unlike Christianity, Islam ranks justice above love, compassion and mercy. This prioritisation of justice over other values in Islam has roots in the founding of Islam. Genyi (2016: 110) shows that 'In Medina where the first Muslim community was founded, it was characterized by an affirmation of human dignity and social justice.' This historical fact makes justice a true central value of Muslims. Quran, *Hadith* and *Sunnah* teach the importance of social justice not just for human relationships, but also for relationships of human beings and God. Quran (Sura An-Nahl, 16:90) makes it clear that justice is what God commands. As Genyi (2016: 110) observes, 'Justice is expected to permeate all actions, speech and thoughts of Muslims.' For example, Quran puts it this way: 'And when you speak, observe justice, even if *the concerned person* be a relative' (Surah Al-An'am 6:153).[4] In regards to relationships, the unjust person, according to Quran (6:158), is the one who turns away from Allah and rejects his signs. Allah punishes such a person. Like love in Christianity, the practice of justice in Islam extends to strangers. Yet, these strangers are Muslims or people of the Book such as Christians and Jews. It rarely extends to pagans (Sookhdeo, 2014). Because of these teachings Muslims strongly believe that believers draw closer to God only through a just society.

4	This translation was taken from Maulawi Sher 'Ali (Trans.). 2015. *The Holy Qur'an: Arabic Text and English Translation* (Islamabad, Sheephatch Lane: Islam International Publications Ltd). Retrieved from: https://www.alislam.org/quran/Holy-Quran-English.pdf

Muslims are universalistic in their worldview, like many Christians. They regard believers all over the world as brothers and sisters. Muslims see believers as people belonging to one community or society (Sookhdeo, 2014). Yet, Islamic society is not like a Christian society. The concept of society in Christianity is the aggregate of people with diverse backgrounds and beliefs living together in a community with common purpose or activity. Islamic society is the *umma* (Sookhdeo, 2014). It is the community of Muslims or believers in Islam only. *Umma* is universal in the sense that it does not limit membership to any state borders. Non-Muslims living together with Muslims in a country like South Sudan are not part of Islamic *umma* with Muslim South Sudanese. South Sudan Muslims consider themselves to be in one *umma* with Muslims in Sudan and Uganda. This also refers to common ancestry. One does not qualify as a member of *umma* simply because his or her parents are part of *umma* if such a person is not a Muslim. The Islamic worldview of *umma* has implications to how Muslims relate to others. If people outside Islam are seen as strangers, then it becomes difficult for radical Muslims to build true consensus for conflict resolution with those who fall outside the *umma*. The issues are even more complicated if people outside *umma* are seen as those who have turned away from God.

In Islamic justice, those who have turned away from God are punished because it is unjust to reject Allah's signs. The Quran (6:158), however, leaves punishment in the hands of Allah only. Radical Muslims who want to pursue justice in a just society often do it on behalf of Allah. It is partly because of this human implementation of justice on God's behalf that Genyi (2016: 107) wonders: 'If the entire humanity depends on God for survival, then it is rather absurd that a helpless humanity would turn against itself in defence of God!' But values are very complicated things to promote and enforce. It is the enforcement of values that would make human beings appear like defending God. Both 'Muslims and Christians hold tenaciously to values considered absolute and superior and hence must be adhered to and protected at all times in all circumstances' (Genyi, 2016: 106). Because of this belief prioritisation of values matters in understanding how people arrive at consensus in conflict resolution.

Reconciling Divergent Enforcement of Values

It is not the prioritisation of values such as justice over love or vice versa that makes consensus-building difficult in some religions but how to reconcile conflicting ways of enforcing such values. Sometimes, the promotion of values could be contradictory. For example, Islamists strongly believe that peace must be based on the principle of equality (Genyi, 2016). Yet, this equality includes differences in righteousness or piety of individuals (Surah Al-Hujurat, 49: 13). This differentiation on the basis of righteousness makes some people more equal than others. Therefore, it is possible that differences within one religion regarding moral convictions can be explained by the contradictory nature of some values and how to reconcile these contradictions. Radicals in any religion would find it easy just to settle in the belief that 'enforcement of the supreme will of God is their responsibility even when they have scant understanding of that will' (Genyi, 2016: 105).

The real issue is that prioritisation of values guides moral judgements and compromises. For example, those who prioritise love over justice believe in persuasion and flexibility in dealing with wrongdoers, while those who prioritise justice over love believe in strict punishment of wrongdoers. Sharia law is full of these punishments. Radical Muslims willingly engage in jihad or holy war to combat internal evil or external injustice (Bangura, 2016). Since Muslims strongly believe in justice and just societies, they stick to their positions on issues to do with moral convictions. It becomes very difficult for some Islamists to compromise on values that they consider to be the will of God. This is because 'The purpose of Islam is to bring society on earth into harmony with the will of God' (Schiffman, 2016: 13).

Christians believe in justice too, but implement it as an agapeic justice to leave room for compassion and mercy. To them, 'What justice reveals is that authentic love always accepts the other as good, as worthy of love and worthy of rights, by virtue of his or her very being' (Gholson, 2016: 131). Agapeic justice focuses more on the wellbeing of others. This is why it does not aim at legalised revenge based on just deserts. Sometimes to arrive at consensus, Christians do not have to agree on the same values with the opposing side. Because of this flexibility South Sudan Churches adopt different models from different traditions to arrive at consensus whenever they work on a resolution to a particular problem. They mainly apply biblical and African traditional methods of consensus building in solving conflicts.

Church leaders in South Sudan do not vote or urge people to vote on issues presented during conflict resolution discussions simply because they often aim at decisions that every member in a meeting could support. This is partly why people regard them as 'the most important peace actors in the country' (Wilson, 2019: 2). The need for cordial relationships guides consensus building in decision-making among religious and traditional leaders and institutions in South Sudan (Kibret, 2015). This means that individuals or minority groups such as Muslims matter in conflict resolution in the country. This consideration of minority groups as important in decision-making would go fairly well with the Muslim principle of equality and a just society. It would be expected that those who discuss issues under the principle of consensus regard one another as equal. Such people would rarely work against one another. Consensus leads to sharing power among religious groups. In discussions guided by consensus, participants talk openly with honesty, knowing that other members will listen to them with respect and seriousness (Kibret, 2015).

What religious discussants aim at in any problem is a win-win settlement that would make each side in the conflict happy. This led to the people-to-people peace agreement that united warring factions of the SPLM/A in Wunlit in 1999. The Church adopted the Lederach pyramid as the model of making the top leaders of the warring factions accept peace after it was clear that 'They were not prepared to reconcile' (Ashworth & Ryan, 2013: 54). Lederach divides the pyramid into three parts. The narrow part on the top is occupied by the top leadership. The middle of the pyramid includes religious leaders, members of parliaments, and army generals, among others. The bottom of the pyramid is occupied by communities and their leaders. The New Sudan Council of Churches (NSCC) decided to work with community leaders at the grassroots to unite communities that were fighting each other in support of SPLM/A leaders who had disagreed and fought. The adoption of the Lederach pyramid also led to the adoption of traditional African methods of consensus building for conflict resolution.

The first thing that Church leaders did was to meet with SPLM/A leaders led by its Chairman Dr. John Garang de Mabior at Kajiko in 1997. Kajiko is a small court centre near the town of Yei in Central Equatoria State. The aim of the meeting was 'to iron out differences which had developed between the church and the movement' (Ashworth & Ryan, 2013: 54). The importance of ironing out misunderstandings before convening any meeting for consensus building is to build trust between the mediating team and conflicting parties. The Kajiko meeting between the Church and the SPLM/A resulted in rebuilding relationships between the two institutions to the point that 'The SPLM/A mandated the church to handle peace and reconciliation, as well as other issues such as the provision of chaplains to the armed forces' (Ashworth & Ryan, 2013: 54).

After meeting with the leadership of the SPLM/A for trust-building, Church leaders convened the Lokichoggio Chiefs Peace Meeting in northern Kenya in June 1998. The chiefs were from the conflicting major ethnic groups of Dinka and Nuer. Most of the Dinka were supporting Dr. John Garang who was the overall leader of the SPLM/A. The majority of Nuer were supporting Dr. Riek Machar who rebelled against Dr. Garang in 1991. At this time, Dr. Riek's group had joined the government in Khartoum to strengthen their fight against the SPLM/A. Therefore, Church leaders were concerned that civilians were going to suffer even more because of Dr. Riek's alliance with the government in Khartoum. Being serious about their plans to stop the suffering of civilians, Church leaders from areas affected by the conflict between the SPLM/A factions accompanied chiefs to the peace meeting in Lokichoggio, Kenya. This meeting became important in helping chiefs from Dinka and Nuer as the two major tribes in South Sudan define their common goal. The definition of a common goal is very important because it encourages compromises for consensus building.

The common goal that the chiefs, community elders and religious leaders agreed upon in the meeting was to live in harmony with one another. During the process of defining it, the chiefs and community elders discussed how their ancestors had dealt with conflict and restored peace and harmony among their communities in the past (Ashworth & Ryan, 2013). This precedence of peace building among conflicting communities helped the chiefs and elders in Lokichoggio agree with Church leaders that it was possible for them to bring peace to the conflicting communities even if Dr. Garang and Dr. Riek were not present in the meeting. Since the chiefs and elders agreed with Church leaders that it was their responsibility to restore peace between the warring factions and communities supporting them, they committed themselves to doing it until they managed to unite the conflicting parties. The Wunlit peace agreement led to the unified SPLM/A that negotiated CPA in Kenya and signed it in 2005.

The need for harmony likely makes religious groups with divergent values work together in South Sudan today. Muslims who prioritise justice over love work together with Christians who prioritise love over justice mainly to restore broken relationships among communities (Wilson, 2019). Even though Muslims do not seem to love harmony when it comes to how they relate to other religious groups, they love harmony within the *umma*. They seem to translate this love of harmony within the *umma* to love of harmony within South Sudan because they feel fully African. Put differently, South Sudan Muslims possibly put their African identity at almost equal level with their religious identity. This is partly because African Muslims in Sudan were regarded as less important than Arab Muslims (Sidahmed, 2012). Religious leaders in South Sudan mostly borrow from their African traditions in valuing harmony above all. The love for harmony is very high in African traditional communities (Okoye, Ezeanya, & Chukwuma, 2018). Africans often arrive at consensus in their conflict resolution for the sake of restoring harmony among their groups in conflict (Issifu, 2016). Therefore, religious leaders in South Sudan often consider their value differences less important than the maintenance of harmonious relationships among communities (Ashworth & Ryan, 2013). They seem to believe that one could still harmoniously relate with others without necessarily accepting their values.

Preliminary Conclusion

We have attempted to answer this question: How might different groups with different moral convictions arrive at consensus in South Sudan? African traditional communities prioritise harmony over other values in their conflict resolutions. If communities or individuals disagree on values, then what matters to mediators and members of the conflicting parties is the restoration of broken relationships. Those who deviate from common values are persuaded rather than forced to follow such common values. Africans believe that deviating from common values affects harmonious relationships in a community, but punishment of those who deviate from these values is not severe. When discussing issues of disagreement during conflict resolution, Africans are often flexible, with the hope of arriving at consensus that would let involved parties lose little and gain little. In issues relating to justice, Africans apply restorative justice in most cases. This is why compensation is often included in cases involving harm done to victims.

Traditional South Sudanese are similar to many African communities. They love harmony. However, the harmony that they love is often limited to communities geographically closer to one another. Yet, politicians are slightly different from traditional South Sudanese. At the local level, politicians seem to value harmony and encourage flexibility at the community level for problem-solving. But, at the national level, they often seem unwilling to relate harmoniously to those who disagree with them. This partly why they worked for secession of South Sudan. The same is true when politicians engage in negotiations to resolve their differences. It is possible that South Sudan politicians learned political inflexibility from the Sudanese in Khartoum who often never wanted to compromise on any political and religious issue at the national level. Nevertheless, the same politicians are influenced by their local values at local levels. That is why they love harmony at community levels and not at the national level.

Religious leaders in South Sudan love harmony like traditional Africans. They therefore borrow from different traditions besides Holy Books on how to solve differences. There is no evidence that religious leaders and groups give up their own values. But they define common goals that help them arrive at consensus without necessarily giving up what they believe in. For example, Christians prioritise love over other values, and Muslims prioritise justice. Yet, they work together now in South Sudan to promote harmony among communities without disagreeing on whether love or justice could come first in conflict resolution. All these differences in belief and practices might explain the reason why the politicians seem confused in implementing legal provisions on state and religion separation. At the national level, politicians may truly believe that institutions could function separately. Yet, at local level they may think that separation of religion and state is less important since harmony is one of major values that guide local decisions and practices.

Possibly, traditional South Sudanese and religious groups arrive at consensus in resolving divergent moral convictions when they aim at restoring harmonious relationships among conflicting parties. However, politicians seem confused between what they believe to be national and local ways of doing things. Yet, it is likely that their local upbringing often trumps their national views. That could be why they seem confused in implementing separation of religion and state. We will next explore what the theology of state and religion separation could be in South Sudan and examine the best possible relationship that could exist between religion and the state in South Sudan from the perspective of a South Sudanese contextual theology.

---- CHAPTER SEVEN ----

SOUTH SUDANESE CONTEXTUAL THEOLOGICAL ETHICS AND STATE-RELIGION SEPARATION

Introduction

What would a South Sudanese contextual theological ethics suggest is the 'best' approach to the separation of religion and state in South Sudan? This question will attempt to establish an approach that South Sudan theologians and religious leaders could use to develop their public theology. Theology that addresses the relationship or the separation of religion and state would fall under public theology. Forster (2020: 18) defines public theology as 'the work of "public reasoning" with, alongside and sometimes in spite of, the diverse publics in which we live.' It is public theology that 'interacts with other disciplines as it seeks to apply theology in areas that are usually covered by disciplines like economics, sociology, ecology and educational and political theory' (Forster, 2020: 18). And what types of values guide public theology, if such theology exists, in South Sudan.

Scholars and religious leaders rarely agree on one principle defining theology of the separation of religion and state. Different worldview traditions and value systems influence theological developments in many areas of public life. Different understandings of reality lead to different theological arguments about state and religion relationships. The notion of the foundation of any theology is often the beginning of disagreements among theologians. Theologians and philosophers from a similar worldview tradition and value system may differ slightly, yet what unites them remains consistent. Premodern thinkers, for example, would argue that the foundation of all theology and the key to reality is God. In line with this belief, theological and philosophical explanations in premodern period are based on essences or forms of things.

Theology and Belief Systems

Belief systems of philosophers and theologians in any particular period play a role in their philosophical and theological arguments. For instance, premodern belief systems influence the philosophies and theologies of thinkers such as Plato, Aristotle, Augustine, and Aquinas. However, theological arguments of modernism differ from those of the premodern period in some fundamental ways.

Modernism started as a reaction against the premodern worldview and value systems. It rejected values of authority and tradition as the means of understanding reality. Modernists rarely believe in formal and final causes in the way that premodern thinkers like Aristotle do.

Aristotle talks of four causes: efficient cause, formal cause, material cause and final cause (Baird, 2016). Modernists only believe in efficient and material causes, so their philosophical and theological explanations of reality put into consideration the role of matter and motion, and they often talk about cause and effect in a mechanical manner.

Mostly, the key to reality for modernists includes nature and human reason which go along with mechanical science of cause and effect. Modernists think that efficient cause is the nature that produces a particular effect. The cause could be the human mind or reason. Some thinkers like Descartes believe that the mind can know God without seeking outside help from tradition or church authority (Baird, 2016). As a result, the modern thinkers would argue that the development of theology should follow a mechanistic fashion of cause and effect. The worldview tradition and value systems of modernism influence philosophies and theologies of thinkers such as Descartes, Spinoza, Leibniz, Locke, and Berkeley. Nevertheless, modernism seems to have failed to define reality satisfactorily. Dissatisfaction with modernism then led to postmodernism.

Postmodernists disagree with a mechanistic interpretation of reality. They believe in the connectedness of things in an organic manner (Baird, 2016). Postmodernism is also a reaction against the foundational rationalistic approach that emphasises dogmatic views guided by deductive reasoning in the process of establishing reality. Mainly, postmodernists believe in developmental processes that depict the reality of change rather than the modernists' notion of a static order that never changes. They think that theology should be understood in relation to the human creative self or self-consciousness which emphasises the self as the foundation and mirror of reality. Belief in the role of human self as key to reality influences philosophies and theologies of German Idealists such as Kant, Hegel, Fichte, Schelling, and Schleiermacher.

Worldview traditions combine with value systems in the development of different theologies. Value systems that influence theological development regarding state and religion relationships include liberalism and secularism. There are liberal and secular states such as the USA, liberal and non-secular states such as South Africa and secular and non-liberal states such as Singapore. Theological understandings in these systems seemingly differ. Differences exist within these states relating to state and religion relationship groupings such as strict separationists, pluralistic separationists, institutional separationists and nonpreferentialists.

Liberal theologians emphasise the role of an individual's experience rather than doctrinal authority in relation to God above that of a faith community in which such individuals participate (Dorrien, 2001). They also stress the importance of individual's reasoning rather than external authority such as Scripture or sacred traditions in understanding ethical life (Robbins & Crockett, 2015). Like modernist thinkers, liberal theologians value intellectual enquiry in the process of establishing reality. Yet, they reject modernist rationalism in doing theology. This is because liberal theology gets its values from both Enlightenment and Romanticism, and in comparison with liberation and feminist theologies, is reformist in nature rather than revolutionary. Its foundational approach is the experience of an individual believer.

Secular theology, a subdivision of liberal theology, has its own approach to these arguments. It gets parts of its influence from premodern thinkers such as Plato and Aristotle. Plato considers God as the Soul of the World (Baird, 2016), the rational Soul who governs the world in the same way that a human rational soul governs human body.[5] This idea first came from Anaxagoras in the pre-Socratic period. Yet,

---

5 This argument is found in Plato. 2008. *Timaeus and Critias*. Oxford, UK: Oxford University Press.

Plato has a dualist interpretation of reality, the idea that eternal Form combines with eternal material element to form the cosmos. Later, Middle- and Neo-Platonism came up with an idealist interpretation of reality in which the cosmos is just a reflection of eternal Form, which is the only existing Being (Baird, 2016).

Aristotle thinks about God as the unmoved mover who causes change through wonder or desire to be like him (Baird, 2016). For Aristotle, material things have always existed. He argues that the unmoved mover is pure actuality who actualises potentials. If God is pure actuality, then he is all good and cannot change.[6] For this reason secular theologians argue against the idea of unchanging Being and also against the dualist interpretation that considers the matter or physical world as evil and the spiritual world or heaven as good. Secular theologians such as Paul Tillich rarely believe in the Christian concept of a personal God. They rarely base their theologies on Christian doctrines. They even dismiss doctrines such as Christology and eschatology as having no historical basis or facts (Spong, 1994). Radical theologians argue like secular theologians. They include Paul Tillich, Gabriel Vahanian, Thomas J. J. Altizer, William Hamilton, Harvey Cox, and Richard Rubenstein (Robbins & Crockett, 2015).

Even though radical theologians reject secularists' belief in restricting religion to private practice, they argue that religion belongs to this world because its authority is removed or disengaged from the church (Gill, 1998; Vattimo, 2007). Radical theology is the theology of emanation that identifies God with the material world. For example, radical theologians argue that 'God is carnal, God is earthen, God is flesh' (Wallace, 2005: 23). They base their arguments on the fact that 'God takes human form in the incarnation, and the Holy Spirit then repeats this move,

---

6   These ideas from Aristotle are taken from his *Metaphysics*, especially books 6, 7, 8, and 9. It is from these ideas that natural theology developed.

incarnating itself in the world' (Robbins & Crockett, 2015: 8). This identification of God with the material world makes radical theology resemble secular theology, or at least political secularism.

Like political secularism, radical theology 'purposely does not advance a particular confessional perspective and it is independent of, and not answerable to, religious authority' (Robbins & Crockett, 2015: 3). Radical theology would fall under genitive theologies. As Vorster (2017: 1) points out, 'a genitive theology has an ulterior motive, aiming at the transformation of a society or the promotion of sound politics and economy.' In most cases, radical theologians believe in the transformation of societies. They think that radical theology is liberation theology with a difference. It is a liberation theology in the sense that 'the more effective and far-ranging theo-political intervention has been that of liberation theology' (Robbins & Crockett, 2015: 5).

Radical theologians seem to combine liberal and secular values in their approach to public theology. Secularists value state neutrality in religion, while liberals value the autonomy of an individual over that of a community or state institutions. On the surface, radical theologians argue that they do not believe in the separation of the private from the public sphere in theological matters. To them, 'political theology, unsurprisingly, has no place in the liberal conception of the state' (Kahn, 2011: 25). Yet, they only believe in the authority of an individual (Robbins & Crockett, 2015). Moreover, radical theologians believe in the autonomy of their theology from the institutions and authority of the church. They seem to argue that the public should not restrict theology to the confines of churches, but that the church should restrict theology to the confine of the public.

Radical theologians believe in postmodernism's epistemology of change. The epistemology of change guides the political theology of radical theologians (Malabou, 2011). Robbins and Crockett (2015:

6) point out that 'radical theology is focused on the change that changes difference.' Radical theologians even argue that God is plastic or changes. This implies that 'If God is plastic then not only is God change, but God makes change and God changes' (Robbins & Crockett, 2015: 7). Partly because of this belief, radical theologians believe in the importance of political changes.

Given the above literature, it seems now that scholars and practitioners develop their theologies in line with dominant worldview traditions that form their central value systems. Some theologians would consider some parts of the Bible as defining what theology of religion and state entails while ignoring other parts that cancel out what they strongly value. Examples of these thinkers include liberation and feminist theologians. Others think that the theology of religion and state relationships should consider the holistic plan of God. The holistic plan of God forms part of the theological imagination in the writings of Lovin and Migliore and starts with creation, sin, reincarnation, redemption and resurrection (Lovin, 2011; Migliore, 2004). Lovin (2011) believes that Augustine was comprehensive in his understanding of the theology of religion and state because he looked at it from creation to resurrection.

Contextual Theological Approach

In the light of these different approaches to theology, it seems any principle regarding religion and state relationships in any country would define theology of religion and state contextually. And each context would apply a particular approach to its theological analysis. There must be a foundation on which each approach is grounded. Premodern theologians seem to base their theological analyses on God as the key to reality. Modernist theologians seem to believe in nature and human reason as the foundation of understanding realities in relation to theology. Postmodernists base their theology of state-church relations on human experience and consciousness. The same applies to values of secularists and liberals who believe in human experience as the key to reality.

No existing literature at this point explores a theological approach that is specific or unique to public theology or theology of religion and state in South Sudan. Major Christian denominations in South Sudan such as the Catholic and Episcopal Churches have theological schools and theologians, but have written little about the theology of state and religion relationships. Because of this lack, it is not clear whether any religious leaders and theologians believe in either *ecclesiocracy* or *erastianism*. *Ecclesiocracy* is the idea that the Church is above the state. Religious leaders assume the leading role above state officials in *ecclesiocracy*. Catholic leaders, to some extent, value *ecclesiocracy*. On the contrary, the Anglican Communion, of which the Episcopal Church of South Sudan is a member, seemingly values *erastianism* in matters of religion and state. *Erastianism* is the belief that the state is above the Church. This means that religious leaders assume subordinate roles in *erastianism*. The third idea is that of David Gitari. Gitari (2014) considers the Church and state as living side by side in a relationship that resembles fire and the human body. For him, one does not go very close to fire to avoid being burned and cannot go very far away from the same to avoid freezing from cold. In Gitari's model, religious and government officials would assume cooperative roles in issues to do with religion and state relationships.

South Sudanese are probably like premodern thinkers in understanding the key to reality, which for them is God. This seems to be the same among the followers of Abrahamic religions such as Christianity (Bernhardt, 2014) and Islam as well as the followers of the African

Traditional Religions. Possibly because of the belief in God as the key to reality the General Assembly of the Presbyterian Church of South Sudan demanded in 2013 that Article 8 in the Constitution be reviewed for better alternatives other than the separation of religion and state (Sudan Tribune, 2013 Feb 25). They probably do not believe in the disconnection of God from state affairs. Muslims also see God as the key to reality (Sidahmed, 2012). Yet, Christians are not like Muslims in South Sudan. Muslims have a clear definition of the foundation of their public theology which Christians still do not have.

Considering the valuing of harmony in South Sudan, it could be argued that the theology dealing with religion and state relationships would be the theology of harmony. This is a recently articulated theology that the Federation of Asian Bishops' Conferences (FABC) developed to go together with the Asians' philosophy of harmony (Wita, 2013). Harmony seems to form central value systems in many Asian societies. They fit it into any relationship issue. Asians even believe 'that religious pluralism is best managed and maintained through the requirements of harmony' (Neo, 2019: 968). Both Christians and Muslims believe in the importance of harmony in Asia. Some Asian Muslim theologians like Alam (2016: 272) argue that 'the Islamic concept of social interaction is more oriented towards achieving "peace" and "harmony" between human beings, regardless of religious background or race.' Since South Sudanese resemble Singaporeans in the love for harmony, public theology in South Sudan would probably resemble this Asian theology.

Every theology is based on a particular foundation. Moltmann (1967), for example, summarises his theology of hope as biblical in foundation, eschatological in orientation and political in responsibility. Theology of harmony in the context of South Sudan has its foundation and starting point in the Trinitarian God. However, the connection between harmony and the Trinitarian God here is mainly imaginative, in the sense (in which we have used this term above) that it equates potential resemblances between substance and community metaphorically instead of using the Trinitarian God as a mere model for communal life in human societies. Using the doctrine of Trinity as a mere model for communal life in human societies could translate to an ethics of imitation which 'fails to take the discontinuity between God's identity and our identities seriously' (Vosloo, 2004: 83). It is obvious that the meaning of 'person or relation within the Triune life is not to be equated uncritically with what we understand about human personhood or relationality' (Vosloo, 2004: 83).

Nonetheless, the theological and ethical imagination for the South Sudanese would differ from that of postmodernists who view with suspicion the modernists' value of foundationalism (Griffin, 2007; Mickey, 2008; Potgieter & Van der Walt, 2015). Vosloo (2004: 84) plausibly argues that theological and ethical imagination would fall short of the moral notion if it is used in an individualistic manner that would disconnect it 'from Christian practices.' The opposite would be true if imagination is used in relation to Christian communal moral life and practices in a way that overlooks individuality of members in such a community. Despite these shortcomings of theological and moral imagination, Vosloo (2004) believes that imagination should be applied critically when used as a tool for understanding moral principles.

Taking into account Vosloo's (2004) argument, the notion of a theological and moral imagination, as used in this study, tries to make sense of the link between the unity of the Triune God and harmonious relationships among people with different functions, but aiming at one goal. Historically it has been argued that Trinitarian harmony is embedded in the substance that forms the foundation of three hypostases of the Triune God. Therefore, unity in the life of the Triune God is both the inspirational model and the source that promotes and sustains harmonious relationships among individuals with diverse roles in a community, while aiming at one goal like loving kindness and order. South Sudanese would understand the foundation of individual identity to be the community. In this case, they may understand the foundation of persons in the Trinity to be the substance of God. Consequently, South Sudanese theology would differ from process theology that emphasises becoming and occurrence over substance (Cobb, 1982). This means that the theology of harmony in South Sudan reflects the oneness of the Trinitarian God in its foundation, eschatological in its orientation and secular in its responsibility. We will, therefore, explore each of these three elements.

Trinitarian God and Harmony

Trinitarian God is one of the perfect examples of harmony. The Trinity is possibly the foundation of the theology of harmony because it is 'the central mystery of Christian faith and life' (Goodey, 2019: 10). However, one's central value systems influence the understanding of the Trinity which in turn, leads to different conclusions regarding harmony. Human minds often find it difficult to grasp diversity in harmony. For example, it is difficult in many communities today to understand how people with different values and personalities could live together in a harmonious relationship. This difficulty in grasping diversity in unity was the main cause of confusion in the understanding of the Trinity in the medieval period. Modalists and Arians, for example, were confused because they believed in one God. Modalists reasoned that if God was one, then the Son must be the Father also (Hippolytus, 2004). That is, the Father is not a different person from the Son. Arians thought that the Son could not be God since God was one (Basil, 2012). They believed that the Son was only the first in the hierarchy of God's creatures. The same confusion about the Son and the Father applies to the Holy Spirit. The Pneumatomachians, for instance, thought that the Holy Spirit was not divine because he was just one of God's creatures (Kariatlis, 2010). Both Modalists and Arians were mainly confused because they thought *substance* and *person* were the same thing. However, St. Basil (2012) was able to demonstrate the difference between the two.

Basil (1980) argues that persons in the Trinity are different from one another. For example, the Father is different from the Son and the Holy Spirit is neither the Father nor the Son. To solve the confusion caused by how three persons could still be one, Basil introduces the distinction between substance and individual. He mainly distinguishes *ousia* (substance or essence) from *hypostasis* (individual) and hypostasis from *prosopon* (person) (Kariatlis, 2010). However, Basil never specifically differentiates the substance from nature or person from hypostasis. The specific differentiation probably appears later in the specialised definitions that John of Damascus provides. Though, in the absence of specificity, Basil (1977) talks of substance and hypostasis as distinct entities. This means that substance is prior to hypostasis in Basil's thought.

Talking of substance and hypostasis only as two distinct entities, Basil (1977) argues that substance is what unites three persons in the Trinity. Yet, such an answer could not be free from confusion. For example, the idea of substance could confuse the Modalists and Arians. The Modalists would think that the substance of the Father would be one. Having the Son as a separate person from the Father would mean that the substance of the Father has been divided into two. Arians would not also believe that the substance would be shared. They would think that the Son's substance was different from that of the Father. Therefore, Basil (1980) had to differentiate the indefinite from definite nouns.

An indefinite noun refers to nonspecific things like human nature. A definite noun is unique to specific bodies like Peter or Paul. Along this line, Basil reasons that God is a substance or essence shared by the Father, the Son and the Holy Spirit in the same way that different human persons such as Peter and Paul share the nature of humanness.

This understanding of humanness resembles part of the definition of *ubuntu* in Africa. Ramose (1999) believes that an individual in Africa is not separable from his or her community. Individuals belong to a community inseparably in the same way that individuals with different personalities and physical appearances share in a common humanity. In African communities, one person depends on other persons in order to be a person. The connection is ontological (Forster, 2010). Ramose (2017: 59) puts it this way: 'For the Africans, the invitation of the dance of be-ing is indeclinable since it is understood as an ontological and epistemological imperative…To dance along with be-ing is to be attuned to be-ing.' Imaginatively, an individual in Africa becomes aware of who he or she is through the community and its surroundings. A community in the ethics of *ubuntu* is the source of individual identity in the same way that the substance of God is the source of the three hypostases in the Trinitarian God. As Forster (2010: 245) points out, 'to be truly human means being in relationship with other persons who give form and substance to one's true humanity.'

Today, a difference between substance and hypostasis is well established (Baird, 2016). Yet, disagreement continues about the prioritisation of either substance over hypostasis or hypostasis over substance. Some scholars even reduce the discussions to the primacy of either nature over person, or person over nature (Zizioulas, 2006). This confusion often leads to different understandings of the Trinity. On the one hand, those who put *person* above *nature* would individualise relationships among the three persons in the Trinity. On the other hand, those who put *nature* above *person* would communalise the relationships among the same persons of the Trinity. Other thinkers would put nature and person side by side in a reciprocal relationship (Loudovikos, 2013). This section will, therefore, explore these differences in relation to what would be the understanding of the Trinitarian God in South Sudan and how such understanding could apply to harmonious relationships among groups with different values.

Nature Above Person

Differences in the prioritisation of either nature over person or person over nature relate to worldview traditions. Premodern tradition, for example, puts nature above person in the sense that universals and common entities come before particulars. Neo-Platonists would even rank the soul above the body in an individual human being, possibly because the human soul has a base or a foundation in the World Soul and the body is connected to the sensible world. Plotinus (1992) starts the ranking of beings backwards to establish what being or reality is prior to the other. In this process of backward ranking Plotinus believes that the body depends on the soul. If that is the case, then he would also like to know what is prior to the soul. Plotinus (1992) thinks that the Intellect, or divine reason, is prior to the soul. The Intellect in Plotinus' understanding is the reason in the mind of God (Baird, 2016). Since Plotinus is working his way backward to establish the ultimate foundation of all beings, he believes that the Intellect depends on the One who is the 'absolute and undivided unity' (Vacura, 2020: 203).

If Plotinus' backward ranking is turned in a way that vertically puts the bottom upward, then the One would automatically rank above all beings. Neo-Platonists put the One above all in the hierarchy of beings (Baird, 2016). Logos follows the One and the World Soul is the third in the hierarchy. Neo-Platonists believe that the Nous or Logos emanates from the Divine Mind of the One, and the World Soul emanates from the Nous or Logos. Unity of goodness informs the Logos or Nous which embodies the Form of the One. That is, 'The totality of the whole being is thus founded (in the last instance) on the One, in which everything is ontologically based and from which everything springs or, to use Plotinus' term, *emanates*' (Vacura, 2020: 203). The World Soul that emanates from the Logos then activates and orders the universe.

It is impossible, according to Plotinus (1992), to describe the One. On this ground human beings describe God in *via negativa* (negative language) such as immortal, among other terms, that describe the indescribable nature of the One. The One is independent in everything, including human understanding. Plotinus (1992) thinks that the One could never relate to created beings. Created beings are the ones that relate to Him. The relationship between the One and created beings is one way. It is an upward-only relationship to the ultimate self-sufficient foundation of all existence. Since the One is beyond human understanding, Neo-Platonists would argue that He does not have shape or form, making Him unlimited or with no boundaries. His power is limitless and His substance can never be divided. The One who is the foundation of all beings 'does not include any multiplicity or diversity' (Vacura, 2020: 203). Yet, He is the ultimate purpose and goal of everything that exists.

The One is the goal and purpose in the sense that things that emanate from Him aim at returning to Him. The return to the One is the opposite of the fall. The fall of humans, in the understanding of Neo-Platonists, comes as a result of the soul's attention to bodily things that are below the higher things of both the Logos and the One. This fall leads to the loss of unity of goodness that is obtained from the Logos. The return to the One, therefore, corresponds to the ultimate Good and is achieved through contemplating the nature that reveals the One in the created things (Baird, 2016). Another view is about self-understanding or self-consciousness to understand the form of humanness that shows the goodness of the One. Moreover, returning to the One requires contemplating the Nous or Logos, which is the intelligence in the mind of God. These contemplations would eventually lead to the ecstatic reunion with the One. So reunion with the One would lead to loss of the individual self in favour of communion with the nature of the One. Nothing at this point would disconnect the self from the indivisible One after the ecstatic reunion.

Even though the One is indivisible, it is still He who produces the multiplicity of beings. However, the multiplicity begins at the level of the Nous or Intellect. As Vacura (2020: 207) puts it, the 'product is primarily Intellect, an intelligible world of varying ideal forms.' Yet, 'it can be argued that although multiplicity is always a non-uniform plurality, the form or idea of multiplicity is itself a unity' (Vacura, 2020: 207). The Intellect is the product, and the product, according to Plotinus, is often less perfect than the producer. Moreover, the Intellect, who is closer to the One in hierarchy, is more perfect than products below Him, since things that are lower in the hierarchy are less good than things that are closer to the One.

The multiplicity produced by the Intellect happen through emanation. The Intellect, according to Plotinus (1992), emanates as a single entity from the One. The multiplicity produced by the Intellect 'is a kind of indeterminate principle of multiplicity, an unformed desire for separate existence, a desire to "be as such" – a regrettable desire because it is a desire for something less than the Good' (Vacura, 2020: 208). Yet, this production of multiplicity does not reduce the energy of the Intellect. What the Intellect produces generates other beings that are lower than the Intellect in strength and perfection. Because of the imperfection of products from producers, it follows that things are either good or evil in relation to their positions in the hierarchy (Lovejoy, 1933). To Neo-Platonists, this hierarchy differentiates moral things from immoral ones, since evil is the privation of the higher form of the Good (Baird, 2016).

The World Soul also produces multiplicity. What generates multiplicity in the World Soul 'is an inner unrest, a desire for constant activity, a movement for movement's sake or a continuous sequence of successive events and experiences' (Vacura, 2020: 208). The World Soul also connects the Intellect to the sensible world. According to Plotinus (1992), a finite soul emanates from the World Soul. This finite soul is like the World Soul (Baird, 2016). The difference is that the World Soul is eternal, and the finite soul is temporal. The finite soul, however, is free from desires and concerns of the body because its nature is that of the eternal World Soul. When the soul is embodied in a finite body, then it would constantly feel threatened and insecure and so pay attention to bodily desires and concerns.

The above-mentioned Neo-Platonist's steps of the return to the One mostly influence theologies of the medieval theologians such as Augustine. Yet, medieval theologians disagree with some of Neo-Platonists' ideas that could not be confirmed from Scripture. For example, Augustine (1955) would not agree with the Neo-Platonists' idea that evil results from how the body would drag humans to lower things. He believes that evil comes from voluntary choice or free will (Baird, 2016). Because of free will, human beings are not saved through the Neo-Platonic mystical path of contemplation on the higher Good, but from the free choice to love the Good. Considering the above-mentioned reasoning, it would be plausible to argue that Augustine (1955) is the one who introduced the distinction between the will and the intellect by saying that human beings are not driven by what they know, but by what they love.

Furthermore, most medieval theologians differ from Neo-Platonists in their understanding of Trinity. Augustine, for instance, does not accept the idea of the inferiority of any one member of the Trinity such as the Holy Spirit below the other two members (Baird, 2016). Three persons in the Trinity are of the same substance, co-equals and are diverse in unity. A helpful way of understanding this diversity in unity is that 'the distinction within the Godhead lay in the three unique hypostatic realities, whereas their unity and community in the *ousia*' (Kariatlis, 2010: 63).

Person Above Nature

Unlike premodern thinkers who put nature over person, thinkers influenced by German idealism put person over nature (Zizioulas, 2006). German idealists argue that a person is the mirror of reality (Baird, 2016). They disagree with the idea that the understanding of reality starts from the absolute and inclusive transcendent Being rather than from the finite creative self or self-consciousness. The difference between German idealists and premodern thinkers is that German idealists believe that 'individual parts are transcended into a greater whole' (Bowie, 2003: 51), while premodern thinkers believe that the whole is what produces individual parts (Plotinus, 1992). This resembles what some Africans assert. Namely, 'a person is a person through, with and for the community' (Forster, 2010: 248).

German idealists further think that reality is just an appearance or a phenomenon. They together with early Romanticists make 'use of a story about particular beings to tell a general story about the meaning and nature of reality' (Bowie, 2003: 55). The implication of this understanding of reality is that no foundation of reality exists. The definition of reality to German idealists is 'not in terms of what is *known* of reality up to now but in terms [of] what reality *ought* to become' (Bowie, 2003: 57). In this view, everything changes in line with individual transitions or changes in self-consciousness. In this sense, if a person understands his or her own self in whatever way, then the understanding of the universe as a whole would follow. This is how nature could be secondary to the creative self of a person.

Unity and Beings

Differences in worldview traditions make people understand and interpret any idea differently. For premodern thinkers, what unites beings is the substance or essence. However, German idealists believe that beings are united by functions. That is, beings are united in action. Scholars who follow this idea of unity through function or action include Pannenberg (1991), Boff (1988) and Moltmann (1981). Slight differences, nevertheless, exist among scholars within one worldview tradition. For example, Barth and Moltmann differ on the nature of the three persons in the Trinity. Barth (1975), on the one hand, contends that the three persons in the Trinity are just three modes that God employs to reveal himself. Moltmann (1981), on the other hand, believes that the three persons in the Trinity are truly distinct, divine individuals. Yet, these theologians are united by the dominant worldview tradition (German Idealism) that forms their central value systems. For instance, both Barth and Moltmann believe that the three persons in the Trinity are united by functions. For Barth, the function or action that unites the Trinity is the self-revelation of God. Moltmann argues that what unites the three distinct persons in the Trinity is the mutual indwelling that comes from the act of reciprocal relationships.

Different Understandings of the Trinitarian God

The above different understandings of the Trinitarian God are mostly the ones that differentiate the ontological view from the economic view of the Trinity. Thinkers influenced by premodern tradition, for example, focus their debate on the ontological realities of the three persons in the Trinity, regardless of their functions and acts of creation and redemption. The ones influenced by German idealism or Romanticism talk about the economic Trinity, which mostly refers to the function of the three persons in relation to creation and redemption. The redemption, like the creation, unites the three persons in the sense that the Father sent the Son into the world to redeem it, and the Holy Spirit safeguards this redemption for God's chosen people on earth. Along these lines of reasoning scholars like Loudovikos (2013) and Zizioulas (2006) differ over St. Maximus the Confessor's understanding of the Trinitarian God.

Maximus' understanding of the Trinity remains the same in his writing, but Loudovikos (2013) and Zizioulas (2006) interpret the Trinity in line with their worldview traditions. Loudovikos (2013) agrees with premodern understanding of the Trinity and Zizioulas follows German idealists' line of reasoning in relation to the Trinity. Zizioulas (2006) separates nature from hypostasis. Loudovikos (2013: 265) puts the two together in what he terms as 'the *co-priority* of person and nature, on the ontological level.' He argues in line with his understanding of Maximus the Confessor that 'between nature and person, neither is *ontologically* prior or above or possessor of the other, precisely because neither really exists even for a moment without the other' (Loudovikos, 2013: 265).

It is not surprising to see Loudovikos argue in favour of nonspecific order of nature and person in accordance with his understanding of Maximus. It is obvious that Maximus' thoughts are often eclectic in the sense that he would always pick 'heterogeneous elements, without always reaching a definitive synthesis' (Skliris, 2017: 5). This is because he was influenced by different schools of thought. As Skliris (2017: 5) points out, Maximus' 'thought is characterized by the tension between the former great centers of the Roman Empire—for example, between Alexandrinian metaphysics, Antiochian historicity, Cappadocian trinitarian theology, Roman anti-Caesarism, and more widely between Hellenism and Judaism, nature and history.' Because of these different influences, Maximus' argument is often asymmetrical or an antinomy. Specifically, it is 'an antinomy in which the two parts are not equal, but the one is preponderant, preserving nevertheless the other in an interior tension with it' (Skliris, 2017: 6).

Other thinkers like John of Damascus would reason in the same manner as Maximus. However, they would differ slightly. Differences between Maximus and John of Damascus would relate to how they define terms. John of Damascus, for example, would define hypostasis as the individual substance that exists in itself. The individual in this sense is something indivisible. That is, you cannot divide an individual body into parts and still maintain its identity as an individual. What differentiates a particular individual from other individuals of the same species are attributes unique to each.

Unlike attributes that differentiate individuals, John of Damascus (1958) would consider a substance as something that individuals that belong to the same species share. For instance, human beings share in the same essence. (Frede, 2002). Alternatively, differences in essence relate to differences in species. For example, a monkey has a different essence because it does not share the same substance with humans. Along this line John (1958) differentiates hypostasis from person in terms of actions specific to a particular individual. Zhyrkova (2009: 108) points out that 'In John's doctrine it is the hypostasis that is the principle of existence, while the person is the way of exhibiting itself as a certain hypostasis.'

Substance, nature and form are also not the same in John's understanding. Substance, as mentioned above, is a general term for a simple being which does not have features and is self-subsistent. Mostly, substance is the source of the existence of accidents. Accidents here could refer to properties or attributes that would not affect substances in which they appear. If substance refers to unqualified basic existence, then nature refers to 'qualified entity or substrate' (Zhyrkova, 2009: 112). Essential differences possibly differentiate one species from another. For example, the mortal nature of human beings differentiates humans from the immortal nature of God. This means that nature corresponds to the idea of specific species such as monkey, human and angel. Unlike substance, form closely relates to nature in the definition of John of Damascus (Frede, 2002).

Hypostasis is not isolated. It relates to the three entities mentioned above in the following manner. Substance, nature and form are general universal entities while the hypostasis is particular. In terms of prioritisation, John would argue that the three entities 'are predicated of particulars subordinated to them' (Zhyrkova, 2009: 113). The order is often that a substance, on the one hand, becomes a nature when it is informed by essential differences. A nature, on the other hand, becomes the hypostasis when it assumes accidents or individual properties and attributes. This means that substance, nature and form would exist within a hypostasis.

Sometimes, two natures such as soul and body unite in the same hypostasis. This unity of natures in one hypostasis applies to Jesus Christ. John of Damascus (1958) believes that the Word, who is Jesus (John: 1-5), is the hypostasis that combines together divine and human natures. Possibly, 'the compound hypostasis is a principle of being and of the union of its composites' (Zhyrkova, 2009: 117). Two natures of different substances that combine in one hypostasis such as the divine and human natures that are combined in the Word are referred to as *enhypostata*. Because of this, the human nature that the divine Word of God assumes is considered as *enhypostaton*. Even though one hypostasis can contain more than one nature, 'neither substance nor nature can be made of diverse substances or natures respectively' (Zhyrkova, 2009: 121).

The union of two natures in one hypostasis can occur without altering either. Since there is no compound nature, two natures in one hypostasis can remain distinctly unconfused and participate in the hypostasis of which they are part. Because the natures participating in one hypostasis are not confused, 'each of the essential characteristics of the respective natures, such as differences and essential properties, are kept unchangeable and unmixed' (Zhyrkova, 2009: 122). For example, soul and body that unite in human hypostasis remain unmixed in their natures. The principle of the union of more than one nature in one hypostasis remains unchanged or undivided even after certain separation, like death, that separates soul from the body in the case of human beings. The argument along this line is that 'since the being of human nature is the being according to the existence of the compound hypostasis, the existence of a human after separation of the soul from the body in death could not be complete and perfect' (Zhyrkova, 2009: 124). This idea led 'to philosophical and theological explanations of the resurrection of the human body' (Zhyrkova, 2009: 124).

What unites divine and human natures in Jesus Christ is the hypostasis of the Word or Logos. However, it is not yet clear what unites three persons in the Trinity. John of Damascus agrees with the Cappadocian Fathers such as St. Basil that what unites the three persons in the Trinity is *ousia* or substance. Hypostasis spells out the mode of existence of each member of the Trinity. Nevertheless, *ousia* unites them. This is because 'substance designates the simple being of entities, while nature is the simple motion of things' (Zhyrkova, 2009: 127). It is not, however, clear that John of Damascus focuses on the ranking of nature and person, or substance and form. He is just trying to explain the principle behind the individuation and nature of human individuals or persons together with that of Jesus.

Unity in Diversity Versus Diversity in Unity

The ambiguity in the prioritisation of either nature over person or person over nature in the postmodern world makes the confusion in the understanding of unity in the Trinitarian God even more complicated. Some would argue in favour of unity in diversity, while others would argue in favour of diversity in unity. Those who approach the unity of the Trinity from the individualist perspective would argue that the three hypostases in the Trinity are brought together by particular shared functions. That is, the diversity brings unity in the Trinity. However, those who approach the same unity of the three hypostases in the Trinity from the communal perspective would reason that the oneness of the three is prior to their diversity. Notably, the substance that unites the three hypostases in the Trinity is very important in defining who they are as distinct divine hypostases. This means that the unity in substance defines the diverse natures of the divine hypostases in the Trinity in the same manner that the hypostasis of the Word defines distinct characteristics of divine and human natures in Jesus.

Those who favour unity in diversity mostly celebrate multiplicity rather than unity. The starting point for them is the variety that Potgieter and Van der Walt (2015: 237) refer to as a 'value supermarket' in which individuals shop around to find values that would unify them with other individuals. It follows from this reasoning that the variety or diversity is the value that forms unity (Turner, 1990). This is why postmodernists think that unity comes from the converged multiplicities. For example, people who believe in unity in diversity argue that 'All of us are obliged to search for and (in constant cooperation with one another) find the basis for peaceful co-existence in a shared set of agreed-upon values, a sort of social contract' (Potgieter & Van der Walt, 2015: 248-249). Diversities that form unity in romanticism and postmodernism have their foundations in individuals who define reality according to their personal self-consciousness (Baird, 2016). The prioritisation of a person over nature, that scholars such as Zizioulas (2006) favour, comes from Andrew North Whitehead's rejection of the modernists' foundationalism (Griffin, 2007; Mickey, 2008). In rejecting the modernists' foundationalism, 'postmodernism emphasizes that a particular reality is a social construction by individuals, a particular group, community, or class of persons' (Potgieter & Van der Walt, 2015: 238). For this reason, believing in nature would imply believing in a foundation from which things originate. Yet, since nothing hangs in the air without a foundation, postmodernists replace the nature with a person who should be the mirror of reality.

The ones who favour diversity in unity celebrate unity over diversity. For example, 'Christian universalism teaches that all human beings share the same nature and possess equal spiritual worth, a worth that does not derive from their particular attributes but rather human nature itself' (Raeder, 2017: 78). The Christians' nature that portrays their equal spiritual worth comes from the hypostasis of Jesus Christ (Galatians 3:28). Along this line the founders of the United States of America favoured 'diversity-within-unity, *e pluribus unum*' (Raeder, 2017: 78) rather than unity in diversity that has now become the way of thinking in the predominantly-postmodernist America. For Christian Universalists as well as premodern thinkers who prioritise diversity in unity over unity in diversity, personal attributes are secondary. What comes first is the essential nature from which diversities are produced (Baird, 2016).

Differences in the prioritisation of either diversity over unity or unity over diversity lead to differences in understanding the important value of tolerance. For example, those who believe in diversity in unity understand tolerance as the ability to endure or put up with pain and difficulties that result from values and practices that conflict with one's deep-seated values and practices. One reason for tolerance is 'the awareness that, since humans are not omniscient, it behoves us to allow for the possibility that one's own viewpoint, no matter how strongly held, might be incorrect or misguided' (Raeder, 2017: 74). Therefore, putting up with what one does not agree with never means accepting it. One could just endure the pain caused by values and practices that conflict with his or her own values for the sake of harmonious relationships. So sometimes one could condemn practices that he or she dislikes, and at other times discussions on value differences could take place for better understanding. Yet, those who prioritise unity in diversity would understand tolerance as accepting without judgement values, practices, beliefs and behaviours that one dislikes or disapproves of (Raeder, 2017). One reason for this belief is that individuals are 'sufficiently mature to develop their own value systems and to live by them' (Potgieter & Van der Walt, 2015: 251). This is why people who condemn values that they disapprove of are restrictive. But the restriction would often be guided by a predominant worldview tradition that forms the underlying values held by many people in a particular community or country.

Foundational Approach in the Context of South Sudan

Considering the above, the best approach for South Sudan theologians and religious leaders to employ to develop the theology of harmony is a foundational approach that considers the Trinitarian God as a foundation for understanding unity among people with different beliefs, values and practices. In Africa generally, a community comes first before an individual. In most cases, 'every member of the community is expected to act in ways that will enhance the good of the entire society' (Okoye, Ezeanya, & Chukwuma, 2018: 10). In a minimal sense, a community is like a common substance that different individuals share. In the Trinity, it is not the diversity of the three persons that results in their unity. It is their unity in one divine substance that produces diversity among them. In the same way, Africans believe that it is not individuals that form a community; it is the community that produces individuals (Mbiti, 1990).

As one thing unifies three persons in the Trinity, one thing that unifies South Sudanese communities is probably the state that all of them share. For example, Article 50(2) of the Constitution makes it clear that the government of South Sudan 'shall be the institution around which the people of South Sudan are politically, economically, socially and culturally organized.' The same was true in the understanding of the United States of America by its founders. As Raeder (2017: 77) points out, 'During the Founding era, the motto generally referred to the welding of a single federal political order out of many individual political communities—originally colonies and then states united under the federal Constitution.' For this reason the laws of central government trump state and local laws within any country. Mostly, 'Law does not command individuals to pursue specific values or ends but merely structures, the means they must employ in pursuing their diverse personal values and purposes' (Raeder, 2017: 77-78). Expanding the idea, it would be plausible to argue that there must be one thing that unifies countries like South Sudan. Possibly, what unifies different countries is the world that they share as humans. It is undoubtedly clear that humans put in place borders dividing nations for administrative reasons. Therefore, the world that human beings share with the rest of God's creatures is the foundation of diversity.

We have seen that worldview traditions influence people's understanding of the Trinitarian God. People influenced by postmodernism prioritise the person over nature. On the other hand, the ones influenced by premodern and modern traditions prioritise nature over person. However, the understanding of premodern nature differs from that of modernism. Some premodern thinkers, for example, associate nature with eternal matter while some do not (Baird, 2016). That is, the nature of created beings is temporal, and the nature of God is eternal. Most modern thinkers believe in the eternity of matter in relation to their mechanical science (Baird, 2016). Yet, many Christian thinkers in both traditions opine that the substance of God is eternal, and the nature of created beings is temporal.

These differences imply that those who prioritise person over nature individualise the relationships among the three persons in the Trinity. The ones who prioritise nature over person communalise the relationships among the same three persons in the Trinity. Moreover, particularised relationships imply unity in diversity, while communalised relationships translate to diversity in unity. South Sudanese mostly understand diversity as the product of oneness, especially in relation to a community. Therefore, they can imaginatively understand the Trinitarian God as the foundation for understanding unity among people with different beliefs, values and practices in the country. The life of the Triune God is both the model and a source for diversity in unity. Partly for this reason a metaphorical foundation for the theology of harmony in the context of South Sudan would be the Trinitarian understanding of God. It is the understanding that 'the very nature of the beings is found through their being in community' (Forster, 2010: 246).

Eschatology and Harmony

Since the foundation for the theology of harmony in the context of South Sudan would be the Trinitarian God, its eschatological orientation would also be grounded in the Trinity. The unity of the three persons in the Trinity is possibly both ontological and teleological in nature. The ontological reality of the Trinity resembles a community that one would have no choice to reject. It is what it is by necessity. For example, three persons of the Trinity are united by the eternal substance of God which is the necessity of their eternal existence. Each of the three divine persons is defined by the essence of eternal existence. This eternal existence of the Trinity is communal in nature.

The nature of the Trinitarian God is that 'each divine person subsists in self-giving to the others' (Venter, 2014: 113). Similarly, human communities in Africa exist by necessity. Individuals who are born in particular communities are defined by such communities even when they choose to relocate to places where communities do not matter. This means that the nature of the community in which a person is born defines the social existence of such a person in Africa. The teleological nature of the Trinity relates to their functions. Each of the three persons in the Trinity focuses on a unified goal in relation to creatures. Schwöbel (2000: 238) refers to this teleological nature of the Trinity as the 'Trinitarian eschatology.' It is the Trinity that focuses attention towards the end.

Eschatology and the End of History

The end in eschatology indicates the finishing line or the end of history. The end of history is the idea that things gradually move from abstract to concrete. It would also mean that they move from general concepts to specific concrete philosophical ideas (Hegel, 1977). The process leading to the end of history, as Hegelians view it, starts with the human spirit, which they consider abstract. This abstract human spirit is like the thesis (Fichte, 1993). Yet, the historical development of the human spirit also involves antithesis that brings into focus the tension between contradictions. Hegelians believe 'that every complex situation contains within itself conflicting elements, which work to destabilize the situation, leading it to break down into a new situation in which the conflicts are resolved' (Shamim, 2018: 2). This antithesis leads to self-consciousness. The resolution to contradictions at this level leads to synthesis, which yields freedom. Therefore, German idealists would connect the end of history to the realisation of freedom. The end would open up another spiral process in which the synthesis becomes a thesis of a higher level of freedom.

The end of history includes the stage of general recognition in which individuals recognise the importance of the other and then form a unity that brings two or more individuals together in a manner that resembles the social contract. Probably, the ultimate goal of the end of history is the perfect freedom that unites different individuals. Freedom unites individuals in the sense that it implies 'being with oneself in another' (Hegel, 1991: 42). However, what German idealists would call the end of history might be the beginning of history in many African societies. This distinction will come later. At this point, we will start with the description of the end of history as understood by German idealists.

The idea of the end of history comes from German idealism,

especially from the philosophy of Georg Wilhelm Friedrich Hegel (1770–1831). Hegel, as Harrison (2005) summarises, developed his philosophy in an effort to understand possible reasons why a perfect God created an imperfect world. He concluded by saying that God who created this imperfect world possibly lacks some perfections. Following this conclusion, 'Hegel arrived at the surprising idea that God needed to create the world in order to attain perfection' (Harrison, 2005: 40). He possibly arrives at this conclusion in relation to his concept of self-knowledge or self-consciousness. To Hegel (1977), self-consciousness comes from one's understanding of the other. That is, you would know exactly who you are if you distinguish yourself from a person that is not you. It follows from this concept that God created the world to distinguish himself from it in order to know exactly who he is. Since God is a Spirit, he created the material world that would be different from himself. This different world would then lead to a complete self-knowledge for God (Bubbio, 2017).

In order for true self-knowledge to take place, one has to be together with the other that helps him or her to self-consciousness (Geniušas, 2008). Thus, God and the material world must become one for him to gain full self-knowledge. One way of understanding this concept is that the world resembles a slave and God resembles a master who gains self-consciousness as the master by distinguishing himself from, yet depending on, the slave. The other way of understanding it could be that God is a subject and the material world is an object.

Since Hegel's (1977) solution to subject and object dichotomy is that they must come together for full self-consciousness, God and the material world must be one for God to gain full self-knowledge and perfection. It is in this process of reasoning that Hegel adopts the Neo-Platonists' idea of emanation (Baird, 2016). The idea of emanation is that the material world and other spiritual beings come out of God

(Vacura, 2020). This means that God and the material world are one in that God is in the material world and the material world is in God.

Neo-Platonists also talk about the process of the return to the One (Vacura, 2020). Hegel (1977), like the Neo-Platonists, talks about the return to God. For example, the idea that God reappropriated the world to himself in order to know everything about it resembles the Neo-Platonists' idea of the return to the One. For Neo-Platonists, beings emanate from and return to the One in a circular manner (Baird, 2016). The only difference is that Hegel puts the need for the return on God rather than on the material beings. That is, the return seemingly aims at helping God understand himself better through the material world. To Hegel, God reappropriates the world 'through the very process of becoming increasingly self-aware' (Harrison, 2005: 41).

What connects all the above to the concept of history is that God 'becomes self-aware through the history of the world' (Harrison, 2005: 41). That is, self-awareness of God is a historical process since it is related to the created world. When God attains full universal consciousness, then history ends. What is interesting in Hegelian thought, as Harrison (2005: 41) points out, is the idea that the Spirit attains his perfection through 'the mind of freely developing human beings.' It is interesting because it seems to be what defines Hegel's prioritisation of person over nature. Possibly, Hegelians would believe that a person is the foundation of reality because it is the means through which God understands his perfection.

A person that Hegelians believe to be the foundation of reality would exemplify the process of history through the process of physical growth and advancement in knowledge. A baby, for example, is a potential grown-up person in both physical appearance and self-consciousness. It means that it is only through the historical process of growing up that a person attains his or her full actuality. Therefore, the Spirit like a baby strives to attain actual freedom, rather than the potential one, by aiming at the end of history of the world in which the minds of human beings freely develop. The end of history for human beings who gradually develop their free minds is the actual accomplishment of a wider knowledge of everything else that takes place in history. Hegel (1977) even believes that freedom is the substance of Spirit. Harrison (2005: 42) summarises this concisely, pointing out that Hegel argues that 'freedom is the essence of Spirit, and history consists in the progress of this freedom from potentiality to actuality.'

The concept of beings moving from potentiality to actuality is not necessarily a modernist or romanticist idea. It is a premodern concept, popular in the philosophies of Plato and Aristotle. Hegel adopts the concept, it seems, to help him explain his philosophy of history. He, however, mixes the premodern concept of moving from potentiality to actuality with the modern concept of freedom.

This mixture of ideas from different worldview traditions shows that change from one worldview tradition to another is never a radical one. It takes place slowly. One may strongly react against beliefs and ideas in a particular school of thought. But the argument developed against such school of thought would sometimes bank on the very ideas that one claims to reject.

Hegel and South Sudanese

Like Hegel, South Sudanese have a mixture of worldview traditions. Most of these worldviews are not developed in an academic manner as in other countries. They naturally come from religious concepts of Abrahamic religions such as Christianity and Islam. Moreover, worldviews of many South Sudanese Christians and Muslims are steeped in old ways of looking at things from the African Traditional Religions

(ATRs). These Christians and Muslims might not be conscious that they are holding onto to their former ATR-related values. Since ATR values were mixed with cultural values, they possibly remain in the central value systems of Christians and Muslims in South Sudan. Nevertheless, South Sudanese rarely resemble Hegel in his understanding of history. It would be extraordinary to find South Sudanese in rural areas who could argue that the end of the world means the end of history. Instead, it would be common to find many who think that the end of the world or the end of time would interrupt history. This is because the end of the world is like the end of an individual's life in the world today. The end of an individual's life does not end history. It only disrupts it since history continues after a person's death.

However, Hegel does not think that history completely ends, but could converge in what seems to be its end and then open up again. For example, the history of the liberation work of the SPLM/A founder John Garang seemed to have ended with his death in 2005. However, it opens up again in a new beginning that tries to define the future of South Sudan on the basis of the work of the same John Garang. It is along the lines of the Hegelians' concept, the spiral movement of history that some theologians talk about as the new beginning or the new creation that brings into existence a new heaven and earth (Moltmann, 1996; Kerovec, 2009). Moltmann (1996) adds a fresh narrative to Hegelianism by rebranding the idea of the return to the One or reappropriation of the material world in the eschatology as the harmonising of the creation with God. Moltmann (1985) believes that this harmony is the reason why God created the world (Harrison, 2005).

Hegel and Moltmann

Moltmann's (1985) argument would potentially resemble the Hegelians' and the Neo-Platonists' theology of emanation in which God is part of everything that comes out of him and everything is in God. He would slightly differ from Hegel in the sense that he hardly sees the reason for creation of the material world as a necessary condition for God's perfection (Moltmann 1990). Further, 'in Moltmann's view, eschatology must be understood in the context of the doctrine of the Trinity' (Harrison, 2005: 44). To him, the end of history does not seem to be the goal of eschatology. It is a reality realised in the life of the Trinity that defines the eschatological goal. Yet, Moltmann still uses the Hegelian language of history in his explanation of the Trinitarian eschatology. For example, he argues that 'Through the sending of Christ and the Spirit, the "history of the Trinity" is opened for the history of the gathering, uniting and glorifying of the world in God and of God in the world' (Moltmann, 1979: 91).

Moreover, Moltmann (1981) connects the Hegelians' freedom to his Trinitarian eschatology. To him, 'freedom means the unhindered participation in the eternal life of the triune God himself, and in his inexhaustible fullness and glory' (Moltmann, 1981: 222). He, however, differs from Hegel in that he thinks that complete freedom is only achieved in God and his Kingdom, instead of Hegel's belief that the Spirit achieves his perfection in freedom. Yet, this difference does not mean that Moltmann has less belief in freedom. He is a product of the same tradition and school of thought of which Hegel is part. Central value systems of Hegel and Moltmann are formed by a mixture of modernism and German idealism.

Eschatological Orientation in South Sudan

Given the above-mentioned views, eschatological orientation in South Sudan is probably distinct from that of Hegel and Moltmann even if South Sudanese share the idea of harmony with Moltmann. First, South Sudanese seem to believe in duty more than freedom (Mickute, 2018). Second, although no existing literature discusses the views of South Sudanese regarding the end of the world, in their unrecorded sermons, South Sudanese Christian leaders rarely think about the end of the world as the end of history. The end of history seems to be a symbolic expression of something that would physically remain unchanged. Yet, Africans generally regard the world in which dead people live as invisible to the living (Mayemba, 2009). Since this world is invisible to the living, it could not be a material world like the current one. Added to this is the fact that God never allowed Moses in his body of flesh and blood to see his face (Exodus 33:20-23). Thus, how can the material world unite with the same God in its current form? Nevertheless, the end of the world seems to suggest the change of the physical existence of the material world and everything associated with its physical existence such as its history.

South Sudanese Christians might have received their view of the end of the world from Christian missionaries influenced by Stoic thought. Stoics believed that the current material world would be destroyed by fire (Kyle, 1998). Stoics further believed that the destroyed world might be reborn or reconstructed in a different form. However, one would argue that the destroyed world will still remain the world, not history. It is not history that would end or be transformed, but the world. Therefore, the view of South Sudanese about the end of the world in their unrecorded sermons might resemble the premodern idea in which the world is destroyed and rebuilt (Weber, 2000). Yet,

South Sudanese religious leaders keep telling their congregations that they should behave each day as if the end of the world would come soon, since nobody knows when it will come. The importance of this caution will be seen later.

It could be true that when the current material world ends, the history of its existence in a current temporal form will end. However, it will not only be the history that will end. It will be the material world in which the current history narrates its existence that will end. The new heaven and the new earth will be new together with the history that explains the nature of their existence. The nature of such history will likely be eternal because it will be the history of the existence of the eternal God. For this reason, this eternal history may not necessarily begin its narrative from the creation as narrated in Genesis 1 and 2, but go all the way back before Genesis 1 and 2. Instead, the beginning of the eternal history after the end of the current material world might not be a continuation of the temporal history that we know now. The eternal history that will come after the current history might not necessarily be new since it might not have ended at all with the end of the current world.

The Hegelians' idea that eschatology or the end of history happens when mutual recognition takes place among individuals may not fit into the understanding of the same in Africa. For Hegelians, 'recognition seems to have two dimensions: on the one hand some sort of concern for the life or well-being of the other, and on the other hand taking the other as having or sharing authority with oneself on the norms whereby interaction and life in common is organized and regulated' (Ikäheimo, 2013: 29). It is what brings individuals together at the end of history. On the contrary, recognition in Africa is an activity within a community. It is the beginning rather than the end of history. The end of history may take place as disruption to growing diversity beyond one community in which the history began.

Africans do not think that diversity comes before oneness. This is why they value a community over an individual (Kibret, 2010). In Africa, individuals are members of society and make sure that one person's freedom grows out of a society's order. No freedom of any individual should disrupt the stability of a community or society. Mostly, 'every member of the community is expected to act in ways that will enhance the good of the entire society' (Okoye, Ezeanya, & Chukwuma, 2018: 11). Individuals exist to make a community more stable. For Africans, 'the society is a series of interrelationships in which each one contributes to the welfare and the stability of the community, and avoids anything that is disruptive or harmful to the community's life' (Okoye, Ezeanya, & Chukwuma, 2018: 10).

Eschatology and Time

Differences in eschatological understanding between premodern and postmodern thinkers may also relate to time. Some thinkers may regard the end as the interruption to the linear progression of time. Others would see the end as the circular return to the point of beginning. Understanding eschatology in relation to linear progression of time could lead to a belief in a new beginning of everlastingness. The end of the current work of God in creation marks the time in which things could transition into everlasting existence so that temporal souls of human beings become eternal like the eternal essence of God. Those who understand the end as a circular return to the point of beginning believe in the reunion of God with his creation in the eschaton. For example, postmodern thinkers influenced by German idealism would regard eschatology as the end of the history of God's work. For them, eschatology 'is about personal, historical and cosmic telos' (Venter, 2014: 114).

Yet, Africans understand time differently. Mbiti (1990) thinks that time is a two-dimensional concept. One is the past and the other is the present. The future, according to Mbiti (1969), is absent in Africans' concept of time. Mbiti (1990) also observes that traditional Africans rarely think about the end of the world or human history because nothing suggests to them such ending. Others differ. Bujo (2003), for example, thinks that Africans have a three-dimensional concept of time. Africans value the past more in that it defines what is taking place in the present and what will likely happen in the future. He points out that Africans love their ancestral tradition because it defines who they are in the present and who they will be in the future. Parratt (1995: 125) also believes in the Africans' three dimensional concept of time as shown by his argument that 'salvation, wholeness, and the meaning of life are inextricably bound up with the ancestors, who are the guardians of the present and the guarantors of the future.' This means that Africans focus on the future of their children. One's bad reputation will affect his or her present time and the future of his or her children.

Traditional South Sudanese seem to understand time in a way that Bujo and Parratt understand it. They seem to believe that one's present behaviour will either negatively or positively affect one's children. In rural areas children are often reminded that they should behave in a way that does not give the family a bad reputation. This means South Sudanese pay attention to short- and long-term behavioural impacts. Their eschatological orientation would focus on present and future implications of harmonious relationships. This brings in another concept of reality in relation to time, one in which the present is what combines the past with the future. Augustine who was an African viewed time in this manner. As Manning, Cassel, and Cassel (2013: 233) point out, Augustine believed in the reality of the past and the future in the present because 'The time present of things past is memory;

the time present of things present is direct experience; the time present of things future is expectation.' Probably, the present is very important in one's behaviour in relation to others.

All the above shows that different worldview traditions, even within one country, lead to different ways of understanding eschatology. For example, South African 'eschatology is dominated by the critical relationship between the eschaton and the present, and by its potential to inspire people amidst oppression' (Venter, 2014: 113). The same is generally true in South Sudan. However, the most important thing in the theology of harmony is that 'The starting-point for eschatology is not time, but God, and the end is not a human ethical project, but is ultimately in the hands of the triune God' (Venter, 2014: 107). Eschatology, as South Sudanese understand it, is not the end of history. It is a literal end of the world. Yet, they still think that eschatology starts today. This is why they believe that whatever one does today affects his or her children in the near future. South Sudan Christians also extend this understanding to the end of the world. What one does now will not only affect his or her children in the near future, it will also affect him or her in the final judgment when the current world ends. For this reason, one's life in a community and in a nation must be guided by the expected short term and long term effects of his or her behaviours as a member of this world as well as a member of the world to come.

Theology of Harmony and Secular Responsibility

The connection between theology and secular responsibility is very elusive in the sense that secular domain is mostly associated with neutrality in matters to do with religion (Neo, 2017; Alexander, 2019). Some people argue that no clear distinction exists between secular practices and the religious ones (Fitzgerald, 2007). Others believe that such distinctions do exist (Alexander, 2019). Moreover, some scholars opine that the distinction between secular and religion may exist, but is fluid (Asad, 2003; Besserman, 2006). Although this debate has been in existence for long, scholars still admit that it remains difficult to arrive at consensus (Agrama, 2010; Starrett, 2010). The difficulty in arriving at consensus regarding the distinction between the domains of religion and the secular seems to relate to either different worldview traditions or the conceptualisation of the problem. This section, nevertheless, does not aim to resolve this slippery problem. It will only attempt to explore literature that would help in understanding how secular responsibility functions as one of the elements defining the nature of the theology of harmony. It will begin with some limited understanding of the distinction between religion and secular domains and then transition to how such limited understanding may shed some light on secular responsibility in the theology of harmony in the context of South Sudan.

Religion and Secular Domains

Balagangadhara (2014) observes that the problem in resolving how the secular domain could relate to religion lies in viewing the distinction as a binary rather than a triadic one. The binary distinction between religion and secular domains associates secularism with idolatry. However, the triadic distinction puts the secular domain in a neutral position. This is because the secular domain emerged as a third option between the dichotomy of true and false religion. This dichotomy is the reason why there are different religions and different beliefs. Christians believe that Christianity is the only true religion because they worship the true God whose Son declares that he is 'the truth, and the life' (John 14:6). Muslims and Jews also think that their respective religions are true and the rest are false (Assmann, 2010). This means that one's religion is true when he or she believes that he or she worships the true God, while others worship false gods (Balagangadhara, 2014). Even atheists have the concept of truth and falsehood of belief.

The tension between true and false religions leads to the secular domain in the sense that it is indifferent to competing claims of true and false beliefs among religious groups. This indifference makes the secular a neutral domain. The Apostle Paul seems to recognise the secular domain in clarifying his prior warning that Christians should not associate with wrongdoers of this world. He opines that never to associate with immoral people of this world, Christians 'would have to leave this world' (1 Corinthians 5:10). Paul mainly cautions that a Christian 'must not associate with anyone who claims to be a brother or sister but is sexually immoral or greedy, an idolater or slanderer, a drunkard or swindler' (1 Corinthians 5:11). The world that Christians cannot leave to immoral people and idolaters seems to be a neutral ground in Paul's understanding. However, Christians cannot share in the practices of immoral people and idolaters in this neutral ground. The Church Fathers such as Tertullian later try to define what practices are idolatrous and should be avoided by Christians in public.

Since the dichotomy between true and false religion remains a major part of religious belief in every period of time, thinkers like John Locke (2003) come up with possible solutions. The solution that Locke suggests aims at making it possible for different religious groups to live together in any country without any of them giving up the truth it holds onto in relation to the worship of God. Accepting a person of different religious conviction as a fellow citizen without agreeing with his or her belief is what Locke (2003) believes to be tolerance. In their secular responsibility, different religious groups tolerate one another for the sake of harmony.

Equal Treatment in Public Services

The tolerance that religious groups should have towards one another could also apply to state institutions and employees of such institutions. State authorities or employees must tolerate competing concepts of truth and falsehood held by different religious groups. State employees will sometimes disagree with certain religious definitions of truth and falsehood but will still provide equal treatment to those with different beliefs from their own (Balagangadhara, 2014). Secular neutrality relates to the principle of non-discrimination in public services which is mandatory for secular employees, regardless of their religious convictions. That is, the secular responsibility of state leaders makes them neutral in relation to different religions within the state. However, they remain committed to their personal religious convictions and the understanding of truth and falsehood that goes with one's religion and religious teachings. The secular domain that any state protects is neutral to religion, but not neutral to the worship of the Divine Being even in public places.

Any person who prevents religious or nonreligious activities in the secular domain assumes that this domain belongs to particular people and not to others. Probably, assigning the secular domain to some activities and not to others makes it not neutral in the truest sense of the word. This was why the United States of America Supreme Court ruled against the Colorado Civil Rights Commission in 2018 for lacking neutrality in the case of Jack Phillips, a baker who refused to sell a wedding cake to a same-sex couple on the basis of his religious beliefs (Alexander, 2019). The Supreme Court considered the Colorado Civil Rights Commission not neutral and even hostile to Phillips because one of its members threatened that Phillips would not be allowed to do business in Colorado if he continued to act based on his religious beliefs.

The Supreme Court seemed to believe at that time that a true neutral secular domain is a place where the state cannot get involved in defining true and false beliefs. Yet, it should not interfere with people who hold onto their various beliefs and definitions. It should also not interfere with those who refuse to accept religious definitions and practices that they regard as false or immoral. The secular domain is a place where people are free to choose what they believe in and refuse what they do not believe in. It is a place where people with different beliefs interact in a non-coercive manner. This means that the state does not protect the feelings of the people from being hurt. It only protects people from being physically harmed by anybody who thinks that his or her definition of what is true or false should remain the only condition in the secular domain.

The secular domain is a neutral place to which any member of a nation belongs. People belong to it as equal human beings, regardless of their diverse backgrounds and beliefs. The secular domain in any state is the oneness that produces diversity. People who worship the Abrahamic God, those who worship idols, atheists and the ones who believe in ideologies as their religions, belong to the same neutral secular domain in any country. It is a place in which anyone can persuade anybody to join his or her own group. Balagangadhara (2014) regards the secular domain as a transitioning station where everybody, including even aliens with their aliens' passports, could spend time with the intention of moving to the next destination. The secular responsibility of state in this station is to provide services to all passengers without asking where they came from and where they are going to. The secular responsibility of religious groups in this station is to persuade only those who have no group or the ones who want to change groups to join them without forcing them to do so. The responsibility of those who are sitting in the secular domain is to choose voluntarily where to go. The state also has the responsibility to make sure that nobody is forced against his or her will to join any group.

It is along this line that South Sudan lawmakers put Article 8 into the Constitution in 2005. Article 8(2) provides a neutral secular domain by stipulating that 'All religions shall be treated equally and religion or religious beliefs shall not be used for divisive purposes.' Religious beliefs mainly become divisive in their competing claims to truth in the worship of God. That problem led to the secession of South Sudan from Sudan in the year 2011. Article 8(2) tries to set the non-discrimination principle in public service. It does not, in any way, prevent the state from providing services to any religious group. Nevertheless, Article 8(2) ensures that any service provided to one religious group could be provided to other religious groups who may have similar needs. Yet, the services must not be provided to silence any religious group from criticising the government. Providing services to silence those who criticise the government would amount to state coercion of religion. This service-related religious coercion, as mentioned above, is popular in Sudan.

Political Power and Religious Roles in Secular Domains

The Islamist-led government in Khartoum, Sudan used many ways to coerce other religious adherents to join Islam (Sidahmed, 2012). One way was to give better services to Muslims than others. Another was to make it hard for Christians to rule Muslims. That means Sudan was an Islamic state, as some Islamists such as Al-Turabi (1983) claimed. In theocratic states like Sudan, the secular domain hardly exists. The state assumes a religious role to advance certain religious beliefs. Religious leaders influence their members to bring to power politicians who will advance their version of religion. For example, Muslims in Sudan would work hard to get the political power 'in order to utilize the authority of the state in its endeavour of Islamic transformation' (Sidahmed, 2012: 182). This is because an Islamic state supports the Islamic theological doctrine of tawhid (Sookhdeo, 2014). The doctrine of tawhid in Islamic theology gives no room for diversity of beliefs and laws. For instance, Islam is the one true religion. The law is sharia. An Islamic state forbids diversity in its recognition of only one true religion. It is, therefore, in line with the tawhidic doctrine in Islamic theology that state institutions and Islamic institutions are never separate in Sudan (D'Angelo, 2010).

On the contrary, South Sudan does not resemble Sudan in how the state relates to religion. This is mainly because of the influence of the African Traditional Religions and customary court systems that South Sudanese have practiced for centuries. In the history of civil governments in Sudan and South Sudan, state authorities interact with religious authorities. As Pendle (2020: 44) points out, 'Not only did governments and governing authorities often justify their power through connections to the divine, but also registers of authority among divine leaders have long been informed by centralized ideas of government.' Yet, religious responsibilities are distinct from customary court responsibility in rural South Sudan. The two roles only converge in making sure that there is harmony in the community. For example, the Nuer prophetess called Nyachol makes 'use of the customary law to resolve disputes and her attempts to distinguish herself from government authority' (Pendle, 2020: 47). At the same time, she uses her spiritual powers to unite Nuer youth (Pendle, 2020). In both cases, harmonious relationship among the Nuer is the main focus of Nyachol's spiritual and secular involvement.

Harmony as a Public Good

As mentioned earlier, South Sudan seems to resemble Singapore in its state- religion relationships. Like Singapore, South Sudan is a secular and non-liberal state. In both countries, harmony is considered a public good (Neo, 2017; Pendle, 2020). It is likely that the main value that mitigates value-clashes in secular and non-liberal states is communal morality that promotes harmony (Walker, 1996). This means that what religious groups must pay attention to in the public domain is harmony among the people.

Yet, South Sudan differs from Singapore in the regulation of religious practices. Singaporean lawmakers prevent religious groups from doing evangelism in public. Mostly, they regulate evangelistic crusades that they regard as harmful to harmonious relationships. For example, 'aggressive proselytization could be regarded as inimical to peaceful coexistence because groups may feel threatened and see such activities as deliberate incursions undermining their religious community' (Neo, 2017: 349). However, there are no such regulations in South Sudan. The assumption in South Sudan is that if the secular domain is neutral, then no one should claim religious injury to their feelings by others in such a setting. In a secular domain, each person is free to defend his or her religious understanding of truth and falsehood without jumping into an argument about injury to their religious feelings.

South Sudan excluded provision for injury to religious feeling from its laws because it was a major issue in the united Sudan's laws. The 1998 Constitution of Sudan, for example, guarantees the freedom of religion without 'injury to the feelings of others' in an attempt to block other religious groups from conducting evangelism. Since differences in religion relate to different definitions of truth and falsehood of beliefs and worship, it is simple for anybody to understand that regulating injury to feelings implies blocking expressions of differences in understanding what is and is not true. A neutral secular domain would assume that we are all responsible for the harmony of a community or of the nation. But we are individuals in our beliefs and worship of God. Anyone who goes into other people's religious domain and insults them would rightly be accused of injuring their feelings, but not in the secular domain that belongs to everybody.

Even though Asians and Africans share strong beliefs in harmonious relationships, they probably differ in what forms their central value systems. Because of this, secularism in South Sudan possibly differs from that of Singapore because it is a customary secularism (Jok, 2012). Customary secularism does not separate the sacred from the secular (Pendle, 2020). It mostly makes use of both customary rules and spiritual powers to promote and maintain harmony among the people within a community or a nation. This means that both spiritual and customary leaders have secular responsibility in promoting and maintaining harmony among people. Moreover, the worldview that forms central value systems in South Sudan is that anyone can have his or her religion, but the community brings us together from our diverse religious beliefs.

To sum up, the problem in understanding the distinction between religion and secular domains comes from the binary view which lumps the secular domain together with idolatry. The triadic view helps clarify the confusion. It shows that the secular domain stands alone as a third option between the conflicting views about true and false religions. The literature further shows that responsibility in the theology of harmony lies in the neutral ground of the secular domain. The secular domain is a ground in which evangelism can take place without any religion forcing people to join it. It is a place of free choice. However, religious and state authorities are responsible for promoting and maintaining harmony among the people in the secular domain. This is because the nation produces diversity; it is not diversity that unites people into a nation. Therefore, it is the responsibility of all the people in the neutral ground to guarantee the oneness of the nation. It is the responsibility of people in a nation with diverse religious convictions to promote and maintain harmonious relationships among God's people.

Preliminary Conclusion

This chapter examined what a South Sudanese contextual theological ethics would suggest as the 'best' approach to the separation of religion and state in the country. It is likely that the best theology that would fit South Sudan as a secular and non-liberal state would be the theology of harmony. The introduction argued that the best approach for the theology of harmony in the context of South Sudan would start with God as the foundation. The theology of harmony in the context of South Sudan reflects the oneness of the Trinitarian God in its foundation, eschatological in its orientation and secular in its responsibility. Each of these three elements was explored. The literature discussed in the chapter supports the above-mentioned assumptions and confirmed the idea that people's understanding of any issue is influenced by their central value systems.

For example, the literature explored in section 2 of this chapter shows that worldview traditions influence people's understanding of the Trinitarian God. On the one hand, people influenced by postmodernism prioritise the person over nature. On the other hand, the ones influenced by premodern and modern traditions prioritise nature over the person. It appears that those who prioritise person over nature individualise the relationships among the three persons in the Trinity. The ones who prioritise nature over person communalise the relationships among the same three persons in the Trinity. Moreover, particularised relationships imply unity in diversity, while communalised relationships translate to diversity in unity. South Sudanese mostly understand diversity as the product of oneness, especially in relation to a community. This is why a sound foundation for a theology of harmony in the context of South Sudan would be the Trinitarian understanding of God.

The perspective influenced by particular traditions is confirmed by the rest of the sections explored in this chapter. For instance, the understanding of eschatology in South Sudan shows that South Sudanese do not understand eschatology as the end of history as German idealists such as Hegel would understand it. They understand it as a literal end of the world. Yet, South Sudanese still think that eschatology starts today. Because of this, they believe that whatever one does today affects his or her children in the near future. South Sudan Christians also extend this understanding to the end of the world in that what one does now would not only affect his or her children in the near future; it will also affect him or her in the final judgment when the current world ends. For this reason, one's life in a community and in a nation must be guided by the expected short- and long-term effects of his or her behaviours as a member of this world, as well as a member of the world to come.

The last section, examining the secular responsibility in the theology of harmony, shows that the secular domain is a neutral field in which anybody from any background can play a role. For example, religious and state authorities are responsible for promoting and maintaining harmony among the people in the secular domain. This is because the nation produces diversity. It is not diversity that unites the people in the nation. Therefore, it is the responsibility of all the people in the neutral ground to guarantee the oneness of the nation. It is the responsibility of people with diverse religious convictions to promote and maintain harmonious relationships among God's people in a nation with diverse beliefs.

CHAPTER EIGHT

CONCLUSIONS

General Synopsis

This study set out to establish what causes likely confusions in the implementation of Article 8 in the Constitution of South Sudan. Article 8 stipulates both the separation of state and religion and equal treatment of all religions. The discrepancies observed in the implementation of Article 8 relate to equal treatment of all religions. Some religions such as Islam seem to get more favourable treatment from the state than others. Yet, the likely favoured religion, Islam, is not the religion of the majority of the leaders of South Sudan. It is even the religion that most of them disagreed with on the theology of state-religion relationships during the North-South civil war that led to the secession of South Sudan from Sudan in the year 2011. For this reason, the study set out to establish what could be behind how South Sudanese leaders make their decisions concerning state and religion relationships. At one time, they fought against Islam and its theology. Now, they favour it by giving it special treatment contrary to constitutional provisions that clearly specify equal treatment for all religions. The study's hypothesis is that central value systems contribute to likely inconsistencies in the decision-making regarding implementation of constitutional provisions such as Article 8. The study employed the phenomenology of religion to explore possible reasons behind probable inconsistencies in the implementation of Article 8.

After analysing potential reasons behind inconsistencies in the implementation of Article 8, I have argued that central value systems guide how people choose what to pay attention to and what to ignore. Central value system is a new concept formulated in this study. No previous study has been identified to have mentioned the concept of a central value system. The conservation value concept that engenders the central value system concept is taken from the existing theory of basic human values developed by Shalom Schwartz, though Schwarz's arrangement of values is different. Schwartz believes that values are fixed in a motivational continuum that he has arranged in a circular chart. What this study considers as central value systems are Schwartz' (2012) conservation values that he placed at the lower part of the circular motivational continuum. The upper part of his circle always indicates liberal values and the lower part indicates conservative values. But this study shows that values are so arranged that conservation values often stay in the centre of values. Conservation values likely fit into conservatism rather than liberalism in that they protect old values that people cherish, rather than new ones.

Cherished values take time to change possibly because central value systems protect them. This study has demonstrated that both conservatives and liberals employ conservation values of conformity, security and tradition to protect whatever values they cherish. For example, liberals would require conformity from their members to secure or protect main values in their liberal tradition. The same is true of conservatives who employ central value systems to shield cherished conservative values. This is why this study shows the conservation value as a central value system for any person or any group of any persuasion or school of thought. Its originality lies in demonstrating that conservation values form central values that direct how people react to values that they are uncomfortable with, regardless of whether they are conservatives or liberals.

Regarding the acquisition of underlying values that guide people's daily activities and decisions, values that individuals learn from childhood directly or indirectly influence their decisions in their daily activities. In line with this understanding, South Sudanese leaders seem confused in the implementation of Article 8 because they are consciously and unconsciously guided by the love for power. Potentially, power value is what most of South Sudanese learn from their surroundings at home and in public. To preserve power, people often activate security, conformity and tradition values to safeguard it, even if that means going against legal provisions. This often results in inconsistencies in the implementation of constitutional provisions such as Article 8 in South Sudan's Constitution.

The study has shown that the power value that politicians promote in South Sudan rarely involves focus on achievement. In Schwartz's (1992) basic theory of human values, power value is a subset of Self-Enhancement value. Achievement is part of this category but is often missing in the exercise of power in South Sudan. There seem to be negative effects from exercising power for its own sake without any focus on achievements for the common good. Power and insecurity generate each other in South Sudan. For example, the love for more power often results in insecurity which increases the use of power for self-defence. In this practice, South Sudan leaders resemble what patriarchal societies do in the exercise of power (Taylor, 2004).

Patriarchal societies love power for both prestige and survival. In the same way, South Sudanese love power for prestige and survival (de Waal, 2014). This overvaluing of power for prestige and survival is part of some cultures in South Sudan (Pendle, 2020). This means that cultural values matter in defining how South Sudanese behave in public. Generally, cultural values influence what leaders do in South Sudan's government regardless of written laws. In many cultures in South Sudan, hierarchy matters. In this, they resemble medieval cultures. Medieval thinkers believed in the hierarchy of beings. This has serious implications for how people exercise power.

In confirming the widespread love for power in South Sudan, this study has shown that the intention behind the inclusion of Article 8 in South Sudan's Constitution is the political survival of the leaders in the country. The need for political survival became the main policy focus for South Sudan politicians because the Sudanese government in Khartoum, together with the Islamists, were thought to have plans for preventing any non-Muslim politician from getting political power in the future. Generally, Islamists who work within political institutions believe it is a dishonour to Islam for non-Muslims to rule Muslims (Sookhdeo, 2014).

Moreover, political survival motivates the teaming up of politicians and the Islamic religion in independent South Sudan. This is because at independence in 2011, Christianity, not Islam, became a potential threat to the unquestioned rule of South Sudan politicians. Government officials see Muslim leaders as trusted partners because Muslims do not condemn unethical activity of the state, as Christians do. There is a shift from the fear of Islam to fear of Christianity in political circles. This shift from the fear of Islam by South Sudanese politicians in united Sudan to favouring the same in an independent South Sudan makes the implementation of Article 8 appear inconsistent, when in fact the politicians are being consistent in their efforts to secure and maintain political power. The shift from what South Sudan politicians favoured to what they stood against in united Sudan clearly indicates the role of central value systems. Central value systems of Sudanese and South Sudanese heavily use the security value to safeguard political and religious interests understood in terms of traditional practices. The need to secure political and religious interests requires conformity of citizens to religious and political requirements in all aspects of life.

Revisiting Research Questions

The exploration of the research questions in this study possibly confirms the claim that central value systems contribute to likely inconsistencies in the implementation of Article 8 in South Sudan's Constitution. The same central value systems influence theological approaches that religious leaders employ to relate to state authorities and institutions. The primary research question, for example, explored how a contextual South Sudanese theology would frame an ethical relationship between religion and state. The study generally showed that Christian theology frames the ethical relationship between religion and state in terms of harmony. Many South Sudanese, regardless of their religious affiliation, value harmony which is therefore one of main values their central value systems protect.

South Sudan is closer to Singapore in the love for harmony. Singapore is a secular and non-liberal state. South Sudan correspondingly appears to be secular and non-liberal even though its Constitution does not mention secularism. The *SPLM Manifesto* of 1983 implies that South Sudanese value customary secularism. Moreover, the separation of state and religion as well as the provisions for equal treatment of all religions in Article 8 of the Constitution imply secular neutrality of the state in religious matters. Besides, Article 1(4) of the Constitution stresses the significance of peaceful co-existence. Yet, the religious and political understandings of harmony seemed slightly different. This sometimes leads to clashes between values of religion and of constitutional governance. One example is the Islamic understanding of harmony as *tawhid* or oneness of Allah that excludes non-Muslims from being part of the united *umma* or Islamic state.

Muslims are not alone in the promotion of harmony as important only for inner groups. At the local level in South Sudan, for example, chiefs believe their powers should be used to reconcile and unite the people they lead (Pendle, 2020). Africans and Asians love harmony but it is often only for inner groups. The literature explored when comparing the love for harmony in Singapore with South Sudan was not sufficient to demonstrate enough similarities and differences between the two nations.

However, it is common for South Sudanese to promote harmony in their inner groups. This is why it is easier to promote harmonious relationships within separate communities at the local level and harder at the national level. Religious leaders often succeed in promoting peaceful coexistence among communities at the local level because they draw on the love for inner harmony that communities already cherish. Ashworth and Ryan (2013: 54) seem to confirm this by observing that religious leaders succeed in cultivating peace in South Sudan because they make use of 'local values and practices.' Local values and practices possibly diminish at the national level where the understanding of power as the ultimate value that unifies all communities under one person in the country cancels out the love for particularised harmony.

The study confirmed the above by showing that religious leaders in South Sudan tend to promote peaceful coexistence among different communities more often than political leaders do. Nonetheless, religious leaders are not effective at all levels. They are more effective at the local level than at the national level in promoting harmony among citizens within and outside religious institutions. The difference is that religious leaders work hard to promote the common good, regardless of whether or not they are promoting it within respective inner groups. They believe it is for the good of such inner groups, while politicians seem to love power without much consideration for the common good or the welfare of all citizens. Like communities that promote harmony only within their inner groups, politicians in South Sudan exercise power in a self-centred manner. Religious leaders focus on promoting harmony between groups and are less focused on harmony within group, which, on its own, may lead to national disharmony.

Because of their love for harmony religious leaders borrow from different traditions in addition to Holy Books on how to mend differences. There is no evidence in the explored literature to show that religious leaders and groups give up their own values. They define common goals that help them arrive at consensus without necessarily giving up what they believe in. For example, Christians prioritise love over other values and Muslims prioritise justice. Yet, they work together now in South Sudan to promote harmony among communities without disagreeing on whether love or justice should come first in conflict resolution. All these differences in belief and practice might explain the reason why South Sudan politicians seem confused in the implementation of legal provisions on state and religion separation.

Examination of the question about roles that religious and government institutions play in cultivating values among South Sudanese indicated that politicians promote separation of state and religion at the national level. The same is true of political power promotion. This is because at the national level, politicians seem to believe that institutions could function separately. Yet, at the local level they think that separation of religion and state is less important since harmony is one of the major values that guide local decisions and practices.

The analysis of the conflict between so-called 'Christian values' and the values of constitutional governance (as prescribed in Article 8) in South Sudan demonstrated that value clashes in different states happen when a constitutionally defined value system in the state and the values of religion do not in practice march together. Mainly, the clashes are influenced by predominant underlying values in the nation even if values in the constitution are slightly different. For example, those who value secularism and liberalism resist values that seem to violate individual autonomy and lack of state neutrality on religious matters. Non-liberal states pay less attention to individual autonomy. However, they resist any value that seems to go against communal values. What Christian values and values of constitutional governance have in common is the avoidance of harm to any human life. Traditional South Sudanese and religious groups arrive at consensus in resolving divergent moral convictions when they aim at restoring harmonious relationships among conflicting parties. However, politicians seem confused between what they believe to be national ways of doing things and local ways of doing things. Nevertheless, it is likely that their local upbringing often trumps their national views. That could be why they seem confused in implementing separation of religion and state.

South Sudan has less defined national values that guide daily activities in the country. The customary secularism for which South Sudan's leaders have been advocating seems to resemble secularism in Singapore. Yet, South Sudan is different from Singapore in value prioritisation. Power value drives almost everything in South Sudan. What the Constitution stipulates is often disregarded when it appears to restrict one's powers. But there is no evidence of this opportunistic shifting of value prioritisation in Singapore, though the literature explored on the concept is insufficient. Secularism in Singapore is guided by love for public order and religious harmony. Heavy use of power by Singaporean leaders relates to maintenance of law and order in the country (Neo, 2020).

The clashes between religious values and values of constitutional governance in Singapore happen when any institution does what would disturb public order or religious harmony. No individual autonomy, as in the USA, justifies one's actions against public order or religious harmony. Communal values trump individual values in both Singapore and the Republic of South Sudan. However, what causes value clashes in South Sudan seems to be any act that is perceived to be a threat to one's hold onto power, be it political or religious. No court cases show these clashes in South Sudan. Yet, some examples show that Islamic religion and African Traditional Religions have been used to demonstrate these power-motivated value clashes in united Sudan and in the current independent South Sudan.

Even though religious and constitutional value clashes do exist in South Sudan, people with differing values still arrive at consensus. What helps them is the love for harmonious relationships among communities. African traditional communities prioritise harmony over other values in their conflict resolutions. If communities or individuals disagree on values, then what matters to mediators and members of the conflicting parties is the restoration of broken relationships. Those who deviate from common values are persuaded rather than forced to follow such common values. Africans believe that deviating from common values affects harmonious relationships in a community, but punishment of those who deviate from these values is not severe. When discussing issues of disagreement during conflict resolution, Africans are often flexible, with the hope and intention of arriving at consensus that would let parties involved lose little and gain little. In issues relating to justice, Africans apply restorative justice in most cases. This is why compensation often applies to cases involving harm done to victims.

Since the love of harmony is one of the traditional values in South Sudan, finding the best approach to the separation of religion and state called for an exploration of the place of harmony in contextual theological ethics. Cited studies established that the theology of harmony in the context of South Sudan reflect the oneness of the Trinitarian God in its foundation, eschatological in its orientation and secular in its responsibility. The literature confirmed the idea that people's understanding of any issue is influenced by their central value systems. South Sudanese mostly understand diversity as the product of oneness, especially in relation to a community. Partly for this reason the foundation for the theology of harmony in the context of South Sudan is grounded on the doctrine of a Trinitarian God.

The same understanding influenced by particular worldview traditions is confirmed by the explored literature. South Sudanese do not understand eschatology as the end of history as German idealists such as Hegel would understand it. They understand it as a literal end of the world. Yet, they still think that eschatology starts today. Because of this, they believe that whatever one does today affects his or her children in the near future. South Sudan Christians also extend this understanding to the end of the world, in that what one does now would not only affect his or her children in the near future, but also in the final judgment when the current world ends. For this reason, one's life in a community and in a nation must be guided by the expected short- and long- term effects of his or her behaviour as a member of this world, as well as a member of the world to come.

The literature that examined secular responsibility in the theology of harmony showed that the secular domain is a neutral field in which anybody from any background may play a role. For example, religions and state authorities are responsible for promoting and maintaining harmony among the people in the secular domain. This is because the nation is what produces diversity. It is not diversity that unites the people in the nation. Therefore, it is the responsibility of all the people in the neutral domain of politics to sustain the oneness of the nation. Put in a different way, it is the responsibility of people with diverse religious convictions to promote and maintain harmonious relationships among people with diverse beliefs.

The current study is significant in that it claims to make a distinct and original contribution to knowledge: namely, the ability of the concept of central value systems to explain inconsistencies in decision-making in relation to policy implementation and other value-related activities. It is the first to examine the concept of central value systems in this context and to point out that values might not be fixed in the circular motivational continuum that Schwartz constructed, but that Conservation values such as conformity, security and tradition form the centre circle of value structure. They protect whatever values that any school of thought cherishes.

The study, therefore, fills two gaps that existed in the theory of basic human values. First, values are not fixed in a way that Schwartz believed: that values in the upper part of the circle belong to liberals and the ones in the lower parts belong to conservatives. Second, conservation values are central values rather than bottom values in the value circular structure. Filling these gaps in existing theories of values creates new understanding in how values consciously and unconsciously influence our decisions in our daily lives. The study also helps us understand that central values are consolidated by dominant surroundings in one's upbringing. Those raised in liberal environments tend to believe in liberal values and those who grow up in a conservative environment believe in conservative values.

Above all, the study demonstrates that no group is free from anxiety. This is contrary to the findings of Schwartz's studies that associate anxiety-avoidance with conservatives and anxiety-free with liberals. No group is free from anxiety in value protection in the sense that those who are in power do not stay in an anxiety free zone in advancing their values until the time they become powerless. Every group activates values of conformity, security and tradition to resist penetration whenever new values try to change values that it cherishes. It is this resistance to penetration of new values that makes implementation of Article 8 in the Constitution of the Republic of South Sudan appear confusing or inconsistent.

---- APPENDIX ----

Limitations and Future Studies

One limitation of the study is that it qualitatively rearranged Schwartz's human basic values in a way that conservation values form central value systems. Yet, Schwartz and those who test his theory of basic human values have repeatedly carried out their studies in quantitative methods. This means that even though the current study has sought to address its own research questions, it might be different if the same questions were answered by quantitative testing of the hypothesis.

The other limitation is that little research, if any, has been done on the intentions of the framers of the constitution when they included Article 8. This made it difficult to access sufficient existing relevant literature which might have deepened understanding of the principles of Article 8 and the potential discrepancies in their implementation. Furthermore, having inadequate available relevant literature on Article 8 and its implementation in South Sudan made it hard to identify different explanations of why South Sudan leaders seem inconsistent in the implementation of the provision. It limited pursuit of the trend that might have consolidated meaningful data-related explanations that could have confirmed or disputed the connection of central value systems to likely inconsistencies in the implementation of Article 8.

To address these limitations, future studies could quantitatively test central value systems to confirm the best approach to state-religion relations, making use of methodologies that researchers who test Schwartz's theory employ. The alternative is to use a quantitative phenomenological approach. It could use hermeneutic phenomenology (Kafle, 2011; Laverty, 2003) in order to focus on how individuals give meaning to their experiences in the implementation of the separation of religion and state. Central value systems would be inferred from how participants express their preferences on how the separation of religion and state should be implemented. Those who value liberalism would share the same way of looking at the issue. The conservatives would have the opposite way of addressing the same issue. The two are sometimes combined in some types of state and religion relationships. For example, some states are ideologically liberal and secular. Others are liberal and non-secular. The rest are secular and non-liberals.

Yet, the variables of liberalism and secularism would not be the only variables for understanding the concept of central value systems. Further studies must correspondingly test people's beliefs in either collectivism or individualism as they matter in how people understand relationships between state and religion. Moreover, the concept of the sovereignty of God in a particular culture should be tested to see whether it influences how people look at the sovereignty of the state and its leaders. Further, questionnaires of such quantitative research could test the understanding of nature and its relationship to persons. The philosophical concept of the ranking between nature and persons matters in appreciating the foundation of the theology of harmony that seems to go together with the value of harmony in the management of value clashes in Africa and Asia.

Alternatively, future studies could qualitatively explore central value systems in different settings, cultures, locations and contexts to determine if the conclusions would be the same. For example, one setting could be one where dominant ideologies include secularism and liberalism, such as in the USA, in relation to state and religion relationships. Another could be liberal and non-secular states such as South Africa. The aim for carrying out studies in these settings would be increased understanding of likely inconsistencies in implementing constitutional provisions for state and religion, or church and state, separation. It would be helpful if adequate literature on the implementation of such constitutional provisions existed. Sufficient existing literature can even be useful in carrying out the same qualitative study in settings that resemble South Sudan. Adequate literature would help a researcher in both settings explore the concept meaningfully. Conclusions of such studies may confirm or dispute the notion that central value systems contribute to confusions or discrepancies in implementation.

Other questions that future studies might consider include the following: What is the place of a theology of harmony in the light of postcolonial theology of reconstruction, with reference to South Sudan? To what extent would a theology of harmony fit in the schema of post-colonial reconstruction phase? How can we achieve a theology of harmony in light of Christian-Muslim divides? Is favouring Islam a temporary stop-gap, as a measure of humanising the former 'oppressors'? These questions could be explored in relation to a central value systems concept. Additionally, future studies might attend to Eduard Tödt's theory of moral decision and judgment (as also appropriated by South African scholars such as Etienne de Villiers and Dirkie Smit), as well as James Gustafson's well-known work on various moral discourses.

REFERENCES

Agrama, H. A. 2010. Secularism, Sovereignty, Indeterminacy: Is Egypt a Secular or a Religious State? *Comparative Studies in Society and History* 52(3):495–523.

Agwella, M. O.L. 2018. Localising peacebuilding in South Sudan? A case of transitional justice and reconciliation. *Unpublished PhD Dissertation*, University of Bradford. https://bradscholars.brad.ac.uk/handle/10454/17138

Ahmed, D. 2017. Religion–State Relations. *International Institute for Democracy and Electoral Assistance (International IDEA) Second edition.* Available at: https://www.idea.int/sites/default/files/publications/religion-state-relations-primer.pdf

Ahmed, D. I., & Gouda, M. 2015. Measuring Constitutional Islamization: The Islamic Constitutions Index. *Hastings International and Comparative Law Review*, 38(1): 1-74. http://papers.ssrn.com/abstract=2523337

Ajayi, A. T., & Buhari, L. O. 2014. Methods of conflict resolution in African traditional society. *African Research Review*, 8(2): 138-157. https://www.ajol.info//index.php/afrrev/article/view/104273

Aktas, B., Yilmaz, O., Bahçekapili, H. G. (2017). Moral pluralism on the trolley tracks: Different normative principles are used for different reasons in justifying moral judgments. *Judgment and Decision Making*, 12(3): 297–307.

Alam, M. 2016. Harmony in religious and cultural diversity, case study of Sungai Penuh city society. Al-Arab 5(2): 265-280.

Alexander, K. W. 2019. The masterpiece cakeshop decision and the clash between nondiscrimination and religious freedom. *Oklahoma Law Review*, 71(4): 1069-1107. Available at: https://digitalcommons.law.ou.edu/olr/vol71/iss4/4

Ali, M. S. (Trans.). 2015. *The Holy Qur'an: Arabic Text and English Translation*. Islamabad, Sheephatch Lane: Islam International Publications Ltd. Retrieved from: https://www.alislam.org/quran/Holy-Quran-English.pdf

Al-Suhrawardy, A. S. A. A. 2013. *The Sayings of Muhammad*. London: John Murray Publishers. https://themuslimtimesdotinfodotcom.files.wordpress.com/2013/11/sayings-of-muhammedsaw.pdf

Al-Turabi, H. 1983. The Islamic State. In Esposito, J. L (Ed.). *Voices of Resurgent Islam* (241–51). New York: Oxford University Press.

Aquinas, T. 1964. *Summa Theologia* (V.2). McDermott, T. (Trans). New York: McGraw-Hill Book Company.

Asad, T. 2003. *Formations of the Secular: Christianity, Islam, Modernity*. Stanford: Stanford University Press.

Ashworth, J. & Ryan, M. 2013. "One nation from every tribe, tongue, and people": The Church and strategic peacebuilding in South Sudan. *Journal of Catholic Social Thought*, 10(1): 47-67. https://www.cmi.no/file/2291-the-church-and-strategic-peacebuilding-in-south-sudan.pdf

Aspelund, A., Lindeman, M., & Verkasalo, M. (2013). Political conservatism and left–right orientation in 28 eastern and western European countries. *Political Psychology*, 34: 409-417. doi:10.1111/pops.12000

Assmann, J. 2010. *The Price of Monotheism*. Stanford, Calif.: Stanford University Press.

Atem, D. A. 2020. How nepotism is undermining social cohesion and prosperity in South Sudan. *PaanLuel Wël*. https://paanluelwel.com/2020/07/27/how-nepotism-is-undermining-social-cohesion-and-prosperity-in-south-sudan/

Augustine, A. 1998. *The Confessions*. Paris, France: Bibliothèque de La Pléiade. Available online: http://www.ourladyswarriors.org/saints/augcon10.htm

_____. 2015. *The City of God against the Pagans*. Cambridge, MA: Harvard University Press.

Awolich, A. 2015. Political parties and the push for political consensus. *The Sudd Institute*. https://reliefweb.int/report/south-sudan/political-parties-and-push-political-consensus

Bafinamene, C.K. 2017. Becoming good in Africa: A critical appraisal of Stanley Hauerwas' ecclesial ethic in the sub-Saharan context. *Verbum et Ecclesia*, 38(1), 1-10. a1716. https://doi.org/10.4102/ve.v38i1.1716

Baird, F. E. (2016). *From Plato to Derrida (6th Ed.)*. New York: Routledge.

Balagangadhara, S. N. 2014. On the Dark Side of the "Secular": Is the Religious-Secular Distinction a Binary? *Numen* 61(1): 33–52.

Bangura, A. K. 2016. The parable of the three rings: An allegory of the interconnections among Judaism, Christianity, and Islam. *The Journal of Living Together*, 2(3): 17-45.

Barth. Karl. 1975. *Church Dogmatics*. Geoffey Bromile & Thomas Torrance (Eds.). Edinburgh: T and T. Clark.

Basil. 1977. Letters (Vol. 1). In A. C. Way (Trans.). *The Fathers of the Church* (1-185). Washington DC: The Catholic University of America Press.

_____. 1980. *On the Holy Spirit.* Translated by David Anderson. Crestwood, NY: SVS Press.

_____. 2012. *Letter XXXVIII: Nicene and Post-Nicene Fathers, Second Series* (Vol. VIII). Edited by Philip Schaff & Henry Wace. Peabody, Massachusetts: Hendrickson Publishers, Inc.

Bayram, A. B. (2015). What drives modern Diogenes? Individual values and cosmopolitan allegiance. *European Journal of International Relations*, 21(2): 451–479. DOI: 10.1177/1354066114541879

Bernard, M. M., Gebauer, J. E., & Maio, G. R. (2006). Cultural estrangement: The role of personal and societal value discrepancies. Personality and Social Psychology Bulletin, 32: 78-92.

Bernhardt, R. 2014. Trinity as a framework for a theology of religions. *Svensk teologisk kvartalskrift* 90 (2): 52-62.

Besserman, L. 2006. Introduction: Sacred and Secular in Medieval and Early Modern Cultures: Issues and Approaches. In L. Besserman (Ed.). *Sacred and Secular in Medieval and Early Modern Cultures: New Essays* (1-18). New York: Palgrave Macmillan.

Biar, Z. M. 2014. Ethics and Globalization. In Maurice Nyamanga Amutabi (Ed.) *Globalization, Identity and Multiculturalism in Africa* (22-34). Nairobi: Research, Catholic University of Eastern Africa and AIDAL. Print

Bilsky, W., & Schwartz, S. H. (1994). Values and personality. *European Journal of Personality*, 8: 163–181. DOI: https://doi.org/10.1002/per.2410080303

Blayney, I. W. 1957. *The Age of Luther: The Spirit of Renaissance-Humanism and of the Reformation.* New York: Vantage Press.

Blum, J. N. 2012. Retrieving phenomenology of religion as a method for religious studies. *Journal of the American Academy of Religion*, 80(4), 1025-1048.

Bobowik, M., Basabe, N., Páez, D., Jiménez, A., & Bilbao, M. Á. (2011). Personal values and well-being among Europeans, Spanish natives and immigrants to Spain: Does the culture matter? *Journal of Happiness Studies*, 12: 401-419.

Boer, D. 2017. Values and affective well-being: How culture and environmental threat influence their association. In S. Roccas & L. Sagiv (Eds.), *Values and behavior: Taking a cross-cultural perspective.*

Boff. L. 1988. *Trinity and Society*. Translated by Paul Burns. Mac knoll.

Bohman, J. 2007. *Democracy across Borders: From Demos to Demoi*. Cambridge, MA: MIT Press.

Bowie, A. 2003. *Aesthetics and subjectivity: From Kant to Nietzsche* (2nd Ed.). Manchester: Manchester University Press.

Bubbio, P. D. 2017. *God and the Self in Hegel: Beyond Subjectivism*. Albany, New York: SUNY Press.

Bujo, B. 2003. *African Theology in its Social Context* (2nd ed.). Nairobi: Paulines Publications Africa.

Burroughs, B. 2013. Reconceiving politics: Soulcraft, statecraft, and the City of God. *Journal of the Society of Christian Ethics*, 33(1), 45-62. http://www.jstor.org/stable/23563065

Calvin, J. 1960. *Institutes of the Christian Religion*. Battles, F. L. (trans.). Philadelphia: Westminster Press.

Caprara, G. V., & Vecchione, M. 2015. Democracy through ideology and beyond: The values that are common to the right and the left. *Ceskoslovenska Psychologie*, 59(1): 2-13.

Caprara, G. V., Vecchione, M., Schwartz, S. H., Schoen, H., Bain, P. G., Silvester, J., & Caprara, M. G. 2017. Basic values, ideological self-placement, and voting: A cross-cultural study. Cross-Cultural Research, 51, 388-411. doi:10.1177/1069397117712194

Caprara, G. V., Vecchione, M., Schwartz, S. H., Schoen, H., Bain, P. G., Silvester, J., Cieciuch, J., Pavlopoulos, V., Bianchi, G., Kirmanoglu, H., Baslevent, C., Mamali, C., Manzi, J., Katayama, M., Posnova, T., Tabernero, C., Torres, C., Verkasalo, M., Lönnqvist, J., Vondráková, E., & Caprara, M. G. 2018. The Contribution of Religiosity to Ideology: Empirical Evidences from Five Continents. *Cross-Cultural Research*, 52(5): 524–541. https://doi.org/10.1177/1069397118774233

Catholic Radio Network. 2012, May 25. Minister asks Akobo church leaders to leave politics. http://catholicradionetwork.org/?q=node/6865

Chapman, N. S. 2013. Disentangling conscience and religion. *University of Illinois Law Review*, 4: 1457-1502. Available at: https://www.illinoislawreview.org/wp-content/ilr-content/articles/2013/4/Chapman.pdf

Chen, J. 2014. Bias and Religious Truth-Seeking in Proselytization Restrictions: An Atypical Case Study of Singapore. *De Gruyter* 8(1): 21-85.

Chuan, T. Y. 2013. Compensate woman fired for adultery, church told. *The Straits Times*. Available at: https://www.straitstimes.com/singapore/compensate-woman-fired-for-adultery-church-told-0

Cieciuch, J, Schwartz, S. H., & Vecchione, M. 2013. Applying the Refined Values Theory to Past Data: What Can Researchers Gain? *Journal of Cross-Cultural Psychology*, XX(X): 1–20. DOI: 10.1177/0022022113487076

Cieciuch, J., Davidov, E., & Algesheimer, R. 2015. The stability and change of value structure and priorities in childhood: A longitudinal study. *Social Development*, doi:10.1111/sode.12147.

Cieciuch, J., Davidov, E., Algesheimer, R., and Schmidt, P. (2017). Testing for approximate measurement invariance of human values in the European Social Survey. *Sociol. Methods Res.* doi: 10.1177/0049124117701478

Ciulla, J. B. 2009. Ethics and leadership effectiveness. https://www.researchgate.net/publication/265568882

Clifford, L. 2017. *Words matter: Hate speech and South Sudan. IRIN.* Available at: https://www.refworld.org/docid/59b8eb654.html [accessed 23 September 2020]

Cobb J. J. B. 1982. *Process Theology as Political Theology.* Manchester: Manchester University Press.

Cohen, J. L. 2015. Pluralism, Group Rights, and Corporate Religion: Reply to Critics. *Netherlands Journal of Legal Philosophy*, 44(3), 264-278.

Collins, R. O. & Daly, M. W. 2016. *A History of South Sudan.* Cambridge: Cambridge University Press.

Constitution of the Republic of Singapore. 1999. Published by the Attorney-General on the authorisation of the President under Article 155(2) of the Constitution. Available at: https://sso.agc.gov.sg/Act/CONS1963

Constitution of The Republic Of Sudan. 1998. Available at: http://www.ilo.org/dyn/natlex/natlex_browse.details?p_lang=en&p_country=SDN&p_classifi cation=01.01&p_origin=COUNTRY&p sortby=SORTBY_COUNTRY [Last accessed 09.04.2014. At 18:14]

Copleston, F. 1993. *A History of Philosophy* (Vol. II). New York: Image Books, Doubleday.

Copleston, F. 1993. *A history of philosophy* (Vol. II). New York: Image Books, Boubleday.

Cox, J. L. 2006. *A guide to the phenomenology of religion: Key figures, formative influences and subsequent debates*. London: T & T Clark International.

D'Agoôt, M. 2019. Why did Sudan lose a small war in Southern Sudan? *Small Wars & Insurgencies*, 30(3): 679-702. DOI: 10.1080/09592318.2019.1601872

D'Angelo, G. 2010. Religion and the Secular State: Sudan National Report. *Religion and the Secular State*. 645-667. https://classic.iclrs.org/content/blurb/files/Sudan.1.pdf

Danchin, P. G. 2008. Suspect Symbols: Value Pluralism as a Theory of Religious Freedom in International Law. *Yale Journal of International Law*, 33(1): 14–15.

Daniel, K. 2012. The applicability of phenomenology in the study of religion. *International Journal of Psychology and Behavioral Sciences*, 2(5), 130-137.

Davidov, E., & Meuleman, B. (2012). Explaining attitudes towards immigration policies in European countries: The role of human values. Journal of Ethnic and Migration Studies, 38, 757–775.

De Waal, A. 2014. When kleptocracy becomes insolvent: Brute causes of the civil war in South Sudan. *African Affairs*, 113(452): 347–369.

Deagon, A. 2017. Secularism as a religion: Questioning the future of the 'secular' state. *The Western Australian Jurist*, 8, 31-94.

DeGirolami, M. O. 2015. Constitutional contraction: Religion and the Roberts Courts. *Stanford Law & Policy Review*, 26, 385-409.

DeGirolami, M. O. 2017. Religious Accomodation, Religious Tradition, and Political Polarization. *Faculty Publications*, 138. https://scholarship.law.stjohns.edu/faculty_publications/138

Delaney, M. J. 2010. John Garang and Sudanism: A Peculiar and Resilient Nationalism. Unpublished Bachelor Dissertation. San Luis Obispo, California: California Polytechnic State University.

Deng, F M. 1995. *War of Visions: Conflict of Identities in the Sudan.* Washington, DC: Brookings Institution.

Deng, D. 2020. Priorities for Peace in South Sudan. *Conflict Research Programme,* LSE. https://www.lse.ac.uk/ideas/Assets/Documents/Conflict-Research-Programme/crp-memos/Deng-Priorities-for-Peace-060820.pdf

Djupe, P. A. & Calfano, B. R. 2013. Divine intervention? The influence of religious value communication on U.S. intervention policy. *Political Behavior,* 35(4), 643-663. http://www.jstor.org/stable/43653167

Dorrien, G. J. 2001. *The Making of American Liberal Theology: Idealism, Realism, and Modernity,* 1900-1950. Louisville, Ky: Westminster John Knox Press.

Doshi, R. M. 2010. Nonincorporation of the establishment clause: Satisfying the demands of equality, pluralism, and originalism. *The Georgetown Law Journal,* 98, 459-502.

Duffel, S. V. 2007. Sovereignty as a religious concept. *The Monist,* 9(1), 126-143. http://www.jstor.org/stable/27904018

Ells, C. 2011. Communicating qualitative research study designs to research ethics review boards. *The Qualitative Report,* 16(3), 881-891. http://www.nova.edu/ssss/QR/QR16-3/ells.pdf

Epstein, R. A. 2018. A not quite contemporary view of privacy. *Harvard Journal of Law & Public Policy,* 41(1): 95-116.

Esbeck, C. H. 1986. Five Views of Church-State Relations in Contemporary American Thought. *Brigham Young University Law Review,* 371-404. http://scholarship.law.missouri.edu/facpubs

Feldman, N. 2009. Religion and the Earthly City. *Social Research,* 76(4): 989-1000. http://www.jstor.org/stable/40972198

Ferreira, P. 1970. *Pedagogy of the Oppressed* (30th Anniversary Edition). New York: The Continuum. Available at: https://envs.ucsc.edu/internships/internship-readings/freire-pedagogy-of-the-oppressed.pdf

Fichte, J. G. 1993. *Fichte: Early philosophical writings*. Ithaca, New York: Cornell University Press.

Fitzgerald, Timothy. 2007. *Discourse on Civility and Barbarity: A Critical History of Religion and Related Categories*. Oxford: Oxford University Press.

Flint-Hamilton, K. 2010. When church becomes state: Electioneering and the culture of fear and race in the 2008 presidential election. *U.S. Catholic Historian*, 28(1), 41-52. http://www.jstor.org/stable/40731253

Forster, D. 2019. From "Prophetic Witness" to "Prophets of Doom"?—The Contested Role of Religion in the South African Public Sphere. In Forster, D., Gerle, E., & Gunner, G. (Eds). *Freedom of Religion at Stake: Competing Claims among Faith Traditions, States, and Persons*. Eugene, OR: Wipf and Stock Publishers. pp. 18-39.

_____. 2019. Social identity, social media, and society: A call for public theological engagement (na).

_____. 2019. New directions in evangelical Christianities. *Theology* 0(0): 1-9.

_____. 2020. The Nature of Public Theology. In S. B. Agang, H. J. Hendriks & D. A. Forster. *African Public Theology* (15-26). Carlisle, Cumbria: Langham Publishing.

_____. 2010. African relational ontology, individual identity, and Christian theology: An African theological contribution towards an integrated relational ontological identity. *African relational ontology* CXIII(874): 243-253.

Garang, K. 2019. Political ideology and organisational espousal: A political-historical analysis of Dr. John Garang de Mabior's "New Sudan Vision." *Modern Africa: Politics, History and Society*, 7(2): 89–122. https://doi.org/10.26806/modafr.v7i2.258

Garnett, R. W. 2007. "Pluralism, Dialogue, and Freedom: Professor Robert Rodes and the Church-State Nexus." *Journal of Law and Religion*, 22(2), 503-525. http://www.jstor.org/stable/27639062

_____. 2013. "The Freedom of the Church": (Towards) an Exposition, Translation, and Defense. *Journal of Contemporary Legal Issues*, 21(33), 31-58. https://scholarship.law.nd.edu/cgi/viewcontent.cgi?article=1284&context=law_faculty_scholarship

Gelvin, J. L. 2005. *The Modern Middle East: A History*. New York and Oxford: Oxford University Press.

Geniušas, S. 2008. Self-Consciousness and Otherness: Hegel and Husserl. *Santalka. Filosofija* 16(3): 27–36.

Genyi, G. A. 2016. Christianity and Islam: What shared values for enhanced religious harmony and global stability. *The Journal of Living Together*, 2(3): 103-115.

Gholson, J. G. 2016. The seat of justice in the house of love: Toward an Ecclesial Theory of Justice. *Unpublished PhD Dissertation*. Loyola University in Chicago. https://ecommons.luc.edu/cgi/viewcontent.cgi?article=3280&context=luc_diss

Gill, S. 1998. Territory. In M. C. Taylor (Ed.). *Critical Terms for Religious Studies*. Chicago, IL: The University of Chicago Press.

Gilpin, C. 2010. Building the "Wall of Separation": Construction Zone for Historians. *Church History*, 79(4), 871-880. http://www.jstor.org/stable/40962872

Giorgi, A., Giorgi, B., & Morley, J. (2017). The Descriptive Phenomenological Psychological Method. In C. Willig & W. Stainton-Rogers, (Eds.), *The SAGE Handbook of Qualitative Research in Psychology* (pp. 176-192). London: Sage Publications Ltd.

_____. 2007. Concerning the Phenomenological Methods of Husserl and Heidegger and their Application in Psychology. *Collection du Cirp*, 1, 63-78.

Gitari, D. 2014. *Troubled but not destroyed: The autobiography of Archbishop David Gitari*. McLean, VA: Isaac Publishing.

Goh, R. B. H. 2009. Christian identities in Singapore: Religion, race and culture between state controls and transnational flows. *Journal of Cultural Geography* 26(1): 1-23.

Goldman, A. 2015. Reliabilism, veritism, and epistemic consequentialism. *Episteme*, 12: 131–143.

Goodey, D. 2019. The Centrality of the Trinity: Exploring the Significance for Christians, Catechists and Deacons. *Rev. Guillermo de Ockham* 17(1): 9-15. doi: https://doi.org/10.21500/22563202.4087

Goren, P., Schoen, H., Reifler, J., Scotto, T., & Chittick, W. 2016. A Unified Theory of Value-Based Reasoning and U.S. Public Opinion. *Polit Behav*, 38: 977–997. DOI 10.1007/s11109-016-9344-x

Graburn, N. H. H. 2001. What is Tradition? *Museum Anthropology*, 24(2/3): 6-11.

Griffin, D. R. 2007. *Whitehead's radically different postmodern philosophy. An argument for its contemporary relevance*. New York: State University of New York Press.

Grim, B. J., & Finke, R. 2011. *The Price of Freedom Denied*. Cambridge: Cambridge University Press.

Guirguis, M. 2014. A Coat of Many Colors: The Religious Neutrality Doctrine from Everson to Hein. *Stetson Law Review*, 43: 67-118.

Hacker-Wright, J. 2010. Virtue Ethics without Right Action: Anscombe, Foot, and Contemporary Virtue Ethics. *J Value Inquiry*, 44: 209–224. DOI 10.1007/s10790-010-9218-0

Hamilton, M. A. 2018. The cognitive dissonance of religious liberty discourse: statutory rights masquerading as constitutional mandates. *Harvard Journal of Law & Public Policy*, 41(1): 79-94.

Harmless, W. (Ed.) 2010. *Augustine in His Own Words*. Washington, D. C: The Catholic University of America Press.

Harrison, V. S. 2005. The metamorphosis of "the end of the world": From theology to philosophy and back again. *Philosophy & Theology* 17(1 & 2): 32-50.

Haslam, N., Whelan, J., & Bastian, B. (2009). Big Five traits mediate associations between values and subjective well-being. *Personality and Individual Differences*, 46: 40-42.

Hauerwas, S. 1985. *Against the nations: War and survival in a liberal society*. Minneapolis: Winston Press.

_____. 2010. *Hannah's child: A theologian's memoir*, Grand Rapids, MI: Wm. B. Eerdmans Publishing Company.

_____. 2013. *With the grain of the universe: The church's witness and natural theology: Being the Gifford Lectures delivered at the University of St. Andrews in 2001*. Grand Rapids, MI: Baker Academic.

_____. 2015. *Performing the faith: Bonhoeffer and the practice of nonviolence*. Eugene, OR: Wipf & Stock.

_____. 2016. *Sanctify them in the truth: Holiness exemplified*. London: Bloomsbury.

Hegel, G. W. F. 1991. *Elements of the Philosophy of Right*. Allen W. Wood (Ed.). Cambridge: Cambridge University Press.

Hegel, G. W. F., & Findlay, J. N. 1977. *Phenomenology of Spirit*. A. V. Miller (Trans.). Oxford: Oxford University Press.

Hegel, G. W. F., & Rauch, L. 1988. *Introduction to the philosophy of history*. Indianapolis: Hackett.

Henrico, R. 2019. Proselytising the Regulation of Religious Bodies in South Africa: Suppressing Religious Freedom? *PER / PELJ*, 22: 1-27. Available at: https://journals.assaf.org.za/index.php/per/article/view/5315

Herdin, T., & Aschauer, W. 2013. Value changes in transforming China. *KOME-An International Journal of Pure Communication Inquiry*, 1(2): 1-22.

Herescu, D. 2019. Secularization, Multiple Modernities, and the Contemporary Challenge of "Multiple Orthodoxies." The Orthodox Christian Studies Center of Fordham University. publicorthodoxy.org/2019/10/29/secularization-multiple-orthodoxies/

Hippolytus of Rome. 2004. *Against the Heresy of One Noetus: Ante-Nicene Fathers* (Vol. V). Edited by Alexander Roberts & James Donaldson. Peabody, Massachusetts: Hendrickson Publishers, Inc.

Hobbes, T. 1999. *Leviathan*. Oregaon: The University of Oregon Press. http://darkwing.uoregon.edu/%7Erbear/hobbes/leviathan.html (1 of 145)4/5/2005 4:42:45 AM

Holyoak, K. J., & Powell, D. 2016. Deontological Coherence: A Framework for Commonsense Moral Reasoning. *Psychological Bulletin*, 142(11): 1179–1203. http://dx.doi.org/10.1037/bul0000075

Horwitz, P. 2013. Defending (Religious) Institutionalism. *Virginia Law Review*, 99: 1049-163. http://www.virginialawreview.org/sites/virginialawreview.org/files/Horwitz_Book.pdf

Ikäheimo, H. 2013. Hegel's Concept of Recognition—What Is It? In C. Krijnen (Ed.). *Recognition—German Idealism as an Ongoing Challenge* (11-38). Leiden and Boston: Brill.

Ireland's Constitution of 1937 with Amendments through 2015. 1937. This complete constitution has been generated from excerpts of texts from the repository of the Comparative Constitutions Project, and distributed on constituteproject.org. Available at: http://extwprlegs1.fao.org/docs/pdf/ire129756.pdf

IRRI. 2018. "We Do Not Honour Agreements" Dialogue and Peace Agreements in South Sudan.

Islam, M. N., & Islam, M. S. 2017. Islam and Democracy: Conflicts and Congruence. *Religions*, 8 (104): 1-19.

Issifu, A. K. 2016. Local peace committees in Africa: The unseen role in conflict resolution and peacebuilding. Africology: *The Journal of Pan African Studies*, 9(1): 141-158.

Jaeckle, T. & Georgakopoulos, A. 2010. Conflict discourse among Sudanese Dinka fefugees: Implications for cross-cultural analysis and resolution. *Journal of Alternative Perspectives in the Social Sciences*, 2, No 1, 57- 87. https://core.ac.uk/download/pdf/25872219.pdf

Johnson, D. H. 1986. Judicial Regulation and Administrative Control: Customary Law and the Nuer, 1898–1954. *The Journal of African History*, 27(1): 59–78.

_____. 2014. Briefing: The crisis in South Sudan. *African Affairs*, 113(451): 300–309.

Johnson, I. 2016. Beyond Orthodox strategies: Managing conflicts and sustaining peace through communal ethics, traditional values and methods in Africa. *Studies in Sociology of Science*, 7(4): 26-33.

Jok, K. M. 2012. Conflict of national identity in Sudan. *Unpublished Doctoral Dissertation*, Helsinki, Finland: University of Helsinki. https://helda.helsinki.fi/bitstream/handle/10138/30239/conflict.pdf?sequence=1

Jok, M. J. 2011. Diversity, unity, and nation building in South Sudan. *United States Institute of Peace*. Special Report.

_____. 2015. Negotiating an end to the current civil war in South Sudan: What lessons can Sudan's Comprehensive Peace Agreement offer? *Berghof Foundation Operations*.

Joshanloo, M., & Ghaedi, G. 2009. Value priorities as predictors of hedonic and eudaimonic aspects of well-being. *Personality and Individual Differences*, 47: 294-298.

Jost, J. T., & Amodio, D. M. 2012. Political ideology as motivated social cognition: Behavioral and neuroscientific evidence. *Motivation and Emotion*, 36: 55–64. http://dx.doi.org/10.1007/s11031-011-9260-7

Jost, J. T., Federico, C. M., & Napier, J. L. 2009. Political ideology: Its structure, functions, and elective affinities. *Annual Review of Psychology*, 60: 307-337.

Jost, J. T., Glaser, J., Kruglanski, A. W., & Sulloway, F. 2003. Political conservatism as motivated social cognition. *Psychological Bulletin*, 129: 339-375.

Kahn, P. 2011. *Political Theology: Four New Chapters on the Concept of Sovereignty*. New York: Columbia University Press.

Kalkandjieva, D. 2011. A comparative analysis on church-state relations in Eastern Orthodoxy: Concepts, models, and principles. *Journal of Church and State*, 53(4), 587-614. http://www.jstor.org/stable/24708220

Karabati, S., & Cemalcilar, Z. 2010. Values, materialism, and well-being: A study with Turkish university students. *Journal of Economic Psychology*, 31: 624-633.

Kariatlis, P. 2010. St Basil's contribution to the Trinitarian Doctrine: A synthesis of Greek Paideia and the Scriptural worldview. *Phronema* XXV: 57-83.

Katongole, E.M. 2008. Eschatology in African perspective. In W.A. Dyrness, & V. M. Kärkkäinen (Eds.) *Global dictionary of theology* (282-285). Downers Grove: Inter-Varsity.

Kelly, R. A. 2011. Public Theology and the Modern Social Imaginary. *Dialog: A Journal of Theology* 50(2): 162-173.

Kerovec, R. 2009. The embrace of justice and peace: concerning the tension between retributive and eschatological justice. *KAIROS - Evangelical Journal of Theology* III(1): 9-22.

Khalid, M. 1990. *The Government They Deserve: The Role of the Elite in Sudan's Political Evolution*. London and New York: Keagan and Paul International.

Khaptsova, A., & Schwartz, S. H. 2016. Life satisfaction and value congruence: Moderators and extension to constructed socio-demographic groups in a Russian national sample. *Social Psychology*, 47: 163-173.

Kibret, B. T. 2015. Conflicts, Conflict Resolution Practices and Impacts of the War in South Sudan. *International Journal of School and Cognitive Psychology* 2(013): 1-11.

Kindersley, N. 2019. Rule of whose law? The geography of authority in Juba, South Sudan. *The Journal of Modern African Studies* 57(1): 61-83

King, P. E., Abo-Zena, M. M, & Weber, J. D. 2017. Varieties of social experience: The religious cultural context of diverse spiritual exemplars. *British Journal of Developmental Psychology*, 35, 127–141.

Knopf, K. A. 2013. Fragility and state-society relations in South Sudan. *Africa Center for Strategic Studies*. Research Paper No. 4

Knopf, K. A. 2013. Fragility and state-society relations in South Sudan. *Africa Center for Strategic Studies*. Research Paper No. 4

Kon, M. 2015. Institutional Development, Governance, and Ethnic Politics in South Sudan. Kon, *J Glob Econ*, 3(2): 1-6. https://www.google.com/search?client=firefox-b-d&ei=hXjYX8KpN5OcUt-7povAO&q=Priorities+for+Peace+in+South+Sudan&oq=Priorities+-for+Peace+in+South+Sudan

Koopman, N. 2010. Some contours for public theology in South Africa. *International Journal for Practical Theology*, 14(1), 123-138. http://dx.doi.org/10.1515/ijpt.2010.9

Kopec, M. 2018. A pluralistic account of epistemic rationality. *Synthese*, 195: 3571–3596. https://doi.org/10.1007/s11229-017-1388-x

Kraus, M. W., Piff, P. K., Mendoza-Denton, R., Rheinschmidt, M. L., & Keltner, D. 2012. Social class, solipsism, and contextualism: How the rich are different from the poor. *Psychological Review*, 119: 546–572. https://doi.org/10.1037/a0028756

Krause, J. 2019. Stabilization and local conflicts: Communal and civil war in South Sudan. *Ethnopolitics*, 18(5): 478-493. DOI: 10.1080/17449057.2019.1640505

Kustenbauder, M. 2012. The politicization of religious identity in Sudan, with special reference to oral histories of the Sudanese diaspora in America. In A. Adogame & S. Shankar (Eds.). *Religion on the Move! New Dynamics of Religious Expansion in a Globalizing World* (397-424). Leiden: Brill.

Kyle, R. G. 1998. *The Last Days Are Here Again: A History of the End Times*. Grand Rapids: Baker Book House

Lamle, E. N., & Aigbovbioisa, F. O. 2019. Symbolic representation and conflict management in Africa. *International Journal of Research and Innovation in Social Science (IJRISS)*, III(XII): 194-204.

Lee, J. T. 2014. According to the Spirit and not to the Letter: Proportionality and the Singapore Constitution. *Vienna Journal on International Constitutional Law* 8(3): 276-304.

Leeuw, G. V. 1963. *Religion in essence and manifestation*. New York, Evanston: Harper & Row.

Lewis, A. R. 2014. Abortion Politics and the Decline of the Separation of Church and State: The Southern Baptist Case. *Politics and Religion*, 7, 521–549.

Liu, Z. 2013. Commentary on "Islamic State" Thoughts of Islamism. *Journal of Middle Eastern and Islamic Studies (in Asia)*, 7(3): 22-42.

Locke, J. 2003. A Letter Concerning Toleration. In I. Shapiro (ed.). *Two Treatises of Government and a Letter Concerning Toleration*. New Haven and London: Yale University Press.

Loh, K. S. 1998. Within the Singapore Story: The Use and Narrative of History in Singapore. *Crossroads: An Interdisciplinary Journal of Southeast Asian Studies* 12(2): 1–22.

Loudovikos, N. 2013. Possession or wholeness? St. Maximus the Confessor and John Zizioulas on person, nature, and will. *Participatio* 4: 258-286.

Lovejoy, A. O. 1933. *The great chain of being: A study of the history of an idea.* Cambridge, Massachusetts: Harvard University Press.

Lovin, R. W. 2011. *An introduction to Christian ethics: Goals, Duties, and Virtues.* Nashville, TN: Abingdon Press.

Lund, C. C. 2017. Religion is special enough. *Virginia Law Review,* 103: 481-524.

Luther, M. 1991. On Secular Authority. In Höpfl, H. (ed. & trans.). *Luther and Calvin on Secular Authority* (viii). Cambridge: Cambridge University Press.

———. 2012. Temporal Authority: To What Extent It Should Be Obeyed. In Lull, T. & Russell, W (Eds.). *Martin Luther's Basic Theological Writings.* Minneapolis: Fortress Press.

———. 2012. The Freedom of a Christian. In Lull, T. & Russell, W (Eds.). *Martin Luther's Basic Theological Writings.* Minneapolis: Fortress Press.

MacIntyre, A. C. 2014. *After virtue: A study in moral theory.* London: Bloomsbury.

Macleod, D. 2009. The influence of Calvinism on politics. *Theology in Scotland,* XVI(2): 5-22.

Magun, V., Rudnev, M., & Schmidt, P. 2016. Within and between-country value diversity in Europe: A typological approach. *European Sociological Review,* 32: 189–202. DOI: https://doi.org/10.1093/esr/jcv080

Malabou, C .2011. *Changing Difference: The Feminine and the Question of Philosophy.* Cambridge, UK: Shred X Trans Polity Press.

Manfredo, M. J., Bruskotter, J. T., Teel, T. L., Fulton, D., Schwartz, S. H., Arlinghaus, R., Sullivan, L. 2017. Why social values cannot be changed for the sake of conservation. *Conservation Biology*, 31: 772– 780. http://dx.doi.org/10.1111/cobi.12855

Manfredo, M. J., Teel, T. L., & Dietsch, A. M. 2016. Implications of human value shift and persistence for biodiversity conservation. *Conservation Biology*, 30: 287–296. https ://doi.org/10.1111/cobi.12619

Manning, L., Cassel, D., & Cassel, J. 2013. St. Augustine's Reflections on Memory and Time and the Current Concept of Subjective Time in Mental Time Travel. *Behavioral Science* 3: 232–243

Manstead, A. S. R. 2018. The psychology of social class: How socioeconomic status impacts thought, feelings, and behaviour. *British Journal of Social Psychology*, 57: 267–291. DOI:10.1111/bjso.12251

Manta, I. D. 2018. Gawking Legally. *Harvard Journal of Law & Public Policy*, 41(1): 117-124.

Mason, J. R. J. 2014. Justice and harmony as complementary ideals: Reconciling the right and the good through comparative philosophy. *Unpublished PhD Dissertation*, University of Hawaii. https://scholarspace.manoa.hawaii.edu/bitstream/10125/100405/1/Mason_Joshua_r.pdf

Matthee, K. 2019. Freedom of Religion: Individual? Collective?—As Perceived by the South African State. In Forster, D., Gerle, E., & Gunner, G. (Eds). *Freedom of Religion at Stake: Competing Claims among Faith Traditions, States, and Persons* (117-134). Eugene, OR: Wipf and Stock Publishers. pp. 117-134.

Mayemba, B. 2009. The notion of eschatology in African ancestral religions: A category of deliverance, promise, remembrance. Available at: https://dlib.bc.edu/islandora/object/bc-ir:102736/datastream/PDF/view

Mbiti, J. S. 1990. *African Religions and Philosophy* (2nd Ed). Oxford: Hienemann.

McAuliff, C. M. A. 2010. Religion and the secular state. *The American Journal of Comparative Law*, 58: 31-49. http://www.jstor.org/stable/20744531

McAuliff, C. M. A. 2010. Religion and the secular state. *The American Journal of Comparative Law*, 58, 31-49. http://www.jstor.org/stable/20744531

McConnell, M. W. 2013. Why protect religious freedom? *Yale Law Journal*, 123(3): 770-810. Available at: https://digitalcommons.law.yale.edu/ylj/vol123/iss3/4

McGregor, A. 2014. South Sudan's Tribal "White Army" - Part One: Cattle Raids and Tribal Rivalries. *Terrorism Monitor*, 12(1). Available at: https://www.refworld.org/docid/52e0e94b4.html [accessed 21 September 2020]

McKinnon, S. 2000. Domestic exceptions: Evans-Pritchard and the creation of nuer patrilineality and equality. *Cultural Anthropology*, 15(1), 35-83. http://www.jstor.org/stable/656640

McMahone, M. 2010. Broadening the Picture of Nineteenth-Century Baptists: How Battles with Catholicism Moved Baptists toward Separationism. *Journal of Law and Religion*, 25(2): 453-486. http://www.jstor.org/stable/20789490

Metz, T. 2011. Ubuntu as a moral theory and human rights in South Africa. *African Human Rights Law Journal*: 532-559.

Mickey, S. 2008. Cosmological postmodernism in Whitehead, Deleuze and Derrida. *Process Studies* 37(2): 24-44.

Mickute, V. 2018. Being a journalist in South Sudan: Practitioners recount experiences covering political, corruption and human rights stories in world's youngest country. *Aljazeera*. https://www.aljazeera.com/news/2018/12/18/being-a-journalist-in-south-sudan

Migliore, D. L. 2004. *Faith seeking understanding: An introduction to Christian theology* (2nd ed.). Grand Rapids, MI: William B. Eerdmans Publishing Company.

Miles, A. (2015). The (Re)genesis of Values: Examining the Importance of Values for Action. *American Sociological Review*, 80(4): 680–704. DOI: 10.1177/00031224155915800 http://asr.sagepub.com

Mo, K. 2014. Contested Constitutions: Constitutional development in Sudan 1953-2005. MA thesis in history Department of AHKR University of Bergen. Available at: http://suffragio.org/2013/12/18/how-to-prevent-south-sudans-impending-civilwar/sudan-map/ [Last accessed 14.05.14]

Moltmann, J. 1967. *Theology of Hope: On the Ground and Implications of Christian Eschatology*. London: SCM.

_____. 1979. *The Future of Creation*. London: SCM.

_____. 1981. *The Trinity and the Kingdom of God*. London: SCM.

_____. 1985. *God in Creation: An Ecological Doctrine of Creation*. London: SCM.

_____. 1990. *The Way of Jesus Christ: Christology in Messianic Dimensions*. London: SCM.

_____. 1996. *The Coming of God: Christian Eschatology*. London: SCM.

Muita, M. M., Yitbarek, M. & Mnguni, S. 2018. South Sudan conflict insight. *IPSS Peace & Security Report*.

Muita, M. M., Yitbarek, M. & Mnguni, S. 2018. South Sudan conflict insight. *IPSS Peace & Security Report*.

Mujuzi, J. D. 2011. Unpacking the law and practice relating to parole in South Africa. *PER / PELJ*, 14(5): 204-240. http://www.scielo.org.za/pdf/pelj/v14n5/v14n5a05.pdf

Muñoz, V. P. 2016. Two Concepts of Religious Liberty: The Natural Rights and Moral Autonomy Approaches to the Free Exercise of Religion. *American Political Science Review*, 110(2): 369-381.

Naylor, M. 2017. God, Evil, and Infinite Value. *Religions*, 9(20): 1-11.

Neo, J. L. 2019. Dimensions of Religious Harmony as Constitutional Practice: Beyond State Control. *German Law Journal*, 20: 966-985. Available at: https://www.cambridge.org/core/journals/german-law-journal/article/dimensions-of-religious-harmony-as-constitutional-practice-beyond-state-control/6595877F3B-75832F6E232FF029FB843F

_____. 2020. Regulating Pluralism: Laws on Religious Harmony and Possibilities for Robust Pluralism in Singapore. *The Review of Faith & International Affairs* 18(3): 1-15.

_____. 2017. Secularism without liberalism: Religious Freedom and Secularism in a Non-Liberal State. *Michigan State Law Review*, 2:333-370.

Nhlapo, T. 2017. Homicide in traditional African societies: Customary law and the question of accountability. *African Human Rights Law Journal*, 17: 1-34. http://dx.doi.org/10.17159/1996-2096/2017/v17n1a1

Nkondo, G. M. 2007. Ubuntu as public policy in South Africa: A conceptual framework. *International Journal of African Renaissance Studies - Multi-, Inter- and Transdisciplinarity* 2(1): 88-100.

Norris, P., & Inglehart, R. 2004. *Sacred and secular: Religion and politics worldwide*. Cambridge, England: Cambridge University Press.

Nyaba, P. A. 1997. *The Politics of Liberation: An Insider's View*. Kampala: Fountain Publishers.

Okoye, U. M., Ezeanya, W. C., & Chukwuma, J. N. 2018. 'Live and let live': The African ["Igbo"] traditional strategy for contemporary conflict resolution. *FAHSANU Journal: Journal of the Arts / Humanities*, 1(1): 1-16. https://fahsanu.com/journal/FAHSANU%20VOL-1/Paper%20Fifteen%20(Okoye,%20Uche%20Miriam).pdf

Ong, B. J. 2019. Special Feature on Symposium on Contemporary Issues in Public Law: Standing Up for Your Rights: A Review of the Law of Standing in Judicial Review in Singapore (2019). *Singapore Journal of Legal Studies*. 316-350, Available at SSRN: https://ssrn.com/abstract=3508483

Palm, S. 2019. Building Bridges or Walls?—Human Rights and Religious Freedom: A South African History. In Forster, D., Gerle, E., & Gunner, G. (Eds). *Freedom of Religion at Stake: Competing Claims among Faith Traditions, States, and Persons*. Eugene, OR: Wipf and Stock Publishers. pp. 175-198.

Pannenberg, W. 1991. *Systematic Theology* (Vol. 1). Translated by Geoffrey W. Bromiley. Grand Rapids: Eerdmans

Parratt, J. 1977. Time in traditional African thought. *Religion* 7(2): 117-126.

Pastura, P. S. V. C., Land, M. G. P. 2016. The perspective of Virtue Ethics regarding the process of medical decision-making. *Rev. bioét. (Impr.)*, 24(2): 243-249. http://dx.doi.org/10.1590/1983-80422016242124

Paul, H. 2013. Stanley Hauerwas: Against secularization in the church. *Zeitschrift* für *Dialektische Theologie*, 29(2): 12-33.

Pendle, N. R. 2020. Politics, prophets and armed mobilizations: competition and continuity over registers of authority in South Sudan's conflicts. *Journal of Eastern African Studies*, 14(1): 43-62. https://www.tandfonline.com/doi/full/10.1080/17531055.2019.1708545

Perkins, A. K. 2010. "Distinct but Inseparable": Church and State in the Writings of Michael Manley. *Caribbean Quarterly*, 56(3): 1-11. http://www.jstor.org/stable/23050671

Pew Research Center. 2019. A Closer Look at How Religious Restrictions Have Risen Around the World.

Piazza, J., & Sousa, P. 2014. Religiosity, Political Orientation, and Consequentialist Moral Thinking. *Social Psychological and Personality Science*, 5(3): 334-342. DOI: 10.1177/1948550613492826

Piazza, J., Russell, P. S., & Sousa, P. 2013. Moral emotions and the envisioning of mitigating circumstances for wrongdoing. *Cognition & Emotion*, 27: 707–722. doi:10.1080/02699931.2012.736859

Pinaud, C. 2014. South Sudan: Civil war, predation and the making of a military aristocracy. *African Affairs*, 113(451): 192–211.

Piurko, Y., Schwartz, S. H., & Davidov, E. 2011. Basic personal values and the meaning of left-right political orientations in 20 countries. *Political Psychology*, 32: 537-561.

Plaatjies van Huffel, M. 2019. Freedom of Religion in South Africa. In Forster, D., Gerle, E., & Gunner, G. (Eds). *Freedom of Religion at Stake: Competing Claims among Faith Traditions, States, and Persons.* Eugene, OR: Wipf and Stock Publishers. pp. 135-156.

Plato. 2008. *Timaeus and Critias.* Oxford, UK: Oxford University Press.

Plotinus. 1992. *The Enneads.* Translated by Stephen MacKenna. London: Larson Publications.

Ponizovskiy, V., Grigoryan, L., Kühnen, U., & Boehnke, K. 2019. Social Construction of the Value–Behavior Relation. *Frontiers in Psychology*, 10: 934. doi: 10.3389/fpsyg.2019.00934

Potgieter, F., & Van der Walt, J. 2015. Postmodern relativism and the challenge to overcome the "value-vacuum". *Stellenbosch Theological Journal* 1(1): 235–254.

Raeder, L. C. 2017. Postmodernism, Multiculturalism, and the Death of Tolerance: The Transformation of American Society. *Humanitas* XXX(1-2): 59-85.

Ramose, M. 1999. *African Philosophy through Ubuntu*. Harare: Mond Books.

_____. 2017. *Ubuntu. Stroom van het bestaan als levensfilosofie*. Utrecht: Ten Have.

Rajah, J. 2012. *Authoritarian Rule of Law: Legislation, Discourse and Legitimacy in Singapore*. Cambridge: Cambridge University Press.

Republic of South Sudan. 2011. *The Transitional Constitution of the Republic of South Sudan, 2011*. Juba: Ministry of Justice Publication.

Republic of South Sudan. 2011. *The Transitional Constitution of the Republic of South Sudan, 2011*. Juba: Ministry of Justice Publication.

Riedl, R. B. 2011. Transforming Politics, Dynamic Religion: Religion's Political Impact in Contemporary Africa. *African Conflict and Peacebuilding Review*, 2(2): 29-50. http://www.jstor.org/stable/10.2979/africonfpeacrevi.2.2.29

Riedl, R. B. 2011. Transforming politics, dynamic religion: Religion's political impact in contemporary Africa. *African Conflict and Peacebuilding Review*, 2(2): 29-50. http://www.jstor.org/stable/10.2979/africonfpeacrevi.2.2.29

Roach, S. C. 2016. South Sudan: A volatile dynamic of accountability and peace. *International Affairs*, 92(6): 1343–1359

Robbins, J. W., & Crockett, C. 2015. A radical theology for the future: five theses. *Palgrave Communications* 1(150): 1-10.

Rolandsen, Ø. H. 2015. Another civil war in South Sudan: the failure of Guerrilla Government? *Journal of Eastern African Studies*, 9(1): 163-174.

Ronzoni, M. 2010. Teleology, Deontology, and the Priority of the Right: On Some Unappreciated Distinctions. *Ethic Theory Moral Practice*, 13: 453–472. DOI 10.1007/s10677-009-9209-z

Ruey, T. 2017. The South Sudanese Conflict Analysis. Conflict Profile, Causes, Actors and Dynamics. *Doctoral Thesis*. Atlantic International University.

Sagiv, L., & Schwartz, S. H. 2000. Value priorities and subjective well-being: Direct relations and congruity effects. European Journal of Social Psychology, 30: 177-198.

Schiffman, L. H. 2016. Peace and reconciliation in the Abrahamic religions: Sources, History and future prospects. *The Journal of Living Together*, 2(3): 4-16.

Schomerus, M. & Aalen, L. 2016. Considering the state: Perspectives on South Sudan's subdivision and federalism debate. *CMI*.

Schwartz S. H., Caprara G. V., & Vecchione, M. 2010. Basic personal values, core political values, and voting: A longitudinal analysis. Political Psychology 31(3): 421–452.

Schwartz, S. H. 1992. Universals in the content and structure of values: Theoretical advances and empirical tests in 20 countries. In M. P. Zanna (Ed.). *Advances in Experimental Social Psychology* (1-65). New York, NY: Academic Press.

_____. 1994. Are there universal aspects in the structure and contents of human values? Journal of Social Issues, 50, 19-45.

_____. (2006). A theory of cultural value orientations: Explication and applications. *Comparative Sociology*, 5, 137–182. http://dx.doi.org/10.1163/156913306778667357

_____. 2012. An overview of the Schwartz theory of basic values. *Online Readings in Psychology and Culture*, 2(1), 11. doi:10.9707/2307-0919.1116.

———. 1992. Universals in the content and structure of values: Theoretical advances and empirical tests in 20 countries. In M. P. Zanna (Ed.). *Advances in Experimental Social Psychology* (pp. 1-65). New York, NY: Academic Press.

———. 2012. An overview of the Schwartz theory of basic values. *Online Readings in Psychology and Culture*, 2(1), 11. doi:10.9707/2307-0919.1116.

Schwartz, S. H., & Bilsky, W. 1987. Toward a psychological structure of human values. *Journal of Personality and Social Psychology*, 53: 550-562.

Schwartz, S. H., & Sortheix, F. M. 2018. Values and subjective well-being. In E. Diener, S. Oishi, & L. Tay (Eds.). *Handbook of well-being*. Salt Lake City, UT: DEF Publishers. DOI: nobascholar.com

Schwartz, S. H., Caprara, G. V., Vecchione, M., Bain, P., Baslevent, C., Bianchi, G., Verkasalo, M. 2013. Basic personal values constrain and give coherence to political values: A cross-national study in 15 countries. Political Behavior, 36, 899-930.

Schwartz, S. H., Cieciuch, J., Vecchione, M., Davidov, E., Fischer, R., Beierlein, C., Konty, M. 2012. Refining the theory of basic individual values. *Journal of Personality and Social Psychology*, 103: 663–688. http://dx.doi.org/10.1037/a0029393

Seedat, F. 2019. Intersections and Assemblages—South Africans Negotiating Privilege and Marginality through Freedom of Religion and Sexual Difference. In Forster, D., Gerle, E., & Gunner, G. (Eds). *Freedom of Religion at Stake: Competing Claims among Faith Traditions, States, and Persons*. Eugene, OR: Wipf and Stock Publishers. pp. 199-220.

Shamim, S. J. 2018. Hegel's Concept of Intellectual Development in Human History. *Asian Research Journal of Arts & Social Sciences* 5(4): 1-6.

Sheeder, R. 2013. Awad V. Ziriax: The Tenth Circuit's Defense against the Power of Religious Majority Factions. *Denver University Law Review*, 90(3): 801-823.

Sheeder, R. 2013. Awad V. Ziriax: The tenth circuit's defense against the power of religious majority factions. *Denver University Law Review*, 90(3): 801-823.

Shutte, A. 2001. *Ubuntu an ethic for a new South Africa*. Pietermaritzburg: Cluster Publications.

Sidahmed, A. S. 2012. Islamism & the state. In J. Ryle, J. Willis, S. Baldo, & J. M. Jok (Eds.). *The Sudan Handbook* (164-184). St Luke's Mews, London: Rift Valley Institute.

Sidenvall, E. 2012. Church and state in Sweden: A contemporary report. *Kirchliche Zeitgeschichte*, 25(2): 311-319. http://www.jstor.org/stable/43751965

Sindima, H. 1990. Liberalism and African Culture. *Journal of Black Studies* 21(2): 190–209.

Skliris, D. 2017. "Eschatological Teleology," "Free Dialectic," "Metaphysics of the Resurrection": The Three Antinomies That Make Maximus an Alternative European Philosopher. In S. Mitralexis, G. Steiris, M. Podbielski, & S. Lalla (Eds.). *Maximus the Confessor as a European Philosopher* (3-23). Eugene, Oregon: Cascade Books.

Smack, A. J., Herzhoff, K., Tang, R., Walker, R. L., & Tackett, J. L. 2017. A Latent Class Analysis of Personal Values in Young Adults. *Collabra: Psychology*, 3(1): 1–10. DOI: https://doi.org/10.1525/collabra.114

Sookdeo, P. 2014. *Dawa: The Islamic strategy for reshaping the modern world*. McLean, VA: Isaac Publishing.

_____. 2019. *Hated without a reason: The remarkable story of Christian persecution over the centuries*. McLean, VA: Isaac Publishing.

Sortheix, F. M., & Lönnqvist, J. E. 2015. Person-group value congruence and subjective well-being in students from Argentina, Bulgaria and Finland: The role of interpersonal relationships. *Journal of Community & Applied Social Psychology*, 25(1): 34-48

Sortheix, F. M., & Schwartz, S. H. 2017. Values that underlie and undermine well-being: Variability across countries. *European Journal of Personality*, 31(2): 187-201.

Spinelli, D. 2019, Sep 23. Trump's UN Speech on Religious Freedom Conveniently Ignored One Major Point: An American ally is persecuting religious minorities at record levels. *Mother Jones*. Available at: https://www.motherjones.com/politics/2019/09/donald-trump-un-religious-freedom-saudi-arabia/

Spong, J. S. 1994. *Resurrection: Myth or reality?: A bishop's search for the origins of Christianity*. San Francisco: Harper San Francisco.

Starks, B., & Robinson, R. V. 2017. Moral cosmology, religion, and adult values for children. *Journal for the Scientific Study of Religion*, 46(1):17–35.

Starrett, G. 2010. The Varieties of Secular Experience. *Comparative Studies in Society and History* 52(3): 626– 651.

Sudan People's Liberation Movement (SPLM). 1983. *Manifesto*. Bilpam, Ethiopia.

Sudan Tribune. 2012. Hundreds of South Sudanese Muslims head to Mecca for pilgrimage. https://sudantribune.com/spip.php?iframe&page=imprimable&id_article=44261

Sudan Tribune. 2013. South Sudan Church calls to review separation of religion and the state. https://www.sudantribune.com/spip.php?article45420

Sudan Tribune. 2014. South Sudan president warns against importing radical Islam. https://sudantribune.com/spip.php?iframe&page=imprimable&id_article=51831

Stephens, N. M., Markus, H. M., & Phillips, L. T. 2014. Social class culture cycles: How three gateway contexts shape selves and fuel inequality. *Annual Review of Psychology*, 65: 611–634. https://doi.org/10.1146/annurev-psych-010213-115143

Tamir, M., Bigman, Y. E., Rhodes, E., Salerno, J., & Schreier, J. 2015. An expectancy-value model of emotion regulation: Implications for motivation, emotional experience, and decision making. *Emotion*, 15: 90–103. http://dx.doi.org/10.1037/emo0000021

Tamir, M., Schwartz, S. H., Cieciuch, J., Riediger, M., Torres, C., Scollon, C., Vishkin, A. (2016). Desired emotions across cultures: A value based account. *Journal of Personality and Social Psychology*, 111: 67– 82. Advance online publication. http://dx.doi.org/10.1037/pspp0000072

Taylor, C. *Modern Social Imaginaries*. Durham, NC: Duke University Press, 2004.

Terry, K. S. 2008. Shifting out of Neutral: Intelligent Design and the Road to Nonpreferentialism. *Public Interest Law Journal*, 18: 67-117.

The Interim National Constitution of the Republic of the Sudan. 2005. Available at: http://www.refworld.org/pdfid/4ba749762.pdf [Last accessed 09.04.2014].

The Juba Conference. 1947. *Minutes EP/SCR/1.A.5/1*. Hai Cinema: Juba.

The Permanent Constitution of the Sudan, 1973. (Issued on the 8th of May 1973). The Attorney Generals Office. The Democratic Republic of the Sudan Gazette. Reference: Mahmoud Salih Collection, UIB, Box P-5 "Parliament, Constitution, Legislature."

The Transitional Constitution of Sudan, 1956. (McCorquodale & Co. (Sudan), Ltd.) Reference: Mahmoud Salih Collection, UIB, Box P-5 "Parliament, Constitution, Legislature."

Thio, L. 2010. Contentious liberty: Regulating religious propagation in a multi-religious secular democracy. *Singapore Journal of Legal Studies*. 484-515.

Tsai, J. L., Sims, T., Qu, Y., Thomas, E., Jiang, D, & Fung, H. H. 2018. Valuing Excitement Makes People Look Forward to Old Age Less and Dread It More. American Psychological Association, 33(7): 975–992. http://dx.doi.org/10.1037/pag00002950882-7974/18/$12.00

Turner, F. 1990. The Meaning of Value: An Economics for the Future. *New Literary History* 21(3): 747-762. Available at: http:// www.jstor.org/stable/469137

U. S. Department of State. 2017. 2017 Report on International Religious Freedom: South Sudan. Available at: https://www.state.gov/reports/2017-report-on-international-religious-freedom/south-sudan/

_____2018 Report on International Religious Freedom: South Sudan. Available at: https://www.state.gov/reports/2018-report-on-international-religious-freedom/south-sudan/

Vacura, M. 2020. The one and differentiating principles of hypostases in Plotinus' metaphysics. *Philosophia: International Journal of Philosophy* 21(2): 202-220.

Vaisey, Stephen, and Omar Lizardo. (2010). Can Cultural Worldviews Influence Network Composition? *Social Forces*, 88(4): 1595–1618.

Van der Walt, C. 2019. Mind the Gap—Freedom of Religion and the "Gay Rights Clause." In Forster, D., Gerle, E., & Gunner, G. (Eds). *Freedom of Religion at Stake: Competing Claims among Faith Traditions, States, and Persons*. Eugene, OR: Wipf and Stock Publishers. pp. 221-238.

Van Manen, M. 2017. But is it phenomenology? *Qualitative Health Research*, 27(6), 775–779. DOI: 10.1177/1049732317699570. journals.sagepub.com/home/qhr

Van Zyl, L. 2011. Qualified-agent virtue ethics. *South African Journal of Philosophy*, 30(2): 219-228, DOI: 10.4314/sajpem.v30i2.67784 https://doi.org/10.4314/sajpem.v30i2.67784

Vandrunen, D. 2007. The Two Kingdoms Doctrine and the Relationship of Church and State in the Early Reformed Tradition. *Journal of Church and State*, 49(4), 743-763. http://www.jstor.org/stable/23922304

Vattimo, G. 2007. A prayer for silence: Dialogue with Gianni Vattimo. In J. W. Robbins (ed). *After the Death of God*. New York: Columbia University Press.

Vecchione, M., Caprara, G. V., Dentale, F., & Schwartz, S. H. 2013. Voting and values: Reciprocal effects over time. Political Psychology, 34, 465-485.

Vecchione, M., Schoen, H., González Castro, J. L., Cieciuch, J., Pavlopoulos, V., & Caprara, G. V. 2011. Personality correlates of party preference: The Big Five in five big European countries. Personality and Individual Differences, 51, 737-742.

Vecchione, M., Schwartz, S. II., Caprara, G. V., Schoen, H., Cieciuch, J., Silvester, J., Alessandri, G. 2015. Personal values and political activism: A crossnational study. *British Journal of Psychology*, 106: 84-106.

Veerachary, P. 2018. Philosophical Dimensions of Postmodernism. *International Journal of Humanities and Social Science Invention*, 7(5): 2319-7722. www.ijhssi.org

Venter, R. Trends in contemporary Christian eschatological reflection. *Missionalia* 43(1): 105–123. Available at: www.missionalia.journals.ac.za | http://dx.doi.org/10.7832/43-1-72

Vorster, J. M. 2018. The church as a moral agent: In dialogue with Bram van de Beek. *HTS Teologiese Studies/Theological Studies* 74(4). 4809. https://doi. org/10.4102/hts.v74i4.4809

Vorster, J.M. 2009. The contribution of deontological Christian ethics to the contemporary human rights discourse. *In die Skriflig*, 43(3): 497-518.

Vosloo, R. 2004. Identity, otherness and the Triune God: Theological groundwork for a Christian ethics of hospitality. *Journal of Theology for Southern Africa* 119: 69-89.

_____. 2002. The gift of participation: On the Triune God and the Christian moral life. *Scriptura* 79: 93-103.

Walker, G. 1996. The mixed constitution after liberalism. *J. INT'L & COMP. L.* 4: 311-319.

Wallace, M. I. 2005. *Finding God in the Singing River: Christianity, Spirit, Nature*. Minneapolis, MN: Fortress Press.

Walsh, E. A. 2017. Shh! State legislators bite your tongues: Semantics dictates the constitutionality of public school "moment of silence" statutes. *The Catholic Lawyer*, 43, 225-254.

Ward, G. 2018. *Unimaginable*. London: I.B.Tauris & Co. Ltd.

Wassara, S. S. 2007. Traditional mechanisms of conflict resolution in Southern Sudan. *Berghof Foundation for Peace Support*: 1-13. https://gisf.ngo/wp-content/uploads/2014/09/0979-Wassara-2007-Traditional-Mechanisms-of-CR-in-South-Sudan.pdf

Weber, E. 2000. *Apocalypses: Prophecies, Cults, and Millennial Beliefs through the Ages*. Cambridge, Massachusetts: Harvard University Press.

Wilson, J. 2019. The Religious Landscape in South Sudan: Challenges and opportunities for engagement. *United States Institute of Peace*. Peace Works, NO. 148.

Wita, G. 2013. *Theology of Harmony in Federation of Asian Bishops' Conferences (FABC) Documents*. Katolicki Uniwersytet Lubelski Jana Pawła II - Wydział Teologii.

Witte, J. 2003. That serpentine wall of separation. *Michigan Law Review*, 101, 1869-1905.

Yobwan, L. 2018. *South Sudan: Sudan Understanding the Culture, People and Their Mindset.* Indianapolis, IN: Next Century Publishing.

Zaccheus, M. 2018. MHA Investigating Foreign Christian Preacher's Comments that Online Site Claims were Anti-Islamic. *The Straits Times,* March 28. Available at: https://www.straitstimes.com/singapore/mha-investigating-foreign-christian preachers-comments-that-online-site-claims-was-anti.

Zhyrkova, A. 2009. Hypostasis - The principle of individual existence in john of Damascus. *Journal of Eastern Christian Studies* 61(1-2): 101-130.

Zilberfeld, T. (2010). *Person-culture fit and subjective well-being among ultra-orthodox and secular Israelis.* Unpublished master's thesis, Hebrew University, Jerusalem, Israel.

Zizioulas, J. 2006. The Father as Cause: Personhood Generating Otherness. In P. McPartlan (Ed.). *Communion and Otherness: Further Studies in Personhood and the Church* (113-154). London: T. & T. Clark.

Zollman, K. (2013). Network epistemology: Communication in epistemic communities. *Philosophy Compass,* 8: 15–27.

---- INDEX ----

Aalen 224-225, 377
Ababa 233-234, 263, 270
Abdel 6, 33
Abdullah 273
Abilene xii, xiv
Abingdon 369
Abrahamic 291, 316, 327, 377
Accommodation 38
Accomodation 358
Adam 274
Addis 233-234, 263, 270
Addis Ababa 59, 78, 177, 216, 234
Adogame 368

Africa xvi, 10-1, 21, 53, 69, 127, 136, 160-7, 169-172, 191, 212, 219, 241-2, 245-6, 250-1, 253-5, 260, 269, 287, 296, 310, 312, 320-1, 349, 354-5, 365, 367-8, 371-2, 375-6, 379, 384
African 1-2, 6-11, 43, 48, 50, 52-4, 56-7, 114, 128, 135, 161-7, 171-2, 178-9, 184, 190, 219, 240-6, 248-252, 254-5, 267, 269, 271, 278-9, 281-2, 291, 296, 313, 316, 322-3, 329, 342, 349, 352, 355, 358, 360, 365-7, 370-1, 373-6, 379, 383

Africans 10, 18, 48-9, 126-8, 172, 177-8, 219, 236, 241, 248-251, 253, 255, 260-2, 266-7, 269, 281-3, 296, 301, 310, 319, 321-2, 331, 339, 342-3, 378
Afshari xiv
Agang 360
Agapeic 278
Agrama, H. A. 351
Agwella 253, 351
Ahmed, D. I. 351
Aigbovbioisa 239, 242, 253, 368
Ajak 54, 73
Ajayi, A. T. 352
Akobo 356
Aktas, B. 352
Alam, M. 292, 352
Albany 355
Alessandri 383
Alexander 153, 155, 323, 352, 364
Alexandrinian 304
Algesheimer 356-357
Ali 73, 352
Alice 18
Aljazeera 371
Allah 45-46, 133-4, 142, 179, 275-6, 339
Allama 273
Allen 363

Altizer 288
Ambiguities 184
America xi, 39, 50, 57, 67, 89, 103, 122, 126-7, 144, 150, 153, 210, 249, 308, 310, 326, 354, 362, 368
American 18, 33, 39, 74-5, 78, 150, 160, 355, 359, 371-3, 376, 380, 382
Americans 67, 127
Amodio 365
Amutabi 354
Anaxagoras 287
Anderson 354
Andre xiv
Andrew 308
Andrews 363
Anglican 20, 291
Anglicans 83
Anscombe 362
Anthropology 362, 371
Antinomies 379
Antiochian 304
Anya 177
Aquinas, T. 200-202, 285, 352
Arab 48, 50-1, 54-6, 58-9, 62, 73, 176-9, 243, 249, 267, 281
Arabia 35, 72, 158-160
Arabic 267, 275, 352
Arabicspeaking 54

Arabization 58, 62
Arabs 48-49, 54-5, 57, 177-8, 266-7
Arama xv
Areteology 90
Argentina 380
Arians 294-295
Aristotelian 39, 90
Aristotle 89, 209, 285-8, 316
Arlinghaus 13, 370
Arts 374, 378
Asad, T. 352
Aschauer 135, 363
Ashworth, J. 235-236, 339, 352
Asia 69, 126-7, 136, 170-2, 292, 349
Asian 6, 114, 170-2, 292, 368, 378, 384
Asians 127, 236, 292, 331, 339
Aspelund, A. 119, 353
Assmann, J. 353
Atem 353
Atlantic 377
Augustine, A. 198-202, 230, 285, 290, 300-1, 322, 353, 362
Augustinianism 230
Augustinus 198
Aurelius 198
Australia 126-127
Australian 358

Australians 126
Authority 369
Autonomy 373
Awad 379
Awolich 262, 353
Babylon 199
Badi xv
Bafinamene 17, 353
Bahr 58
Bain 356, 378
Baird 89, 353
Balagangadhara 6, 324, 327, 353
Baldo 379
Bangura 353
Bantus 250-251
Barach 72
Barnabas xiv
Barth 302, 353
Basabe 355
Basil 295-296, 306, 354
Baslevent 356, 378
Bastian 363
Baudrillard 167
Bayram 126-127, 354
Beek 383
Behav 362
Beierlein 378
Belinda xi, xii, xiv
Bentiu 257
Bergen 372

Berghof 365, 384
Berkeley 286
Bernard, M. M. 354
Bernhardt 354
Besserman 324, 354
Bianchi 356, 378
Biar xv, xix, xxi, xxi, xxv, 3, 5, 7, 9, 11, 13, 15, 17, 19, 21, 23, 25, 27, 29, 31, 33, 35, 37, 39, 41, 43, 45, 47, 49, 51, 53, 55, 57, 59, 61, 63, 65, 67, 69, 71, 73, 75, 77, 79, 81, 83, 85, 89, 91, 93, 95, 97, 99, 101, 103, 105, 107, 109, 111, 113, 115, 117, 119, 121, 123, 125, 127, 129, 131, 133, 135, 137, 139, 141, 143, 145, 147, 149, 151, 153, 155, 157, 159, 161, 163, 165, 167, 169, 171, 173, 175, 177, 179, 181, 183, 185, 187, 189, 191, 195, 197, 199, 201, 203, 205, 207, 209, 211, 213, 215, 217, 219, 221, 223, 225, 227, 229, 231, 233, 235, 237, 239, 241, 243, 245, 247, 249, 251, 253, 255, 257, 259, 261, 263, 265, 267, 269, 271, 273, 275, 277, 279, 281, 283, 285, 287, 289, 291, 293, 295, 297, 299, 301, 303, 305, 307, 309, 311, 313, 315, 317, 319, 321, 323, 325, 327, 329, 331, 333, 335, 337, 339, 341, 343, 345, 349, 353-5, 357, 359, 361, 363, 365, 367, 369, 371, 373, 375, 377, 379, 381, 383, 385
Bigman 381
Bilbao 355
Bilpam 380
Bilsky, W. 103, 354, 378
Binary 353
Biology 370
Bior 73
Blayney 354
Bloomsbury 363, 369
Blue 55-56
Blum 30, 355
Bob xi, xii
Bobowik, M. 122, 355
Boehnk 100
Boehnke 375
Boer 355
Boff 302, 355
Bohman 355
Bonhoeffer 363
Books 271, 283, 340, 357, 376, 379
Bor 45
Boubleday 357
Bowie 355
Bradford 351
Bram 383

Brigham 359
Brill 364, 368
British 39, 43, 54-6, 76, 177, 185, 243, 265, 367, 370, 383
Britisheducated 55
Broadening 371
Bromile 353
Bromiley 374
Brookings 359
Bruskotter 13, 370
Bubbio 355
Buhari 352
Bujo 322, 355
Bul 233, 258
Bulgaria 380
Burroughs, B. 355
Buth 54
Cairo 69
Calfano 9, 359
Calif 353
Calvin, J. 204-205, 207, 355, 369
Calvinism 369
Cambridge 353, 355, 362, 369, 373, 384
Cappadocian 304, 306
Caprara, G. V. 99-100, 102, 112, 118-120, 355-6, 377-8, 383
Caribbean 375
Carlisle 360
Cassel 322, 370

Castro 383
Catechists 362
Catholicism 371
Cemalcilar 122, 366
Centrality 362
Ceskoslovenska 355
Chan 174
Chantepie 29
Chapman 356
Charles 6, 8
Chen 356
Cheong 175
Chicago 361
Children 137
China 363
Chinese 260-261
Chittick 362
Christ 11, 18, 38, 175, 201, 273, 305-6, 308, 318
Christian xii, xxv, 2, 4-5, 7-8, 13, 16-20, 22-3, 25, 29-31, 36, 38-9, 43, 48, 52, 57-8, 73-5, 77, 79-81, 85, 98-9, 120, 133, 135, 139-142, 147-8, 161, 165, 167, 187, 191, 196, 198-9, 227-231, 234, 246-7, 271, 274, 276, 288, 291, 293-4, 308, 311, 319, 325, 338, 341, 355, 360, 362, 364, 369, 372, 379, 383-5
Christianities 360

Christianity 2, 4, 7, 36, 49-50, 56, 73-4, 85-6, 98, 133-5, 138, 141-2, 166, 177-8, 180-1, 187, 190, 198, 227-230, 271-6, 291, 316, 324, 337-8, 352-3, 361, 380, 384

Christianization 58

Christians xvi, xx, xxi, 1-2, 5, 13, 16-8, 20, 22, 25-6, 39-40, 43, 47-54, 75, 77, 79, 85, 93-4, 119, 134-5, 138-9, 142-3, 159, 174-5, 177, 190, 198-9, 203, 227-230, 235, 249, 266-7, 273, 275-8, 281, 283, 292, 316-7, 319, 323-5, 328, 333, 337, 340, 343, 362

Christology 288, 372

Christopher xiv

Chuan, T. Y. 356

Chukwuma 170, 241-2, 249, 260, 269, 281, 310, 321, 374

Cieciuch, J 102, 104-5, 123, 356-7, 378, 381, 383

Cirp 361

Ciulla 218, 357

Civility 360

Clark 353, 358, 385

Clifford 357

Cobb 357

Cohen, J. L. 208, 357

Colin 174

Collins, R. O. 357

Colorado 153-154, 326

Columbia 103, 366, 383

Commonsense 364

Confessor 303, 369, 379

Conscience 150, 152

Consequentialist 375

Continuum 121, 359

Cooperation 69

Copleston 357

Corinthian 273

Corinthians 231, 325

Cornell 360

Cosmological 371

Courtney 16, 19

Cox, J. L. 288, 358

Creation 372

Crestwood 354

Critias 287, 375

Crockett 287-290, 376

Cronin 251

Crux 23

Daly 226, 357

Damascus 295, 304-7, 385

Danbury 64

Danchin 358

Daniel 233, 358

Darfur 55, 57, 179

Darfuris 48

David xi, xii, 291, 354, 362

Davidov, E. 99-100, 102, 118, 135, 356-8, 375, 378
De Waal 358
Deagon 8, 358
Deconstructionism 167
Dee xi, xii
Delaney 179, 358
Deleuze 371
Democracy 351, 355
Demoi 355
Demos 355
Deng xii, 58, 233-4, 359
Dentale 383
Denver 379
Deontological 96, 98, 364
Deontologists 89-90
Deontology 90, 377
Derrida 167-168, 353, 371
Descartes 203, 286
Detroit 19
Dhimmi 52
Dialektische 374
Diener 378
Dietsch 370
Dinka 189, 234, 257-9, 268, 270, 280, 365
Diocesan xv
Diocese xv, 233
Diogenes 354
Dion xiv, 6
Dirkie 349
Dit 258
Diu 54
Diversities 308
Djupe, P. A. 9, 359
Doctoral 365, 377
Dogmatics 353
Donaldson 364
Doom 164
Dorrien, G. J. 359
Doshi 359
Doubleday 357
Downers 366
Dualism 230
Duffel, S. V. 359
Duke 381
Durham 381
Dyrness 366
Early 143, 354, 360, 383
Earthly 359
Eastern 354, 366, 368, 374, 376, 385
Ecclesia 353
Ecclesial 361
Ecclesiocracy 83, 291
Econ 367
Economic 159, 366
Economics 382
Eduard 349
Edward 233

Eerdmans 363, 372, 374
Egypt 39, 351
Egyptian 1
Electioneering 360
Eliade 29
Ells 359
Emeritus 233
England xvi
English xiv, 43-4, 275, 352
Enneads 375
Enock 233
Episcopal xv, 233, 291
Episteme 362
Epstein 146, 359
Equality 24
Equatoria 58, 251, 279
Erastianism 83, 291
Esbeck 359
Eschatological 319
Eschatology 312-313, 321, 323, 366, 372
Esposito 352
Ethic 377
Ethics 16, 91, 98, 219-220, 354-5, 357, 362, 374
Ethnic 358, 367
Ethnicity 57
Ethnopolitics 368
Etienne 349

Eugene 360, 363, 370, 374-5, 378-9, 382
Europe 82, 126-8, 172-3
European 108, 353-4, 357-8, 369, 377, 379-380, 383
Europeans 355
Everson 362
Evil 373
Explication 377
Ezeanya 170, 241-2, 249, 260, 269, 281, 310, 321, 374
Faculty 358
Federico 366
Feldman, N. 359
Ferreira 359
Fichte, J. G. 286, 360
Filosofija 361
Findlay 363
Fink xiv
Fischer 13, 378
Fitzgerald 360
Fordham 364
Forster xiv, 6, 11, 14, 164, 284, 296, 360, 370, 374-5, 378, 382
Fortress 369, 384
Foucault 146, 167
Fragility 367
Francois 167
Friedrich 314
Fulton 13, 370

Fung 382
Gabriel 288
Garang 33, 50, 74-5, 177-180, 187-8, 217-9, 225-6, 267, 279-280, 317, 358, 360
Gardeang 258
Garnett, R. W. 361
Gatdeang 258-259
Gebauer 354
Geert 103
Gelvin 188, 361
Genesis 320
Geneva 16-17
Genyi 275-276, 361
Geoffey 353
Geoffrey 374
Georg 314
Georgakopoulos 24, 365
Georgetown 359
Gerle 360, 370, 374-5, 378, 382
German 129, 148, 167, 286, 301-3, 313, 318, 321, 333, 343, 373
Ghaedi 122, 365
Ghazal 58
Gholson 274, 361
Gianni 383
Gifford 363
Gill 361
Gilpin 361

Giorgi, A. 361
Gitari 291, 362
Glaser 366
Globalization 354
Globalizing 368
God xix, xxv, 10-2, 16, 18-21, 38, 47, 82-4, 94, 96, 98-9, 101, 133, 140-3, 150, 152, 166, 169, 181, 183, 196-206, 208-9, 212, 228-9, 231, 271-8, 285-294, 296-9, 302-3, 305-7, 310-2, 314-5, 317-321, 323-5, 327-8, 331-3, 343, 348, 353, 355, 372-3, 383-4
Godhead 301
Goh, R. B. H. 362
Goldman, A. 362
Goodey 362
Goren, P. 362
Gouda 142, 351
Governance 163, 173, 367
Graburn, N. H. H. 132, 362
Graham 6
Greek 89, 129, 133, 141, 366
Griffin 362
Grigoryan 100, 375
Grim, B. J. 362
Gruyter 356
Guillermo 362
Guirguis 362
Gwynne xv

Hackett 363
Hadith 272, 275
Hai 381
Halbert xi, xii
Hamilton 157, 288, 362
Happiness 93, 355
Harambe 254
Harmon xi, xii, xiv
Harper 368, 380
Harrison 314-316, 363
Harvard 353, 359, 362, 369-370, 384
Harvey 288
Haslam, N. 122, 363
Hassan 1, 40, 44, 53, 59-60, 77, 179
Hastings 351
Hauerwas 16-17, 363
Health 382
Hegel, G. W. F. 286, 314-9, 333, 343, 361, 363
Hegelian 315, 318
Hegelianism 317
Hegelians 313, 315, 320
Heidegger 361
Hein 362
Helsinki 365
Hendrickson 354, 364
Hendrik xiv
Hendriks 360

Henrico 163-164, 363
Henry 354
Herdin, T. 135, 363
Hereafter 181
Herescu, D. 134, 364
Herzhoff 379
Hiang 174
Hienemann 371
Hiiboro 233-234
Hippo 198
Hippolytus 364
Hipponensis 198
Hobbes 96, 364
Hofstede 103
Holiness 363
Holyoak, K. J. 90, 99, 364
Horwitz 210, 364
Hospitality 12
Huffel 162-163, 165-6, 375
Humanism 354
Humanitas 376
Humanities 374, 383
Humanity 10
Hungary 119
Husserl 361
Hussin 147
Hutchinson 170, 258
Hypostasis 305-306, 385
Ibrahim 40
Idealism 129, 359, 364

Ideology 177
Illinois 356
Imaginaries 381
Imaginary 366
Imagination 14, 221, 251
Imaginations 195
Imaginatively 296
Incoherence 91
Indianapolis 385
Inglehart 20, 373
Institutionalism 364
Interdisciplinary 368
Iran 159-160
Iranian 160
Irish 173
Isaac 362, 379
Islam, M. N. xvi, 2, 4-5, 36, 38, 42, 45-6, 48-51, 53, 55-7, 59-60, 62, 69, 71-4, 79, 84-6, 98, 133-4, 136, 141-2, 175, 178-181, 183, 188, 190, 227, 267, 271-2, 275-6, 278, 291, 316, 328-9, 334-5, 337-8, 349, 352-3, 364, 380
Islamabad 352
Islamisation 182
Islamism 39, 41, 59-60, 79, 368, 379
Islamist 39-42, 44, 49, 58, 60, 62, 74, 77-8, 137

Islamization 45-46, 58, 61-2, 71, 75, 77, 79
Israel 17, 103, 118, 385
Israelis 385
Issifu 170, 365
Italy 100
Ithaca 360
Jaafar 44
Jack 153, 326
Jaclyn 6, 171
Jacques 167
Jaeckle, T. 24, 365
James 349, 364
Jana 384
Jean 167
Jefferson 64
Jehovah 174
Jerusalem 103, 199, 385
Jesus 11, 17-8, 22, 272-4, 305-8, 372
Jewish 52, 274
Jews 20, 51-2, 275, 324
Jiang 382
John xiv, 16, 19, 33, 74-5, 150, 173, 177-9, 187-8, 217, 225, 267, 273, 279-280, 295, 304-7, 317, 325, 352, 358-360, 369
Johns xii
Johnson 241, 365
Jok, M. J. 238, 267, 365, 379

Jones 380
Joshanloo, M. 365
Joshva xiv
Jost, J. T. 365-366
Juba 54, 233, 367, 381
Judaism 271-272, 304, 353
Judgments 45
Juma 73
Jurist 358
Justin xv
Kahn 366
Kajiko 279
Kalkandjieva 366
Kant 286, 355
Karabati, S. 122, 366
Kariatlis 366
Karl 353
Kassala 55-57
Katayama 356
Katie 16-17
Katolicki 384
Katongole 366
Keagan 366
Kelly 80-82, 366
Keltner 367
Kenya xxi, 2, 21, 32, 78, 212, 216, 280-1
Kenyans 21
Kerovec 317, 366
Ket 185

Khalid 366
Khaptsova, A. 100, 367
Khartoum 1-2, 4, 23, 39, 42, 47-8, 50, 53, 57, 59-62, 73-8, 81, 85, 216-7, 234, 263, 265-6, 270, 280, 282, 328, 337
Kian 175
Kibret, B. T. 170, 260, 367
Kiir 72-73, 259, 268
Kindersley 266, 268, 367
Kirchliche 379
Kirmanoglu 356
Kitayama 13
Knopf 263, 367
Knowledge 25
Knox 359
Kolang 185
Kon, M. 265, 269, 367
Konty 378
Koopman 30, 367
Kopec, M. 95, 367
Kordofan 57
Kraus, M. W. 367
Krause 368
Krijnen 364
Kristensen 29
Kruglanski 366
Kuhn 168
Kuol 186
Kussala 233

Kustenbauder 44, 48, 54, 57-9, 74, 77, 249, 368
Kyle 368
Lalla 379
Lamle, E. N. 239, 368
Langham 360
Lapponya 54
Larry xiv
Larson 375
Lastly 170
Latin 198
Laverty 348
Law 43, 200-1, 220, 272, 351-2, 356, 358-9, 361-2, 364-5, 368-371, 373-4, 379, 381, 384
Lederach 279
Lee 368
Leeuw, G. V. 29-30, 368
Legislation 376
Legitimacy 376
Leibniz 286
Leiden 364
Leng 174
Letting 117
Leuith 54
Lewis 8, 368
Liberation xx, 33, 45-6, 59-60, 73, 87, 179, 189, 380
Lifeline 161
Lindeman 353
Liu 179, 368
Lizardo 123, 382
Lobbyists 249
Lochapi 73
Locke 286, 325, 368
Logos 297-299, 306
Loh 368
Lokichoggio 280
Lokudu 233-234
Lombard xiv
London 366
Loro 233
Lotende 73
Loudovikos 303, 369
Louisville 359
Lovejoy 369
Lovin, R. W. 6-7, 16-9, 22, 290, 369
Loyola 361
Luak 186
Lual xii
Lubelski 384
Lueth 73
Luis 358
Lull 369
Lund, C. C. 369
Luther, M. 133, 203-5, 369
Lyotard 167-168
Mabior 33, 74, 279
Mac 355

Machar 3, 268, 280
Macleod 369
Macmillan 354
Madison 103
Magun, V. 107-108, 121, 369
Mahmoud 381
Mahmud 59
Maio 354
Malabou 369
Mamali 356
Manchester 357
Manen 29, 382
Manfredo, M. J. 370
Manicheian 230
Manley 375
Manning, L. 322, 370
Manpower 175
Manstead 109, 370
Manta 370
Manyok xv, xix, xxi, xxi, xxv, 3, 5, 7, 9, 11, 13, 15, 17, 19, 21, 23, 25, 27, 29, 31, 33, 35, 37, 39, 41, 43, 45, 47, 49, 51, 53, 55, 57, 59, 61, 63, 65, 67, 69, 71, 73, 75, 77, 79, 81, 83, 85, 89, 91, 93, 95, 97, 99, 101, 103, 105, 107, 109, 111, 113, 115, 117, 119, 121, 123, 125, 127, 129, 131, 133, 135, 137, 139, 141, 143, 145, 147, 149, 151, 153, 155, 157, 159, 161, 163, 165, 167, 169, 171, 173, 175, 177, 179, 181, 183, 185, 187, 189, 191, 195, 197, 199, 201, 203, 205, 207, 209, 211, 213, 215, 217, 219, 221, 223, 225, 227, 229, 231, 233, 235, 237, 239, 241, 243, 245, 247, 249, 251, 253, 255, 257, 259, 261, 263, 265, 267, 269, 271, 273, 275, 277, 279, 281, 283, 285, 287, 289, 291, 293, 295, 297, 299, 301, 303, 305, 307, 309, 311, 313, 315, 317, 319, 321, 323, 325, 327, 329, 331, 333, 335, 337, 339, 341, 343, 345, 349, 353, 355, 357, 359, 361, 363, 365, 367, 369, 371, 373, 375, 377, 379, 381, 383, 385

Manzi 356
Marginalisation 49, 62-3
Marginality 378
Markus 381
Matip 215
Matthee 163, 370
Matthew 272-273, 275
Maulawi 275
Maurice 354
Maximus 303-304, 369, 379
Mayardit 259

Maybe 4, 76
Mayemba 370
Mbiti 322, 371
Mecca xvi, xx, 25, 35, 380
Mechanistic 130
Medieval 9, 143, 197, 236, 337, 354
Medina 275
Memory 370
Mennonites 17
Mental 370
Messianic 372
Metaphysics 288
Metz 10, 371
Meuleman 358
Mews 379
Michael xiv, 375
Michel 167
Michigan 19, 103, 373, 384
Mickey, S. 293, 308, 371
Mickute 371
Migliore 290, 372
Mike 159
Military 217
Millennial 384
Minneapolis 384
Misinterpretation 34
Missionalia 383
Mitralexis 379
Mnguni 213, 238, 372

Mo 177, 181-3, 372
Modalists 294-295
Moderators 367
Modernism 129-130, 168, 285
Modernist 129-130, 147, 290
Modernists 285-286
Modernities 364
Modernity 352, 359
Mogobe 6
Mohammed 59
Moltmann 292, 302, 317-9, 372
Mond 376
Monist 359
Monotheism 353
Morley 361
Moses 319
Mosque 46
Mouton 18
Muhammad 133-134, 272-3, 352
Muita, M. M. 238, 372
Mujuzi 372
Murle 234
Murray 16, 19, 273, 352
Muslim 1, 5, 38-41, 43-5, 47-8, 53, 56-7, 59-60, 62-3, 68, 74, 79, 85, 133, 174, 187, 189, 227, 231, 265, 267, 275-6, 278, 292, 337
Muslimdominated xxi, 250

Muslims xx, 1, 5, 24-5, 35, 40, 42-3, 45-57, 59, 62, 72-3, 76, 79-80, 83, 85, 94-5, 133-5, 138-9, 141-3, 158, 174-7, 179, 182-3, 189, 249-250, 266-7, 270, 275-8, 281, 283, 292, 316-7, 324, 328, 337, 339-340, 380
Napier 366
Nashville 369
Nasir 225
Nationalism 358
Naylor, M. 373
Neo 6, 145, 170-3, 373
Netherlands 357
Neutrality 362
Nexus 361
Nhlapo 373
Nicaragua 158
Nicene 11, 354, 364
Niebuhr 16, 18-9
Nietzsche 355
Nile 55-56, 58
Nilotic 255
Nilotics 250
Nimeiri 40, 44-5, 58, 78, 177, 183
Nkondo 373
Nobody 14, 220
Nonetheless 3, 293, 340
Nonincorporation 359
Nonpreferentialism 9, 381
Nonpreferentialists 211
Normative 82
Norris, P. 20, 373
Northerner 54
Northerners 54-56
Nous 298-299
Nuba 179
Nuer 184-185, 189, 219-220, 222, 234, 255-9, 266, 270, 280, 329, 365
Numayri 183
Numeiri 45, 59
Numen 353
Nya 177, 217
Nyaba 373
Nyachol 184-185, 255-8, 329
Nyamanga 354
Nyaruac 185-186
Nylapo 259
Obispo 358
Obscurity 34
Ockham 133, 362
Oct 25
Offenses 245
Oishi 13, 378
Okoye, U. M. 246, 374
Omar 41-42, 382
Oneness 45
Ong 175, 374

Oregon 364
Orthodox 365
Orthodoxies 364
Otherness 385
Otto 29
Overviewing 161
Oxford xiv, xvi, 287, 352, 375
Paideia 366
Paine 96
Palgrave 354, 376
Pannenberg 302, 374
Paride 233
Paris 353
Parratt 322, 374
Participatio 369
Pastura, P. S. V. C. 374
Patriarchal 235, 337
Patrick xiv
Paul 17, 30, 273, 288, 296, 325, 355, 366, 374
Paulines 355
Paulino 215, 233
Pavlopoulos, V. 356, 383
Pawla 384
Peabody 354, 364
Peacebuilding 376
Pedagogy 359
Penal 245
Pence 159

Pendle, N. R. 170, 184, 189-190, 221, 255-9, 329-330, 374
Penuh 352
Personality 354, 363, 365, 375, 378, 380-1, 383
Personhood 385
Peter 296
Pew 158, 375
Phenomenological 361
Phenomenology 167, 363
Philips 155
Phillips 153-155, 326, 381
Phronema 366
Piazza, J. 88, 375
Piff 367
Pinaud, C. 263, 375
Piurko, Y. 102, 112, 120, 375
Plaatjles 162, 375
Plato 285, 287-8, 316, 353, 375
Plotinus 202, 297-300, 375
Pluralism 357-358, 373
Pneumatomachians 295
Podbielski 379
Poland 119-120
Polit 362
Polity 369
Polytechnic 358
Ponizovskiy, V. 100-101, 110, 122, 125, 128, 375
Porto 13

Posnova 356
Postmodern 167, 375
Postmodernism 130-131, 148, 167-8, 286, 376, 383
Postmodernist 129-130, 167
Postmodernists 130, 168, 286, 291
Potgieter, F. 293, 307, 375
Powell 89-90, 92, 96, 98-9, 364
Preliminary 85, 137, 191, 235, 282, 332
Presbyterian 3-4, 292
Priorities 359
Prioritisation 144, 246
Prof xiv
Prophecies 384
Proportionality 368
Proselytization 356
Protestant 17, 20, 205
Protestants 18-20
Psychologie 355
Psychology 353-354, 356, 358, 361, 366-7, 370, 375, 377-381, 383
Qu 382
Quarterly 375
Quran 38, 59, 66, 133, 182, 275-6
Radley 163
Raeder, L. C. 310, 376

Rajaf 233
Rajah, J. 173, 376
Ramose 6, 11, 296, 376
Rauch 363
Rawls 150
Rawlsian 93
Realism 359
Reconceiving 355
Redford 13
Reifler 362
Reinhold 16, 18
Relationships 197-198, 203, 205-6
Reliabilism 362
Renaissance 8-9, 129, 373
Rene 203
Repressions 58
Rheinschmidt 367
Rhodes 381
Richard 288
Riediger 381
Riedl, R. B. 376
Riek 3, 268, 280
Roach 376
Robbins, J. W. 289, 376, 383
Robert 6, 361
Roberts 358, 364
Robinson 20, 257, 380
Roccas 355
Rodes 361

Rolandsen 266, 268, 376
Roman 233, 304
Romans 17
Romanticism 287, 303
Rome 364
Ron xii
Ronzoni, M. 88, 92, 377
Rousseau 231
Rubenstein 288
Rudnev 104, 106-7, 369
Ruey, T. 377
Russell 369, 375
Russian 367
Ruth xiv
Ryan 232-233, 235-6, 239, 262, 279-281, 339, 352
Ryle 379
Sadiq 41
Saeed 73
Sage 361
Sagiv, L. 355, 377
Salam 6, 33
Salerno 381
Salih 381
Salva 72-73, 259
Samuel xiv
San 358, 380
Santalka 361
Sara xiv
Satan 202

Saudi 35, 72, 158-160
Schaff 354
Schelling 286
Schiffman 271, 274, 377
Schleiermacher 29, 286
Schmidt 104, 106-7, 357, 369
Schoen 356, 362, 383
Schomerus, M. 377
Schreier 381
Schwartz, S. H. xvi, xix, xxi, 6, 13, 99-100, 102-5, 111, 118-123, 128, 130, 135, 193, 335, 344, 347, 354, 356, 367, 370, 375, 377-8, 380-1, 383
Scollon, C. 381
Scotland 369
Scotto 362
Scriptura 384
Scriptural 366
Secular 149, 169, 171, 287-8, 323-4, 326, 328, 351, 354, 358, 369, 380
Secularism 172, 192, 342, 351, 358, 373
Secularization 364
Seedat 167, 378
Sep 73, 380
Separationism 9, 371
Sexual 378

Shalom xvi, xxi, xxi, 6, 88, 103, 335
Shamim 378
Shankar 368
Shapiro 368
Sharia 43-44, 56, 58, 182-3, 188-9, 277
Sheeder 8, 379
Sheephatch 275, 352
Sheik 73
Sheikh 73
Sher 275
Shia 158
Shutte 10, 379
Sidahamed 33
Sidahmed 6, 40-1, 49, 249, 379
Sidenvall 379
Silvester, J. 356, 383
Sims 382
Sindima 379
Singapore 170-175, 187-8, 191-2, 236, 287, 330-1, 338-9, 341-2, 356-7, 368, 373-4, 376, 382
Singaporean 330, 342
Singaporeans 172, 292
Sir 273
Skliris 304, 379
Skriflig 384
Slovenia 119
Smith xiv

Socialism 180
Sociol 357
Sociological 369, 372
Sociology 365, 377
Sookdeo 379
Sookhdeo xiv, 38, 42, 46-8, 52, 56, 59, 69, 119
Sortheix, F. M. 99, 101-2, 104, 120-3, 378, 380
Soul 287, 297-8, 300
Soulcraft 355
Sousa 88-90, 375
Southeast 368
Southerner 54
Sovereignty 194, 351, 359, 366
Spanish 355
Spinelli, D. (019 158, 380
Spinoza 286
Spong 380
Stabilization 368
Stanford 353, 358
Stanley 16, 353, 374
Starks, B. 20, 380
Starrett 324, 380
Steiris 379
Stellenbosch xii, xiv, xvi, 375
Stephen 375, 382
Stephens, N. M. 381
Stipulation 34
Stroom 376

Structuralism 167
Subjectivism 355
Sudan xii, xv, xvi, xix, xx, xxi, xxi, xxi, xxi, xxv, 1-5, 7, 12-3, 22-9, 31-6, 39-67, 69-89, 92, 98, 124, 135-141, 148, 161-2, 171, 176-180, 182-4, 186-197, 212-236, 238-241, 243-252, 255-7, 262-271, 276, 278-285, 291-2, 294, 297, 310-2, 317, 319, 323-4, 328-334, 336-343, 345, 347, 349, 351-3, 357-360, 364-5, 367-8, 372, 376, 379-382, 384
Sudanese xvi, xx, xxv, 1-2, 5, 7-8, 12, 23-8, 33-6, 39-42, 44-5, 47-63, 65-6, 73, 75, 77-88, 135, 176-9, 182-3, 186, 188, 190, 193-6, 213-4, 218, 221, 223-6, 230, 232, 235-6, 240, 242-3, 245-7, 249, 251-2, 262-7, 269-270, 276, 282-4, 291-4, 310-1, 316-7, 319-320, 322-3, 329, 332-3, 335-341, 343, 365, 368, 377, 380
Sudanic 250
Sudanism 178-180, 188
Sudans 194
Sudd 353
Sugden xiv

Sullivan 13, 370
Sulloway 366
Summa 352
Sungai 352
Sunnah 275
Svensk 354
Sweden 20
Synopsis 334
Synthese 367
Taban 233
Tabernero, C. 356
Tackett 379
Taha 59
Tamazuj 73
Tamir, M. 102, 114, 116, 381
Tang 379
Tay 378
Taylor 6, 8, 14-5, 22, 70, 81, 195, 214, 228, 231, 361, 381
Teel 13, 370
Teleologists 89
Teleology 91, 377, 379
Tenth 379
Teny 3
Teologiese 383
Teologii 384
Territory 361
Terrorism 371
Terry 381
Tertullian 325

Texas xii, xiv
Theologia 352
Theologie 374
Thio 382
Thirdly 170
Tillich 30, 288
Timaeus 287, 375
Timothy 360
Tombe 233-234
Torit 233
Torrance 353
Torres 356, 381
Trans 369
Transdisciplinarity 373
Treatises 368
Tribal 224, 371
Tribalism 266
Tribune xx, xxi, 2-4, 23, 25, 32, 72, 292, 380
Trinitarian xix, xxv, 10, 12-3, 292-4, 296-7, 303, 307, 310-2, 318, 332-3, 343, 366
Trinity 11-12, 293-7, 301-3, 306-7, 310-2, 318, 332, 354-5, 372
Triune 293, 311, 384
Tsai, J. L. 382
Turabi 179
Turkish 366
Turks 177

Turner 382
Ubuntu 10-11, 371, 373, 376, 379
Uganda 276
Umma 40-41, 44, 71, 189, 276
Unappreciated 377
Understandings 303
Unionist 40
Unity 298, 302, 307
Universalism 110-112
Universalists 308
Uniwersytet 384
Uskul 13
Vacura 299, 382
Vahanian 288
Vaisey 382
Vandrunen 383
Vargas 13
Variability 380
Vattimo 288, 383
Vecchione, M. 102-103, 105, 128, 355-6, 377-8, 383
Veerachary 168, 383
Venezuela 158
Venter 383
Verbum 353
Verkasalo 353, 356, 378
Vice 3, 159
Vienna 368
Villiers 349

Vinay xiv
Violent 52-53
Virginia 364, 369
Vishkin 381
Vorster 98-99, 168, 289, 383-4
Vosloo, R. 6, 10, 12, 293, 384
Waal 215-216, 220, 236, 263, 337
Wace 354
Wallace, M. I. 384
Walsh 8, 384
Walt 166, 293, 307-9, 375, 382
Wanglei xv
Warrap 258-259
Washington 75, 354, 359, 362
Wassara 251, 384
Weber, E. 16, 367, 384
West 39, 69, 189, 242-4, 260
Westernborrowed 245
Westminster 355, 359
Whelan 122, 363
Whitehead 371
Wilhelm 314
William 133, 288, 372
Willig 361
Willis 379
Wilson 232-233, 263, 384
Winston 363
Wipf 360, 363, 370, 374-5, 378, 382

Wita 384
Witte 20, 384
Wm 363
Wunlit 262, 270, 279, 281
Wydzial 384
Yak 233
Yale 171, 358, 368, 371
Yambio 233-234
Yei 279
Yilmaz 94-95, 352
Yitbarek 213, 238, 372
Yobwan, L. 385
Zaccheus 170, 385
Zanna 377-378
Zechariah xv, xix, xxi, xxi, xxv, 3, 5, 7, 9, 11, 13, 15, 17, 19, 21, 23, 25, 27, 29, 31, 33, 35, 37, 39, 41, 43, 45, 47, 49, 51, 53, 55, 57, 59, 61, 63, 65, 67, 69, 71, 73, 75, 77, 79, 81, 83, 85, 89, 91, 93, 95, 97, 99, 101, 103, 105, 107, 109, 111, 113, 115, 117, 119, 121, 123, 125, 127, 129, 131, 133, 135, 137, 139, 141, 143, 145, 147, 149, 151, 153, 155, 157, 159, 161, 163, 165, 167, 169, 171, 173, 175, 177, 179, 181, 183, 185, 187, 189, 191, 195, 197, 199, 201, 203, 205, 207, 209, 211, 213, 215, 217, 219, 221,

223, 225, 227, 229, 231, 233,
235, 237, 239, 241, 243, 245,
247, 249, 251, 253, 255, 257,
259, 261, 263, 265, 267, 269,
271, 273, 275, 277, 279, 281,
283, 285, 287, 289, 291, 293,
295, 297, 299, 301, 303, 305,
307, 309, 311, 313, 315, 317,
319, 321, 323, 325, 327, 329,
331, 333, 335, 337, 339, 341,
343, 345, 349, 353, 355, 357,
359, 361, 363, 365, 367, 369,
371, 373, 375, 377, 379, 381,
383, 385

Zeitgeschichte 379

Zeitschrift 374

Zhyrkova 11, 304, 385

Zilberfeld 385

Zizioulas 303, 308, 369, 385

Zollman 385

Zyl 383

www.ingramcontent.com/pod-product-compliance
Lightning Source LLC
Chambersburg PA
CBHW030250010526
44107CB00053B/1649